W9-BYN-333

8194961

# American Accent Training

# 美语发音秘诀

（美）Ann Cook・著

群言出版社
QUNYAN PRESS
北京

**图书在版编目(CIP)数据**

美语发音秘诀 /（美）库克编著；吕明，李莘，张
倩译. —北京：群言出版社，2013（2017.2重印）
书名原文：American Accent Training
ISBN 978-7-80256-397-1

Ⅰ.①美… Ⅱ.①库… ②吕… ③李… ④张… Ⅲ.
①英语—发音—美国 Ⅳ.①H311

中国版本图书馆CIP数据核字（2012）第293376号

**版权登记：图字 01—2012—6928**

AMERICAN ACCENT TRAINING (THIRD EDITION) by ANN COOK
Copyright: © 2012 BY Ann Cook
This edition arranged with American Accent Training, Inc.
through BIG APPLE AGENCY, INC., LABUAN, MALAYSIA.
Simplified Chinese edition copyright:
2013 Qunyan Press
All rights reserved.

**责任编辑：** 张　倩
**封面设计：** 大愚设计

**出版发行：** 群言出版社
**社　　址：** 北京市东城区东厂胡同北巷1号（100006）
**网　　址：** www.qypublish.com
**自营网店：** http://xdfdytushu.tmall.com（天猫旗舰店）
　　　　　　http://qycbs.shop.kongfz.com（孔夫子旧书网）
　　　　　　http://www.qypublish.com（群言出版社官网）
**电子信箱：** dywh@xdf.cn　qunyancbs@126.com
**联系电话：** 010-62418641　62605019　65267783　65263836
**经　　销：** 全国新华书店
**法律顾问：** 北京天驰君泰律师事务所

**印　　刷：** 北京海石通印刷有限公司
**版　　次：** 2013年2月第1版　2017年2月第12次印刷
**开　　本：** 889mm×1194mm　1/16
**印　　张：** 17.25
**字　　数：** 368千字
**书　　号：** ISBN 978-7-80256-397-1
**定　　价：** 42.00元

# Table of Contents　目录

# Read This First

Welcome to *American Accent Training*. This book and CD is designed to get you started on your American accent. We'll follow the book and go through the 25 lessons and all the exercises step-by-step. Everything is explained and a complete Answer Key is in the back of the text.

## What Is Accent?

Accent is a combination of four main components: *voice quality*, *intonation* (speech music), *liaisons* (word connections), and *pronunciation* (the spoken sounds of vowels, consonants, and combinations). As you go along, you'll notice you're being asked to look at accent in a different way. You'll also realize that the grammar you studied before and this accent you're studying now are completely different.

Part of the difference is that grammar and vocabulary are systematic and structured—the *letter* of the language. Accent, on the other hand, is free form, intuitive, and creative—more the *spirit* of the language. So, thinking of music, feeling, and flow, let your mouth relax into the American accent.

## Can I Learn a New Accent?

Can a person actually learn a new accent? Many people feel that after a certain age, it's just not possible. Can classical musicians play jazz? If they practice, of course they can! For your American accent, it's just a matter of learning and practicing techniques this book and CD will teach you. It is up to you to use them or not. How well you do depends mainly on how open and willing you are to sounding different from the way you have sounded all your life.

A very important thing you need to remember is that you can use your accent to say *what* you mean and *how* you mean it. Word stress conveys meaning through tone or feeling, which can be much more important than the actual words that you use. We'll cover the expression of these feelings through intonation in the first lesson.

You may have noticed that I talk fast and often run my words together. You've probably heard enough "English-teacher English"—where...everything...is...pronounced without having to listen too carefully. That's why on the CD we're going to talk just like the native speakers that we are, in a normal conversational tone.

Native speakers often tell people who are learning English to "slow down" and to "speak clearly." This is meant with the best of intentions, but it is exactly the opposite of what a student really needs to do. If you speak fairly quickly, with strong intonation and good voice quality, you will be understood more easily. To illustrate this point, you will hear a Chinese gentleman first trying to speak slowly and carefully and then repeating the same two sentences quickly and with clear intonation. The difference makes him sound like a completely different person.

*Hello, my name is Raymond Choon.*

You may have to listen to this CD a couple of times to catch everything. To help you, every word on the CD is also written in the book. By seeing and hearing simultaneously, you'll learn to reconcile the differences between the *appearance* of English (spelling) and the *sound* of English (pronunciation and the other aspects of accent).

The CD leaves a rather short pause for you to repeat into. The point of this is to get you responding quickly and without spending too much time thinking about your response.

## Accent Versus Pronunciation

Many people equate *accent* with *pronunciation*. I don't feel this to be true at all. America is a big country, and while the pronunciation varies from the East Coast to the West Coast, from the southern to the northern states, two components that are uniquely American stay basically the same—the speech music, or *intonation*, and the word connections, or *liaisons*. Throughout this program, we will focus on them. In the latter part of the book we will work on pronunciation concepts, such as Cat? Caught? Cut? and Betty Bought a Bit of Better Butter; we also will work our way through some of the difficult sounds, such as **TH**, the American **R**, the **L**, **V**, and **Z**.

## "Which Accent Is Correct?"

*American Accent Training* was created to help people "sound American" for lectures, interviews, teaching, business situations, and general daily communication. Although America has many regional pronunciation differences, the accent you will learn is that of standard American English as spoken and understood by the majority of educated native speakers in the United States. Don't worry that you will sound slangy or too casual because you most definitely won't. This is the way a professor lectures to a class, the way a national newscaster broadcasts, the way that is most comfortable and familiar to the majority of native speakers.

## "Why Is My Accent So Bad?"

Learners can be seriously hampered by a negative outlook, so I'll address this very important point early. First, your accent is *not* bad; it is nonstandard to the American ear. There is a joke that goes: What do you call a person who can speak three languages? *Trilingual.* What do you call a person who can speak two languages? *Bilingual.* What do you call a person who can speak only one language? *American.*

Every language is equally valid or good, so every accent is *good.* The average American, however, truly does have a hard time understanding a nonstandard accent. George Bernard Shaw said that the English and Americans are two people *divided* by the same language!

Some students learn to overpronounce English because they naturally want to say the word as it is written. Too often an English teacher may allow this, perhaps thinking that colloquial American English is unsophisticated, unrefined, or even incorrect. Not so at all! Just as you don't say the **T** in *listen*, the **TT** in *better* is pronounced **D**, *bedder.* Any other pronunciation will sound foreign, strange, wrong, or different to a native speaker.

## Less than It Appears...More than It Appears

As you will see in Exercise "Squeezed-Out Syllables," some words appear to have three or more syllables, but all of them are not actually spoken. For example, *business* is not (*bi•zi•*ness), but rather (*biz•*ness).

Just when you get used to eliminating whole syllables from words, you're going to come across other words that look as if they have only one syllable but really need to be said with as many as three! In addition, the inserted syllables are filled with letters that are not in the written word. I'll give you two examples of this strange phenomenon: *Pool* looks like a nice, one-syllable word, but if you say it this way, at best it will sound like *pull* and at worst will be unintelligible to your listener. For clear comprehension, you need to say three syllables (pu/wuh/luh). Where did that **W** come from? It's certainly not written down anywhere, but it is there just as definitely as the **P** is there. The second example is a word like *feel.* If you say just the letters that you see, it will sound more like *fill.* You need to say (fee/yuh/luh). Is that really a **Y**? Yes. These mysterious semivowels are explained under Liaison in Chapter 11. They can appear either inside a word as you have seen or between words as you will learn.

## Language Is Fluent and Fluid

Just like your own language, conversational English has a very smooth, fluid sound. Imagine that you are walking along a dry riverbed with your eyes closed. Every time you come to a rock, you trip over it, stop, continue, and trip over the next rock. This is how the average foreigner speaks English. It is slow, awkward, and even painful. Now imagine that you are a great river rushing through that same riverbed—rocks are no problem, are they? You just slide over and around them without ever breaking your smooth flow. It is *this* feeling that I want you to capture in English.

Changing your old speech habits is very similar to changing from a stick shift to an automatic transmission. Yes, you continue to reach for the gearshift for a while, and your foot still tries to find the clutch pedal, but this soon phases itself out. In the same way, you may still say "telephone **call**" (kohl) instead of (kahl) for a while, but this too will soon pass.

You will also have to think about your speech more than you do now. In the same way that you were very aware and self-conscious when you first learned to drive, you will eventually relax and deal with the various components simultaneously.

A new accent is an adventure. Be bold! Exaggerate wildly! You may worry that Americans will laugh at you for putting on an accent, but I guarantee you, they won't even notice. They'll just think that you've finally learned to "talk right." Good luck with your new accent!

## A Few Words on Pronunciation                                    Track 002

I'd like to introduce you to the pronunciation guide outlines in the following chart. There aren't too many characters that are different from the standard alphabet, but just so you'll be familiar with them, look at the chart. It shows eight *tense* vowels and six *lax* vowels and semivowels.

## Tense Vowels? Lax Vowels?

In some books, tense vowels are called *long* and lax vowels are called *short*. Since you will be learning how to lengthen vowels when they come before a voiced consonant, it would be confusing to say that *hen* has a long, short vowel. It is more descriptive to say that it has a lax vowel that is doubled or lengthened.

## Tense Vowels | Lax Vowels

| Symbol | Sound | Spelling | Example | Symbol | Sound | Spelling | Example |
|---|---|---|---|---|---|---|---|
| ā | ɛi | take | tāk | ɛ | eh | get | gɛt |
| ē | ee | eat | ēt | i | ih | it | it |
| ī | äi | ice | īs | ü | ih + uh | took | tük |
| ō | ou | hope | hōp | ə | uh | some | səm |
| ū | ooh | smooth | smū<u>th</u> | | | | |
| ä | ah | caught | kät | | Semivowels | | |
| æ | ä + ɛ | cat | kæt | ər | er | her | hər |
| æo | æ + o | down | dæon | ᵊl | ul | dull | dəᵊl |

Although this may look like a lot of characters to learn, there are really only four new ones: æ, ä, ə, and ü. Under Tense Vowels, you'll notice that the vowels that say their own name simply have a line over them: ā, ē, ī, ō, ū. There are three other tense vowels. First, ä, is pronounced like the sound you make when the doctor wants to see your throat, or when you loosen a tight belt and sit down in a soft chair—*aaaaaaaah!* Next, you'll find æ, a combination of the tense vowel ä and the lax vowel ɛ. It's similar to the noise that a goat or a lamb makes. The last one is æo, a combination of æ and o. This is a very common sound, usually written as *ow* or *ou* in words like *down* or *round.*

A *tense vowel* requires you to use a lot of facial muscles to produce it. If you say ē, you must stretch your lips back; for ū you must round your lips forward; for ä you drop your jaw down; for æ you will drop your jaw far down and back; for ā bring your lips back and drop your jaw a bit; for ī drop your jaw for the *ah* part of the sound and pull it back up for the *ee* part; and for ō round the lips, drop the jaw, and pull back up into ū. An American ō is really ōū.

▶ Now you try it. Repeat after me. ē, ū, ā, æ, ä, ī, ō.

A *lax vowel,* on the other hand, is very reduced. In fact, you don't need to move your face at all. You only need to move the back of your tongue and your throat. These sounds are very different from most other languages.

Under Lax Vowels, there are four reduced vowel sounds, starting with the Greek letter epsilon ɛ, pronounced *eh*; the letter i pronounced *ih*; and ü pronounced *ü*, which is a combination of *ih* and *uh*; and the schwa, ə, pronounced *uh*—the softest, most reduced, most relaxed sound that we can produce. *It is also the most common sound in English.* The semivowels are the American R (pronounced *er*, which is the schwa plus R) and the American L (which is the schwa plus L).

## Voiced Consonants? Unvoiced Consonants?

A consonant is a sound that causes two points of your mouth to come into contact, in three locations—the *lips*, the *tip of the tongue*, and the *throat*. A consonant can either be *unvoiced* (whispered) or *voiced* (spoken), and it can appear at the beginning, middle, or end of a word. You'll notice that for some categories, a particular sound doesn't exist in English.

| Beginning | | Middle | | End | |
|---|---|---|---|---|---|
| Whispered | Spoken | Whispered | Spoken | Whispered | Spoken |
| parry | bury | apple | able | mop | mob |
| ferry | very | afraid | avoid | off | of |
| stew | zoo | races | raises | face | phase |
| sheet | ▬ | pressure | pleasure | crush | garage |
| two | do | petal | pedal | not | nod |
| choke | joke | gaucho | gouger | rich | ridge |
| think | that | ether | either | tooth | smooth |
| come | gum | bicker | bigger | pick | pig |
| ▬ | ▬ | accent | exit | tax | tags |
| ▬ | yes | ▬ | player | ▬ | day |
| ▬ | wool | ▬ | shower | ▬ | now |
| his | ▬ | ahead | ▬ | ▬ | ▬ |
| ▬ | late | ▬ | collect | ▬ | towel |
| ▬ | rate | ▬ | correct | ▬ | tower |
| ▬ | me | ▬ | swimmer | ▬ | same |
| ▬ | next | ▬ | connect | ▬ | man |
| ▬ | ▬ | ▬ | finger | ▬ | ring |

## Pronunciation Points

1. In many dictionaries, you may find a character that looks like an upside-down V (ʌ) and another character that is an upside-down *e* (ə), the *schwa*. There is a linguistic distinction between the two, but they are *pronounced* exactly the same. Since you can't hear the difference between these two sounds, we'll just be using the upside-down *e* to indicate the schwa sound. It is pronounced *uh*.

2. The second point is that we do not differentiate between **ä** and **ɔ**. The **ä** is pronounced *ah*. The backward C (**ɔ**) is more or less pronounced *aw*. This *aw* sound has a "back East" sound to it, and as it's not common to the entire United States, it won't be included here.

3. **R** can be considered a *semivowel.* One characteristic of a vowel is that nothing in the mouth touches anything else. **R** definitely falls into that category. So in the exercises throughout the book it will be treated not so much as a consonant but as a vowel.

4. The *ow* sound is usually indicated by **äu**, which would be *ah + ooh.* This may have been accurate at some point in some locations, but the sound is now generally **æo.** *Town* is **tæon,** *how* is **hæo,** *loud* is **læod,** and so on.

5. Besides *voiced* and *unvoiced*, there are two words that come up in pronunciation. These are *sibilant* and *plosive.* When you say the **s** sound, you can feel the air *sliding* out over the tip of your tongue—this is a sibilant. When you say the **p** sound, you can feel the air *popping* out from between your lips—this is a plosive. Be aware that there are two sounds that are sometimes mistakenly taught as sibilants but are actually plosives: **th** and **v.**

6. For particular points of pronunciation that pertain to your own language, refer to the Nationality Guides in the back of the book.

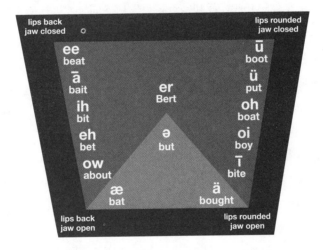

Throughout this text, we will be using three symbols to indicate three separate actions:

▶ Indicates a command or a suggestion.

◀ Indicates the beep tone.

✗ Indicates that you need to turn the CD on or off, back up, or pause.

# 致读者

欢迎阅读《美语发音秘诀》。本书及其配套CD都是为你的美音学习而设计的。我们将通过25章的内容及其练习一步一步地跟随这本书来学习美音。本书对所有的发音问题进行了解释，书后配有完整的答案。

## 什么是口音？

口音主要包括四个成分：音质、语调（说话的音调）、连音（词的连读）和发音（元音、辅音和混合音的发音）。当你学习这本书的时候，要换一个角度来看待口音。你也会注意到以前学的语法和现在学的口音是完全不同的。

这些不同一方面在于语法和单词是系统性和结构性的——是语言的文字，另一方面在于口音是一种自由的、直觉性的、具有创造性的形式——更多的是语言的精神。所以，想想音调、感觉和气流的流动，让你的嘴放松地发出美音。

## 我能学会一种新的口音吗？

一个人真的能学会一种新的口音吗？很多人认为过了一定的年龄，学习新的口音是不可能的。古典音乐家能演奏爵士乐吗？如果他们练习的话，当然能！那么对于你的美语发音来说，就只是一个学习和练习技巧的问题了。这些技巧本书及其配套CD都会教你，主要取决于你是否使用它们。你能学到多好，主要取决于你的开放程度和是否乐意发出不同于你以往所发出的声音。

有件重要的事你要记住：你可以用你的口音表达你的意思并决定你所要表达的程度。单词的重音是通过声调或情感来传达意思的，这一点比你实际使用的词要重要得多。我们将在第一章讲解如何通过语调来表达这些情感。

你也许已经注意到了，我说话时语速很快，而且经常连读。你也许已经听了太多"英语老师的英语"——这种英语把每个音都发出来，我们不必太专注就能听得清。那也是为什么我们在CD中用以英语为母语者的自然表达方式、用一种正常的对话语调来说话的原因。

以英语为母语者经常会告诉那些正在学习英语的人要"说慢点"、"说清楚点"。这是出于好心，但这样的要求确实和学生们真正需要做的相反。如果你说得相当快，而且带有强烈的语调和较好的音质，别人将更容易听懂你的话。为了说明这一点，你将会听一位中国男士先试着很仔细地慢速说话，然后用清晰的语调快速地重复同样的两个句子。这种不同让他听起来判若两人。

*Hello, my name is Raymond Choon.*

你也许要把这张CD多听几遍才能透彻地理解。为了帮助你理解，CD上的每个单词在本书中都有体现。通过听和看的同步进行，你的书面英语（拼写）和口头英语（发音以及其他方面）将会达到和谐一致的程度。

CD中供你进行重复的停顿时间非常短。这样做的目的是让你能快速作答，并且不花费太多的时间来思考你的回答。

## 口音与发音的区别

很多人把发音和口音等同起来。我认为这是不对的。美国是个大国，从东海岸到西海岸，从南部各州到北部各州，人们的发音是不同的，但是美语的两个独特成分——说话的音调，或叫做语调，以及单词的连读，或叫做连音——基本上是相同的。在本书中，我们将重点讲解这两个方面。在本书的后半部分，我们将讲解发音概念，如：Cat? Caught? Cut? 和 Betty Bought a Bit of Better Butter；我们还会涉及一些难发的音，如：TH，美音R，L，V 和 Z。

## "哪种口音是正确的？"

《美语发音秘诀》这本书的写作初衷是帮助人们在进行讲座、面试、授课、商务交流和一般的日常会话时发出纯正的美音。虽然美国有很多地区性的发音差别，但你将要学习的是标准美语发音，它能够为美国大多数受过教育的母语者所使用和理解。不要担心你的发音太俚语化或太随意，因为事实上人们并不会这么认为。这是教授在课堂上讲课的方式，是国家新闻广播员播报的方式，也是大多数母语者感觉最舒服和最熟悉的方式。

## "为什么我的口音这么糟糕？"

学习者有可能受负面观点的严重影响，所以我要先说明此点。首先，你的口音并不糟糕，只是在美国人听起来不标准而已。有这样一个笑话：我们把能讲三种语言的人叫做什么？三语者。我们把能讲两种语言的人叫做什么？双语者。我们把只能讲一种语言的人叫做什么？美国人。

每一种语言都是有效而美好的，所以每一种口音也都是美好的，虽然一般的美国人确实很难理解非标准口音。萧伯纳曾说过，英国人和美国人是用同一种语言分开的两类人！

有些学生在发音时往往会咬文嚼字，因为他们很自然地想要按照单词的拼写方式去发音。大多数情况下英语老师会允许这种情况的发生，也许他们认为美式英语是浅显的、粗俗的，甚至不正确的。但事实绝对不是这样！正如listen这个单词中没有T这个音，而better中的TT发D音一样。对于母语者来说，把这两个单词发成其他任何的音听起来都是格格不入的、奇怪的、错误的或者不同的。

## 少发和多发的音节

正如你将在练习"被挤出来的音节"中看到的（见第58页），有些词看起来有三个或三个以上的音节，但并不是每个音节都发音。例如，business并不是读作(bi·zi·ness)，而是读作(biz·ness)。

当你习惯了不读出单词的所有音节，你将会遇到其他一些看起来似乎只有一个音节的单词，但实际上却要发三个音节的音！在单词的拼写中并未出现的某个字母带来了插入的音节。我将举两个例子来说明这个奇怪的现象。Pool看起来是个很一般的单音节单词，但如果你按照字面发音，最好的情况是听起来像是pull，最坏的情况是你的听众根本不理解。为了能被准确地理解，你需要发出三个音节(pu/wuh/luh)。 那个W音从哪儿来呢？当然它并没有被写在任何地方，但它就像P一样，是确实存在的。 第二个例子是单词feel。如果你只按照拼写来发音，那么听起来就会像fill。你需要这样发音(fee/yuh/luh)。真的有个Y音吗？是的。这些神秘的半元音将在第11章的连音中进行解释。它们会出现在单个的单词中，这一点你已经见过了；也会出现在单词之间，这一点你将在后面学到。

## 语言既要流利，也要流畅

就像你的母语一样，英语口语有着非常顺滑而流畅的发音。想象一下，你正闭着眼睛行走在一片干涸的河床上。每次遇到一块石头，你都会被它绊倒，然后停下来，接着又继续走，然后又会被下一块石头绊倒。这就是普通的外国人说英语的方式。它会非常缓慢，非常笨拙，甚至非常痛苦。现在，想象一下，你是一条大河，正在通过同样的河床——石头不是问题，对吗？你只要从它们上面和周围滑过去，而无需打破你顺滑的水流。这就是我想让你在说英语时所具有的感觉。

改变你过去的说话习惯与从手动挡改为自动挡十分相似。是的，有一段时间你仍然在找变速杆，脚也在寻找离合器踏板，但是不久你就会停止这么做。同样，在一段时间内你仍然将call(kahl)说成"telephone **call**"(kohl)，但是这个阶段将很快过去。

你也会不得不比现在更多地想到所说的内容。类似的，当你第一次学习开车时，你非常清醒和敏感，但你最终会放松下来，并能同时应付不同的情况。

学习一种新的口音就是一次冒险。勇敢些！夸张些！你也许会担心美国人会笑话你带上了口音，但我向你保证，他们根本不会注意到。他们只会认为你终于学会正确地说话了。祝你在学习新口音的道路上一切顺利。

## 浅谈发音

下面我介绍一下下方表格中的发音指南概要。表中有些音标与标准的字母表不同，但你会熟悉它们的。我们来看看表格吧。表格中含有8个紧元音、6个松元音和半元音。

## 紧元音？松元音？

有些书把紧元音称为长元音，把松元音称为短元音。因为你即将学习如何拉长浊辅音前的元音，所以如果你说hen有一个长的短元音就会令人迷惑不解。更准确的描述是，它有一个被加倍发音或延长发音的松元音。

| Tense Vowels | | | | Lax Vowels | | | |
| Symbol | Sound | Spelling | Example | Symbol | Sound | Spelling | Example |
|---|---|---|---|---|---|---|---|
| ā | εi | take | tāk | ε | eh | get | gεt |
| ē | ee | eat | ēt | i | ih | it | it |
| ī | äi | ice | īs | ü | ih + uh | took | tük |
| ō | ou | hope | hōp | ə | uh | some | səm |
| ū | ooh | smooth | smū<u>th</u> | | | | |
| ä | ah | caught | kät | | Semivowels | | |
| æ | ä + ε | cat | kæt | ər | er | her | hər |
| æo | æ + o | down | dæon | ᵊl | ul | dull | dəᵊl |

虽然看上去要学习很多音标，其实只有4个是要新学的：æ, ä, ə, ü。在紧元音里，你会注意到5个发音为其字母读音的音标就只在其字母上方标了一条线：ā, ē, ī, ō, ū。另外还有 3 个其他的紧元音。首先，ä的发音就像医生要看你的喉咙时你发出的声音，或者像你松开紧勒的腰带惬意地坐到软椅上时发出的声音——aaaaaaaah！下一个是æ，是紧元音ä和松元音ε的结合体，很像山羊或绵羊发出的声音。最后一个是æo，它是æ和o的结合体。这个音很普通，通常在单词中被写成ow或ou，如：down或round。

发紧元音时，你需要使用很多面部肌肉。发ē这个音时，你必须向后拉紧双唇；发ū音时，你要把双唇向前收圆；发ä音时，你要把下颚向下拉；发æ音时，你要把下颚向下、向后拉；发ä音时，你要把双唇向后拉，下颚稍向下拉；发ī音时，你要把下颚向下拉发出ah的音，然后将下颚向上拉回，发ee的音；发ō音时，你要收圆嘴唇，把下颚向下拉，然后再向上拉回发出ū的音。美音的ō实际上发的是ōū音。

现在你来试一下。跟我一起念：ē，ū，ā，æ，ä，ī，ō。

另一方面，松元音是弱读音。事实上，你一点都不需要使用面部肌肉。你只需使用你的舌头后部和喉咙。这些音和其他大多数语言的发音有着很大的不同。

在松元音中，有4个弱读音，第一个是ɛ，发eh的音；第二个是i，发ih的音；第三个是ü，发ü的音，它是ih和uh的结合体；第四个是非中央元音ə，发uh的音——它是我们能够发出的最轻、最弱、最放松的音，也是英语中最常出现的音。半元音是指美音R（发er的音，由非中央元音加上R组成）和美音L（由非中央元音加上L组成）。

### 浊辅音？清辅音？

辅音是使你口中的两点相接触于三个地方——双唇、舌尖以及喉咙——的音。辅音分为清辅音（不发声）和浊辅音（发声），出现于词首、词中和词尾。在下表的某些分类中，你会注意到，英语中并不存在与之相对应的音。

| Beginning | | Middle | | End | |
|---|---|---|---|---|---|
| **Whispered** | **Spoken** | **Whispered** | **Spoken** | **Whispered** | **Spoken** |
| parry | bury | apple | able | mop | mob |
| ferry | very | afraid | avoid | off | of |
| stew | zoo | races | raises | face | phase |
| sheet | ▬ | pressure | pleasure | crush | garage |
| two | do | petal | pedal | not | nod |
| choke | joke | gaucho | gouger | rich | ridge |
| think | that | ether | either | tooth | smooth |
| come | gum | bicker | bigger | pick | pig |
| ▬ | ▬ | accent | exit | tax | tags |
| ▬ | yes | ▬ | player | ▬ | day |
| ▬ | wool | ▬ | shower | ▬ | now |
| his | ▬ | ahead | ▬ | ▬ | ▬ |
| ▬ | late | ▬ | collect | ▬ | towel |
| ▬ | rate | ▬ | correct | ▬ | tower |

| | me | | swimmer | | same |
|---|---|---|---|---|---|
| | next | | connect | | man |
| | | | finger | | ring |

## 发音要点

1. 在很多词典中，你会发现像倒v和倒e的音标ʌ和ə（非中央元音）。在语言学中，这两个音标是不同的，但它们的发音是完全相同的。既然听不出这两个音有什么不同，我们就用倒e来表示那个非中央元音。它发uh的音。

2. 第二点是我们并不区分ä和ɔ。ä发ah音。反写的c即ɔ大致发aw音，aw音带有东部发音的特色，并不能代表整个美国的发音，所以在此不作讲述。

3. 可以把R音看做半元音。元音的特点在于发音时嘴的任何部位没有相互接触，发R音时也是如此。因此在本书的练习中我们将它看做元音而非辅音。

4. ow这个音通常用äu来表示，äu是由ah加上ooh音组成的。在某些地区这样发音是正确的，但现在这个音通常被发成æo，如town读作tæon音，how读作hæo，loud读作læod，等等。

5. 除了清辅音和浊辅音，我们还将讲述齿擦音和爆破音。当你发s音时，可以感受到气流从舌尖处滑过——这就是齿擦音。当你发p音时，你能感受到气流从双唇间冲出——这就是爆破音。要注意的是，有时th和v音也会被当做齿擦音来教，这是不对的，它们实际上是爆破音。

6. 要具体了解与你的母语相对应的发音要点，请参考"汉语发音与美音的对比"部分。

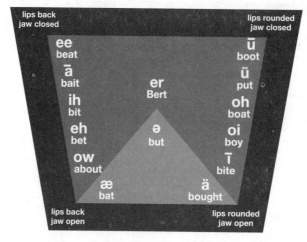

在本书中，我们将应用以下三种符号来表示三种单独的行为：

▶ 表示命令或建议。

◀ 表示"嘟嘟"声。

✗ 表示你需要打开或关闭CD，回听或暂停。

# Telephone Tutoring
# 电话指导

## Preliminary Diagnostic Analysis
## 初级诊断分析

This is a speech analysis to identify the strengths and weaknesses of your American accent. If you are studying American Accent Training on your own, please contact (800) 457-4255 or AmericanAccent.com for a referral to a qualified telephone analyst. The diagnostic analysis is designed to evaluate your current speech patterns to let you know where your accent is standard and nonstandard.

这是一种语音分析，旨在识别你的美语发音的优缺点。如果你在自学本书，在中国大陆地区请拨打001-800-457-4255，在美国本土请拨打800-457-4255，或登录www.AmericanAccent.com，会有专业的分析师对你的发音进行诊断。诊断分析的目的在于评价你目前的语言特点，并让你知道自己的发音是否标准。

Hello, my name is _____. I'm taking American Accent Training. There's a lot to learn, but I hope to make it as enjoyable as possible. I should pick up on the American intonation pattern pretty easily, although the only way to get it is to practice all of the time.

1. walk, all, long, caught      5. ice, I'll, sky          9. tuck, fun, medicine, indicate      13. out, house, round

2. cat, matter, laugh          6. tick, fill, will        10. too, fool, wooed                  14. loyal, choice, oil

3. take, say, fail             7. teak, feel, wheel       11. took, full, would

4. get, any, says, fell        8. work, first, learn, turn 12. woke, told, so, roll

| A | B | C | D | E | F |
|---|---|---|---|---|---|
| 1. pit | 1. bit | 1. staple | 1. stable | 1. cap | 1. cab |
| 2. fear | 2. veer | 2. refers | 2. reverse | 2. half | 2. have |
| 3. sue | 3. zoo | 3. faces | 3. phases | 3. race | 3. raise |
| 4. sheer | ▓▓▓ | 4. cashew | 4. casual | 4. rush | 4. rouge |
| 5. tin | 5. din | 5. metal | 5. medal | 5. hat | 5. had |
| 6. chin | 6. gin | 6. catcher | 6. cadger | 6. rich | 6. ridge |
| 7. thin | 7. then | 7. ether | 7. either | 7. bath | 7. bathe |
| 8. cut | 8. gut | 8. bicker | 8. bigger | 8. tack | 8. tag |
| 9. yellow | 9. race | 9. million | 9. correction | 9. say | 9. sore |
| 10. would | 10. breed | 10. coward | 10. surprise | 10. how | 10. peeper |
| 11. him | 11. man | 11. reheat | 11. summer | 11. soul | 11. palm |
| 12. lace | 12. name | 12. collection | 12. runner | 12. people | 12. can |
| 13. bleed | ▓▓▓ | 13. supplies | 13. kingdom | 13. sink | 13. sing |

1. Make him get it.
2. Let her get your keys.
3. You've got to work on it, don't you?
4. Soup or salad?

1. Maykim **ged**dit.
2. Ledder getcher **keez**.
3. Yoov gädda **wr** kä nit, doan choo?
4. Super **salad**?

1. Betty bought a bit of better butter.

2. Beddy bada bida bedder budder.

3. Italian        Italy
4. attack         attic
5. atomic         atom
6. photography    photograph

7. bet            bed

> Shoulders back, chin up, deepen your voice and project out!
>
> 昂首挺胸，
> 压低声音，
> 大胆说出来！

# The American Sound
# 美音

## Voice Quality

## 音质

You know how you hear a voice across a crowded room and you can just tell that it's American? What's at play there? To answer that question, let's first define our terms: What *is* voice quality and the American sound? It's a combination of vocal placement and cadence. This means a throaty sound and a stairstep intonation.

你应该遇到过这种情况：在一个拥挤的房间里，远远地听到一个人的声音，马上就能判断出那是美音。这是什么原因呢？在回答这个问题之前，我们先来定义一下这两个术语：什么是音质和美音？它们受发声位置和节奏，也就是喉音和阶梯状语调的共同影响。

Listen to British comedian Eddie Izzard imitate the American accent. Notice how his voice moves back in his throat and down in his chest when he's imitating the American accent. This throaty quality is an essential characteristic. There's even a fancy word to describe it—*rhoticity*—which is that solid **R** as in *hard* and *far*. There are regional dialects that are notable for lacking rhoticity, such as the classic Bostonian *Pahk yah cah in Hahvahd Yahd* for *Park your car in Harvard Yard*, but the overwhelming majority of Americans growl out the **R**.

听一下英国喜剧演员埃迪·伊泽德模仿美语发音，注意在他模仿时，声音是如何回到他的喉咙并进入胸腔的。这种喉音音质是美语的一个重要的特点。它甚至有个很花哨的名字——卷舌化——也就是hard和far里清晰可辨的R音。也有些地区方言的显著特点就是没有卷舌化的现象，一个典型的例子就是波士顿人把Park your car in Harvard Yard（把你的车停在哈佛校园里）说成Pahk yah cah in Hahvahd Yahd，但是绝大多数美国人的R音还是很浓重的。

Intonation, voice quality, and phrasing all contribute to the uniquely American voice, along with a casual, relaxed attitude. This relaxation causes American English to differ from the crisper sounds of British English. Within voice quality, you'll be adjusting your volume (a little louder vs. muted or murmured), pitch (high pitched vs. a deeper register), air flow (popped, hissed, or buzzed), and where the voice is generated (throat and chest vs. head and nose).

语调、音质和断句以及一种悠闲、放松的态度造就了独特的美音。这种放松的感觉使得美音和干脆的英音不同。在一定的音质条件下，你可以调节自己的音量（稍大的声音或者哑音、喃喃细语），音高（高音调或者低音域的声音），气流（爆破音、清音或者浊音）以及发音的位置（喉咙和胸腔或者头部和鼻子）。

Americans tend to be a little louder than you're accustomed to. The stereotypical American is louder, a little brasher, more boisterous, immediately friendly, informal, and slightly jokey. It's important to project your voice out with more force than usual and you'll need more breath to push it out. Kids are loud, right? Things stick in their heads because

1

they yell them out. Yell this out! In the privacy of your home, car, or mountaintop, get out and yell some of these sounds and practice sentences so that you can get it really in your head. Don't be afraid to exaggerate and go away further than you think the American accent actually is. This will help you embrace the sound.

　　美国人的声音往往比你通常认为的要大一些。典型的美国人声音更大、有些急躁、更加活跃、能很快和人熟悉、不拘礼节，而且爱开玩笑。用比平时更大的力气发出声音是很重要的一点。同时，你需要吸入更多的空气，以便发出声来。孩子们声音都很大，对吧？因为他们喊出来了，所以事情会停留在脑海里。大声喊出来吧！当你在自己家里、车里或山顶时，大声喊出这些声音吧。通过这种方式练习英文句子，你就可以真正地把它们记在脑子里。别担心自己太过夸张，也别担心发出的美音比你想象的要过火。这样才有助于你领会美音。

## Music　　　　　　　　　　　　　　　　　　　　　　　　　　　Track 005
音乐

Even if you can't sing, you'll recognize the correlation between song and speech music. We're going to listen to a range from high to low.

　　即便不会唱歌，你也可以认识到歌曲和语言韵律之间的联系。我们将会听到一系列从高到低的音。

The singer's natural voice is in the middle range, so for him, the highs and lows don't feel natural, just as deepening your voice won't feel natural for you in the beginning. You'll have to practice and get comfortable with it. (See also Chapter 4)

　　歌手的自然嗓音处于中间音域，因此，对他来说高音和低音都会感觉不自然，就像如果你压低自己的声音，一开始也会感觉不自然一样。你需要多加练习来适应它。（也见第4章）

## Pitch / Sound　　　　　　　　　　　　　　　　　　　　　　　　Track 006
音高 / 音

Let's transition from song to speech. Interestingly, languages are spoken at different pitches, so it's important to recognize the pitch you're coming from as well as the pitch you're heading toward. Even though there are millions of English speakers, both male and female, there is a general pitch range into which English falls. Listen to this audio clip, ranging from a Japanese woman speaking at a very high pitch, to an Arabic man speaking in a much deeper register. You'll notice that English is in the middle.

　　让我们从歌曲转到语言。有趣的是，人们说不同的语言所用的音高不同，所以要分辨出自己所使用语言的音高和将要学习的语言的音高就很重要。虽然说英语的人数量众多，有男有女，但他们说出来的英语都处于一定的音高范围内。听这段音频，从一位音调非常高的日本女人到一位音域低得多的阿拉伯男人，你会发现英语的音高处于中间。

Generally speaking, to Americans, a higher pitch indicates stress or tension, and they will respond accordingly, even if you are not stressed. Of course, speaking in a second language can be stressful, so make a conscious effort to match your speaking voice in English to your deepest voice in your own language.

　　总的来说，美国人认为高音调暗示着压力或紧张，即便你并不紧张，他们也会做出相应的反应。当然，说第二语言会充满压力，所以要有意识地用你说母语时最低沉的声音来说英语。

## The Daddy Voice

爸爸的声音

Americans are culturally programmed to trust the deep voices of authority. In a study from McMaster University in Canada, published in the *Journal of Evolution and Human Behavior*, researchers found that men with lower-pitched voices are found to be more dominant and attractive than are men with higher-pitched voices. They found that lower-pitched voices were associated with favorable personality traits more often than were higher-pitched voices. Listeners were asked to assess the attractiveness, honesty, leadership potential and intelligence—among other qualities—of the speakers. For nearly every attribute they were asked to rate, participants were significantly more likely to prefer the deeper voice.

美国人的固有文化中把深沉的声音视为权威的象征。在加拿大麦克马斯特大学的一项发表在《进化与人类行为》期刊上的研究中，研究者们发现音调低的男人比音调高的男人更具主导性，也更有魅力。他们发现相较于高音调的声音，人们往往容易将低音调的声音与更好的个性特质联系起来。听声音的受试者被要求评估说话者的吸引力、诚信度、潜在领导力、智慧以及其他品质。对于几乎每项被要求评估的特质，受试者都明显更喜欢音调低的人。

Think of national broadcasters and the deep mellifluous tones they use. If you deepen your voice, you'll find that Americans become more respectful and attentive. To capture this voice, hark back to when your Dad would call you in for dinner (even if this was never the case). Put your shoulders back, your chest out, take a deep breath and say, *Hey! Get in here!* Notice how that feels physically and mentally. If you come in through the Daddy Voice, you'll probably have a less negative reaction than just by deepening your voice randomly, to which we've had people say, *I sound like a monster! I sound like a gangster!* This is not the direction we want to push you in, but rather the calm, reassuring voice of authority figure. Shoulders back, chin up, chest out, project from your diaphragm, and relax your throat.

想一想国家播音员和他们柔美的音色。如果压低自己的声音，你会发现美国人对你变得更加尊重和有礼貌。为了掌握这种声音，回想一下你爸爸是如何叫你吃饭的（虽然这种情况几乎没有）。肩膀向后，挺胸，深吸一口气，说"嘿！进来吃饭了！"注意一下身体和精神上的感觉。如果你是通过模仿爸爸的声音练习发声的，那你的反应可能就不会像仅通过随意压低声音练习那样消极了。我们曾听到人们说："我听起来像个怪物！我听起来像个流氓！"这可不是我们想让你发展的方向。我们想让你练就的是权威人物所拥有的那种平静的、可靠的声音。肩膀向后，抬头挺胸，从膈肌发出声音，然后放松喉咙。

## Sound / Pronunciation

音 / 发音

In the pronunciation sections, we'll be working on a sound that is produced deep in the throat—the American **R**. In Chapter 12, we study two tense vowels, æ and ä, and the completely neutral schwa, ə (*cat, caught, cut*). The æ sound has a tendency to sound a little nasal all on its own, and when other vowels are nasalized as well, it puts your whole voice in the wrong place. This is an opportune moment, then, to go into the quality of your voice. In my observation, when people speak a foreign language, they tense up their throat, so their whole communication style sounds forced, pinched, strained, artificial, or nasal. The foreign speaker's voice is also generally higher pitched than would be considered desirable. To practice the difference between high pitch and lower pitch, work on **uh-oh**. In addition to pitch, this exercise will let you discover the difference between a tinny, nasal tone and a deep, rich, mellifluous, basso profundo tone. The tilde (~) is used to indicate a nasal sound. If you try to deepen your voice by expanding your throat, you'll end up with an odd, hollow sound.

在发音部分，我们将练习喉咙深处的发音——美音R。在第12章，我们将学习两个紧元音æ和ä，以及完全中性的非中央元音ə（cat，caught，cut）。æ音本身听起来有点鼻音化的倾向，但如果其他元音也是鼻音化的，它会使你发错所有的音。那么，这正是时候来探究你的音质了。据我观察，人们说外语时会喉部紧张，因而他们的整个交流方式听起来是不自然的、挤压的、紧张的、矫揉造作的，或鼻音化的。同时，说外语的人的声音通常比人们所认为的适宜的音高要高。为了掌握高音调和低音调之间的区别，练习uh-oh的发音。除了音高，这个练习还将让你发现微弱的鼻音和深沉、圆润、优美的最低音之间的区别。波形号"~"用来表示鼻音。如果你试图通过扩张喉咙来压低声音，你会发出一种奇怪的、空洞的声音。

---

**Exercise 1-1: Shifting Your Voice Position**                                   **Track 009**

---

*Pinch your nose closed and say* **æ**. *You should feel a high vibration in your nasal passages, as well as in your fingers. Now, continue holding your nose, and completely relax your throat—allow an* **ah** *sound to flow from deep in your chest. There should be no vibration in your nose at all. Go back and forth several times. Next, we practice flowing from one position to the other, so you can feel exactly when it changes from a nasal sound to a deep, rich schwa. Remember how it was imitating a man's voice when you were little? Do that, pinch your nose, and repeat after me.*

| Nose | | | Throat | | Chest |
|------|------|------|------|------|------|
| ãæ ▶ | ãæ ▶ | ãä ▶ | ä ▶ | ə ▶ | ə |

*Here, we will practice the same progression, but we will stick with the same sound,* **æ**.

| Nose | | | Throat | | Chest |
|------|------|------|------|------|------|
| ãæ ▶ | ãæ ▶ | æ ▶ | æ ▶ | æ ▶ | æ |

*As you will see in Chapter 24, there are three nasal consonants,* **m**, **n**, *and* **ng**. *These have nonnasal counterparts,* **m/b**, **n/d**, **ng/g**. *We're going to practice totally denasalizing your voice for a moment, which means turning the nasals into the other consonants. We'll read the same sentence three times. The first will be quite nasal. The second will sound like you have a cold. The third will have appropriate nasal consonants but denasalized vowels. Repeat after me.*

| Nasal | Hollow | Normal |
|-------|--------|--------|
| Mãry might need money. | Berry bite deed buddy. | Mary might need money. |

## The Underlying Hum

不明显的哼哼声

The underlying hum is quite important and it, too, has to do with your throat. You want to keep the vibration going from one word to the next, gluing the whole phrase together. If words are the train, the hum is the tracks. After applying this technique, a Lebanese doctor was told by his own wife, "Your accent has changed! You're adding extra sounds as if you are filling in the blanks between the words. There's like this background music going on." Exactly! There are no blanks between the words, and there is a continuous hum. (See also Chapter 11)

　　不明显的哼哼声很重要，它也跟你的喉咙有关。你需要让喉咙从一个单词到下一个单词一直保持振动，让整个短语连接起来。如果单词是火车，哼哼声就是铁轨。自从黎巴嫩的一位医生用了这个技巧后，他的妻子告诉他："你的发音变了！你加了一些音，好像要把单词之间的空隙填满。就像现在放的这种背景音乐一样。"没错！单词之间不再有空隙，而是有了一种连续不断的哼哼声。（也见第11章）

## I Closed My Eyes and Listened Carefully

我闭上眼睛，仔细听

The secret to finally getting the American accent you want is just to *listen*. The most successful speakers say, "I closed my eyes and listened carefully." So while the sentence **Bob and Sam brought a good book** may be hard to pronounce at first as **Bäb an Sæm brädə güd bük**, if you close your eyes and listen to the individual sounds, you will hear the way it actually *is* and not the way it's *spelled*. (See also Chapter 8)

　　获得你想要的美语发音的秘诀就是"听"。最成功的说话者说："我闭上眼睛，仔细听。"所以，对于句子Bob and Sam brought a good book（鲍勃和萨姆带来了一本好书），一开始你可能很难将其发音为Bäb an Sæm brädə güd bük，但如果你闭上眼睛，仔细听每个音，你就会听到真正的发音方式，而不是按照拼写来发音。（也见第8章）

## Listening Comprehension

听力理解

We perceive based on past experiences. We're more likely to hear what we *expect* to hear. Everyone thinks that native speakers catch everything when they listen, but actually, they don't. An American listening to the lyric in the classic hymn, **Gladly the cross-eyed bear** might not realize that the actual words are **Gladly the cross I'd bear**, or others like **There's a bathroom on the right** (There's a bad moon on the rise) from *Bad Moon Rising*, and **'Scuze me while I kiss this guy** ('Scuze me while I kiss the sky) from *Purple Haze*. How you hear the language determines how you will speak it. Let's listen for some pure sounds.

　　我们基于以往的经验来认知。我们更倾向于听到我们期望听到的。大家都以为说母语的人能听懂他们听到的一切，但实际上并非如此。一个美国人在听经典的赞美诗的歌词时，听到Gladly the cross-eyed bear（很高兴的斗鸡眼的熊），可能并不会意识到歌词实际上是Gladly the cross I'd bear（很高兴戴上十字架）；或者会把歌曲Bad Moon Rising（《非常时期》）中的歌词There's a bad moon on the rise（邪恶之月正在升起）听为There's a bathroom on the right（右边有个洗手间）；又或者会把

*Purple Haze*（《紫雾》）中的歌词'Scuze me while I kiss the sky（原谅我亲吻天空）听为'Scuze me while I kiss this guy（原谅我亲吻这个人）。你如何听这种语言决定了你如何去说。我们来听一些纯粹的发音吧。

---

**Exercise 1-2: The American Sound**　　　　　　　　　　　　　　　　　　　　　**Track 013**

*Listen to each of the sounds in **bäbee bädə bäik**. Now, say it quickly and smoothly, and write what you think the standard English spelling is.*

_____

Now when you hear, **Bobby bought a bike**, you'll know that it's spelled one way and pronounced another. **Bäbee bädə bäik** doesn't *look* like English, but if you pronounce the words according to the spelling, it really, really won't *sound* like English!

　　现在当你听到Bobby bought a bike（博比买了一辆自行车）时，你就会知道它的拼写是一回事，而发音又是另一回事。Bäbee bädə bäik看起来不像英语，但是如果你按照拼写的方式发音，它听起来真的一点也不像英语！

## Go-To Phrase　　　　　　　　　　　　　　　　　　　　　　　　　　　　　　**Track 014**
Go-To短语

Here's a quick trick. When I put on a German accent, I pick out a few sounds that are particular to that language, and a phrase that contains them, such as **Germans will have to work on the V & W**. I then tighten my lips and from the front of my mouth say, **Cheumans vill haff too veuk ohn zee Fee ent Doppel yu**. It may not be perfect, but it certainly gets me in the ballpark.

　　下面我告诉大家一个小窍门。当我使用德语发音时，我会挑一些这种语言特有的音，以及包含这些音的一个语句，例如Germans will have to work on the V&W（德国人需要努力学习V和W的发音）。接着，我紧闭双唇，用口腔靠前的部位发出Cheumans vill haff too veuk ohn zee Fee ent Doppel yu。可能不是很完美，但是它无疑让我接近了正确的发音。

American English is generated in the back of the mouth and the throat. A couple of go-to phrases in English, to get you in the zone, are *Bob got a water bottle*, *Sam sat back and laughed*, or *Rory ran around*.

　　美式英语由口腔靠后的部位以及喉咙发音。一些可以让你感受到这个发音区域的go-to短语有Bob got a water bottle, Sam sat back and laughed或Rory ran around。

## Variety Is the Spice of Life　　　　　　　　　　　　　　　　　　　　　　　**Track 015**
多样化是生活的调味品

There's the American sound, and then there's sounding American. An important aspect of the American sound is the heavy use of synonyms. We consider it awkward, both in speech and in writing, for a single word or phrase to be repeated more than twice. Twelve times is disconcerting, as in this writing sample from a Vietnamese physiologist.

　　有美式发音，也有空洞的美语。美式英语的一个重要的特点是大量使用同义词。我们觉得无论在口头上还是书面表达中，重复使用一个单词或词组两次以上都很别扭。像下面这位越南生理学家写的文章中，把一个词重复12次简直让人无法接受。

*I live in **Dorchester**, Massachusetts which is in the Northeast of the United States. **Dorchester** is just south of Boston. As an urban city, **Dorchester** is very crowded. **Dorchester** is a poor city. It is known for crimes, drugs and gangsters. Most of people living in **Dorchester** are African American, Hispanic, and Asian. There is still a good number of white people living in **Dorchester**. JFK library and University of Massachusetts Boston are located in **Dorchester**. Every year, **Dorchester** residents celebrate **Dorchester** Day on the first Sunday of June. The parade on **Dorchester** Avenue is the main event of the celebration. The Mayor of Boston, Massachusetts Governor and other local political candidates usually attend the event to gain support from **Dorchester** residents. **Dorchester** Day Parade usually lasts until 2PM in the afternoon.*

Rewritten to have an acceptable number of synonyms:

下面是改写后的文章，它的同义词在可接受的范围内：

*I live in **Dorchester**, Massachusetts which is in the Northeast of the United States. This urban satellite is just south of Boston. As an urban city, it's very poor and crowded. It is known for crimes, drugs and gangsters. Most of people living here are African American, Hispanic, and Asian, but there is still a good number of white people. JFK library and University of Massachusetts Boston are located here. Every year, the residents celebrate **Dorchester** Day on the first Sunday of June. The parade on **Dorchester** Avenue is the main event of the celebration. The Mayor of Boston, Massachusetts Governor and other local political candidates usually attend the event to gain support from local residents. The parade usually lasts until 2PM in the afternoon.*

Variety also applies to active listening, so instead of having one phrase and overusing it, have at least five to ten different responses that you've practiced.

多样化也适用于积极倾听，因此，不要反复使用一个词组，至少要有5到10个你提前练习好的不同的回答方式。

| | | |
|---|---|---|
| 1. Ah, I see... | 6. Really? | 11. Is that a fact? |
| 2. Oh, that's interesting! | 7. Oh, yeah! | 12. You don't say. |
| 3. Hmm, tell me more. | 8. Right. | 13. Wow, that's weird! |
| 4. Got it! | 9. Fair enough. | 14. Oh, no! |
| 5. Gotcha! | 10. Good point, I can see that. | 15. That's too bad. |

## Intonation and Attitude
**Track 016**

语调和态度

There are certain sounds in any language that are considered nonsense syllables yet impart a large amount of information to the informed listener. Each language has a different set of these sounds, such as **eto ne** in Japanese, **em** in Spanish, **eu** in French, and **um** in English. In this particular case, these are the sounds that a native speaker makes when he is thinking out loud—holding the floor, but not yet committing to actually speaking.

在任何语言中，都有某些发音被认为是无意义的音节，然而，这些发音向信息接收者传递了大量的信息。每种语言都有一系列这样的发音，比如日语中的eto ne，西班牙语中的em，法语中的eu，以及英语中的um。以此为例，当说母语的人正在努力思考但尚未付诸实际言语时，他发出这些音以拖长发言时间。

**Exercise 1-3: Nonverbal Intonation**      **Track 017**

*The top eight are the most common nonword communication sounds. They can all be nasalized or not, and said with the mouth open or closed. Intonation is the important factor here. Repeat after me.*

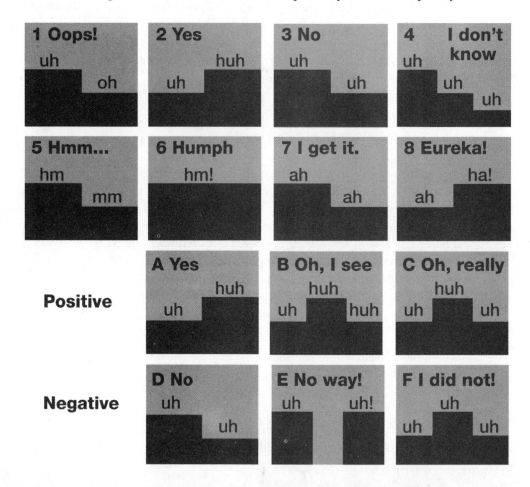

**Exercise 1-4: Sounds of Empathy**      **Track 018**

*Let's see how well you interpret emotionally meaningful words.*

1. Okay
   A. ☑ Got it!
   B. ❑ Uneasy
   C. ❑ Depressed

2. Okay
   A. ❑ Surprised
   B. ☑ Cheerful
   C. ❑ Impatient

3. Okay
   A. ☑ What a good idea!
   B. ❑ Whatever
   C. ❑ Doubtful

4. Thanks
   A. ❑ Sarcastic
   B. ☑ Appreciative
   C. ❑ Unsure

5. Fine
   A. ☑ Great!
   B. ❑ Annoyed
   C. ❑ I don't care...

6. Uh-huh
   A. ❑ Sure, no problem
   B. ❑ I do, too!
   C. ☑ Really?

7. No
A. ☑ Absolutely not!
B. ❑ How ridiculous
C. ❑ Defensive

8. Sure
A. ❑ Disbelieving
B. ❑ Worried
C. ☑ Quickly agreeable

9. Yeah
A. ☑ Positive
B. ❑ Unsure
C. ❑ Supportive

10. Sooo
A. ☑ Expecting more info
B. ❑ Impatient
C. ❑ Uneasy

11. What
A. ☑ That's funny
B. ❑ Not caring
C. ❑ Uh-oh, not again

12. Really
A. ❑ Barely attentive
B. ☑ Is that true?
C. ❑ Bored

13. Well
A. ☑ Sorta/kinda
B. ❑ Annoyed
C. ❑ Happy

14. I don't know
A. ❑ Curious
B. ❑ Casual
C. ☑ Why ask me?!

15. Hey
A. ❑ Shy
B. ☑ Canned enthusiasm
C. ❑ Bored

16. Yes
A. ❑ Confused
B. ☑ Go on...
C. ❑ Great joy

17. Sorry
A. ❑ Not sorry at all
B. ☑ Apologetic
C. ❑ Perky

18. Okay
A. ❑ Resigned
B. ❑ Excited
C. ☑ Sure, why not?

19. Hmmm
A. ☑ What?!
B. ❑ Not so sure
C. ❑ Thinking

20. I know
A. ❑ Nonchalant
B. ☑ Knowing
C. ❑ Defensive

21. Oh
A. ❑ Happy
B. ☑ Disappointed
C. ❑ Confused

## Warm Up with Run-Up Phrases

Track 019

用前奏短语预热

Another trick to oil the joints is to pick some general intro phrases and string them all together with as strong an American accent as possible, without ever actually saying anything, just focusing on creating that rich, round, deep American sound... **Well, you know, I was just thinking, and it kinda seems like, uhh, what do you think about...**

　　另外一个让表达流利的秘诀是加入一些普通的引入语，并且用尽可能浓重的美音把它们连接起来，不需要真正地说出什么内容，只需专注地发出那种饱满、圆润、深沉的美音即可…… Well, you know, I was just thinking, and it kinda seems like, uhh, what do you think about...（嗯，你知道的，我正在想，看起来好像是，呃，你怎么看……）

> Don't overthink it —
> just do it.
>
> 别想太多——
> 只管去做。

# Chapter 2
# 第2章

# Psycholinguistics
# 心理语言学

Track 020

## So You're In a Tough Relationship with English; Let's Talk About That!
## 这么说你学习英语很有困难；那我们来谈谈吧！

Maybe you've tried to pick up an American accent before and it made you uncomfortable. Maybe your family thinks that you shouldn't change. Maybe you've tried and failed, and now you're frustrated. Whatever the reason, you've got an unsatisfying relationship with English. We're here to fix that.

也许你之前尝试过学习美语发音，但是学习的过程让你不舒服；也许你的家人认为你不必改变自己的发音；也许你尝试过但失败了，而你现在很沮丧。不论是什么样的原因，你在英语学习方面都存在困难。我们现在就来克服它。

## Let's Get Your Head in the Right Place
## 我们一起来帮你树立正确的观点

Learning a whole language is indeed a big deal, but you've already done all the heavy lifting, having learned the grammar and vocabulary. Right now, we're just doing the fine-tuning and working on your accent. Here's what you should expect after the first one to six weeks (depending on your diligence).

Track 021

学习一门新的语言确实是一件不容易的事，但你已经克服了最难的部分，你已经学会了语法和词汇。现在，我们只是做些调整，来帮助你改进发音。下面是你在学习了一到六周后应该会达到的程度（取决于你的勤奋程度）。

There are two ways to pick up the accent: all at once or step-by-step.

Track 022

有两种学习发音的方式：一步到位和按部就班。

There's the do-it-now people and the people who like to change slowly, thinking that there is no validity to things that happen quickly to them. People don't think it's real if it's fast. But that's the Nike® slogan, "Just do it!" You know you can, and even if it is faster than you expect, it's still valid. It's all about behavior modeling. You don't have to believe it, you just have to do it.

有的人喜欢立刻行动，有的人喜欢慢慢改变，后者认为对他们来说太快发生的事情没有效果。人们认为太快发生的事情是不真实的。但是正如耐克的广告语"只管去做！"一样，你知道自己可以的。即便它比自己想象的快，也依然是有效的。这就是所谓的行为模仿。你不需要相信它，去做就行。

## All at Once

Just do it! Listen to the sounds and rhythms. Capture some essential elements, and go!

只管去做！听发音和节奏。抓住一些重要特征，说出来！

## Step-by-Step

Apply each technique one by one to develop your voice quality, pronunciation, intonation, phrasing, and linking. After you have mastered each of these elements, work on integrating them into speech.

一次使用一种发音技巧，使你的音质、发音、语调、断句和连读不断提高。在掌握了每种技巧后，把它们融入到你的口头表达中去。

Which method will work best for you? We'll try the all-at-once way first to see if we can jump-start you with this shortcut. This isn't so much about the American accent as much as it's about you doing pure mimicry. Don't think. Don't overanalyze. Just imitate exactly what you hear in every aspect—voice quality, pronunciation, rhythm, phrasing, and word flow.

哪种方法最适合你？我们先来试试一步到位的方法，看我们能否通过这种捷径让你快速开始。这种方式与其说是练习美语发音，不如说是进行纯粹的模仿。不要思考。不要过多地分析。只是正确地模仿你所听到的一切——音质、发音、节奏、断句和单词流。

| Exercise 2-1: Pure Mimicry | Track 023 |
|---|---|

*Listen to this heavy Australian accent, record yourself, and compare the two. (If you don't have a recorder handy, go to AmericanAccent.com/recorder.)*

**Track 024**

**Please call Stella.**

**Track 025**

When comparing your recording with our Aussie friend, see if you copied his nasality, used **plays** for the pronunciation of **please**, and included the distinctive phrasing as he finishes up the sentence. If your recording matches closely and you were comfortable with the process, go to Chapter 3 and get started. If it wasn't entirely satisfying for you, or your recording didn't sound like him, let's take a moment to think about who you are, and how you learn best.

把你自己的录音和我们这位澳大利亚朋友的做比较，看看你是否重现了他的鼻音，是否把please发音为plays，是否像他一样在说完这句话后有明显的断句。如果你的录音非常吻合，而且你觉得过程很轻松，那么直接进入第3章开始学习。如果你觉得不是很满意，或者你的录音听起来不像他，那我们就花些时间想一想你的水平，以及你用什么样的方式学习最好。

**Exercise 2-2: Are You Steadfast or Freewheeling?**  **Track 026**

*Answer the following questions with a checkmark in the appropriate box.*

1. Would you rather answer...
   - ❑ An essay question
   - ☑ A multiple-choice question

2. Do you...
   - ❑ Start from yes
   - ❑ Start from no

3. Do you prefer solutions that are...
   - ❑ Open-ended, abstract, and subject to interpretation
   - ❑ Clear-cut, precise, and objective

4. Are you...
   - ❑ Comfortable with a flexible time frame with constant updates
   - ❑ More deadline oriented

5. Do you prefer to...
   - ❑ Follow another person's lead
   - ❑ Do things your own way

1. 你更愿意回答
   - ❑ 一个论述性的问题
   - ❑ 一个多项选择题

2. 你的回答以
   - ❑ "是" 开始
   - ❑ "不" 开始

3. 你更喜欢的解决方法是
   - ❑ 开放式的、抽象的、需要进行解读的
   - ❑ 清晰的、准确的、客观的

4. 你是否
   - ❑ 习惯于灵活的时间规划，随时可进行调整
   - ❑ 更倾向于明确的截止时间

5. 你更愿意
   - ❑ 听从别人的引导
   - ❑ 用自己的方式做事

If you selected the second option two or more times, try this experiment. Just for today, when someone says something to you, practice temporarily suspending judgment. Respond with, "Hmm, that's interesting," "Tell me more," or "You could be right." Not only will this help you listen better, it will also make you a better conversationalist and open your mind to picking up and using this accent.

如果你选择第二个选项的次数在两次或两次以上，试着做下面这个实验吧。就在今天一天，当有人对你说了一些事情，练习暂时地延长做出判断的时间。用下面这些话来回答："嗯，听起来很有意思""再多给我讲一些"或"你可能是对的"。这样不仅能帮助你更好地倾听，也能使你成为更好的谈话者，同时打开心扉，学习和使用美语发音。

**Exercise 2-3: Mimicry**  **Track 027**

*Say the following sentence out loud:*

**Track 028**

**There was a time when people really had a way with words.**

**Track 029**

Did you say it out loud (not to yourself, actually out loud)? If you did, go on to the next exercise. If not, let's talk about why you didn't. As we all know, *stubborn* is a negative word, and nobody wants to attribute a negative word to himself or herself. As the famous curmudgeon Bertrand Russell said, "**I** am firm. **You** are obstinate. **He** is a pig-headed fool." Interestingly, stubbornness has both *positive* (consistent, reliable, persistent) and *negative* (stubborn, inflexible, rigid) aspects.

你是不是大声说出来了（不是对你来说的大声，而是真正的大声）？如果是这样，就接着做下一个练习。如果不是，我们来谈谈你为什么没有。我们都知道，"固执"是一个贬义词，没有人愿意把贬义词用在自己身上。著名的坏脾气伯特兰·罗素说过："我很坚定。你很倔强。他是个顽固的笨蛋。"有趣的是，"固执"是既有褒义（一贯的、可靠的、坚持的）也有贬义的（顽固的、不变通的、死板的）。

Think back in your life to a time when persistence paid off. It may have been following through on an idea to successful fruition or overcoming apparently insurmountable odds on something important to you. Own that, it's yours. One of my favorite responses was when I asked a successful businessman if he'd had everything handed to him, if building his business had been easy or if he'd had to fight to succeed. "Fight?!" he barked, "I've had to kill!"

回想一下自己的生活，是否有一段时间你的坚持很有成效。可能是坚持一个想法直到它成功实现，或者是在一件对你来说很重要的事情上克服了似乎不可逾越的障碍。坚持吧，那是属于你的。有一次，我问一个成功的商业人士，他的所有收获是不是手到擒来，他创业的过程是否轻松、是否需要努力奋斗才得以成功，他的回答是我最喜欢的回答之一。"奋斗？"他咆哮道，"我得拼命！"

Now, however, we're going to look at how stubbornness can get in your way. Stubbornness isn't necessarily something that just happens later in life, but is often an innate trait. Many of us have a deep-seated feeling of what is *right*, and it's hard to go against this. If you're a visual learner, chances are you did well on spelling tests, and so you have a sense of the *rightness* of spelling. It can be checked and validated. Speech, however, may seem very fluid and free form to you. For this process, however, you need to embrace the *rightness* of phonetic spelling for speech as much as you embrace the *rightness* of spelling for written English and the *rightness* of mathematical notation for numbers.

但是现在，我们要看看固执是如何阻止你成功的。固执并不是今后的生活中必须发生的事情，通常是一种与生俱来的特质。我们中的很多人对于什么是"正确的"都有一种根深蒂固的感觉，这点很难改变。如果你是个视觉型学习者，你可能在拼写测试中表现很好，那么你就有一种在拼写方面"正确"的感觉。它是可以被检查和证实的。而说话对你来说可能是一种非常不固定的、自由的形式。对于这个过程，你需要把音标拼写的"正确性"和说话结合起来，就像你把拼写的"正确性"和书面英语结合起来以及把数学符号的"正确性"和数字结合起来一样。

Sometimes you're not being stubborn—you really *do* forget because you're focusing on **what** you're saying instead of **how** you're saying it. To illustrate this, a researcher had a problem with the door of the lab refrigeration unit, whose tall upright handle had come loose. Not having time to fix it, he decided to open it by pulling on the side. Not five minutes later, he went back to grab some more vials and opened the fridge with the handle. It came completely loose and clonked him on the head! This time, he knew he had to remember, so he put a note right on the handle to remind himself. And again, a few minutes later, when he went back to get another vial, he grabbed the handle and hit himself on the head again. Clearly he needed a more dramatic solution. He took a whole page of newspaper and covered the entire handle of the fridge, so that the next time he mindlessly grabbed the handle, the newspaper crackled, and he realized what he was about to do. It's not like he *wanted* to get hit in the head, he just kept forgetting because he was focused on the **goal** and not the **process**. Sometimes people speaking English are so focused on the end product of using words in conversation, like he was in the end product of getting vials out of the fridge, that they forget to include the accent and pronunciation.

有时候，你并不是固执——你是真的忘了，因为你专注于说的内容，而不是说的方式。我们举个例子来说明这点。有位研究员，他实验室里的冷藏设备的门出了点问题——位于高处的长把手松了。由于没有时间去修，研究员决定抓着门边打开冷柜。不到五分钟后，他再次回来取一些小瓶时，又抓着门把手开冷柜。把手完全松掉了，重重地砸在了他的头上。这次，他知道他下次必须得记住，于是在门把手上贴了个便条提醒自己。但是几分钟后，他再次回来取另一个小瓶时，又抓住门把手，把手又一次砸在了他头上。显然，他需要一种更显著的解决方法。他拿了一整张报纸盖住了整个门把手，这样下次在他不小心又抓到门把手时，报纸会发出声响，他就会意识到自己正要做的事情。他并不想被把手打到头，他只是一直忘记，因为他只专注于"目的"，而不是"过程"。人们说英语时，有时会过于关注在对话中使用词语所达到的最终结果，就像研究者过于关注最后把小瓶子拿出冷柜这一结果，他们忘了同时还要注意语音和发音。

## Think, Then Act
### 先思考，后行动

When you have learned the techniques, but forget to apply them in speech, you are **acting** before **thinking**. In order to train yourself to think first, devise a strategy that works for you. For the researcher, it was putting a sheet of newspaper over the fridge handle. For you, it might be taking a deep breath before speaking, counting to three, pulling on a rubber band, or even the old school standby: a string around your finger. The point is, while you are internalizing these new sounds and rhythms, to create a stopgap measure to get you to focus on the process and not so much the goal.

如果你已经学会了技巧，但是忘了把它们用在语言中，你就是行动先于思考。为了训练你先思考，这里设置了一种可以帮助你的策略。对于上面的研究员来说，在冷柜把手上放一张报纸很管用。对于你来说，以下这些方法可能管用：在说话之前先深吸一口气、数到三、拉橡皮条，或者甚至是学校里老式的替换办法——在手指上缠一根线。这样做的用意是，当你在内化这些新的声音和节奏时，创造出一种权宜措施来使你关注过程而不是过多地关注结果。

## The Four Stages of Learning
### 学习的四个阶段

Let's look at the transition you're going to be going through.

我们来看一看你需要经历的转变。

1. Unconscious incompetence (you don't even know you're making mistakes).

无意识的错误（你甚至不知道自己在犯错）。

2. Conscious incompetence (you're aware, but you don't know how to fix them).

有意识的错误（你知道自己出错了，但是不知道如何修正）。

3. Conscious competence (when you focus really hard, you're actually pretty good).

有意识的能力（当你努力注意时，你做得非常好）。

4. Unconscious competence (you've internalized the concepts, and it's second nature).

无意识的能力（你已经内化了概念，变成了习惯）。

You're most likely edging from **2** to **3**. To get to **4**, the key is consistent practice—a minimum of 15 minutes per day, plus applying the techniques whenever you talk.

你最有可能处于第2或第3阶段。要达到第4阶段，关键是坚持不懈地练习——每天至少练习15分钟，再加上每次说话时都注意使用学过的技巧。

| Exercise 2-4: Correlating Sounds & Phonetic Transcription | Track 031 |
| --- | --- |

*Listen to this sound and correlate it with this phonetic transcription:*

**Track 032**

### gäddit

Repeat this sound and notice the open **ah** sound of **gä**, the way the tip of your tongue flicks on the bumps on the top of your mouth, and the fact that the air doesn't pop out at the end of the word. Listen to the audio and say this out loud ten times. (See also Chapter 8)

重复这个音，注意gä里张开的ah音，感受舌尖轻弹上颚的隆起处，同时注意气流并没有在词尾爆破。听音频，大声念十次。（也见第8章）

| Exercise 2-5: Correlating Phonetic Transcription & Regular Spelling | Track 033 |
| --- | --- |

*Listen to this sound and correlate it with this phonetic transcription:*

### gäddit        Got it!

Using the exact same sounds as before, observe how different the spelling is. Listen to the audio and say this out loud ten times.

使用跟前面一样的发音，观察与实际拼写的差别。听音频，大声念十次。

## Skidiz
**Track 034**

Let me tell you a little story about how I came to "get" word connections in French, or as they like to call them, liaisons. I stumbled upon the word **skidiz** and was amazed that it could represent **ce qu'ils disent**. *Wow! That looks different!* I thought to myself. *They'll never understand me if I say it like that.* Fortunately, my empirical side prevailed and I thought, *Okay, fine, I'll try it, even if it's just to prove that it doesn't work.*

让我来告诉你一个小故事，关于我如何"获得"法语中的词的连读，或者他们喜欢称为的"连音"。我偶然碰到了skidiz这个单词，并且惊奇地发现它可以表达为ce qu'ils disent。"哇！这看起来可真不一样！"我自己这么想。"如果我这么说，他们肯定听不懂。"幸运的是，我喜欢尝试的一面占了上风，而且我想："好吧，我还是试一下吧，即便就是为了证实一下这么说真的不行。"

I was in Marseilles, so I combined it with the local pronunciation of **Je ne sais pas** and managed to work **Sheh pah skidiz** in as a conversational response. Whoa! To my huge surprise it worked, and the person started talking to me in real French and not baby language. That led me to part two of the epiphany: *Yikes, if I do this, it'll totally raise their expectations of how well I speak*, and then, *Ahh, I'm talking the way I want them to talk to me, so I can understand them more easily!*

我当时在马赛，于是我把它和当地的发音Je ne sais pas结合起来，并且尝试在和别人谈论的回答中夹杂了Sheh pah skidiz。哇哦！令我大为吃惊的是，对方居然听懂了，并开始用真正的法语跟我交谈，而不再用婴儿语。这让我进入了顿悟的第二阶段："呀，如果我这么说，会完全提高他们对我语言能力的预期，"接着是，"啊，我在用我希望他们跟我说话的方式说话，因此我可以更容易听懂他们的话！"

Once I realized how I'd been sabotaging myself, I started trusting the phonetics and stopped basing my pronunciation on spelling. My confidence went up because thought follows behavior, and my new behavior resulted in more sophisticated, intelligent conversations. People didn't have to talk down to my language level but could actually talk with me at my conversational level. It's my goal that you have that same realization with **gäddit**. My job is to give the epiphany. Your job is to hold on and use it. (See also Chapter 10)

当我意识到我一直在妨碍自己时，立刻开始相信音标，而放弃基于单词拼写来发音。因为行为影响想法，我的新行为引起了更加成熟、有智慧的交谈，自信心也增加了。人们不再迁就我的语言水平来跟我交谈，而是可以在我的交谈水平上和我进行真正的谈话。我的目的是想让你们从gäddit这个例子得到同样的认识。我要做的是给出顿悟。你要做的是坚持使用它。（也见第10章）

### Exercise 2-6: Gathering that Empirical Evidence — Track 035

*Trusting in this method is an important component of how successful you will be, so we're going to do a short trust exercise. Take this phrase out into the world, and use it exactly the way it's presented here. Try it out on coworkers and friends. Watch how they respond to you now that they can hear you playing with the language a little.*

#### gäddit / Got it!

 We tend to think of language primarily as a *tool*,
我们往往把语言当成一种工具，

 or as a *weapon*.
或者武器。

 Instead, start playing around in the English *toy box*.
其实不然，学着把英语当做一个装满玩具的箱子来对待吧。

Play with the sounds, rhythms, and patterns. Have fun! You'll find that some of the inhibitions fall away, and your linguistic adaptability kicks in.

和发音、节奏、模式一起，好好玩吧！你会发现一些压抑逐渐消失，语言的适应性也显现了出来。

# Phonetic Transcription = Mathematical Notation

标音法 = 数学符号

If you accept that **2 x 2** can also be written **2²**, you are comfortable with multiple labels for a single concept. This is the same principle as the word **cat** also being written as **kæt**.

如果你能接受2×2也可以写为2²，那么你就能接受一个概念有不同的表示法。这和单词cat也可以写为kæt的原理一样。

Here is a simple two-part rule for the letter **o**:

下面是关于字母o的两个简单的规则：

> **1.** In a *one-syllable* word, **o** sounds like **ä** (unless the word ends in **e**):
>
> 在单音节单词中，o听起来像ä（除非单词以e结尾）：
>
> hot, lost, Tom, Bob, dot com

> **2.** In a *stressed* syllable, **o** also sounds like **ä**:
>
> 在重音节里，o听起来也像ä：
>
> possible, Holland, philosophy

Here is a two-part rule for the letter **a**:

下面是关于字母a的两个规则：

> **1.** In a *one-syllable* word, **a** sounds like **æ** (unless the word ends in **e**):
>
> 在单音节单词中，a听起来像æ（除非单词以e结尾）：
>
> cat, Sam, drab

> **2.** In a *stressed* syllable, **a** sounds like **æ**:
>
> 在重音节里，a听起来也像æ：
>
> rational, manager, catastrophe

(For more on these two vowels, see Chapter 12)

（想更多地了解这两个元音，见第12章）

Once you have internalized the basic rules of phonetics, you need to diligently, persistently, and *stubbornly* apply them universally. In computing terms, think of doing a global **Search All** and **Replace**.

一旦你内化了语音学的基本规则，就需要勤奋地、坚持不懈地、"固执地"广泛使用它们。用电脑术语来说，就是进行全面的"查找"和"替换"。

Some people have an initial aversion to reading phonetics because it's new and confusing. *It doesn't even look like English!* This is where we're going to have you practice some of that open-mindedness and trust. Accept that if you read the phonetics, you *will* have an American accent.

有些人一开始读这些音标时会有些反感，因为它们是全新的，而且令人困惑。"它看起来甚至不像英语！"这正是我们将会让你练习的思想开放性和信任的一方面。接受吧，当你读出这些音标时，你会拥有美语发音的。

An accountant kept making the same pronunciation errors in English over and over again. Asked why, her response was consistently, "I forgot!" When asked if she forgot arithmetic, the answer was, "Of course not, that would make my life miserable."

一位会计师在说英语时总是一次又一次出现相同的发音错误。当问她原因时，她的回答总是"我忘了！"当问她是否会忘记算术时，她回答："当然不会，那样会让我的生活很悲惨。"

Well, not applying the phonetics was making her life miserable!

可是，不正确使用这种音标一直让她的生活很悲惨！

## Over-Confidence                                          Track 037
过度自信

Counterintuitively, it's sometimes overconfidence that gets in a person's way. You're used to the positive rewards of doing things quickly and independently—an algebraic equation, a sales report with a high closing rate, a dissertation. Because you're good at what you do, you can skip over certain details. However, if you try to rush through speaking English you'll end up skipping crucial details. Furthermore, if you only rely on your *own* judgment about your accent, particularly if it's spelling based, you're going to fall far short of the mark.

与直觉相反的是，有时候过度自信会成为一个人的阻碍。你习惯于快速、独立地完成工作，并且得到积极的肯定——一个代数方程，一个有着高收盘汇率的销售报告，一篇论文。因为你擅长自己所做的事情，所以可以略过某些细节。但是，如果你仓促地说英语，你最终会错过一些重要的细节。另外，如果你仅仅依赖自己对自己发音的判断，特别是这种发音还是基于拼写的，你会远远达不到目的。

What to do about it? Start from scratch and make a conscious effort to get rid of your preconceptions. Put yourself in the position of knowing nothing about pronunciation, intonation, voice quality, word connections, etc. Then, lay the foundation with basic sounds and rhythms. Rebuild a new strong structure, using the grammar and vocab you've worked so hard to acquire.

怎么做呢？从零开始，有意识地努力摆脱以前的观念。假设自己对发音、语调、音质以及词的连读等一无所知。接着，用基本的语音和节奏打好基础。使用你之前下了很大的工夫学到的语法和词汇重新建立一种坚实的结构。

## The "What" Factor                                        Track 038
"What" 因素

Let's do a quick assessment of what other people think of your accent. How often during a day does someone ask you to repeat yourself? How long does it take to give your e-mail address, and how many times do you have to spell your name? That's your "What?" factor. But the real question is, how does this affect you? How does it affect your working situation, your home life, your life as a whole? Does it make you feel discouraged, or does it encourage you to change? Or does it make you feel like everyone else needs to change around you? Let me tell you a story about someone who felt this way. We'll call her Mei Li.

我们来做一个快速的评估，看看别人认为你的发音怎么样。一天之内有多少人让你重复一遍说过的话？你告诉别人自己的邮箱地址要花多长时间？你拼写自己的名字时需要说几遍？这就是你的"what"因素。但是真正的问题是，它对你有什么影响？它如何影响你的工作情况、家庭生活以及整个生活？它让你感觉很沮丧，还是让你想要改变？或者它是否让你觉得你周围的所有人都应该改变？我来给你讲个故事，故事的主人公就是这么感觉的。我们叫她Mei Li。

A Chinese professor was studying English in the United States, and her instructor had suggested that, for convenience, she Americanize the pronunciation of her name, and she flew into a rage. She excoriated him in a long e-mail about how disrespectful this was to 5,000 years of her Chinese ancestors. The American instructor was stunned and passed her on upstairs.

一位中国教授在美国学习英语。她的导师建议她，为了方便，把她名字的发音美国化，而这让她勃然大怒。她给导师写了一封很长的邮件，痛斥这种做法对于她五千年来的列位祖先来说是多么的不敬。这位美国导师非常震惊，把她交给了上一级的导师处理。

The senior instructor set about finding out what was going on. To say Dr. Li was linguistically rigid is a profound understatement. The instructor would ask, "But let's say you're at the DMV. The clerk doesn't know from Chinese ancestors. Don't you just want him to catch your name the first time and to process the transaction?" "No!" she would declare. "It's my *name*!"

这位级别较高的导师打算找出原因。如果说李教授在语言方面比较死板，那都算是轻描淡写了。导师问："我们假设你在机动车辆管理局，而办事员不懂汉语。你难道不想让他一次就听懂你的名字，并帮你开始办理业务吗？""不！"她郑重地说，"那可是我的名字！"

The instructor finally told her that they simply had to make a breakthrough, so her entire homework would consist of leaving a voice mail with her name Americanized so it would be easier to understand by any random person. She left eight to ten identical Chinese-sounding attempts. Finally, she left one that started with a deep sigh and a deeper voice, "My name is Mei Li." It was a thing of beauty. Unfortunately, 30 seconds later, she left another *very* nasal one, "My name is Mei Liiiiiiiiiiiiiiiiii!"

最后，导师告诉她，他们必须做个突破，而她的所有作业就是给导师发送一封语音邮件，把她自己的名字发音美音化，让任何一个人都能轻松地听明白。她尝试着留了8到10个相似的中国式发音的名字。在她最后留的一个语音邮件里，她先长叹了一声，然后用一种深沉的嗓音说："我的名字是Mei Li。"听起来很不错。遗憾的是，30秒之后，她又留了另外一条鼻音很重的语音邮件："我的名字是Mei Liiiiiiiiiiiiiiiii！"

## Go On, Change Your Name                                    Track 039
来吧，改变你的名字

No, not permanently or legally, but get comfortable with saying your own name differently than you have for your entire life. It may feel weird, unreal, surreal, or just plain dumb, but it's an invaluable mental exercise. Every time I landed in a new country, my first order of business was to find out who I was, or at least how my name was pronounced. I went from Madrid (*Me llamo Anita*) to Paris (*Je m'appelle Annie*) to Tokyo (私はアニーです).

不需要永远改变或从法律上改变你的名字，而是接受用一生都没有用过的不同的方式来说自己的名字。它可能让你感觉奇怪、不真实、荒诞或者简直愚不可及，但这是一种宝贵的精神体验。我每到一个新的国家，第一要务就是定位自己，或者至少知道我的名字是怎么发音的。我到马德里时说Me llamo Anita，到巴黎时说Je m'appelle Annie，到了东京又会说私はアニーです。

## Drop the Baggage!
放下包袱！

For a lot of people, the American accent comes with a lot of emotional baggage. *Americans are loud! Emotionally immature! Unsophisticated!* It may be conflicting for an educated sophisticate such as yourself to work toward actually sounding like this. But you need to fit in and be understood, so drop off the baggage. Just focus on the pure sounds.

对很多人来说，美式发音伴随着许多情感包袱。"美国人声音很大！感情不成熟！不懂世故！"对于像你自己这样受过教育、久经世故的人来说，要学习这种发音可能有些抵触。但是你必须适应，必须让人听得懂，所以放下包袱吧。集中注意力在纯粹的发音上。

## Emotional Investment in Particular Sounds
对于特殊发音的情感投入

A man with a distinctly Spanish accent had trouble distinguishing *iPod* from *iPad*. He learned the **æ** sound for iPad but didn't extrapolate that sound to other words, such as **cat**, **laugh**, or **dance**. It would be natural to think that he simply didn't know where to use it. But surprisingly, when asked why he didn't use the **æ** sound, he laughingly responded, "Because I hate it."

一个有明显西班牙口音的男人在区分iPod和iPad的发音上有困难。他学会了iPad中的æ音，但是不会把那个音延伸运用到其他单词里，例如cat, laugh或dance。你可能会自然地觉得他仅仅是不知道什么时候该发这个音。但是，让人惊奇的是，当问他为什么不发æ音时，他大笑着回答："因为我讨厌这个音。"

Some people have a strong identification with their pronunciation, considering it part of their identity or personal brand. They may reject a single sound or the entire accent. Unless the change wells from within, the accent won't take root and become a true part of them.

有些人的发音有很强的辨识度，他们把这个当成是一种特点或个人特色的一部分。他们可能会拒绝某个发音或某种口音。除非从内心决定改变，否则这种发音是无法扎根并真正成为他们的一部分的。

## Motivation
动机

 Sofia Vergara, a Colombian actor in the American sitcom "Modern Family," was doing an interview, explaining that her 21-year-old son had seen a video of her many years earlier and said, "Mom, you're the only person who's come to America and your accent got worse!" Her utterly charming response was, "It's the moh-nee; I don't have to do eet anymore!" In another interview, Oprah Winfrey asked why her accent seems to be getting heavier, even though she'd been living in America for some time. Sofia explained that she actually does it for comedic effect, "I realized that sometimes it was funnier to say **YOOOUHH** rather than **you**." She's very self-aware and has excellent reasons for maintaining her brand.

索菲娅·贝尔加拉是出演过美国情景喜剧《摩登家庭》的一名哥伦比亚演员。在一次访谈中，她说她21岁的儿子看过她许多年前的一个视频后跟她说："妈妈，你是唯一一个来到美国后发音变差的人！"她非常可爱地回答道："当时是为了挣钱，我现在不用那样做了！"在另外一次访谈中，奥普拉·温弗里问她，她在美国生活也有些日子了，为什么口音还越来越重。索菲娅解释说她其实是为了喜剧效果："我发现有时候说YOOOUHH比you更有意思。"她非常有自我意识，而且她有充分的理由继续维持她的特色。

Over the years, however, we've heard pretty much every excuse from people who have demonstrated that they are able to *create* the sounds in isolation but don't go on to the next step of universally *applying the rules*.

很多人是能够单独地发出每个音的，但是却没有继续进行下去，没有把发音规则加以广泛应用。多年以来，我们听到了各式各样的理由。

| I feel uncomfortable.<br>我觉得不舒服。 | It's not possible.<br>这不可能。 | I tried and can't.<br>我试过但是不行。 |
|---|---|---|
| I don't understand the rules.<br>我不理解发音规则。 | Why should I have to?<br>我为什么要那么做？ | It's not "right."<br>它是不"正确的"。 |
| I wasn't thinking about it.<br>我没想过。 | It makes me sound arrogant.<br>那样让我听起来很傲慢。 | I forgot.<br>我忘了。 |
| I was focusing on what I was saying.<br>我把注意力集中在了我要说的事情上。 | People will laugh at me.<br>人们会笑话我的。 | I was rushing.<br>我当时很着急。 |

## Does Pronunciation Really Matter?
发音真的重要吗？

People say, *It's just a detail...does it really matter? Isn't "okay" good enough for what's needed and not worth the effort of going to the next level? We don't have that sound in my language, and we communicate just fine without it.* This may be true, but if you're, let's say, a doctor, don't you want your patients to know the difference between your saying, "He's in urology" and "He's in neurology" or "We did a below-knee amputation" and not "We did a baloney amputation"? So yes: Pronunciation matters!

人们说，"它只是个细节……真的这么重要吗？难道'还可以'还不能满足需求，不可以进入下一个阶段？我的语言里没有那个音，但是不发它我们也可以很好地交流。"听起来也许有道理，但是我们假设一下，如果你是位医生，难道你不想让你的病人听出你说"他在泌尿科"和"他在神经科"的区别吗？或者让他知道你说的是"我们做了膝下截肢"而不是"我们做了熏肠截肢"？所以，没错：发音很重要！

## Go to Extremes                                                Track 041
走极端

As an exercise, we have people put on a caricature of an American accent, and generally it's quite accurate. They are reluctant, however, to use it because of the inherent mockery involved. It's okay! I can assure you that Americans won't even notice when you're putting on a superheavy American accent. They'll just think your English got better.

作为练习，我们让人们用一种夸张的美音说话，通常听起来很标准。但是，由于它有点自我嘲笑，人们不愿意这样说话。没关系的！我可以向你保证，美国人根本不会发现你用了超级浓重的美国口音，他们只会觉得你的英语说得更好了。

Your family and friends may react negatively and make fun of your nascent attempts to modify your speech. They like you the way you are. They may think your accent is cute. They may think that if you change how you talk you may change who you are. The bottom line is that you will sound different, and they may not like it.

你的家人和朋友可能会有消极的反应，嘲笑你为了修正语音所做的初期尝试。他们喜欢原来的你。他们可能觉得你的口音很可爱，觉得如果你改变了说话方式，就可能也会改变你自己。根本问题就是你会听起来不一样，他们可能不会喜欢。

We recommend practicing on strangers. They don't have a baseline and can accept you at face value. At this point, it may be hard for you to conceive how differently you will be treated. A lot of Americans, I regret to say, turn off when they hear a foreign accent, or are less than kind. Since we can't change all of them, we can make a small change in you.

我们建议和陌生人练习。他们没有衡量标准，会认为你说话就是那样的。这时候，可能对你来说很难料到别人对待你的差别。遗憾地说，很多美国人听到外国口音，会掉头就走或不太友好。既然我们无法改变他们，我们可以让你做一些小的改变。

## Your Own True Voice                                           Track 042
你自己真正的声音

There is not, of course, just one American voice, even for one person. People associate their voices with themselves but have many different voices throughout their lives. You have a different voice as a child than as an adult, different in business than at a party, and so on.

当然，即使对于同一个人来说，也不会只有一种美音。人们把发出的声音和自己联系起来，但是可能一生中会有许多不同的声音。你还是孩子的时候和成年后的声音不同，你在商务场合和聚会场合的声音不同，等等。

Stephen Hawking, the British astrophysicist, had an English accent prior to the paralyzation of his vocal cords. After using a robotic voice with an American accent, he came to associate himself with that voice. Several years later, when production of the DECtalk DCT01 voice synthesizer was discontinued, he declined to switch to a model with a British accent. He identified with the American voice and associated it with himself. "I would not want to change, even if I were offered a British-sounding voice. I would feel I had become a different person," he said.

英国天体物理学家史蒂芬·霍金在他的声带瘫痪之前是英式发音。在使用了美音作为他的机器人声音之后，他开始把自己和那个声音联系起来。多年以后，当DECtalk DCT01型号的语音合成器停产之后，他不愿意更换成英式发音的型号。他认同了美式发音，并把它和自己联系了起来。他说："即使我能获得英式发音的声音，我也不想改变。我会感觉自己变成了另外一个人。"

## 7 Steps to a Perfect Accent                                      Track 043
7步让你拥有完美发音

1. Yep, I have an accent, I want to change it, and I'm sure this program will work for me.

   是的，我有口音，我想改变它，而且我确信这本教程对我有用。

2. I'm making a conscious effort to apply the techniques in an orderly, step-by-step manner.

   我正在有意识地做出努力，循序渐进地使用这些发音技巧。

3. I have taken an inventory of the sounds and rhythm patterns.

   我已经做了发音和节奏模式的自我鉴定。

4. I am keeping a daily log of the "**What Factor**."

   我每天都会记录"what因素"。

5. I record myself once a week, compare it with my original recording, and take specific and detailed notes of changes.

   我每周给自己录音，并将它与原来的录音作对比，并记下具体的、详细的变化。

6. When I talk to people, I consciously and conscientiously apply the techniques.

   当和人们说话时，我有意识地、认真地使用这些技巧。

7. I read aloud for 15 minutes a day with a phonetic transcription or imitate an audio text.

   我每天都用新的标音法或模仿一段声音文本大声朗读15分钟。

## The Pledge
誓言

"It's not the duration; it's the consistency. I'm training my mouth, lips, tongue, and mind."

    "重要的不是一次练多长时间，而是坚持不懈。我正在训练自己的口腔、双唇、舌头和头脑。"

# Chapter 3
# 第3章

> Your lips don't move
> much in English
>
> 说英语时你的双唇
> 不用怎么动。

# General Pronunciation
# 一般发音

## Let's Start at the Beginning
## 让我们从头开始

**Track 044**

As the philosophers say, start with yourself and define your terms. What are the parts of your mouth? How do they interact? What is a consonant? What is a vowel? Let's take a tour of the mouth, starting with the most basic sound.

正如哲学家所说，从自己开始，定义自己。你的口腔有哪些部分？它们是如何相互作用的？什么是辅音？什么是元音？让我们从最基本的音开始，进行一次口腔的旅行。

### Exercise 3-1: The Starting Point—Mmmm...

*Let's start with the **mmmm** sound. It's super easy to do. All you do is put your lips together and hum. You'll notice a couple things here. Your lips are touching and the air is coming out through your nose in a continuous stream. Put your hand on your throat and say **mmmm**, and observe that you can feel a vibration in your fingertips. This means that the **M** sound is spoken and not whispered.*

**Mmmmmm**

This exercise tells you four important things about the consonant **M**:

这个练习告诉你关于辅音M的四个要点：

1. Point of contact (*lips*)

   接触点（双唇）

2. Where the air comes out of your mouth (*nose*)

   气流从哪里流出口腔（鼻腔）

3. How the air comes out (*glide*)

   气流如何流出（滑出）

4. If the sound is spoken or whispered (*spoken*)

   发声还是不发声（发声）

## Exercise 3-2: Combining Sounds — Track 045

*Now that you know where things are, let's turn it into something. In a deep voice, say the following out loud. We're adding two more consonants at the lip position, **P** & **B**.*

Mmm

Ah

1. mah
2. mah-mah
3. pah
4. pah-pah
5. bah
6. bah-bah

## Exercise 3-3: Pronunciation & Cadence — Track 046

*In your deepest voice, repeat these syllables. To get the physical experience of intonation, either stretch a rubber band, snap your fingers, or tap the table. Repeat this ten times. (See also Chapter 4)*

1. **MAH**-mah   2. mah-**MAH**   3. **PAH**-pah   4. pah-**PAH**   5. **BAH**-bah   6. bah-**BAH**

## Exercise 3-4: Pure Sound — Track 047

*Let's put this in context. Using the **äh** sound, repeat the following sounds. Don't worry about what it means; just repeat the sounds in a deep, confident voice. That little upside-down e sounds like **uh**.*

1. bä bläs diz jäb        2. skät tädə lät        3. dän bädə bäik

At this point, you may be thinking, *What the heck is this? It's nonsense! It doesn't even look like English! I really need to know what I'm saying, and I don't know what this means! This is gibberish, and I might just sound like a fool here! I need the confidence of understanding what I'm saying. I'm afraid I'll sound completely foolish! I'm not confident with this because it's so different from what I've been taught. I just want to see what it looks like in regular English.*

看到这里，你可能会想，"这到底是什么？完全看不懂！它看起来甚至不像英语！我必须知道我在说什么，我都不知道这是什么意思！这简直是胡言乱语，我可能听起来就像个傻瓜！我知道自己在说什么时才有自信，我需要这样的自信。我担心自己听起来完全像个傻子！我对这个很没信心，因为它跟我学到的东西太不一样了。我就想看看它在常规英语中是什么样子的。"

## Exercise 3-5: Regular English　　　　　　　　　　　　　　　　Track 048

*OK, go ahead and decipher it into regular English as best as you can. Listen to the audio in the previous section to make sure you're getting all the words.*

1. _____　　2. _____　　3. _____

## Exercise 3-6: Pure Sound　　　　　　　　　　　　　　　　　　Track 049

*This time, listen and imitate the speaker, while reading the first line. Notice that in the second line, it's spelled out for you, but focus on correlating the sounds with the new letters, including the **T** that turns into a **D**. (This is only a temporary transition, and once you've imprinted the sounds, you'll go back to regular spelling.) The intonation is marked for you, so continue with the physical tapping and snapping. (See also Chapter 8)*

1. **bä** bläs diz **jäb**　　2. **skät** tädə **lät**　　3. **dän** bädə **bäik**
　 Bob lost his job.　　　 Scott taught a lot.　　 Don bought a bike.

## You're Visual
你是视觉型学习者

If you **see** it, you've **got** it, and it's hard to catch sounds if you can't get a look at them. Now that you've seen the sentences in proper English, you can imprint with the visual representation (a fancy way of saying spelling).

　　如果你看到了才知道说的什么，你就很难在不看它们的情况下学会发音。既然你已经看到了常规英语下的句子，你就会记住这种视觉表征（是"拼写"的一种好听的说法）。

## Exercise 3-7: Rhyme Time　　　　　　　　　　　　　　　　　Track 050

*Let's check your understanding of the differences between the **appearance** of English and the **pronunciation** of spoken American English. Say each pair of words out loud to yourself. If the two words rhyme, check the first box. If they don't rhyme, check the second box. Unless you score 100% on your first try, spend at least an hour on Exercise 3-8.*

| Does it rhyme? | Yes | No | Does it rhyme? | Yes | No |
|---|---|---|---|---|---|
| 1. give – hive | ❑ | ❑ | 8. been* – seen | ❑ | ❑ |
| 2. have – save | ❑ | ❑ | 9. great – heat | ❑ | ❑ |
| 3. come – gum | ❑ | ❑ | 10. eight – height | ❑ | ❑ |
| 4. been – tin | ❑ | ❑ | 11. done – gone | ❑ | ❑ |
| 5. know – now | ❑ | ❑ | 12. mother – bother | ❑ | ❑ |
| 6. use (v) – choose | ❑ | ❑ | 13. bruise – stews | ❑ | ❑ |
| 7. monkey – donkey | ❑ | ❑ | 14. froze – clothes | ❑ | ❑ |

| | | | |
|---|---|---|---|
| 15. her – sure* | ❏ ❏ | 33. would – stood | ❏ ❏ |
| 16. where – were | ❏ ❏ | 34. flood – stood | ❏ ❏ |
| 17. hour – flower | ❏ ❏ | 35. has – was | ❏ ❏ |
| 18. good – food | ❏ ❏ | 36. food – rude | ❏ ❏ |
| 19. come – dome | ❏ ❏ | 37. enough – though | ❏ ❏ |
| 20. turn – earn | ❏ ❏ | 38. allow – below | ❏ ❏ |
| 21. beard – weird | ❏ ❏ | 39. debt – let | ❏ ❏ |
| 22. comb – tomb | ❏ ❏ | 40. says – pays | ❏ ❏ |
| 23. taste – waist | ❏ ❏ | 41. dance – pants | ❏ ❏ |
| 24. anger – danger | ❏ ❏ | 42. eagle – legal | ❏ ❏ |
| 25. cupboard – blubbered | ❏ ❏ | 43. know – though | ❏ ❏ |
| 26. goes – does (v) | ❏ ❏ | 44. thought – taught | ❏ ❏ |
| 27. glove – move | ❏ ❏ | 45. laugh – half | ❏ ❏ |
| 28. oxen – dachshund | ❏ ❏ | 46. first – worst | ❏ ❏ |
| 29. beard – heard | ❏ ❏ | 47. full – wool | ❏ ❏ |
| 30. sew – few | ❏ ❏ | 48. fool – wool | ❏ ❏ |
| 31. flew – through | ❏ ❏ | 49. drawer – floor | ❏ ❏ |
| 32. little – middle | ❏ ❏ | 50. maître d' – undersea | ❏ ❏ |

\*been (typically pronounced *bin*) is also pronounced *ben* or *been* in various locales.

\*been（通常发音为bin）在不同地方也可发音为ben 或been。

\*sure (typically pronounced *shrr*) is also heard in some places as *shore, shoo-er,* or *shoo-wah*.

\*sure（通常发音为shrr）在有些地方也会发为shore, shoo-er或者shoo-wah。

## Vowel & Consonant Mouth Positions                    Track 051
元音&辅音口腔位置

The vowels are in a continuous stream from **e** to **ooh**, and the consonants are in three categories based on the point of contact.

元音从e到ooh是一个连续的气流，辅音根据接触点的不同分为三类。

Al A. Gator

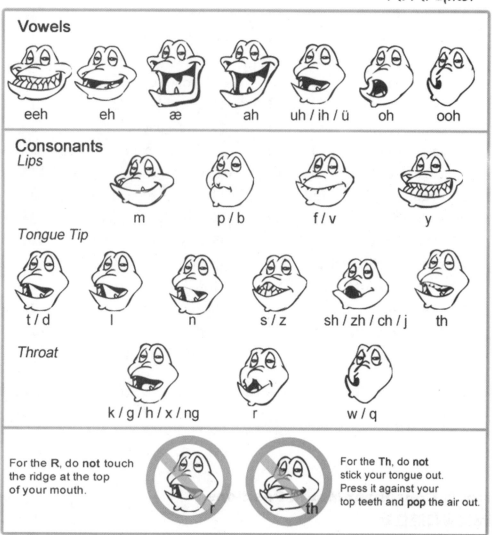

| Vowels | | | | | | |
|---|---|---|---|---|---|---|
| eeh | eh | æ | ah | uh / ih / ü | oh | ooh |

**Consonants**
*Lips*

| m | p / b | f / v | y |
|---|---|---|---|

*Tongue Tip*

| t / d | l | n | s / z | sh / zh / ch / j | th |
|---|---|---|---|---|---|

*Throat*

| k / g / h / x / ng | r | w / q |
|---|---|---|

For the **R**, do **not** touch the ridge at the top of your mouth.

For the **Th**, do **not** stick your tongue out. Press it against your top teeth and **pop** the air out.

The first step is to reprogram you away from **spelling** to the actual **sounds** of English. Start by mastering these sounds, combining initial consonants and vowels. This will give you a strong leg up on pronunciation.

第一步是把你原来依靠"拼写"发音的方式纠正为用真正的英语"音"来发音。从掌握这些发音开始，把开首辅音和元音连起来念。这样会对你的发音有很大的帮助。

The first column is **ä** because it's going to be easy for you. I'm going to say that again. Ready? It's going to be **easy** for you. Why? Because as far as I can tell, every language on earth has an "ah" sound. Some of the consonants may be a little tricky (**Th** and **R** spring to mind) but listen and repeat, repeat, repeat...in a deep voice. (Final consonants, diphthongs, and consonant blends such as **BL** and **CR** are covered in later chapters.)

第一列是ä，因为这对你来说很简单。我会再说一遍。准备好了吗？它对你来说很简单。为什么呢？因为据我所知，地球上的每种语言都有"ah"音。有些辅音可能有点难（我脑子里想到了Th和R），但是听它，并用深沉的声音重复，重复，重复……（词尾的辅音、双元音和辅音连读，如BL和CR，会在之后的章节中讲到。）

---

| **Exercise 3-8: The Pure Sound Jump-Start** | **Track 052** |
|---|---|

*As you go through this chart, pronouncing all the sounds, deepen your voice and make the vowels a little longer than you are inclined to. Some of these will sound like real words, but most of them are just fragments. Observe that for **ä**, you drop your jaw; for **ē**, you stretch your lips back a bit; for **ū**, you round your lips. There are only five new characters: **ä, æ, ɛ, ə, ü**. Listen carefully, and repeat this whole chart at least five times in columns, and five times across. Record yourself, listen back, and compare.*

|  | ä | æ | ɛ | i | ə | ü | ē | ō | ū | ā | ī |
|---|---|---|---|---|---|---|---|---|---|---|---|
| **b** | bä | bæ | bɛh | bih | bə | bü | bē | bō | bū | bā | bī |
| **ch** | chä | chæ | chɛh | chih | chə | chü | chē | chō | chū | chā | chī |
| **d** | dä | dæ | dɛh | dih | də | dü | dē | dō | dū | dā | dī |
| **f** | fä | fæ | fɛh | fih | fə | fü | fē | fō | fū | fā | fī |
| **g** | gä | gæ | gɛh | gih | gə | gü | gē | gō | gū | gā | gī |
| **h** | hä | hæ | hɛh | hih | hə | hü | hē | hō | hū | hā | hī |
| **j** | jä | jæ | jɛh | jih | jə | jü | jē | jō | jū | jā | jī |
| **k** | kä | kæ | kɛh | kih | kə | kü | kē | kō | kū | kā | kī |
| **l** | lä | læ | lɛh | lih | lə | lü | lē | lō | lū | lā | lī |
| **m** | mä | mæ | mɛh | mih | mə | mü | mē | mō | mū | mā | mī |
| **n** | nä | næ | nɛh | nih | nə | nü | nē | nō | nū | nā | nī |
| **p** | pä | pæ | pɛh | pih | pə | pü | pē | pō | pū | pā | pī |
| **r** | rä | ræ | rɛh | rih | rə | rü | rē | rō | rū | rā | rī |
| **s** | sä | sæ | sɛh | sih | sə | sü | sē | sō | sū | sā | sī |
| **sh** | shä | shæ | shɛh | shih | shə | shü | shē | shō | shū | shā | shī |
| **t** | tä | tæ | tɛh | tih | tə | tü | tē | tō | tū | tā | tī |
| **th** | thä | thæ | thɛh | thih | **thə\*** | thü | thē | thō | thū | thā | thī |
| **v** | vä | væ | vɛh | vih | və | vü | vē | vō | vū | vā | vī |
| **w** | wä | wæ | wɛh | wih | wə | wü | wē | wō | wū | wā | wī |
| **y** | yä | yæ | yɛh | yih | yə | yü | yē | yō | yū | yā | yī |
| **z** | zä | zæ | zɛh | zih | zə | zü | zē | zō | zū | zā | zī |

\*Most commonly used word in English.
\*英语中最常使用的单词。

## "We don't have some of those sounds in my language..."
### "这里面的有些音，我的语言里没有⋯⋯"

This is undoubtedly true, but you can see that you only need to pick up a limited number of new sounds (ä, æ, ε, ə, ü). Given what you've already accomplished in life, this is not a big deal. A Chinese speaker was once bemoaning how hard it was for him to say the **R**. When asked if he went to college, he said, "Of course, I have a PhD in physics from Caltech." After a beat, he realized that compared to that...the **R** is not harrrrrrrd.

这毫无疑问是对的，但是你会发现，你只用学习为数不多的几个新的音（ä, æ, ε, ə, ü）。想想你生活中已经取得的成就，这根本不算什么。曾经有一位中国人抱怨说发R这个音对他来说太困难了。当被问到是否上了大学时，他说："当然，我在加州理工学院获得了物理学博士学位。"沉默片刻后，他意识到跟那个相比⋯⋯发R音真的不难。

### Exercise 3-9: Other Characters      **Track 054**

*If you use one of these character sets, compare it with English.*

| American Phonics | ä | bä | chä | dä | fä | gä | hä | jä | kä | lä | mä | nä | pä | rä | sä | shä | tä | thä | vä | wä | yä | zä |
|---|---|---|---|---|---|---|---|---|---|---|---|---|---|---|---|---|---|---|---|---|---|---|
| Japanese | あ | ば | ちゃ | だ | | が | は | じゃ | か | | ま | な | ぱ | | さ | し | た | | | わ | や | ざ |
| Chinese | 啊 | 八 | 茶 | 大 | 发 | 嘎 | 哈 | 家 | 卡 | 拉 | 马 | 拿 | 怕 | | 洒 | 沙 | 他 | | | 哇 | 压 | 匝 |
| Korean | 아 | 바 | 차 | 다 | | 가 | 하 | 자 | 카 | | 마 | 나 | 파 | | 사 | | 타 | | | 와 | 야 | |
| Vietnamese | a | ba | cha | đa | pha | ga | ha | tra | ca | la | ma | na | pa | | xa | sa | ta | | va | oa | ia | da |
| Arabic | ا | ب | | د | ف | | ه | ج | ك | ل | م | ن | | | س | ش | ت | ث | | و | ي | ز |
| Russian | а | ба | ча | да | фа | га | ха | джа | ка | ла | ма | на | па | | са | ша | та | | | ва | ува я | за |

Let me give a quick explanation of why we're using these sounds. When you come in through your own language, you are coming from a place of total and absolute confidence. You *know* that sound. So, we're taking something you know and doing a lateral transference to a set of letters in English. If, on the other hand, you start from scratch, you'll be wondering if you're doing it right, and this will drain your confidence and your energy.

让我来快速解释一下我们为什么要用这些音。当你说自己的语言时，你有着绝对的自信。你"认识"那个音。因此，我们就用你所熟悉的东西来学习，并将它横向转移到英语中的一些字母上。另一方面，如果你从头开始，你会担心自己说的是否正确，而这会耗尽你的自信和精力。

Now that you've worked hard and successfully imitated the sounds, you're going to go on to the next step, which is regular spelling.

既然你已经努力学习并成功模仿了这些音，你将进入下一个阶段，那就是普通拼写。

## Exercise 3-10: Changing to Regular Spelling — Track 055

*Apply the **phonetic** sound to the entire column, no matter what the **spelling** is. Then, read each row across, making the vowel distinctions.*

| | ä | æ | ɛ | i | ü | ə | ē | ō | ū | ā | ī |
|---|---|---|---|---|---|---|---|---|---|---|---|
| | ought | at | etch | it | | um | eat | oat | oops | ate | I'm |
| **b** | Bob | bat | bet | been | book | but | beat | boat | boot | bait | bite |
| **ch** | chop | chat | check | chin | | chuck | cheat | choke | choose | chase | child |
| **d** | Don | Dad | dead | did | | done | deal | don't | do | day | die |
| **f** | fawn | fat | fetch | fit | foot | fun | feet | phone | food | fail | find |
| **g** | gone | gap | get | give | good | gun | geese | go | ghoul | gate | guy |
| **h** | hot | had | head | his | hood | hut | he | hold | who | hey | hi |
| **j** | jaw | Jack | Jeff | gin | | jump | jeans | joke | jewel | jail | giant |
| **k** | call | cat | Ken | kid | could | come | key | cold | cool | cane | kite |
| **l** | law | laugh | left | lick | look | luck | lead | load | lose | lay | lie |
| **m** | Mom | mad | men | mix | | much | me | most | moon | make | mine |
| **n** | not | Nan | net | knit | nook | none | need | note | new | name | knife |
| **p** | pot | pat | pet | pick | put | putt | peak | pole | pool | pay | pie |
| **r** | raw | ran | red | rib | rook | rub | reed | row | room | raise | rise |
| **s** | saw | sat | said | sin | soot | such | see | so | suit | say | sigh |
| **sh** | shawl | shack | shed | shill | should | shut | she | show | shoe | shape | shine |
| **t** | tall | tack | ten | tin | took | tub | tea | toe | tube | take | try |
| **th** | thought | that | then | this | | the | these | though | through | they | thigh |
| **v** | Von | vat | vex | vim | | vug | veal | voice | voodoo | veil | vie |
| **w** | walk | wax | when | with | would | was | we | won't | woo | whales | why |
| **y** | yawn | yap | yes | yip | you'll | young | yield | yo-yo | you | Yale | yikes |
| **z** | czar | zap | zen | zig | | zug | zeal | Zoey | zoo | zany | zygote |

### The Most Common Sound in English: Uh — Track 056
英语中最普遍的音：Uh

As you may know, the schwa ə is the most commonly used sound in English. **The** is the most commonly used word: **thə**. Just by mastering these two sounds—**th** and **ə**—you'll make a 30% improvement in your pronunciation.

你可能知道，非中央元音ə是英语中最常用的音。the是最常用的单词：thə。只要掌握了这两个音——th和ə——你的发音就已经获得了30%的进步。

Let's start with the schwa **ə** sound. Fortunately, it's an easy one. Don't move your lips or tongue; just let a completely neutral sound come out—**uh**. It's pretty much a little grunt. It's the sound Americans use when they're thinking—**um, uh, uh-huh, uh-uh, hum**. It's also used for agreeing, disagreeing, expressing interest, or conveying confusion. It appears as any vowel (actu**a**l, happ**e**n, possibl**e**, c**o**mmunity, **u**nusual) or even where there is no vowel (chasm, spasm, rhythm) just before the **m**. (See also Chapters 12 and 18)

我们从非中央元音ə开始学习。幸运的是，它是个很好发的音。不要移动你的双唇或舌头，仅仅发出一个完全中性的音——uh。它差不多就是一个哼哼声。它是美国人在思考的时候发出的声音——um, uh, uh-huh, uh-uh, hum。它也用来表示同意、不同意、感兴趣或困惑。它以任何元音的形式出现（actual, happen, possible, community, unusual）或者甚至在没有元音的情况下在m之前出现（chasm, spasm, rhythm）。（也见第12和18章）

## *The Second Most Common Sound: Tee Aitch*

第二普遍的音：Tee Aitch

To pronounce **Th** correctly, think about your tongue position. You don't want to take a big relaxed tongue; throw it out of your mouth for a long distance, and leave it out there for a long time. Make only a very quick, sharp little movement. Keep your tongue's tip very tense. It darts out between your teeth and snaps back very quickly—**thing, that, this**. The tongue tip is pressed against the back of your top teeth, and the sound *pops* out. It's not a breathy sound at all. Just as with most of the other consonants, there are two types—*voiced* and *unvoiced*. The voiced **Th** is like a **D**, but instead of being on the roof of the mouth, it's ¼ inch forward, *against* the teeth. The unvoiced **Th** is like a **T** between the teeth. If you mistakenly replace the unvoiced **Th** with **S** or **T** and the voiced one with **Z** or **D**, instead of *thing,* you'll say *sing* or *ting,* and instead of *that,* you'll say *zat* or *dat.* (See also Chapter 13)

　　为了正确地发Th音，想一下舌头的位置。你不需要把又大又松弛的舌头伸出口腔之外很久。只需要快速、敏锐地稍微移动一下。保持舌尖的紧张度。舌头从齿间快速伸出，并且十分迅速地缩回——thing，that，this。舌尖抵住上齿背，这个音就爆发出来了。它根本不是呼吸音。就像大多数其他的辅音一样，Th有两种发音类型——浊音和清音。浊音Th就像是D音，但舌头不是抵住上颚，而是向前伸了1/4英寸，抵住了牙齿。清音Th就像是发在齿间的T音。如果你常常错误地用S音或T音代替清音Th音，用Z音或D音代替浊音Th音，你会把thing发成sing或ting，把that发成zat或dat。（也见第13章）

---

**Exercise 3-11: Theodore Thurston's Theory**　　　　　　　　　　**Track 057**

*I'm going to read the following paragraph once straight through, so you can hear that no matter how fast I read it, all the Ths are still there. It is a distinctive sound, but when you repeat it, don't put too much effort into it. Listen to my reading.*

**The th**eory **th**at **Th**eodore Thurston **th**ought **th**at **th**ree-**th**irds was worth **th**ree **th**ousand dollars meant **th**at one-**th**ird was wor**th** a **th**ousand dollars.

I'd like you to consider words as rocks for a moment. When a rock first rolls into the ocean, it is sharp and well-defined. After tumbling about for a few millennia, it becomes round and smooth. A word goes through a similar process. When it first rolls into English, it may have a lot of sharp, well-defined vowels or consonants in it, but after rolling off a few million tongues, it becomes round and smooth. This smoothing process occurs when a tense vowel becomes reduced and when an unvoiced consonant becomes voiced. The most common words are the smoothest, the most reduced, the most often voiced. There are several very common words that are all voiced: *this, that, the, those, them, they, their, there, then, than, though.* The strong words such as *thank, think,* or *thing,* as well as long or unusual words such as *thermometer* or *theologian,* stay unvoiced.

我想让你暂时把单词看做岩石。当一块岩石刚刚滚入海中，它是锋利且轮廓清晰的。在海中翻滚几千年后，它变得圆润而光滑。单词也经历着相似的过程。一个单词刚进入英语中时，可能有很多明显、清晰的元音或辅音，但经过数百万人之口以后，它变得圆润而平滑。当一个紧元音变成弱读音，一个清辅音变成浊辅音，这种打磨语音的过程就产生了。最常用的单词是最平滑、最弱读的音，而且常为浊音。有几个非常常用的单词，它们都是浊音：this, that, the, those, them, they, their, there, then, than, though。强音单词，如thank, think或thing，以及较长或不常用的单词，如thermometer或theologian，则保持清音。

## Four More Important Sounds

### 四个更重要的音

Earlier, you learned the ə sound (*uh*), and now we're going to take a look at two related sounds. First say **uh**, then drop your jaw and say **ah**. This **ah** sound is used for the letter **O** in one-syllable words (**hot, lost, cop**) and with the **O** in stressed syllables (**possible, hospital, college**). (See also Chapter 12)

之前，你学习了ə音（uh），现在我们来看看两个相关的音。先发出uh音，然后把你的下颚向下拉发出ah音。字母O在单音节单词（hot, lost, cop）以及重读音节（possible, hospital, college）中发ah音。（也见第12章）

Now say **ah** again, but pull your lips back a bit. This gives you the æ sound, used for the letter **a** in one-syllable words (**chance, laugh, dance**) and in stressed syllables (**plastic, fantastic, imaginable**). (See also Chapter 12)

现在，再次发ah音，但是将双唇稍向后拉。这样就发出了æ音。字母a在单音节单词（chance, laugh, dance）以及重读音节（plastic, fantastic, imaginable）中发æ音。（也见第12章）

Another high value sound is the **R**. This growly sound is so very American. It always sounds the same, whether it's at the beginning, middle, or end of the word, and it's always pronounced, especially at the end of a word, such as **carrr, doorrr,** and **hearrr**. In most languages the **R** is a consonant because the tip of the tongue touches the roof of the mouth. This is **not** the case in American English. The tongue does not touch **anywhere** in the mouth, and the sound is formed back in the throat. (See also Chapter 15)

另外一个很值得掌握的音是R音。这个咆哮式的音是非常典型的美音。不论在单词的开头、中间还是结尾，它听起来总是一样的，而且比较明显，尤其是在词尾，例如carrr, doorrr或hearrr。在大部分的语言中，R音属于辅音，因为舌尖会碰触上颚。在美语中却不一样。发R音时舌头不触及口腔的任何部位，并且从喉咙深处发出。（也见第15章）

The letter **T**, as you will learn, has six different pronunciations, but right now we're only going to look at the case of **T** in the middle of a word, where it sounds like a **D**. This is why **metal, medal, mettle,** and **meddle** all sound identical, despite the wide variation in spelling. (See also Chapter 14)

你将会学到字母T有六种不同的发音，但是现在我们只看看T位于单词中间时的情况，它听起来像D音。这就是为什么metal，medal，mettle和meddle的拼写大不相同，但发音听起来都一样的原因。（也见第14章）

## Anticipating the Next Word
**Track 059**
### 预想下一个单词

The anticipation of each following sound brings me to the subject that most students raise at some point—one that explains their resistance to wholly embracing liaisons and general fluency. People feel that because English is not their native tongue, they can't anticipate the next sound because they never know what the next word is going to be. Accurate or not, for the sake of argument, let's say that you do construct sentences entirely word by word. This is where those pauses we'll study in Chapter 7 come in handy. During your pause, line up in your head all the words you want to use in order to communicate your thought, and then push them out in groups. If you find yourself slowing down and talking...word...by...word, back up and take a running leap at a whole string of words.

对每个接下来的发音的预想，使我想起大多数学生在某个时候都会提出的问题——这个问题解释了他们不能发出完整而流畅的连音的原因。人们感到，由于英语不是他们的母语，所以他们无法预想下一个音，因为他们从来不知道下一个单词会是什么。不管正确与否，为了论证，我们假设你完全是逐词来构造句子。这正是我们在第7章所要学习的停顿迟早会派上用场的地方。在停顿期间，在头脑中整理出你想用来交流思想的所有单词，然后将它们成组地说出来。如果你发现自己语速减慢，一个单词一个单词地说话，那么就回到开头，把整串单词连起来快速说出来。

## Run Them All Together (runnemälld'gether)
### 把它们连读起来

As I was reading, I hope you heard that in a lot of places, the words ran together, such as *runnemälld'gether*. You don't have to go way out of your way to make a huge new sound, but rather create a smooth flowing from one word to the next by leaving your tongue in an anticipatory position. (See also Chapter 11)

在我读的时候，我希望你在很多地方也听到过这样的发音，就像在runnemälld'gether中一样，单词是连读的。你不必费力重新发音，而是通过把你的舌头放在预想的位置，产生从一个单词到下一个单词的平滑语流。（也见第11章）

# Chapter 4

Change pitch
on important information.

说到重要信息时提高音量。

# American Intonation
# 美音语调

**Track 060**

## The American Speech Music
美语韵律

### *What to Do with Your Mouth to Sound American*
如何使你听上去像美国人

One of the main differences between the way an American talks and the way the rest of the world talks is that we don't really move our lips. (So, when an American says, "Read my lips!" what does he really mean?) We create most of our sounds in the throat, using our tongue very actively. If you hold your fingers over your lips or clench your jaws when you practice speaking American English, you will find yourself much closer to native-sounding speech than if you try to pronounce every...single...sound...very...carefully.

美国人与世界上其他地方的人说话方式的主要区别之一就是美国人说话时不怎么动嘴唇。（那么，当一个美国人说"看我的嘴形！"时，他到底在表达什么意思呢？）美国人的大多数音都是从喉部发出的，且十分积极地使用舌头。在练习发美音时，如果你把手放在嘴唇上或者用手托住下颚，你会发现你的发音更接近地道的美音，这要比你很仔细地发每一个音接近得多。

If you can relate American English to music, remember that the indigenous music is jazz. Listen to their speech music, and you will hear that Americans have a melodic, jazzy way of producing sounds. Imagine the sound of a cello when you say *Beddy bada bida bedder budder* (Betty bought a bit of better butter), and you'll be close to the native way of saying it.

如果你能够把美音跟音乐联系起来，那么记住，美国的本土音乐是爵士乐。倾听他们语言的韵律，你会发现美国人用带有旋律的爵士乐的方式发音。当你说"Beddy bada bida bedder budder (Betty bought a bit of better butter)"时，想象一下大提琴的声音，你就会接近地道的美语发音方式了。

Because most Americans came from somewhere else, American English reflects the accent contributions of many lands. The speech music has become much more exaggerated than British English, developing a strong and distinctive intonation. If you use this intonation, not only will you be easier to understand, but you will sound much more confident, dynamic, and persuasive.

由于大多数美国人来自其他地方，所以美语能反映出许多地方的口音。比起英式英语，美语的韵律已经变得夸张得多，形成了一种有力而且独特的语调。如果你使用这种语调，不仅会让自己更容易被别人听懂，而且听起来会更加自信、更有活力、更具说服力。

Intonation, or speech music, is the sound that you hear when a conversation is too far away to be clearly audible but close enough for you to tell the nationality of the speakers. The American intonation dictates liaisons and pronunciation, and it indicates mood and meaning. Without intonation, your speech would be flat, mechanical, and very confusing for your listener. What is the American intonation pattern? How is it different from other languages? *Foa egzampuru, eefu you hea ah Jahpahneezu pahsohn speakingu Ingurishu*, the sound would be very choppy, mechanical, and unemotional to an American. *Za sem vey vis Cheuman pipples*, it sounds too stiff. *A mahn frohm Paree ohn zee ahzer ahnd, eez intonashon goes up at zee end ov evree sentence* and has such a strong intonation that he sounds romantic and highly emotional, but this may not be appropriate for a lecture or business meeting in English.

当一段对话远到令你听不清它的内容，但却足以让你分辨出说话人的国籍时，你听到的就是语调，或者说是语言韵律。美语语调以连音和其独特的发音为特征，并且能够表情达意。如果没有语调，你的语言就会平淡无味、机械呆板，让你的听众很费解。那么美语语调的形式是什么样的呢？它跟其他语言又有什么不同呢？例如，假若你听一个日本人说英语，他的发音在美国人听起来是突兀、呆板、缺乏感情的。德国人说英语也一样，听起来很僵硬。一个来自巴黎的人，他的语调在每句话的末尾都会上升，并且十分有力，这使他听起来非常浪漫且富有感情。但这在英文讲座或者商务会议上就不适宜了。

## American Intonation Do's and Don'ts
美音语调准则

### *Do Not Speak Word by Word*

Bob... is... on... the... phone

---

### *Connect Words to Form Sound Groups*

### bä bizän the foun

---

### *Use Staircase Intonation to Stress Important Information*

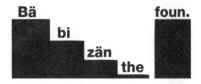

Start a new staircase
when you want to emphasize
that information, generally a *noun*.

---

▶ **Do not speak word by word.**
不要逐字发音。

If you speak word by word, as many people who learned "printed" English do, you'll end up sounding mechanical and foreign. You may have noticed the same thing happens in your own language: when someone reads a speech, even a native speaker, it sounds stiff and stilted, quite different from a normal conversational tone.

如果你像许多学习书面英语的人那样逐字发音，你的发音就会既呆板又不地道。或许你在自己的母语中也已发现了相同的情况：当某人朗读一篇演讲稿时，即使他说的是母语，听起来也是僵硬、呆板的，与正常的会话语调有很大的差别。

▶ **Connect words to form sound groups.**
连接单词，形成音群。

This is where you're going to start doing something *completely different* than what you have done in your previous English studies. This part is the most difficult for many people because it goes against everything they've been taught. Instead of thinking of each word as a unit, think of *sound units.* These sound units may or may not correspond to a word written on a page. Native speakers don't say *Bob is on the phone,* but say *bäbizän the foun.* Sound units make a sentence flow smoothly, like peanut butter— never really ending and never really starting, just flowing along. Even chunky peanut butter is acceptable. So long as you don't try to put plain peanuts directly onto your bread, you'll be OK. (See also Chapters 8 and 11)

在这里，你将开始做一些与过去的英语学习截然不同的事情。这部分对许多人来讲都是最难的，因为这与他们曾经学过的一切背道而驰。不要把每个单词作为一个单位，而要把音群作为单位。音群可能与页面上的一个单词对应，也可能不对应。以英语为母语的人不会说Bob is on the phone, 而会说bäbizän the foun。音群使句子变得流畅，就像是花生酱——从来没有真正地结束，也没有真正地开始，只是在不断地流动。即使是小块的花生酱也是可以的。只要你不试图将生花生直接放到你的面包上，就万事大吉。（也见第8章和第11章）

▶ **Use staircase intonation.**
使用阶梯状语调。

Let those sound groups floating on the wavy river in the figure flow downhill and you'll get the staircase. Staircase intonation not only gives you that American sound, it also makes you sound much more confident. Not every American uses the downward staircase. A certain segment of the population uses rising staircases—generally, teenagers on their way to a shopping mall: *"Hi, my name is Tiffany. I live in La Cañada. I'm on the pep squad."*

如上一页最后一幅图所示，让那些漂浮在波澜起伏的河面上的音群向下流动，你就会得到阶梯状语调了。阶梯状语调不仅让你的发音有美国味，还使你听起来更加自信。并非每个美国人都使用下降式阶梯状语调，一些人会使用上升式阶梯状语调——通常情况下，一群青少年在去购物中心的路上会说："Hi, my name is Tiffany. I live in La Canada. I'm on the pep squad."

# What Exactly Is Staircase Intonation?
## 到底什么是阶梯状语调呢？

In saying your words, imagine that they come out as if they were bounding lightly down a flight of stairs. Every so often, one jumps up to another level and then starts down again. Americans tend to stretch out their sounds longer than you may think is natural. So to lengthen your vowel sounds, put them on two stairsteps instead of just one.

在你说话时，想象说出的语言沿着一段阶梯轻快地向下弹跳。有时一个单词向上跳到另一个高度，然后又开始下降。美国人常常延长他们的发音，比你认为自然的发音要长。因此，为了延长你的元音发音，将元音发音放在两个而不是一个台阶上。

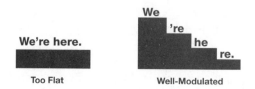

The sound of an American speaking a foreign language is very distinctive, because we double sounds that should be single. For example, in Spanish or Japanese, the word *no* is, to our ear, clipped or abbreviated.

美国人说外语时的发音是很特别的，因为我们会加倍延长本应该是单音的发音。例如，在日语或西班牙语中，单词 no 在我们听来是省略、简短的。

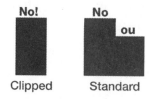

When you have a word ending in an *unvoiced consonant*—one that you "whisper" (t, k, s, x, f, sh)—you will notice that the preceding vowel is said quite quickly, and on a single stair step. When a word ends in a vowel or a *voiced consonant*—one that you "say" (b, d, g, z, v, zh, j), the preceding vowel is said more slowly, and on a double stair step.

当你遇到以清辅音（清辅音是你"低语"时发出的音，不振动声带，例如 t, k, s, x, f, sh）结尾的单词，你会发现清辅音前的元音说得很快，在一个台阶上。当一个单词以元音或浊辅音（浊辅音是你"说"出的音，振动声带，例如 b, d, g, z, v, zh, j）结尾时，浊辅音前的元音说得较慢，在两个台阶上。

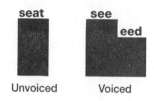

There are two main consequences of not doubling the second category of words: either your listener will hear the wrong word, or even worse, you will always sound upset. Consider that the words *curt, short, terse, abrupt,* and *clipped* all literally mean *short.*

When applied to a person or to language, they take on the meaning of *upset* or *rude*. For example, the expressions *"His curt reply...,"* *"Her terse response...,"* or *"He was very short with me"* all indicate a less than sunny situation.

如果不加倍延长上面第二类单词的发音，会产生两个主要的后果：要么听你说话的人会听错单词，要么更糟糕，你的发音会让人听着很不舒服。想想这些单词：curt，short，terse，abrupt和clipped，它们的字面意思都为"短的"。当它们用来形容人或语言时有"心烦"或"粗鲁"的意思。例如，"His curt reply..." "Her terse response..." 或 "He was very short with me"这些表达，都暗示了一种不愉快的情境。

## Three Ways to Make Intonation
## 构成语调的三种方式

About this time, you're coming to the point where you may be wondering, what exactly are the mechanics of intonation? What changes when you go to the top of the staircase or when you put stress on a word? There are three ways to stress a word:

现在，你正接近问题的关键，这也许正是你想知道的：语调的规则到底是什么？当你到达阶梯状语调的顶部或强调一个单词时，又是什么在发生变化呢？有三种方式来强调单词。

▸ The first way is to just get *louder* or raise the volume. This is not a very sophisticated way of doing it, but it will definitely command attention.
第一种方式只需大声点或提高音量。这种方式做起来不太复杂，但绝对会引起别人的注意。

▸ The second way is to *streeeeetch* the word out or lengthen the word that you want to draw attention to (which sounds very insinuating).
第二种方式是延长单词的发音或延长你想要引起注意的单词（这听起来很有暗示的味道）。

▸ The third way, which is the most refined, is to change *pitch.* Although pausing just before changing the pitch is effective, you don't want to do it every time, because then it becomes an obvious technique. However, it will make your audience stop and listen because they think you're going to say something interesting.
第三种方式，也是最完善的方式，就是改变音高。虽然在改变音高前停顿一下很有成效，但你不会每次都想停顿，因为这会成为一种太过明显的技巧。然而，它会让你的听众停下来去听，因为他们会认为你要说些有意思的事。

---

**Exercise 4-1: Rubber Band Practice with Nonsense Syllables**　　　　　　　　**Track 061**

*Take a rubber band and hold it with your two thumbs. Every time you want to stress a word by changing pitch, pull on the rubber band. Stretch it out gently; don't jerk it sharply. Make a looping ∞ figure with it and do the same with your voice. Use the rubber band and stretch it out every time you change pitch. Read first across, then down.*

| A | B | C | D |
|---|---|---|---|
| 1. **duh** duh **duh** | 1. **la** la la | 1. **mee** mee **mee** | 1. **ho** ho **ho** |
| 2. duh duh **duh** | 2. la la **la** | 2. mee mee **mee** | 2. ho ho **ho** |
| 3. duh **duh** duh | 3. la **la** la | 3. mee **mee** mee | 3. ho **ho** ho |
| 4. **duh** duh duh | 4. **la** la la | 4. **mee** mee mee | 4. **ho** ho ho |

*Read each column down, keeping the same intonation pattern.*

| A | B | C | D |
|---|---|---|---|
| 1. **duh** duh **duh** | 1. duh duh **duh** | 1. duh **duh** duh | 1. **duh** duh duh |
| 2. **ABC** | 2. impre**cise** | 2. con**di**tion | 2. **al**phabet |
| 3. **123** | 3. a hot **dog** | 3. a **hot** dog | 3. **hot** dog stand |
| 4. **Dogs** eat **bones**. | 4. They eat **bones**. | 4. They **eat** them. | 4. **Give** me one. |

## The American Speech Music

美音韵律

All cultures gesture. A developmental physiologist at University of Wisconsin, Dr. Alibali, put forth that gestures accompany speech because our mouths and hands are closely linked in the brain. You may have noticed babies saying **ga-ga-ga** and moving their hands to the beat. It's not necessary for you to gesticulate wildly, but it **is** important to integrate the rhythm of your speech music with physical gestures. To this end, you'll be tapping the table, snapping your fingers, and maybe even stretching a rubber band.

所有的文化都包含手势。威斯康星大学的一位发展生理学家，阿利巴利博士，提出手势伴随着语言，因为控制口腔和双手的神经在大脑中是紧密相连的。你可能已经注意到了，婴儿在说ga-ga-ga时双手会跟着节奏拍动。你没有必要做出非常夸张的手势，但是把你的语言韵律的节奏和肢体动作结合起来是重要的。为此，你可以拍桌子、打响指，甚至还可以拉橡皮筋。

## Not in My Language

我的语言里没有

A Pakistani database analyst said, "I didn't think about my own language in this way before. There is intonation when we speak, but not as much as in American English. Now that I've analyzed it, I found my language to be rhythmic too. In many places, we do the same up and down intonation. I must not have realized it because I speak without thinking about the language itself! It's really interesting to compare both language styles and then to extract certain resemblances from them. I never thought of it in that way."

一位巴基斯坦的数据库分析师说："我以前没有以这种方式思考过我的语言。我们说话的时候也有语调，但是不如美式英语中的多。由于我现在开始分析它，我才发现我的语言也是有节奏的。在许多地方，我们也有同样的高音调和低音调。我没有注意到，一定是因为我在讲话的时候不会去想语言本身！比较两种语言的特点，并且从中提炼出特定的相似点真的很有趣。我从来没有那样想过。"

## Staircase Intonation
### 阶梯状语调

So what is intonation in American English? What do Americans do? We go up and down staircases. We start high and end low.

那么美音语调是什么样的？美国人是怎么做的？我们在阶梯上上上下下，以高音开始，以低音结束。

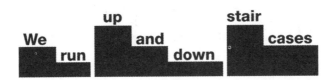

Every time we want to stress a word or an idea, we just start a new staircase. That sounds simple enough, but when and where do you start a new staircase?

每当我们想强调一个单词或一种想法，我们就开始一段新的阶梯。这听起来很容易，但你要在何时何处开始一段新阶梯呢？

## Statement Intonation with Nouns
### 带名词的陈述句语调

Intonation or pitch change is primarily used to introduce *new information.* This means that when you are making a statement for the first time, you will stress the *nouns.*

语调或音高变化主要是用来引出新信息。这就意味着，当你第一次作陈述时，要强调名词。

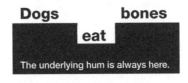

### Exercise 4-2: Noun Intonation

*Practice the noun stress pattern after me, using pitch change. Add your own examples.*

1. **Dogs** eat **bones.**
2. **Mike** likes **bikes.**
3. **Elsa** wants **a book.**
4. **Adam** plays **pool.**
5. **Bobby** needs some **money.**
6. **Susie** combs her **hair.**
7. **John** lives in **France.**
8. **Nelly** teaches **French.**

| | | | |
|---|---|---|---|
| 9. | **Ben** writes **articles.** | 15. | **Ann** and **Ed** call the **kids.** |
| 10. | **Keys** open **locks.** | 16. | The **kids** like the **candy.** |
| 11. | **Jerry** makes **music.** | 17. | The **girls** have a **choice.** |
| 12. | **Jean** sells some **apples.** | 18. | The **boys** need some **help.** |
| 13. | **Carol** paints the **car.** | 19. | _____ |
| 14. | **Bill** and I fix the **bikes.** | 20. | _____ |

✕ Pause the CD.

▶ Practice the patterns five more times on your own, using your rubber band.

## Statement Intonation with Pronouns 　　　　　　　　　Track 065
带代词的陈述句语调

When you replace the nouns with pronouns (i.e., *old information*), stress the verb.
当你用代词（也就是旧信息）代替名词时，强调动词。

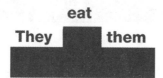

As we have seen, *nouns* are *new* information; *pronouns* are *old* information. In a nutshell, these are the two basic intonation patterns.
正如我们所见，名词是新信息；代词是旧信息。简而言之，这是两种基本的语调形式。

---

### Exercise 4-3: Noun and Pronoun Intonation 　　　　　　　Track 066

*In the first column, stress the nouns. In the second column, stress the verb. Fill in your own examples at the bottom.*

| | | | |
|---|---|---|---|
| 1. | **Bob** sees **Betty.** | 1. | He **sees** her. |
| 2. | **Betty** knows **Bob.** | 2. | She **knows** him. |
| 3. | **Ann** and **Ed** call the **kids.** | 3. | They **call** them. |
| 4. | **Jan** sells some **apples.** | 4. | She **sells** some. |
| 5. | **Jean** sells **cars.** | 5. | She **sells** them. |
| 6. | **Bill** and I fix the **bikes.** | 6. | We **fix** them. |
| 7. | **Carl** hears **Bob** and me. | 7. | He **hears** us. |
| 8. | **Dogs** eat **bones.** | 8. | They **eat** them. |
| 9. | The **girls** have a **choice.** | 9. | They **have** one. |

| | |
|---|---|
| 10. The **kids** like the **candy**. | 10. They **like** it. |
| 11. The **boys** need some **help**. | 11. They **need** something. |
| 12. **Ellen** should call her **sister**. | 12. She should **call** someone. |
| 13. The **murderer** killed the **plumber**. | 13. He **killed** a man. |
| 14. The **tourists** went **shopping**. | 14. They **bought** stuff. |
| 15. _____ | 15. _____ |
| 16. _____ | 16. _____ |
| 17. _____ | 17. _____ |
| 18. _____ | 18. _____ |
| 19. _____ | 19. _____ |
| 20. _____ | 20. _____ |

## Statement Versus Question Intonation      **Track 067**
陈述句语调与疑问句语调的对比

You may have learned at some point that questions have a rising intonation. They do, but usually a question will step upward until the very end, where it takes one quick little downward step. A question rises a little higher than a statement with the same intonation pattern.

你可能已经学过疑问句要用升调。确实是这样，但通常一个问句到句末时语调才升起，升起后又马上向下降一点。疑问句比相同语调形式的陈述句的语调略高。

## Emotional or Rhetorical Question Intonation
表达情绪的问句或反问句语调

If you know that your car is parked outside, however, and someone doesn't see it and asks you where it is, you might think that it has been stolen, and your emotion will show in your intonation as you repeat the question. As your feelings rise in an emotional situation, your intonation rises up along with them.

假如你知道你的车在外面停着，然而有个人没看见它，还问你车在哪儿。你或许以为车被偷了，当你重述问句时，你的情绪会体现在语调中。随着你的情绪变得激动，你的语调也随之升高。

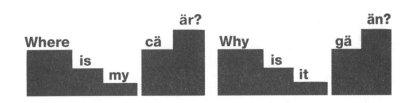

**Exercise 4-4: Sentence Intonation Test**          **Track 068**

*Pause the CD and underline or highlight the words that you think should be stressed.*

| | |
|---|---|
| 1. Sam sees Bill. | 11. He sees him. |
| 2. She wants one. | 12. Mary wants a car. |
| 3. Betty likes English. | 13. She likes it. |
| 4. They play with them. | 14. They eat some. |
| 5. Children play with toys. | 15. Len and Joe eat some pizza. |
| 6. Bob and I call you and Bill. | 16. We call you. |
| 7. You and Bill read the news. | 17. You read it. |
| 8. It tells one. | 18. The news tells a story. |
| 9. Bernard works in a restaurant. | 19. Mark lived in France. |
| 10. He works in one. | 20. He lived there. |

**Exercise 4-5: Four Main Reasons for Intonation**          **Track 069**

*Depending on the situation, a word may be stressed for any of the following reasons:*

**New Information**      **Opinion**      **Contrast**      **"Can't"**

### 1. New Information

新信息

*It sounds like **rain**.*

*Rain* is the new information. It's the most important word in that sentence and you could replace everything else with *duh-duh-duh. Duh-duh-duh **rain*** will still let you get your point across.

rain是新信息。它是这个句子中最重要的部分。你可以用duh-duh-duh代替其他的部分。Duh-duh-duh rain依然能够清楚地表明你的观点。

▶ Repeat: *Duh-duh-duh **rain**. / It sounds like **rain**.*

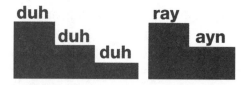

▶ Make *rain* very musical and put it on two notes: *ray-ayn.*
     *Duh-duh-duh **ray-ayn** / It sounds like **ray-ayn**.*

### 2. Opinion

观点

*It **sounds** like rain, but I don't think it is.*

In this case, intonation makes the meaning the opposite of what the words say: *It **looks** like a diamond, but I think it's a **zircon**. It **smells** like Chanel, but at that price, it's a* *knock-off. It **feels** like... It **tastes** like...* These examples all give the impression you mean the *opposite* of what your senses tell you.

在这种情况下，语调使实际表达的意思与字面意思相反：It **looks** like a diamond, but I think it's a **zircon**. It **smells** like Chanel, but at that price, it's a **knock-off**. It **feels** like... It **tastes** like... 这些例子都让人觉得你要表达与你的感觉相反的意思。

▶ Practice the intonation difference between *new information* and *opinion*:

*It sounds like **rain**. (It's rain.)*
*It **sounds** like rain, (but it's not.)*

## 3. Contrast
对比

*He **likes** rain, but he **hates** snow.*

*Like* and *hate* are contrasted and are the stronger words in the sentence.

like和hate形成对比，因而在句中需重读。

## 4. Can't
Can't

*It **can't rain** when there're no **clouds**.*

Contractions *(shouldn't, wouldn't, etc.)* and negatives *(no, not, never)* are important words since they totally negate the meaning of a sentence, but they are usually not stressed.

缩略词（shouldn't，wouldn't等）和否定词（no，not，never）是重要的单词，因为它们完全否定了句子的意思，但通常不用重读它们。

*Can't* is the exception.

Can't 是个例外。

---

**Exercise 4-6: Pitch and Meaning Change**                    **Track 070**

*Practice saying the four sentences after me. Pay close attention to the changes in pitch that you must make to convey the different meanings intended. The words to be stressed are indicated in boldface.*

1. It sounds like **rain**.
2. It **sounds** like rain.
3. He **likes** rain, but he **hates** snow.
4. It **can't rain** on my **parade**! He **can't do** it. *(See also Exercise 4-17 for negatives.)*

---

**Exercise 4-7: Individual Practice**                    **Track 071**

*Practice saying the sentences after the suggestion and the beep tone. You will be given only a **short** time in which to reply so you won't have the leisure to overthink. Start speaking as soon as you hear the tone because I'll be saying the sentence only a few seconds later.*

1. Convey the information that it really does sound as if rain is falling. ◀

2. Convey the opinion that although it has the sound of rain, it may be something else. ◀

3. Convey the different feelings that someone has about rain and snow. ◀

4. Convey the fact that rain is an impossibility right now. ◀

  ✗  Pause the CD.

  ▶  Practice the four sentences on your own ten times.

  ✗  Once you're familiar with moving the stress around and feeling how the meaning changes, turn the CD on to continue with the next exercise.

| **Exercise 4-8: The Meaning of "Pretty"** | Track 072 |
|---|---|

*Native speakers make a clear distinction between pretty **easily** (easily) and **pretty** easily (a little difficult). Repeat the answers after me, paying close attention to your stress.*

Question:    How did you like the movie?

Answer:      1. *It was pretty **good**.* (She liked it.)

              2. *It was **pretty** good.* (She didn't like it much.)

| **Exercise 4-9: Inflection** | Track 073 |
|---|---|

*Notice how the meaning changes, while the actual words stay the same.*

1. **I** didn't say he stole the money. Someone **else** said it.

2. I **didn't** say he stole the money. **That's** not true at **all**.

3. I didn't **say** he stole the money. I only **suggested** the **possibility**.

4. I didn't say **he** stole the money. I think someone **else** took it.

5. I didn't say he **stole** the money. Maybe he just **borrowed** it.

6. I didn't say he stole **the** money, but rather some **other** money.

7. I didn't say he stole the **money**. He may have taken some **jewelry**.

**I**       I didn't say he stole the money. Someone **else** said it.
          It's true that somebody said it, but I wasn't that person.

**Didn't**  I **didn't** say he stole the money. **That's** not true at **all**.
          Someone has accused me, and I'm protesting my innocence.

**Say**     I didn't **say** he stole the money. I only **suggested** the **possibility**.
          Maybe I hinted it. Maybe I wrote it. In some way, I indicated that he stole the money, *but* I didn't say it.

**He**      I didn't say **he** stole the money. I think someone **else** took it.
          I think someone stole the money, only not the person you suspect did it.

**Stole**   I didn't say he **stole** the money. Maybe he just **borrowed** it.
I agree that he took it, but I think his motive was different.

**The**   I didn't say he stole **the** money, but rather some **other** money.
We agree that he stole some money, but I don't think it's this money.

**Money**   I didn't say he stole the **money**. He may have taken some **jewelry**.
We agree that he's a thief, but we think he stole different things.

Notice that in the first half of these sentences nothing changes but the intonation.
注意在以上句子的第一句中，只有语调发生了变化。

▸ Repeat after me.

**Exercise 4-10: Individual Practice**                                   **Track 074**

*Now, let's see what you can do with the same sentence, just by changing the stress around to different words. I'll tell you which meaning to express. When you hear the tone ◂, say the sentence as quickly as you can, then I'll say the sentence for you. To test your ear, I'm going to repeat the sentences in random order. Try to determine which word I'm stressing. The answers are given in parentheses, but don't look unless you really have to. Here we go.*

1. Indicate that he borrowed the money and didn't steal it. (5) ◂
2. Indicate that you are denying having said that he stole it. (2) ◂
3. Indicate that you think he stole something besides money. (7) ◂
4. Indicate that you were not the person to say it. (1) ◂
5. Indicate that you don't think that he was the person who stole it. (4) ◂
6. Indicate that you didn't say it outright but did suggest it in some way. (3) ◂
7. Indicate that he may have stolen a different amount of money. (6) ◂

**Exercise 4-11: Sticky Note Exercise**                                   **Track 075**

*Imagine that you are being held hostage by a mad bomber, and the only way to communicate with the outside is with notes stuck to the bank window.*

*If you give each word of your plea equal value, the message will be lost in the barrage of information.*

*To clearly convey your message, you'll need to emphasize the most important words. This way, any random passerby can, at a glance, immediately catch your meaning.*

*This is the same with intonation. Repeat the sentence, clearly stressing the marked words.*

Please **help** me! I'm being held **captive** by a mad **bomber**!

## Overdo It

Track 076

夸张地做

Practice these sentences on your own, really exaggerating the word that you think should be stressed. In the beginning, you're going to feel that this is ridiculous. *(Nobody stresses this hard! Nobody talks like this! People are going to laugh at me!)* Yet as much as you may stress, you're probably only going to be stressing about half as much as you should.

自己练习这些句子，真正地夸张你认为需要强调的单词。起初，你会觉得这很荒谬。（"没有人强调得这么重！没有人像这样说话！人们会笑话我的！"）然而即使你尽力地强调，你可能也只用了你该强调的力度的一半。

✗ Pause the CD and practice the sentences in random order ten times.

Another reason you must overexaggerate is because when you get tired, emotional, or relaxed, you will stop paying attention. When this happens, like a rubber band, you're going to snap back to the way you originally were sounding (10%). So, if you just stretch yourself to the exact position where you ideally want to be, you'll go back almost completely to the old way when you relax. For practice, then, stretch yourself far *beyond* the normal range of intonation (150% or so), so when you relax, you relax back to a standard American sound (100%). (See also Chapter 1)

你必须夸张地说话的另一个原因在于当你困倦、激动或放松时，你就不注意了。当这些情况发生时，就像是根橡皮筋，你会很快恢复原来的发音方式（10%）。所以，如果你只夸张到你理想中想要达到的位置，当你放松时，你的发音将几乎恢复原状。所以练习时你要远远超过正常的调域（大约150%），这样当你放松时，你就会恢复成标准的美语发音（100%）。（也见第1章）

## We All Do It
我们都这样做

Possibly about this time you're thinking, *Well, maybe you do this in English, but in* **my** *language, I just really don't think we do this.* I'd like you to try a little exercise.

或许此刻你在想，"唉！也许说英语时是这样。可我觉得在我的母语中，我们不会这样做的。" 我想让你来做个小练习。

| Exercise 4-12: Translation | Track 077 |
| --- | --- |

*Take the sentence* **I didn't say he stole the money** *and translate it into your native language. Write it down below, using whatever letters or characters you use in your language.*

Now that you have written your sentence down, try shifting the stress around in your own language by going through the stress patterns 1–7 in Exercise 4-9. Don't try to put on a particularly American or other accent; just concentrate on stressing a different word in the sentence each time you say it.

既然你已写下了句子，请试着用你的母语，通过练习4-9中1-7的重音形式来变换重音。每次读句子时，不要试图带有美音或其他口音，只需集中精力重读不同的词。

For example, if your language is German, *Ich habe nicht gesagt daß er das Geld gestohlen hat,* you would change the stress to: *Ich habe nicht gesagt daß er das Geld gestohlen hat,* or *Ich habe* **nicht** *gesagt daß er das Geld gestohlen hat.*

例如，如果你的母语是德语，Ich habe nicht gesagt daß er das Geld gestohlen hat，你可能会把重音变为**Ich** habe nicht gesagt daß er das Geld gestohlen hat，或Ich habe **nicht** gesagt daß er das Geld gestohlen hat.

If you translated it into French, you would say, *Je* **n'ai pas** *dit qu'il a volé l'argent,* or *Je n'ai pas dit qu'il a* **volé** *l'argent.*

如果你将它翻译成法语，你可能会说Je **n'ai pas** dit qu'il a volé l'argent, 或 je n'ai pas dit qu'il a **volé** l'argent.

In Japanese, many people think that there are no intonation changes, but if you hear someone say, *wak**ka**nai,* you'll realize that it has similarities to every other language. *Watashi wa* **kare** *ga okane o nusunda to wa iimasen deshita.* Or perhaps, *Watashi wa kare ga okane o nusunda to wa* **iimasen** *deshita.*

很多人认为日语中没有语调的变化，但如果你听到有人说wak**ka**nai，你就会意识到日语与其他所有语言有着相似之处。如果翻译成日语，可能是Watashi wa **kare** ga okane o nusunda to wa iimasen deshita. 或 Watashi wa kare ga okane o nusunda to wa **iimasen** deshita.

No matter how strange it may sound to you, stress each different word several times in your language. You may notice that with some words it sounds perfectly normal, but with other words it sounds very strange. Or you may find that in your language, rather than stressing a word, you prefer to change the word order or substitute another word. Whatever you do is fine, as long as you realize where your language patterns are similar to and different from the American English intonation patterns. Then, when you do it again, in English, it will be much easier.

无论听起来有多奇怪，请用你的母语针对每个不同的单词重读几遍。你可能会注意到将重音放在有些单词上听起来很正常，但放在另外一些单词上听起来就很奇怪。或者你会发现在你的母语中，你更喜欢改变词序或用其他词代替，而不是重读单词。只要你能认识到你的母语和美语的语调形式在哪些地方相似，又在哪些地方不同，无论怎么做都行。这样，当你再用英语进行重读时，就会变得容易得多。

**Note** *An excellent exercise is to practice speaking your native language with an American accent. If you can sound like an American speaking your native language, imagine how easy it would be to speak English with an American accent.*

注意：用美音来说你的母语是一个很好的训练。如果你说母语时听起来像个美国人，想象一下用美音来说英语会变得多么简单。

✗ Pause the CD and practice shifting the stressed words in your native language.

## Intonation Contrast
### 语调对比

Below are two sentences—the first is stressed on the most common, everyday word, *book.* Nine times out of ten, people will stress the sentence in this way. The second sentence has a less common, but perfectly acceptable intonation, since we are making a distinction between two possible locations.

在下面两个句子中，第一个句子的重音落在了最常见的日常单词book上，绝大多数情况下人们会用这种方式来重读句子；第二个句子具有不太常见、但完全可以令人接受的语调，因为我们在区别两个可能的位置。

*Normal intonation*        Where's the **book**? It's on the **table**.

*Changed intonation*       Is the book **on** the table or **under** it? It's **on** the table.

✗ Pause the CD and repeat the sentences.

---

**Exercise 4-13: Create Your Own Intonation Contrast**          **Track 080**

*Write a short sentence and indicate where you think the most normal intonation would be placed. Then, change the meaning of the sentence slightly and change the intonation accordingly.*

*Normal intonation*        _____

*Changed intonation*       _____

## Question Types
### 疑问句类型

There are three types of questions: *Yes/No, Either/Or,* and *The Five W Questions.* They each have a different inflection pattern, so even if you don't catch all of the words, you can

**Track 079**

**Track 081**

still tell what type of question it was. The Five W Questions are *Who?*, *What?*, *Where?*, *When?*, and *Why?* (and *How?*).

有三种类型的疑问句：一般疑问句、选择疑问句和特殊疑问句。它们有各自的语调变化方式，所以即便你没有听懂所有的单词，也可以辨别出是哪种疑问句。特殊疑问句有：Who?，What?，Where?，When?，和Why?（以及How?）。

As you heard in the question and response above, "Where's the book? It's on the table.", the inflection goes up on the question and down on the statement. A query like "Would you like tea or coffee?" could be an Either/Or question (Tea? Coffee?) or a Yes/No question (Hot beverage?).

正如你在上面的疑问句和回答中听到的："Where's the book? It's on the table."（"书在哪里？它在桌子上。"），问句的语调上升，答语的语调下降。而像"Would you like tea or coffee?"（你想喝茶还是咖啡？）这样的询问，则既有可能是选择疑问句（Tea? Coffee? 茶？咖啡？），也有可能是一般疑问句（Hot beverage? 需要热饮吗？）。

A classic, probably apocryphal story spells out the consequences of misinterpreting the question type. An immigrant was passing through Ellis Island and was asked the then-standard question, "Are you planning to overthrow the United States by force or violence?"

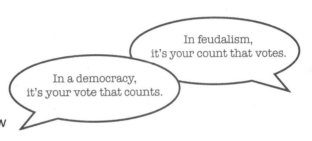

In feudalism, it's your count that votes.

In a democracy, it's your vote that counts.

有一个经典的、可能不真实的故事清楚地说明了误解疑问句类型的后果。一位移民从埃利斯岛通关时被问到当时的一个标准问题："你打算用武力或暴力推翻美国吗？"

The man pondered deeply for a moment and tentatively replied, "By force?" Of course, he was not let in, as the only acceptable answer was, "No."

那个男人沉思了一会儿，尝试着回答："用武力？"当然，他没有被允许入境，因为唯一可接受的答案是："不。"

---

**Exercise 4-14: Variable Stress**　　　　　　　　　　　　　　　　　　**Track 082**

*Notice how the meaning of the following sentence changes each time we change the stress pattern. You should be starting to feel in control of your sentences now.*

### 1. **What would you like?**

This is the most common version of the sentence, and it is just a simple request for information.

这是该句最常见的重读方式，只是简单地询问以获取信息。

### 2. **What would you like?**

This is to single out an individual from a group.

这种重读方式是为了将某个人从一群人中区分开来。

### 3. What **would** you like?

You've been discussing the kinds of things he might like, and you want to determine his specific desires: "*Now that you mention it, what **would** you like?*"

你们之前一直在讨论他会喜欢的东西，现在你想确定他的所需："既然你已经提到了，那么你想要什么呢？"

*or*
或者，

He has rejected several things, and a little exasperated, you ask, "*If you don't want any of these, what **would** you like?*"

他已经拒绝了很多东西而且已经有些生气了，这时你问："如果你不想要这些，你想要什么呢？"

### 4. **What** would you like?

You didn't hear, and you would like the speaker to repeat herself.

你没听清对方的话，想让她重复一遍。

*or*
或者，

You can't believe what you just heard: "*I'd like strawberry jam on my asparagus.*" "***What** would you like?*"

你不能相信你所听到的："我想给我的芦笋加点草莓酱。""你想要什么？"

◀ Turn off the CD and repeat the four sentences.

---

**Exercise 4-15: Make a Variable Stress Sentence**                    **Track 083**

*Now **you** decide which words should be emphasized. Write a normal, everyday sentence with at least seven words and put it through as many changes as possible. Try to make a pitch change for each word in the sentence and think about how it changes the meaning of the entire sentence.*

1. _____

2. _____

3. _____

4. _____

5. _____

6. _____

7. _____

**Exercise 4-16: Yes, You *Can* or No, You *Can't*?**     **Track 084**

*Next you use a combination of intonation and pronunciation to make the difference between **can** and **can't**. Reduce the positive **can** to **k'n** and stress the verb. Make the negative **can't** (**kæn**[(t)]) sound very short, and stress both **can't** and the verb. This will contrast with the positive, emphasized **can**, which is doubled—and the verb is not stressed. If you have trouble with **can't** before a word that starts with a vowel, such as **open**, put in a very small* [(d)]—*The keys **kæn**[(d)] **open** the locks. Repeat.*

| I can **do** it. | I k'n **do** it | positive |
| I **can't do** it. | I **kæn**[(t)]**do** it | negative |
| I **can** do it. | I **kæææn** do it | extra positive |
| I **can't** do it. | I **kæn**[(t)]do it | extra negative |

**Exercise 4-17: Can or Can't Quiz**     **Track 085**

*Listen to how each sentence is said, and select positive, negative, extra positive, or extra negative.*

1. I can see it. ◀
❑ A. positive
❑ B. negative
❑ C. extra positive
❑ D. extra negative

2. I can't see it. ◀
❑ A. positive
❑ B. negative
❑ C. extra positive
❑ D. extra negative

3. I can see it. ◀
❑ A. positive
❑ B. negative
❑ C. extra positive
❑ D. extra negative

4. I can't see it. ◀
❑ A. positive
❑ B. negative
❑ C. extra positive
❑ D. extra negative

5. He can try it. ◀
❑ A. positive
❑ B. negative
❑ C. extra positive
❑ D. extra negative

6. I can't understand him. ◀
❑ A. positive
❑ B. negative
❑ C. extra positive
❑ D. extra negative

7. We can call you. ◀
❑ A. positive
❑ B. negative
❑ C. extra positive
❑ D. extra negative

8. She can't buy one. ◀
❑ A. positive
❑ B. negative
❑ C. extra positive
❑ D. extra negative

9. She can do it. ◀
❑ A. positive
❑ B. negative
❑ C. extra positive
❑ D. extra negative

Rule of Grammar

Double negatives are a no-no.

## Application of Intonation
语调的运用

There is always at least one stressed word in a sentence, and frequently you can have quite a few if you are introducing a lot of new information or if you want to contrast several things. Look at the paragraph in Exercise 4-18. Take a pencil and mark every word that you think should be stressed or sound stronger than the words around it. I'd like you to make just an accent mark (') to indicate a word you think should sound stronger than others around it.

　　在一个句子中，至少会有一个重读的单词，如果你在介绍大量的新信息或想对比几个事物，通常会有多个重读的单词。看练习4-18中的段落，用铅笔标出你认为应该重读或读音应比周围单词重的单词。我想让你用重音符号"'"来标示它们。

**Reminder:** The three ways to change your voice for intonation are:
提示：以下是三种通过声音改变语调的方式：

(1) **Volume** (speak louder)
　　音量（说得大声点）
(2) **Length** (stretch out a word)
　　音长（延长单词的发音）
(3) **Pitch** (change your tone)
　　音高（改变音调）

✖ Pause the CD and work on the paragraph below.

---

### Exercise 4-18: Application of Stress　　　　　　　　　　　　Track 087

*Mark every word or syllable with ´ where you think that the sound is stressed. Use the first sentence as your example. Pause the CD.*

Héllo, my' name is_____. I'm taking American Accent Training. There's a lot to learn, but I hope to make it as enjoyable as possible. I should pick up on the American intonation pattern pretty easily, although the only way to get it is to practice all of the time. I use the up and down, or peaks and valleys, intonation more than I used to. I've been paying attention to pitch, too. It's like walking down a staircase. I've been talking to a lot of Americans lately, and they tell me that I'm easier to understand. Anyway, I could go on and on, but the important thing is to listen well and sound good. Well, what do you think? Do I?

▶ Listen and make any corrections. After you've put in the accent marks where you think they belong, take a highlighter, and as I read very slowly, mark the words that I stress. I am going to exaggerate the words far more than you'd normally hear in a normal reading of the paragraph. You can mark either the whole word or just the strong syllable, whichever you prefer, so that you have a bright spot of color for where the stress should fall.

**Note** *If you do the exercise only in pencil, your eye and mind will tend to skip over the accent marks. The spots of color, however, will register as "different" and thereby encourage your pitch change. This may strike you as unusual, but trust me, it works.*

注意：如果你只用铅笔来做这个练习，你的眼睛和大脑常常会略过重音符号。而色块则会表示"不同"，从而会促进你的音高的变化。这可能让你觉得不可思议，但相信我，这很有效。

✕ Pause the CD and practice reading the paragraph out loud three times on your own.

## How You Talk Indicates to People How You Are   Track 088
你的说话方式表明你是怎样的人

### Beware of "Revealing" a Personality that You Don't Have!
谨防显现出你并不具备的性格

There is no absolute right or wrong in regard to intonation because a case can be made for stressing just about any word or syllable, but you actually reveal a lot about yourself by the elements you choose to emphasize. For example, if you say, *Hello,* this intonation would indicate doubt. This is why you say, *Hello?* when answering the telephone because you don't know who is on the other end. Or when you go into a house and you don't know who's there because you don't see anyone. But if you're giving a speech or making a presentation and you stand up in front of a crowd and say *Hello,* the people would probably laugh because it sounds so uncertain. This is where you'd confidently want to say *Hello,* **my** *name is* **So-and-so.**

关于语调没有绝对的正确或错误，因为重读任何单词或音节都有充分的理由，但是通过你选择强调的成分，你的很多信息确实会暴露出来。比如，如果你说Hello，这种语调会暗示疑惑。这就是为什么当你接电话时会说Hello，因为你不知道电话另一端是谁。或者当你走进一栋房子，不知道谁在那儿时会说，因为你谁也没看见。然而，如果你在演讲或陈述，当你站在众人的面前说Hello时，人们或许会发笑，因为这听起来很不确定。在这里你应自信地说Hello, **my** name is So-and-so。

A second example is, **my** *name is*—as opposed to *my* **name** *is*. If you stress *name,* it sounds as if you are going to continue with more personal information: *My* **name** *is So-and-so, my* **address** *is such-and-such, my* **blood** *type is O.* Since it may not be your intention to give all that information, stay with the standard—*Hello,* **my** *name is* **So-and-so.**

第二个例子是，**my** name is 和 my **name** is。如果你重读name，那么听起来像是你要继续讲更多的个人信息：我的名字是什么，我的地址是什么，我的血型是O型。由于你的本意可能不是提供所有那些信息，所以就保持标准音吧——Hello, **my** name is So-and-so。

If you stress *I* every time, it will seem that you have a very high opinion of yourself. Try it: ***I'm*** *taking American Accent Training.* ***I've*** *been paying attention to pitch, too.* ***I*** *think* ***I'm*** *quite wonderful.*

如果你总是重读I，那你似乎对自己有极高的评价，试着说：**I'm** taking American Accent Training. **I've** been paying attention to pitch, too. **I** think I'm quite wonderful.

An earnest, hard-working person might emphasize words this way: *I'm **taking** American Accent Training* (Can I learn this stuff?). *I hope to **make** it as enjoyable as possible* (I'll force myself to enjoy it if I have to). *Although the only way to get it is to practice **all** of the time* (24 hours a day).

一个认真勤勉的人可能会这样强调单词：I'm **taking** American Accent Training.（我能学会吗？ ）I hope to **make** it as enjoyable as possible.（如果我不得不喜欢它，我会让自己喜欢的。）Although the only way to get it is to practice **all** of the time.（一天24小时）。

A Doubting Thomas would show up with: *I **should** pick up on* (but I might not) *the American intonation pattern **pretty** easily* (but it looks pretty hard, too). *I've been talking to a lot of Americans lately, and they **tell** me that I'm easier to understand* (but I think they're just being polite). (See also Chapter 1)

一个人的多疑可能会这样显现出来：I **should** pick up on （但我可能没这样）the American intonation pattern **pretty** easily.（但它看起来也很难。）I've been talking to a lot of Americans lately, and they **tell** me that I'm easier to understand （但我想他们只是出于礼貌）。（也见第1章）

---

### Exercise 4-19: Paragraph Intonation Practice      Track 089

▸ *From your color-marked copy, read each sentence of the paragraph in Exercise 4-18 after me. Use your rubber band, give a clear pitch change to the highlighted words, and think about the meaning that the pitch is conveying.*

✘ *Back up the CD and practice this paragraph three times.*

✘ *Pause the CD and practice three times on your own.*

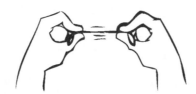

---

### Exercise 4-20: Reading with Staircase Intonation      Track 090

*Read the following with clear intonation where marked.*

Hello, **my** name is_____. I'm taking American **Accent** Training. There's a **lot** to **learn**, but I **hope** to make it as **enjoyable** as possible. I should pick **up** on the American **intonation** pattern pretty **easily,** although the **only** way to **get** it is to **practice** all of the time. I use the **up** and down, or **peaks** and valleys, **intonation** more than I **used** to. I've been paying attention to **pitch, too.** It's like **walking** down a **stair**case. I've been **talking** to a lot of **Americans** lately, and they tell me that I'm **easier** to under**stand. Any**way, I could go **on** and on, but the **important** thing is to **listen** well and sound **good. Well,** what do you **think**? **Do** I?

**Exercise 4-21: Spelling and Numbers**      Track 091

*Just as there is stress in words or phrases, there is intonation in spelling and numbers. Americans seem to spell things out much more than other people. In any bureaucratic situation, you'll be asked to spell names and give all kinds of numbers—your phone number, your birth date, and so on. There is a distinct stress and rhythm pattern to both spelling and numbers—usually in groups of three or four letters or numbers, with the stress falling on the last member of the group. Acronyms (phrases that are represented by the first letter of each word) and initials are usually stressed on the last letter. Just listen to the words as I say them, then repeat the spelling after me.*

| Acronym | Pronunciation | Spelling | Pronunciation |
|---|---|---|---|
| IBM | Eye Bee **Em** | Box | Bee Oh **Ex** |
| MIT | Em Eye **Tee** | Cook | See Oh Oh **Kay** |
| Ph.D. | Pee Aitch **Dee** | Wilson | Dubya You Eye **El**, Ess Oh **En** |
| MBA | Em Bee **ɛi** | | |
| LA | Eh **Lay** | | |

| IQ | Eye **Kyu** | Numbers | Pronunciation |
|---|---|---|---|
| RSVP | Are Ess Vee **Pee** | Area Code | 21**3** |
| TV | Tee **Vee** | Zip Code | 9160**4** |
| USA | You Ess **ɛi** | Date | 9/6/6**2** |
| ASAP | ɛi Ess ɛi **Pee** | Phone Number | **1**(800)-457-425**5** |
| CIA | See Eye **ɛi** | | |
| FBI | Eff Bee **Eye** | | |

| USMC | You Ess Em **See** | Time | Pronunciation |
|---|---|---|---|
| COD | See Oh **Dee** | Nine-fifteen | 9:1**5** |
| SOS | Ess Oh **Ess** | Two-thirty | 2:3**0** |
| X, Y, Z | Ex, Why, **Zee** | Names | **mid**night, after**noon** |

**Exercise 4-22: Sound/Meaning Shifts**      Track 092

*Intonation is powerful. It can change meaning and pronunciation. Here you will get the chance to play with the sounds. Remember, in the beginning, the meaning isn't that important—just work on getting control of your pitch changes. Use your rubber band for each stressed word.*

| | | |
|---|---|---|
| my **tie** | **mai**-tai | **Might** I? |
| my **keys** | **Mi**key's | My **keys**? |
| inn **key** | in **key** | **ink**y |
| my **tea** | **migh**ty | My **D** |
| I have **two**. | I have, **too**. | I **have** to. |

| | |
|---|---|
| How many **kids** do you have? | I have **two**. |
| I've been to **Europe**. | I have, **too**. |
| Why do you **work** so hard? | I **have** to. |

## Exercise 4-23: Squeezed-Out Syllables

*Intonation can also completely get rid of certain entire syllables. Some longer words that are stressed on the first syllable squeeze weak syllables right out. Cover up the regular spelling and read the phonetics.*

| | | | | |
|---|---|---|---|---|
| accidentally | æk•sə•**dent**•lee | | favorite | **fāv**•rit |
| actually | **æk**•chully | | finally | **fyn**•lee |
| aspirin | **æs**prin | | general | **jɛn**r'l |
| average | **æv**r'j | | groceries | **gross**reez |
| bakery | **bā**•kree | | history | **hiss**tree |
| basically | **ba**•sə•klee | | interest | **intr**'st |
| beverage | **bev**•r'j | | jewelry | **jool**ree |
| boundary | **bound**•ree | | liberal | **libr**'l |
| broccoli | **brä**klee | | mathematics | **mæth**mædix |
| business | **biz**ness | | memory | **mɛm**ree |
| cabinet | **cæb**•net | | natural | **næch**•rul |
| camera | **kæm**ruh | | Niagara | **nyæ**•grə |
| catholic | **cæth**•l'k | | nursery | **nr**•sree |
| chocolate | **chäk**l't | | onion | **ən**y'n |
| comfortable | **k'mf**•t'bl | | opera | **äp**rə |
| conference | **cän**frns | | orange | **ornj** |
| corporal | **corp**r'l | | preference | **pref**•rənce |
| coverage | **c'v**r'j | | probably | **präb**lee |
| desperate | **dɛsp**r't | | realize | **ri**•lize |
| diamond | **däi**m'nd | | restaurant | **rɛs**tränt |
| diaper | **däi**per | | separate | **sɛp**r't |
| different | **diff**r'nt | | several | **sɛv**r'l |
| emerald | **ɛm**r'ld | | theory | **thi**ree |
| emory | **ɛm**ree | | threatening | **thrɛt**ning |
| every | **ɛv**ree | | vegetable | **vej**•t'bl |
| family | **fæm**lee | | victory | **vic**•tree |

**Note** *The* **-cally** *ending is always pronounced* **-klee**; **-tory** *turns into* **-tree**.

注意：词尾-cally 通常发音为-klee；-tory通常发音为-tree。

## Exercise 4-24: Regular Transitions of Nouns and Verbs

*In the list below, change the stress from the first syllable for* **nouns** *to the second syllable for* **verbs**. *This is a regular, consistent change. Intonation is so powerful that you'll notice that when the stress changes, the pronunciation of the vowels do, too.*

| **Nouns** | | **Verbs** | |
|---|---|---|---|
| an accent | **æks**'nt | to accent | æk**sɛnt** |
| a concert | **kän**sert | to concert | k'n**sert** |
| a conflict | **kän**flikt | to conflict | k'n**flikt** |
| a contest | **kän**test | to contest | k'n**test** |

| a contract | **kän**træct | | to contract | k'n**trækt** |
|---|---|---|---|---|
| a contrast | **kän**træst | | to contrast | k'n**træst** |
| a convert | **kän**vert | | to convert | k'n**vert** |
| a convict | **kän**vikt | | to convict | k'n**vict** |
| a default | **dee**fält | | to default | d'**fält** |
| a desert* | **dɛz**'rt | | to desert | d'**z'rt** |
| a discharge | **dis**chärj | | to discharge | d'**schärj** |
| an envelope | **änv**'lop | | to envelop | en**vel**'p |
| an incline | **in**kline | | to incline | in**kline** |
| an influence | **influ**(w)'ns | | to influence | in**flu**(w)ns* |
| an insert | **in**sert | | to insert | in**sert** |
| an insult | **in**s'lt | | to insult | in**səlt** |
| an object | **äb**ject | | to object | ə**bject** |
| perfect | **prf**'ct | | to perfect | pr**fekt** |
| a permit | **pr**mit | | to permit | pr**mit** |
| a present | **prɛz**'nt | | to present | pr'**zɛnt** |
| produce | **pro**duce | | to produce | pr'**duce** |
| progress | **prägr**'s | | to progress | pr'**grɛss** |
| a project | **präj**ect | | to project | pr'**jɛct** |
| a pronoun | **pro**noun | | to pronounce | pr'**nounce** |
| a protest | **pro**test | | to protest | pr'**test** |
| a rebel | **rɛ**bəl | | to rebel | r'**bɛl** |
| a recall | **ree**käll | | to recall | r'**käll** |
| a record | **rɛk**'rd | | to record | r'**cord** |
| a reject | **re**ject | | to reject | r'**jɛct** |
| research | **re**s'rch | | to research | r'**srch** |
| a subject | **s'bj**ekt | | to subject | s'**bjekt** |
| a survey | **s'r**vei | | to survey | s'**rvei** |
| a suspect | **s's**pekt | | to suspect | s's**pekt** |

* *The désert is hot and dry. A dessért is ice cream. To desért is to abandon.*

* désert（作名词，意为"沙漠"）又干又热；dessért（意为"餐后甜点"）是指冰激凌之类的东西；desért（作动词）表示离弃。

* *Pronunciation symbols (w) and (y) represent a glide sound. This is explained on page 111.*

* 符号（w）和（y）表示滑音。见第111页。

## Exercise 4-25: Regular Transitions of Adjectives and Verbs       Track 095

*A different change occurs when you go from an adjective or a noun to a verb. The stress stays in the same place, but the -**mate** in an adjective is completely reduced to -**m't**, whereas in a verb, it is a full sound: -**mɛit**.*

| Nouns/Adjectives | | Verbs | |
|---|---|---|---|
| advocate | ædv'k't | to advocate | ædv'kɛit |
| animate | æn'm't | to animate | æn'mɛit |
| alternate | ältern't | to alternate | älternɛit |
| appropriate | əpropre⁽ʸ⁾'t | to appropriate | əpropre⁽ʸ⁾ɛit |
| approximate | əpräks'm't | to approximate | əpräks'mɛit |
| articulate | ärticyul't | to articulate | ärticyəlɛit |
| associate | əssosey't | to associate | əssoseyɛit |
| deliberate | d'libr't | to deliberate | d'liberɛit |
| discriminate | d'skrim'n't | to discriminate | d'skrim'nɛit |
| duplicate | dupl'k't | to duplicate | dupl'kɛit |
| elaborate | elæbr't | to elaborate | əlæberɛit |
| an estimate | ɛst'm't | to estimate | ɛst'mɛit |
| graduate | græjyu⁽ʷ⁾'t | to graduate | græjyu⁽ʷ⁾ɛit |
| intimate | int'm't | to intimate | int'mɛit |
| moderate | mäder't | to moderate | mäderɛit |
| predicate | prɛd'k't | to predicate | prɛd'kɛit |
| separate | sɛpr't | to separate | sɛperɛit |

## Exercise 4-26: Regular Transitions of Adjectives and Verbs          Track 096

*Mark the intonation or indicate the long vowel on the boldfaced word, depending which part of speech it is. Pause the CD and mark the proper syllables.*

1. You need to **insert** a paragraph here on this newspaper **insert**.
2. How can you **object** to this **object**?
3. I'd like to **present** you with this **present**.
4. Would you care to **elaborate** on his **elaborate** explanation?
5. The manufacturer couldn't **recall** if there'd been a **recall**.
6. The religious **convert** wanted to **convert** the world.
7. The political **rebels** wanted to **rebel** against the world.
8. The mogul wanted to **record** a new **record** for his latest artist.
9. If you **perfect** your intonation, your accent will be **perfect**.
10. Due to the drought, the fields didn't **produce** much **produce** this year.
11. Unfortunately, City Hall wouldn't **permit** them to get a **permit**.
12. Have you heard that your **associate** is known to **associate** with gangsters?
13. How much do you **estimate** that the **estimate** will be?
14. The facilitator wanted to **separate** the general topic into **separate** categories.

Whenever there is more than one syllable, one will be stronger.

如果单词中有两个或两个以上的音节，
其中一个音节的发音就会变强。

# Chapter 5
# 第5章

# Syllable Stress
# 音节重音

## Syllable Count Intonation Patterns

**Track 097**

音节计数语调模式

In spoken English, if you put the em**pha**sis on the wrong syl**la**ble, you totally lose the meaning, when you need to put the em**pha**sis on the right **sy**llable.

在英语口语中，如果你重读了错误的音节，就会使一个单词完全失去意义，所以你需要将重音放在正确的音节上。

At this point, we won't be concerned with *why* we are stressing a particular syllable—that understanding will come at the end of this chapter.

在这里，我们暂不解释为什么要重读特定的音节——我们会在本章的最后一部分进行解释。

## Exercise 5-1: Syllable Patterns

**Track 098**

*In order to practice accurate pitch change, repeat the following columns. Each syllable will count as one musical note. Remember that words that end in a vowel or a voiced consonant will be longer than ones ending in an unvoiced consonant (p, f, s, t, k, x, sh, th, ch).*

| | A | B | C |
|---|---|---|---|
| **1 Syllable** | | | |
| **Pattern 1a** | la! | get | stop |
| | cat | quick | which |
| | jump | choice | bit |
| | box | loss | beat |
| **Pattern 1b** | **la**-a | law | bid |
| | dog | goes | bead |
| | see | choose | car |
| | plan | lose | know |
| **2 Syllables** | la-**la** | Bob **Smith** | for **you** |
| **Pattern 2a** | a **dog** | my **car** | Who **knows**? |
| | a **cat** | some **more** | cas**sette** |
| | des**troy** | red **tape** | bal**let** |
| | a **pen** | en**close** | va**let** |
| | pre**tend** | con**sume** | to **do** |
| | your **job** | my **choice** | to**day** |
| | pea **soup** | How's **work**? | to**night** |

| Pattern 2b | la-la | wristwatch | phone book |
|---|---|---|---|
| | hot dog | textbook | doorknob |
| | icy | bookshelf | notebook |
| | suitcase | sunshine | house key |
| | project | place mat | ballot |
| | sunset | stapler | valid |
| | Get one! | modern | dog show |
| | Do it! | modem | want ad |

a hot **dog** is an overheated canine 🐕 ; a **hot**dog is a frankfurter 🍴

## Exercise 5-1: Syllable Patterns *continued* 。                     Track 098

| 3 Syllables | A | B | C |
|---|---|---|---|
| Pattern 3a | la-la-**la** | **Worms** eat **dirt**. | **Joe** has **three**. |
| | **Bob's** hot **dog** 🐕 | **Inch**worms **inch**. | **Bob** has **eight**. |
| | **Bob** won't **know**. | **Pets** need **care**. | **Al** jumped **up**. |
| | **Sam's** the **boss**. | **Ed's** too **late**. | **Glen** sat **down**. |
| | **Susie's nice**. | **Paul** threw **up**. | **Tom** made **lunch**. |
| | **Bill** went **home**. | **Wool** can **itch**. | **Kids** should **play**. |
| | **Cats** don't **care**. | **Birds** sing **songs**. | **Mom** said, "**No!**" |
| | **Stocks** can **fall**. | **Spot** has **fleas**. | **Mars** is **red**. |
| | **School** is **fun**. | **Nick's** a **punk**. | **Ned** sells **cars**. |
| Pattern 3b | la-la-**la** | Make a **cake**. | IBM |
| | a hot **dog** 🐕 | He for**got**. | a good **time** |
| | I don't **know**. | Take a **bath**. | Use your **head**! |
| | He's the **boss**. | We're too **late**. | How are **you**? |
| | We cleaned **up**. | I love **you**. | We came **home**. |
| | in the **bag** | over **here** | on the **bus** |
| | for a **while** | What a **jerk**! | engi**neer** |
| | I went **home**. | How's your **job**? | She fell **down**. |
| | We don't **care**. | How'd it **go**? | They called **back**. |
| | It's in **March**. | Who'd you **meet**? | You goofed **up**. |
| Pattern 3c | la-**la**-la | per**cen**tage (%) | O**hi**o |
| | a **hot**dog 🍴 | ad**van**tage | his **foot**ball |
| | I **don't** know! | It's **star**ting. | They're **lea**ving. |
| | Jim **killed** it. | Let's **try** it. | How **are** you? |
| | to**mo**rrow | fi**nan**cial | em**pha**tic |

| a **fruit**cake | I **thought** so. | Dale **planned** it. |
| the **eng**ine | on **Wednes**day | You **took** it. |
| a **wine**glass | in **A**pril | ex**ter**nal |
| po**ta**to | I **love** you. | a **bar**gain |
| what**ev**er | Let's **tell** him. | Don't **touch** it. |

**Pattern 3d**

| la-**la**-la | **al**phabet | **phone** number |
| **hot**dog stand | **pos**sible | **think** about |
| **I** don't know. | **Show** me one. | **com**fortable |
| **an**alyze | **ar**ea | **wait**ing for |
| **ar**ticle | **punc**tuate | **pit**iful |
| **din**nertime | **em**phasis | **ev**erything |
| **dig**ital | **syl**lable | **or**chestra |
| **an**alog | **Post**-It note | **ig**norant |
| **cell** structure | **Ro**lodex | **Rub**bermaid |

## Exercise 5-1: Syllable Patterns *continued*                    Track 098

| **4 Syllables** | **A** | **B** | **C** |
|---|---|---|---|
| **Pattern 4a** | la-la-la-**la** | **Nate** needs a **break**. | **Max** wants to **know**. |
| | **Spot's** a hot **dog**. | **Ed** took my **car**. | **Al's** kitchen **floor** |
| | **Jim** killed a **snake**. | **Jill** ate a **steak**. | **Bill's** halfway **there**. |
| | **Joe** doesn't **know**. | **Spain's** really **far**. | **Roses** are **red**, |
| | **Nate** bought a **book**. | **Jake's** in the **lake**. | **Violets** are **blue**, |
| | **Al** brought some **ice**. | **Sam's** in a **bar**. | **Candy** is **sweet**, |
| | | | and *so* are *you*. |
| **Pattern 4b** | la-la-la-**la** | She asked for **help**. | I want to **know**. |
| | It's a hot **dog**. | We took my **car**. | the kitchen **floor** |
| | He killed a **snake**. | We need a **break**. | We watched **TV**. |
| | He doesn't **know**. | It's really **far**. | She's halfway **there**. |
| | We came back **in**. | I love you, **too**. | We played all **day**. |
| | He bought a **book**. | They got a**way**. | Please show me **how**. |
| **Pattern 4c** | **la**-la-**la**-la | **Boys** ring **door**bells. | **Phil** knows **mail**men. |
| | **Bob** likes **hot**dogs. | **Bill** ate **break**fast. | **Joe** grew **egg**plants. |
| | **Ann** eats **pan**cakes. | **Guns** are **le**thal. | **Hump**ty **Dump**ty |
| | **Cats** eat **fish** bones. | **Inch**worms **bug** me. | **Hawks** are **vi**cious. |
| | **Bears** are **fuzz**y. | **Rag**tops **cost** more. | **Home**work **bores** them. |
| | **Plan**ets **ro**tate. | **Sales**men **sell** things. | **Mike** can **hear** you. |

| **Pattern 4d** | la-la-**la**-la | an **alarm** clock | He said, "**Light**bulb." |
| | It's my **hot**dog. 𝄞 | I don't **need** one. | What does "**box**" mean? |
| | imi**ta**tion | Ring the **door**bell. | Put your **hands** up. |
| | ana**ly**tic | What's the **matter**? | Where's the **mail**man? |
| | We like **science**. | intro**duc**tion | an as**sem**bly |
| | my to-**do** list | my re**port** card | defi**ni**tion |

| **Pattern 4e** | la-**la**-la-la | po**ta**to chip | What **time** is it? |
| | a **hot** dog stand | Whose **turn** is it? | my **phone** number |
| | Jim **killed** a man. | We **worked** on it. | Let's **eat** something. |
| | a**nal**ysis | How **tall** are you? | How **old** are you? |
| | in**vis**ible | in**san**ity | un**touch**able |
| | a **plat**ypus | a**bil**ity | a **man**iac |

| **Pattern 4f** | **la**-la-la-la | **su**pervisor | **light**house keeper |
| | **per**manently | **win**dow cleaner | **cough** medicine |
| | **de**monstrated | **race** car driver | **bus**iness meeting |
| | **cat**egory | **Jan**uary (jæn-yə-wery) | **Feb**ruary (feb•yə•wery) |
| | **off**ice supplies | **prog**ress report | **ba**by-sitter |
| | **ed**ucator | **thing**amajig | **dic**tionary |

## Syllable Rules

音节规则

The good news is that most of the words used in English are only one syllable.

值得高兴的一点是，英语中的大部分单词都只有一个音节。

**Rule of Thumb:** Stress **nouns** on the **first** syllable and **verbs** on the **second** syllable.

经验法则：对于名词，重读第一个音节；对于动词，重读第二个音节。

**The 95% Rule:** When in doubt, stress the **next to last**.

| 2<br>Syllables | 3<br>Syllables | 1<br>Syllable Suffix | 2<br>Syllable Suffix | Multiple<br>Syllable Suffix |
|---|---|---|---|---|
| **pa**per | po**ta**to | eco**nom**ic ic | **poss**ible ible | **crit**ically i+cal+ly |
| **nap**kin | com**pu**ter | ad**mon**ish ish | **syll**able able | **ver**ifying i+fy+ing |
| **hot**dog | per**sua**sive | **vis**ion ion | com**mun**ity ity | astro**nom**ical nom+i+cal |
| **con**test | con**di**tion | **cru**cial ial | bi**ol**ogy logy | edu**ca**tionally tion+al+ly |
| **ang**ry | di**ver**sion | **pho**tograph graph | pho**tog**raphy graphy | photo**graph**ically ic+al+ly |

## The 5% Rule: Stress the **last syllable**.

Most **two-syllable verbs** stress the **last** syllable, as well as words starting with the prefixes **a-** and **be-**, and words that end in **French suffixes**.

对于大部分双音节的动词，重读最后一个音节；以前缀a-和be-开头的单词，以及以法语后缀结尾的单词也是如此。

| 2-Syllable Verbs | Prefixes a- and be- | French Suffixes |
|---|---|---|
| be**gin** | a**bove** | refe**ree** |
| con**test** | be**low** | engi**neer** |
| de**ny** | a**bout** | clien**tele** |
| con**tain** | be**neath** | bal**let** |
| re**fuse** | a**cross** | ga**rage** |

## Exercise 5-2: Intonation Shifts                                     Track 100

*Practice the following intonation shifts.*

| 1st to 3rd | 1st to 4th | 1st to 2nd to 3rd | 2nd to 3rd |
|---|---|---|---|
| **ac**cident | **quan**tity | **an**alyze | con**demn** |
| acci**den**tal | **quan**tify | a**nal**ysis | con**dem**natory |
| acci**den**tally | quantifi**ca**tion | ana**ly**tic | condem**na**tion |
| **pres**ident | **max**imum | **cat**alyze | re**volve** |
| presi**den**tial | **max**imize | ca**tal**ysis | re**vol**ver |
| presi**den**tially | maximi**za**tion | cata**ly**tic | revo**lu**tionary |
| de**vel**op | **or**igin | **real** | cre**ate** |
| de**vel**opment | o**rig**inal | **re**alize | cre**a**tive |
| develop**men**tal | o**rig**inate | re**al**ity | cre**a**tion |
| develop**men**tally | origi**na**tion | reali**za**tion | crea**tiv**ity |

When in doubt,
stress the noun

不确定时，重读名词。

# Chapter 6
# 第6章

# Complex Intonation
# 综合语调

**Track 101**

This is the beginning of an extremely important part of spoken American English—the rhythms and intonation patterns of the long streams of nouns and adjectives that are so commonly used. These exercises will tie in the intonation patterns of **adjectives** (*nice, old, best,* etc.), **nouns** (*dog, house, surgeon,* etc.), and **adverbs** (*very, really, amazingly,* etc.).

这是美语口语一个极其重要的部分的开始——常用的长串名词和形容词的节奏以及语调模式。这些练习将把形容词（nice, old, best 等）、名词（dog, house, surgeon 等）和副词（very, really, amazingly 等）的语调模式结合在一起。

One way of approaching sentence intonation is not to build each sentence from scratch. Instead, use patterns, with each pattern similar to a mathematical formula. Instead of plugging in numbers, however, plug in words.

有一种处理句子语调的方法，不是从零开始构造每一个句子，而是使用各种模式，因为每种模式类似于一个数学公式，只是插入的是单词，而不是数字。

In Exercise 4-2, we looked at simple noun•verb•noun patterns, and in Exercises 5-1 and 5-2, the syllable-count intonation patterns were covered. Here, we'll examine intonation patterns in two-word phrases.

在练习4-2中，我们看到了简单的名词-动词-名词模式；在练习5-1和5-2中，我们学习了音节计数语调模式。在这里，我们将测验二词短语的语调模式。

It's important to note that there's a major difference between *syllable stress* and *compound noun stress* patterns. In the syllable count exercises, each *syllable* was represented by a single musical note. In the noun phrases, each individual *word* will be represented by a single musical note—no matter how many total syllables there may be.

音节重音模式和复合名词重音模式有一个主要的区别，注意到这一点很重要。在音节计数练习中，一个单独的音符代表一个音节。在名词短语中，一个单独的音符将代表一个单独的单词——不管其中总共有多少个音节。

At times, what appears to be a single-syllable word will have a "longer" sound to it—*seed* takes longer to say than *seat,* for example. (This was introduced on page 38, where you learned that a final voiced consonant causes the previous vowel to double.)

有时，表面看上去是单音节的单词会有较长的读音，比如seed发的音要比seat的长。（这在第38页做过介绍，那部分内容使你认识到结尾的浊辅音会使它前面元音的发音延长一倍。）

*Repeat the following noun and adjective sentences.*

| | **Noun** | **Adjective** |
|---|---|---|
| 1. | It's a **nail**. | It's **short**. |
| 2. | It's a **cake**. | It's **chocolate**. (chäkl't) |
| 3. | It's a **tub**. | It's **hot**. (hät) |
| 4. | It's a **drive**. | It's **härd**. |
| 5. | It's a **door**. | It's in **back**. (bæk) |
| 6. | It's a **cärd**. | There are **four**. |
| 7. | It's a **spot**. (spät) | It's **smäll**. |
| 8. | It's a **book**. (bük) | It's **good**. (güd) |

*Write your own noun and adjective sentences below. You will be using these examples throughout this series of exercises.*

9. It's a _____ It's _____

10. It's a _____ It's _____

11. It's a _____ It's _____

# Two-Word Phrases
二词短语

## Descriptive Phrases
描述性短语

Nouns are "heavier" than adjectives; they carry the weight of the new information. An adjective and a noun combination is called a *descriptive phrase,* and in the absence of contrast or other secondary changes, the stress will always fall naturally on the noun. In the absence of a noun, you will stress the adjective, but as soon as a noun appears on the scene, it takes immediate precedence—and should be stressed.

　　名词比形容词要"重"；它们担负着承载新信息的重任。形容词和名词的组合叫做描述性短语，在没有对比或其他次重音变化时，重音总是自然地落在名词上。如果没有名词，你会重读形容词，但名词一出现，你就需要立即将它放在优先地位——并重读它。

**Exercise 6-2: Sentence Stress with Descriptive Phrases**                    Track 104

*Repeat the following sentences.*

| | Adjective | Adjective and Noun |
|---|---|---|
| 1. | It's **short**. | It's a short **nail**. |
| 2. | It's **chocolate**. | It's a chocolate **cake**. |
| 3. | It's **good**. | It's a good **plan**. |
| 4. | It's **guarded**. | It's a guarded **gate**. |
| 5. | It's **wide**. | It's a wide **river**. |
| 6. | There're **four**. | There're four **cards**. |
| 7. | It was **small**. | It was a small **spot**. |
| 8. | It's the **best**. | It's the best **book**. |

*Pause the CD and write your own adjective and noun/adjective sentences. Use the same words from Exercise 6-1.*

| | | | |
|---|---|---|---|
| 9. | It's _____ | It's a _____ |
| 10. | It's _____ | It's a _____ |
| 11. | It's _____ | It's a _____ |

**Exercise 6-3: Two Types of Descriptive Phrases**                    Track 105

*Repeat.*

| | Adjective/Noun | Adverb/Adjective |
|---|---|---|
| 1. | It's a short **nail**. | It's really **short**. |
| 2. | It's a chocolate **cake**. | It's dark **chocolate**. |
| 3. | It's a hot **bath**. | It's too **hot**. |
| 4. | It's a hard **drive**. | It's extremely **hard**. |
| 5. | It's the back **door**. | It's far **back**. |
| 6. | There are four **cards**. | There are only **four**. |
| 7. | It's a small **spot**. | It's laughably **small**. |
| 8. | It's a good **book**. | It's amazingly **good**. |

*Pause the CD and write your own adjective/noun and adverb/adjective sentences, carrying over Exercise 6-2.*

9. It's a _____ It's _____
10. It's a _____ It's _____
11. It's a _____ It's _____

---

**Exercise 6-4: Descriptive Phrase Story—The Ugly Duckling**　　　　**Track 106**

*The following well-known story has been rewritten to contain only descriptions. Stress the second word of each phrase. Repeat after me.*

There is a *mother **duck***. She lays *three **eggs***. Soon, there are three *baby **birds***. Two of the birds are *very **beautiful***. One of them is *quite **ugly***. The *beautiful **ducklings*** make fun of their *ugly **brother***. The *poor **thing*** is *very **unhappy***. As the *three **birds*** grow older, the *ugly **duckling*** begins to change. His *gray **feathers*** turn *snowy **white***. His *gangly **neck*** becomes *beautifully **smooth***.

In *early **spring***, the *ugly **duckling*** is swimming in a *small **pond*** in the *back**yard*** of the *old **farm***. He sees his *shimmering **reflection*** in the *clear **water***. What a *great **surprise***! He is no longer an *ugly **duckling***. He has grown into a *lovely **swan***.

## Set Phrases　　　　　　　　　　　　　　　　　　　　　　　　**Track 107**
固定短语

### *A Cultural Indoctrination to American Norms*
美语准则的文化教化

When I learned the alphabet as a child, I *heard* it before I *saw* it. I heard that the last four letters were *dubba-you, ex, why, zee*. I thought that *dubbayou* was a long, strange name for a letter, but I didn't question it anymore than I did *aitch*. It was just a name. Many years later, it struck me that it was a *double U*. Of course, a **W** is really **UU**. I had such a funny feeling, though, when I realized that something I had taken for granted for so many years had a background meaning that I had completely overlooked. This "funny feeling" is exactly what most native speakers get when a two-word phrase is stressed on the wrong word. When two individual words go through the cultural process of becoming a set phrase, the original sense of each word is more or less forgotten and the new meaning completely takes over. When we hear the word ***pain**killer,* we think *anesthetic*. If, however, someone says *pain**killer**,* it brings up the strength and almost unrelated meaning of *kill*.

　　　我小时候学习字母时，先听到字母的发音而后才看到写法。我听到最后四个字母是dubba-you，ex, why, zee。那时我想dubbayou对于一个字母来说真是一个又长又奇怪的名字，而我对它产生的疑问也没有对aitch多。它只是个名字。多年后，令我深有感触的是它原来是double U。当然，字母W确实是UU。当我意识到自己很多年来认为是理所当然的事情，却有着被我完全忽略的背景意义时，这种感觉真的很滑稽。当一个二词短语被重读在错误的单词上时，这种滑稽的感觉正是大多数说母语的人的感觉。当两个独立的单词历经了成为固定短语的文化历程后，每个单词的本意几乎都已被忘却，而被新意义完全代替。当我们听到单词**pain**killer时，我们会想到麻醉。然而，如果有人说pain**killer**，就会使人想到"力量"和几乎毫不相关的意义"杀死"。

When you have a two-word phrase, you have to either stress on the first word, or on the second word. If you stress both or neither, it's not clear what you are trying to say. Stress on the first word is more noticeable and one of the most important concepts of intonation that you are going to study. At first glance, it doesn't seem significant, but the more you look at this concept, the more you are going to realize that it reflects how we Americans think, what concepts we have adopted as our own, and what things we consider important.

当你见到一个二词短语，要么重读第一个单词，要么重读第二个单词。如果你两个都重读或都不重读，就会让人搞不清楚你想要表达什么。重读第一个单词更能引起人的注意，也是你要学习的最重要的语调概念之一。乍看之下，这似乎并不重要，但你越仔细地观察这个概念，就会越深刻地意识到它反映了我们美国人是怎么想的，什么理念为我们所接受，以及什么事情在我们看来是重要的。

Set phrases are our "cultural icons," or word images; they are indicators of a *determined use* that we have internalized. These set phrases, with stress on the first word, have been taken into everyday English from descriptive phrases, with stress on the second word. As soon as a descriptive phrase becomes a set phrase, the emphasis shifts from the *second* word to the *first.* The original sense of each word is more or less forgotten, and the new meaning takes over.

固定短语是我们的"文化图标"或文字形象；它们是我们内化形成的固定用法的标示。这些固定短语是从描述性短语变为日常英语的，重音在第一个单词上，而描述性短语的重音在第二个单词。描述性短语一旦成为固定短语，重音就从第二个单词转移到第一个单词上。每一个单词的原意几乎被忘却，而被新的意义所代替。

Set phrases indicate that we have internalized this phrase as an *image,* that we all agree on a concrete idea that this phrase represents. A hundred years or so ago, when Levi Strauss first came out with his denim pants, they were described as *blue **jeans**.* Now that we all agree on the image, however, they are ***blue** jeans.*

固定短语表明我们已把这个短语内化为一种形象，并且都认同这个短语所代表的具体概念。大约一百年前，当李维斯·施特劳斯最先展出牛仔裤时，人们都将它描述为blue **jeans**。现在我们都认可了这个形象，它就成了**blue** jeans。

A more recent example would be the descriptive phrase, *He's a real party animal.* This slang expression refers to someone who has a great time at a party. When it first became popular, the people using it needed to explain (with their intonation) that he was an *animal* at a *party.* As time passed, the expression became cliché and we changed the intonation to *He's a real **party** animal* because "everyone knew" what it meant.

描述性短语He's a real party animal算是近年来的一个例子。这个俚语表达指的是把大量时间用在社交聚会上的人。当它最初流行时，使用它的人需要（用他们的语调）解释说he was an *animal* at a *party*。随着时间的推移，这种表达成了套语，我们也把语调变成了He's a real **party** animal，因为每个人都已知道它的含义。

Clichés are hard to recognize in a new language because what may be an old and tired expression to a native speaker may be fresh and exciting to a newcomer. One way to look at English from the inside out, rather than always looking from the outside in, is to get a feel for what Americans have already accepted and internalized. This starts out as a purely language phenomenon, but you will notice that as you progress and undergo the relentless cultural indoctrination of standard intonation patterns, you will find yourself expressing yourself with the language cues and signals that will mark you as an insider—not an outsider.

在一种新的语言中，套语是难以识别的，因为那些对说母语的人来说可能是陈词滥调的表达，在初学者看来却可能是新鲜和令人兴奋的。一种由内向外而非总是由外向内审视英语的方式，就是要去感知美国人已经接受和内化的东西。这起初是纯粹的语言现象，但你会注意到，当你经历了标准语调模式不间断的文化教化，你会发现自己能用语言的暗示和信号来表达自己的思想了，而这些暗示和信号会表明你是个知情人——而非局外人。

When the interpreter was translating for the former Russian President Gorbachev about his trip to San Francisco in 1990, his pronunciation was good, but he placed himself on the outside by repeatedly saying, *cable **car**. The phrase **cable** car* is an image, an established entity, and it was very noticeable to hear it stressed on the second word as a mere description.

当那位口译员为前苏联总统戈尔巴乔夫1990年的旧金山之行做翻译时，他的发音不错，可他多次说到cable **car**，这表明他并没有真正理解这个短语的含义。短语**cable** car是一种形象，一种确定了的实体，所以听到有人将它作为描述性短语而将重读放在第二个单词上时，就会觉得很突兀。

An important point that I would like to make is that the "rules" you are given here are not meant to be memorized. This discussion is only an introduction to give you a starting point in understanding this phenomenon and in recognizing what to listen for. Read it over; think about it; then listen, try it out, listen some more, and try it out again.

我想指出重要的一点，那就是不要刻意去记忆我在这里教给你的"规则"。这段讨论只是个介绍，给你一个出发点来理解这一现象，并且让你意识到要留意听什么。读一读，想一想，然后再听一听，试一试，多听一些，再试一试。

As you become familiar with intonation, you will become more comfortable with American norms, thus the cultural orientation, or even cultural indoctrination, aspect of the following examples.

当你熟悉了语调，你就会对美语准则更加熟悉，这样对下面例子涉及的文化介绍甚至文化教化也能更好地理解。

**Note** *When you get the impression that a two-word description could be hyphenated or even made into one word, it is a signal that it could be a set phrase—for example, **flash** light, **flash**-light, **flash**light. Also, stress the first word with Street (**Main** Street) and nationalities of food and people (**Mexican** food, **Chinese** girls).*

注意：当你觉得一个由两个词构成的描述性短语可以由连字符连接，甚至可以成为一个单词，这就是个信号，即它可能是个固定短语——例如，**flash** light, **flash**-light, **flash**light。另外，重读和Street在一起的第一个单词（**Main** Street）、食物的产地以及人们的国籍（**Mexican** food，**Chinese** girls）。

## Exercise 6-5: Sentence Stress with Set Phrases — Track 108

Repeat the following sentences.

| | Noun | Noun/Adj. | Set Phrase |
|---|---|---|---|
| 1. | It's a **finger**. | It's a **nail**. | It's a **finger**nail. |
| 2. | It's a **pan**. | It's a **cake**. | It's a **pan**cake. |
| 3. | It's a **tub**. | It's **hot**. | It's a **hot** tub. (Jacuzzi) |
| 4. | It's a **drive**. | It's **hard**. | It's a **hard** drive. |
| 5. | It's a **bone**. | It's in **back**. | It's the **back**bone. (spine) |
| 6. | It's a **card**. | It's a **trick**. | It's a **card** trick. |
| 7. | It's a **spot**. | It's a **light**. | It's a **spot**light. |
| 8. | It's a **book**. | It's a **phone**. | It's a **phone** book. |

Pause the CD and write your own noun and set phrase sentences, carrying over the same nouns you used in Exercise 6-2. Remember, when you use a noun, include the article (a, an, the); when you use an adjective, you don't need an article.

9. It's a_____   It's a_____   It's a_____

10. It's a_____   It's a_____   It's a_____

11. It's a_____   It's a_____   It's a_____

## Exercise 6-6: Making Set Phrases — Track 109

Pause the CD and add a noun to each word as indicated by the picture.

1. a chair    a **chair**man
2. a phone    _____
3. a house    _____
4. a base    _____
5. a door    _____
6. the White    _____
7. a movie    _____
8. the Bullet    _____
9. a race    _____
10. a coffee    _____

11. a wrist    _____
12. a beer    _____
13. a high    _____
14. a hunting    _____
15. a dump    _____
16. a jelly    _____
17. a love    _____
18. a thumb    _____
19. a lightning    _____
20. a pad    _____

**Exercise 6-7: Set Phrase Story—The Little Match Girl**      **Track 110**

*The following story contains only set phrases, as opposed to the descriptive story in Exercise 6-4. Stress the first word of each phrase.*

The little **match** girl was out in a **snow**storm. Her feet were like **ice** cubes and her **finger**tips had **frost**bite. She hadn't sold any matches since **daybreak,** and she had a **stomach**ache from the **hunger** pangs, but her **step**mother would beat her with a **broom**stick if she came home with an empty **coin** purse. Looking into the bright **living** rooms, she saw **Christmas** trees and warm **fire**places. Out on the **snow**bank, she lit a match and saw the image of a grand **dinner** table of food before her. As the **match**stick burned, the illusion slowly faded. She lit **another** one and saw a room full of happy **family** members. On the last match, her **grand**mother came down and carried her home. In the morning, the **passers**by saw the little **match** girl. She had frozen during the **night**time, but she had a smile on her face.

## Contrasting a Description and a Set Phrase

对比描述性短语和固定短语

We now have two main intonation patterns—*first word stress* and *second word stress*. In the following exercise, we will contrast the two.

    现在我们有两种主要的语调模式——重读第一个单词的和重读第二个单词的。在以下练习中，我们将对二者进行对比。

**Exercise 6-8: Contrasting Descriptive and Set Phrases**      **Track 111**

*Repeat after me.*

| Descriptive Phrase | Set Phrase |
|---|---|
| 1. It's a short **nail**. | It's a **finger**nail. |
| 2. It's a chocolate **cake**. | It's a **pan**cake. |
| 3. It's a hot **bath**. | It's a **hot** tub. |
| 4. It's a long **drive**. | It's a **hard** drive. |
| 5. It's the back **door**. | It's the **back**bone. |
| 6. There are four **cards**. | It's a **card** trick. |
| 7. It's a small **spot**. | It's a **spot**light. |
| 8. It's a good **book**. | It's a **phone** book. |

*Pause the CD and rewrite your descriptive phrases (Exercise 6-2) and set phrases (Exercise 6-5).*

    9. It's a _____    It's a _____

   10. It's a _____    It's a _____

   11. It's a _____    It's a _____

*Repeat the following pairs.*

| **Descriptive Phrase** | **Set Phrase** |
|---|---|
| a light **bulb** | a **light**bulb |
| blue **pants** | **blue** jeans |
| a cold **fish** | a **gold**fish |
| a gray **hound** | a **grey**hound |
| an old **key** | an **inn** key |
| a white **house** | the **White** House |
| a nice **watch** | a **wrist**watch |
| a sticky **web** | a **spider** web |
| a clean **cup** | a **coffee** cup |
| a sharp **knife** | a **steak** knife |
| a baby **alligator** | a **baby** bottle |
| a shiny **tack** | **thumb**tacks |
| a wire **brush** | a **hair**brush |
| a new **ball** | a **foot**ball |
| a toy **gun** | a **machine** gun |
| a silk **bow** | a **Band**-Aid |
| a bright **star** | a **fire**cracker |
| Mary **Jones** | a **mail**box |
| Bob **Smith** | a **spray** can |
| foreign **affairs** | a **wine**glass |
| down **payment** | a **foot**print |
| New **York** | a **straw**berry |
| Social **Security** | a **fig** leaf |
| City **Hall** | an **ice** cream |

## Summary of Stress in Two-Word Phrases                    **Track 113**
二词短语重音总结

| | | |
|---|---|---|
| **First Word** | set phrases | *light**bulb*** |
| | streets | ***Main** Street* |
| | Co. or Corp. | ***Xerox** Corporation* |
| | nationalities of food | ***Chinese** food* |
| | nationalities of people | ***French** guy* |
| **Second Word** | descriptive phrases | *new **information*** |
| | road designations | *Fifth **Avenue*** |
| | modified adjectives | *really **big*** |
| | place names and parks | *New **York**, Central **Park*** |
| | institutions, or Inc. | *Oakland **Museum**; Xerox, **Inc**.* |
| | personal-names and titles | *Bob **Smith**, Assistant **Manager*** |
| | personal pronouns and possessives | *his **car**, Bob's **brother*** |
| | articles | *the **bus**, a **week**, an **hour*** |
| | initials and acronyms | *U.S., IQ* |
| | chemical compounds | *zinc **oxide*** |
| | colors and numbers | *red **orange**, 26* |
| | most compound verbs | *go **away**, sit **down**, fall **off*** |
| | percent and dollar | *10 **percent**, 50 **dollars*** |
| | hyphenated nationalities | *African-**American*** |
| | descriptive nationalities | *Mexican **restaurant*** |

## Nationalities                                            **Track 114**
国籍

When you are in a foreign country, the subject of nationalities naturally comes up a lot. It would be nice if there were a simple rule that said that all the words using nationalities are stressed on the first word. There isn't, of course. Take this preliminary quiz to see if you need to do this exercise. For simplicity's sake, we will stick with one nationality—American.

　　当你在外国，国籍的话题自然会经常出现。如果有个简单的规则，指出所有被国籍修饰的单词都重读第一个单词，那该多好啊。这样的规则当然没有。来做个初步测试，看看你是否需要做这个练习。为了简单起见，我们将一直使用美国这个国籍。

**Exercise 6-10: Nationality Intonation Quiz**                **Track 115**

*Pause the CD and stress one word in each of the following examples. Repeat after me. (See also Chapter 5)*

        1. an American guy
        2. an American restaurant

3. American food
4. an American teacher
5. an English teacher

When you first look at it, the stress shifts may seem arbitrary, but let's examine the logic behind these five examples and use it to go on to other, similar cases.

乍看之下，重音的改变似乎是任意的，但让我们来仔细研究一下这五个例子背后的逻辑，并将它运用到其他类似的例子中。

## 1. an Américan guy

The operative word is *American; guy* could even be left out without changing the meaning of the phrase. Compare *I saw two **American** guys yesterday,* with *I saw two **Americans** yesterday.* Words like *guy, man, kid, lady, people* are de facto pronouns in an anthropocentric language. A strong noun, on the other hand, would be stressed—*They flew an American **flag**.* This is why you have the pattern change in Exercise 5-1: 4e, *Jim **killed** a man;* but 4b, *He killed a **snake**.*

有效单词是American；guy甚至可以省去，也不会改变短语的意思。比较I saw two **American** guys yesterday和 I saw two **Americans** yesterday。像guy，man，kid，lady，people这样的单词在以人类为中心的语言中是事实上的代词。另一方面，一个有力的名词会被重读——They flew an American **flag**。这是练习5-1中模式变化的原因：在4e中，Jim **killed** a man；但在4b中，He killed a **snake**。

## 2. an American réstaurant

Don't be sidetracked by an ordinary descriptive phrase that happens to have a nationality in it. You are describing the restaurant: *We went to a good **restaurant** yesterday* or *We went to an American **restaurant** yesterday.* You would use the same pattern where the nationality is more or less incidental in *I had French **toast** for breakfast. **French fry**,* on the other hand, has become a set phrase.

不要被碰巧含有国籍的一般性描述短语转移了注意力。当你说We went to a good **restaurant** yesterday或We went to an American **restaurant** yesterday时，你是在描述那个饭店。当你说I had French **toast** for breakfast时你使用的是相同的模式，在这里国籍几乎是附加的。而**French** fry已经成为了一个固定短语。

## 3. Américan food

*Food* is a weak word. *I never ate **American** food when I lived in Japan. Let's have **Chinese** food for dinner.*

Food是一个弱读词。比如：I never ate **American** food when I lived in Japan. Let's have **Chinese** food for dinner.

## 4. an American téacher

This is a description, so the stress is on *teacher*.

> 这是一个描述性短语，所以重音在teacher上。

## 5. an Énglish teacher

This is a set phrase. The stress is on the subject being taught, not the nationality of the teacher: *a **French** teacher, a **Spanish** teacher, a **history** teacher.*

> 这是一个固定短语。重音落在所教的科目上而非教师的国籍上：a **French** teacher，a **Spanish** teacher，a **history** teacher。

| Exercise 6-11: Contrasting Descriptive and Set Phrases | Track 116 |
|---|---|

*Repeat the following pairs.*

| Set Phrase | Descriptive Phrase |
|---|---|
| An **English** teacher... | An English **teacher**... |
| ...teaches English. | ...is from England. |
| An **English** book... | An English **book**...is on any subject, |
| ...teaches the English language. | but it came from England. |
| An **English** test... | An English **test**... is on any subject, |
| ...tests a student on the English language. | but it deals with or came from England. |
| **English** food... | An English **restaurant**... |
| ...is kippers for breakfast. | ...serves kippers for breakfast. |

Intonation can indicate completely different meanings for otherwise similar words or phrases. For example, an **English** *teacher* teaches English, but an *English* **teacher** is from England; **French** *class* is where you study French, but *French* **class** is Gallic style and sophistication; an **orange** *tree* grows oranges, but an *orange* **tree** is any kind of tree that has been painted orange.

> 语调能够使在其他方面相近的单词或短语表达完全不同的意义。例如：**English** teacher是指教英语的老师，而English **teacher**则指来自英国的老师；**French** class是指学习法语的地方，而French **class**则指法国人的方式和世故；**orange** tree是指生长橘子的树，而orange **tree**则指任何一种被涂成橘红色的树。

| Exercise 6-12: Contrast of Compound Nouns | Track 117 |
|---|---|

*In the following list of words, underline the element that should be stressed. Pause the CD. Repeat after me.*

| 1. | the **White** House | 21. | convenience store | 41. | a doorknob |
|---|---|---|---|---|---|
| 2. | a white **house** | 22. | convenient store | 42. | a glass door |
| 3. | a darkroom | 23. | to pick up | 43. | a locked door |
| 4. | a dark room | 24. | a pickup truck | 44. | ice cream |
| 5. | Fifth Avenue | 25. | six years old | 45. | I scream. |
| 6. | Main Street | 26. | a six-year-old | 46. | elementary |
| 7. | a main street | 27. | six and a half | 47. | a lemon tree |
| 8. | a hot dog 🐕 | 28. | a sugar bowl | 48. | Watergate |
| 9. | a hotdog 🍴 | 29. | a wooden bowl | 49. | the back gate |
| 10. | a baby blanket | 30. | a large bowl | 50. | the final year |
| 11. | a baby's blanket | 31. | a mixing bowl | 51. | a yearbook |
| 12. | a baby bird | 32. | a top hat | 52. | United States |
| 13. | a blackbird | 33. | a nice hat | 53. | New York |
| 14. | a black bird | 34. | a straw hat | 54. | Long Beach |
| 15. | a greenhouse | 35. | a chairperson | 55. | Central Park |
| 16. | a green house | 36. | Ph.D. | 56. | a raw deal |
| 17. | a green thumb | 37. | IBM | 57. | a deal breaker |
| 18. | a parking ticket | 38. | MIT | 58. | the bottom line |
| 19. | a one-way ticket | 39. | USA | 59. | a bottom feeder |
| 20. | an unpaid ticket | 40. | ASAP | 60. | a new low |

## Exercise 6-13: Description and Set Phrase Test                    Track 118

*Let's check and see if the concepts are clear. Pause the CD and underline or highlight the stressed word. Repeat after me.*

1. He's a **nice guy**.

2. He's an **American guy** from **San Francisco**.

3. The **cheerleader** needs a **rubber band** to hold her **ponytail**.

4. The **executive assistant** needs a **paper clip** for the **final report**.

5. The **law student** took an **English test** in a **foreign country**.

6. The **policeman** saw a **red car** on the **freeway** in **Los Angeles**.

7. My **old dog** has **long ears** and a **flea problem**.

8. The **new teacher** broke his **coffee cup** on the **first day**.

9. His **best friend** has a **broken cup** in his **other office**.

10. Let's play **football** on the **weekend** in **New York**.

11. **"Jingle Bells"** is a **nice song**.

12. Where are my **new shoes**?

13. Where are my **tennis shoes**?

14. I have a **headache** from the **heat wave** in **South Carolina**.

15. The **newlyweds** took a **long walk** in **Long Beach**.

16. The **little dog** was sitting on the **sidewalk**.

17. The **famous athlete** changed clothes in the **locker room**.

18. The **art exhibit** was held in an **empty room**.

19. There was a **class reunion** at the **high school**.

20. The **headlines** indicated a **new policy**.

21. We got **online** and went to AmericanAccent **dot com**.

22. The **stock options** were listed in the **company directory**.

23. All the **second graders** were out on the **playground**.

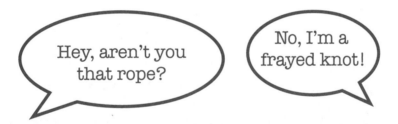

---

**Exercise 6-14: Descriptions and Set Phrases—Goldilocks**                    **Track 119**

*Read the story and stress the indicated words. Notice if they are a **description**, a **set phrase**, or contrast. Repeat after me. (For the next level of this topic, go to page 174.)*

There is a *little girl*. Her name is *Goldilocks*. She is in a *sunny forest*. She sees a *small house*. She *knocks* on the door, but *no one* answers. She *goes inside*. In the *large room*, there are *three chairs*. *Goldilocks* sits on the *biggest chair*, but it is *too high*. She sits on the *middle-sized* one, but it is *too low*. She sits on the *small chair* and it is *just right*. On the table, there are *three bowls*. There is *hot porridge* in the bowls. She tries the *first one*, but it is *too hot*; the *second one* is *too cold*; and the *third one* is *just right*, so she eats it all. *After that*, she goes *upstairs*. She *looks around*. There are *three beds*, so she *sits down*. The *biggest bed* is *too hard*. The *middle-sized* bed is *too soft*. The *little one* is *just **right**,* so she *lies **down**.* Soon, she *falls **asleep**.* In the ***meantime,*** the family of *three **bears*** comes home — the ***Papa** bear,* the ***Mama** bear,* and the ***Baby** bear.* They *look **around**.*

They say, "Who's been sitting in our chairs and eating our porridge?" Then they *run **upstairs**.* They say, "Who's been sleeping in our beds?" ***Goldilocks** wakes **up**.* She is *very **scared**.* She *runs **away**. **Gold**ilocks* never *comes **back**.*

## Phrasal Verbs
短语动词

When you have a *verb* and a *preposition*, it's called a *phrasal verb*. These are idiomatic expressions that can't be translated literally. They tend to be stressed on the second word, such as sit **down**, fall **off**, get **up**, put **away**, come **back**, etc. If you have a phrasal verb, such as pick **up**, and you put the stress on the first word, it turns into a noun meaning **truck**, as in, "He was driving a **pick**up truck."

动词加上介词，就组成了短语动词。它们是习语，不能按字面意思翻译。它们通常在第二个单词上重读，例如sit **down**，fall **off**，get **up**，put **away**，come **back**等。如果你碰到一个短语动词，例如pick **up**，但是你把重音放在了第一个单词上，它就变成了名词，是"卡车"的意思，在"He was driving a **pick**up truck.（他那时正在开卡车。）"这句话中就是这个意思。

| | |
|---|---|
| Don't come **back**! | He's planning his big **come**back. |
| Let's back **up** and start again. | Do you have a **back**up plan? |
| The children have run **off**. | The sewer **run**off polluted the stream. |
| Could you print this **out**? | Could you make a **print**out? |
| They broke **up** last week. | It was a terrible **break**up. |
| Could you call me **back**? | I'm still waiting for a **call**back. |
| We're going to have to cut **back**. | The **cut**backs are ruining the program. |
| Sure, go **ahead**. | We got the **go**-ahead. |
| We need to work **around** the problem. | He came up with a good **work**-around. |
| The heirlooms were handed **down**. | I won't wear **hand**-me-downs! |
| How much was left **over**? | What? **Left**overs again! |
| It didn't work **out**. | It was a great **work**out. |
| The dogs ran **away**. | It was a **run**away best seller. |
| He knocked me **down** and dragged me **out**. | It was a **knock**-down, **drag**-out fight. |

# Chapter 7

Use punctuation for phrasing
Commas sound different from periods.

通过标点符号来断句。
逗号和句号听起来是不同的。

# Phrasing
# 断句

## Word Groups and Phrasing

词群和断句

### *Pauses for Related Thoughts, Ideas, or for Breathing*
因为相关想法、概念或呼吸而进行的停顿

By now you've begun developing a strong intonation, with clear peaks and reduced valleys, so you're ready for the next step. You may find yourself reading the paragraph in Exercise 4-18 like this:

到现在为止，你已开始形成强语调，有明显的音高高点和弱化的音高低点，你已为下一步练习做好了准备。你可能发现自己像这样朗读练习4-18中的段落：

*HellomynameisSo-and-SoI'mtakingAmerican**Accent**Training.*
*There'sa**lot**tolearnbutI**hope**tomakeitasen**joy**ableaspossible.*

If so, your audience won't completely comprehend or enjoy your presentation.
如果是这样，你的听众就不会完全理解或欣赏你的陈述。

In addition to intonation, there is another aspect of speech that indicates meaning. This can be called *phrasing* or *tone.* Have you ever caught just a snippet of a conversation in your own language and somehow known how to piece together what came before or after the part you heard? This has to do with phrasing.

除了语调，语言中还有另一个方面可以传达意思。我们可以把它叫做断句或音调。你碰到过只听到用你的母语进行的只言片语，就知道怎样把未听到的前、后部分连接起来的情况吗？这就与断句有关。

In a sentence, phrasing tells the listener where the speaker is at the moment, where the speaker is going, and if the speaker is finished or not. Note that the intonation stays on the nouns. (See also Chapter 4)

在一个句子中，断句告诉听者说话人此刻在说什么，将来想说什么，以及是否说完。注意语调保持在名词上。（也见第4章）

## Exercise 7-1: Phrasing Track 122

*Repeat after me.*

| | |
|---|---|
| **Statement** | **Dogs** eat **bones**. |
| **Clauses** | **Dogs** eat **bones**, but **cats** eat **fish**, *or* As we all **know**, dogs eat **bones**. |
| **Listing** | **Dogs** eat **bones**, **kibbles**, and **meat**. |
| **Question** | Do **dogs** eat **bones**? |
| **Repeated Question** | Do **dogs** eat **bones**?!! |
| **Tag Question** | **Dogs** eat bones, **don't** they? |
| **Tag Statement** | **Dogs** eat bones, **DON'T** they! |
| **Indirect Speech** | He asked if **dogs** ate **bones**. |
| **Direct Speech** | "Do **dogs** eat **bones**?" he **asked**. |

For clarity, break your sentences with pauses between natural word groups of related thought or ideas. Of course, you will have to break at every comma and every period, but besides those breaks, add other little pauses to let your listeners catch up with you or think over the last burst of information and to allow you time to take a breath. Let's work on this technique. In doing the following exercise, you should think of using *breath groups* and *idea groups.*

为了清晰明了，将句子在相关想法或概念的自然词群间用停顿断开。当然，你必须在每一个逗号和句号处停顿，除了这些中断，还要有其他的小停顿，让你的听众理解你的意思或思考最后一串信息，也让你有时间来换气。让我们来练习这个技巧。在做以下练习时，你应该想着使用"呼吸群"和"大意群"。

## Exercise 7-2: Creating Word Groups Track 123

*Break the paragraph into natural word groups. Mark every place where you think a pause is needed with a slash.*

**He**llo, **my** name is_____. I'm taking American **Accent** Training. There's a **lot** to **learn**, but I **hope** to make it as **enjoyable** as possible. I should pick **up** on the American **intonation** pattern pretty **easily**, although the **only** way to **get** it is to **practice** all of the time. I use the **up** and down, or **peaks** and valleys **intonation** more than I **used** to. I've been paying attention to **pitch, too**. It's like **walking** down a **stair**case. I've been **talking** to a lot of **Americans** lately, and they tell me that I'm **easier** to under**stand**. **Any**way, I could go on and on, but the **important** thing is to **listen** well and sound **good**. **Well**, what do you **think**? Do I?

**Note** *In the beginning, your word groups should be very short. It'll be a sign of your growing sophistication when they get longer.*

注意：刚开始，你的词群应该是很短的。当词群变长时，也标志着你变得熟练了。

✖ Pause the CD to do your marking.

## Exercise 7-3: Practicing Word Groups　　　　　　　　　　　　　　　Track 124

*When I read the paragraph this time, I will exaggerate the pauses. Although we're working on word groups here, remember, I don't want you to lose your intonation. Repeat each sentence group after me.*

Hello, my name is _____ . I'm taking American Accent Training. There's a lot to learn, but I hope to make it as enjoyable as possible. I should pick up on the American intonation pattern pretty easily, although the only way to get it is to practice all of the time. I use the up and down, or peaks and valleys intonation more than I used to. I've been paying attention to pitch, too. It's like walking down a staircase. I've been talking to a lot of Americans lately, and they tell me that I'm easier to understand. Anyway, I could go on and on, but the important thing is to listen well and sound good. Well. What do you think? Do I?

✖ Next, back up the CD and practice the word groups three times using strong intonation.

✖ Then, pause the CD and practice three more times on your own. When reading, your pauses should be neither long nor dramatic—just enough to give your listener time to digest what you're saying. Be sure to take a breath for each phrase, not for each word or indeed the entire paragraph.

## Exercise 7-4: Punctuation & Phrasing　　　　　　　　　　　　　　　Track 125

*Take this quick quiz to make sure you can hear the punctuation-based phrasing.*

1. I did it
A. ❑ . B. ❑ , C. ❑ ? D. ❑ !

2. I did it
A. ❑ . B. ❑ , C. ❑ ? D. ❑ !

3. I did it
A. ❑ . B. ❑ , C. ❑ ? D. ❑ !

4. I did it
A. ❑ . B. ❑ , C. ❑ ? D. ❑ !

## Exercise 7-5: Tag Endings　　　　　　　　　　　　　　　　　　　　Track 126

*Pause the CD and complete each sentence with a tag ending. Use the same verb, but with the opposite polarity—positive becomes negative, and negative becomes positive. (See also Chapter 11)*

## Intonation

With a *query*, the intonation rises.
With *confirmation*, the intonation drops.

## Pronunciation

| | |
|---|---|
| Did he? | **Di**dee? |
| Does he? | **Du**zzy? |
| Was he? | **Wu**zzy? |
| Has he? | **Ha**zzy? |
| Is he? | **I**zzy? |
| Will he? | **Wil**ly? |
| Would he? | **Woo**dy? |
| Can he? | **Can**ny? |
| Wouldn't you? | **Woo**den chew? |
| Shouldn't I? | **Shü**dn näi? |
| Won't he? | **Woe** knee? |
| Didn't he? | **Did**n knee? |
| Hasn't he? | **Has** a knee? |
| Wouldn't he? | **Woo**den knee? |
| Isn't he? | **Is** a knee? |
| Isn't it? | **Is** a nit? |
| Doesn't it? | **Du**zza nit? |
| Aren't I? | **Are** näi? |
| Won't you? | **Wone** chew? |
| Don't you? | **Done** chew? |
| Can't you? | **Can** chew? |
| Could you? | **Cü**joo? |
| Would you? | **Wü**joo? |

1. The new **clerk** is very **slow**, <u>isn't he</u>!
2. But he can **improve**, _____ ?
3. She doesn't **type** very well, _____ !
4. They lost their **way**, _____ ?
5. You don't **think** so, _____ !
6. I don't think it's **easy**, _____ ?
7. I'm your **friend**, _____ ?
8. You won't be **coming**, _____ !
9. He keeps the **books**, _____ !
10. We have to close the **office**, _____ ?
11. We have closed the **office**, _____ ?
12. We had to close the **office**, _____ !
13. We had the **office** closed, _____ ?
14. We had already closed the **office**, _____ ?
15. We'd better close the **office**, _____ !
16. We'd rather close the **office**, _____ ?
17. The office has **closed**, _____ ?
18. You couldn't **tell**, _____ !
19. You'll be working **late** tonight, _____ ?
20. He should have **been** here by now, _____ !
21. He should be **promoted**, _____ !
22. I didn't send the **fax**, _____ ?
23. I won't get a **raise** this year, _____ ?
24. You use the **computer**, _____ ?
25. You're used to the **computer**, _____ !
26. You used to use the **computer**, _____ ?
27. You never used to work **Saturdays**, ____ ?
28. That's **better**, _____ !

The basic techniques introduced so far, are *pitch, stress,* the *staircase* and *musical notes, reduced sounds,* and *word groups and phrasing.* In Chapters 12 through 25, we refine and expand this knowledge to cover every sound of the American accent.

目前为止介绍的基本技巧有音高、重音、音阶和音符、弱读音、词群及断句。从第12章到第25章，我们将通过讲解美音的每一个发音来精练、扩展这些知识。

# Chapter 8

> Listen for the actual sounds,
> not what you *think* they are.
>
> 听每个音的真实发音，而非你所
> 认为的发音。

# The Miracle Technique
# 神奇的技巧

**Track 127**

As you saw in Chapter 1 with **Bobby bought a bike (bäbee bädə bäik)**, and in Chapter 2 with **Got it (gäddit)**, there is a difference between pure sound and spelling.

如你在学习第一章的Bobby bought a bike（Bäbee bädə bäik）和第二章的Got it（gäddit）时所发现的，单纯的发音和拼写之间是有区别的。

## Regaining Long-Lost Listening Skills
## 重获遗失已久的听力技巧

The trouble with starting accent training after you know a great deal of English is that you know a great deal *about* English. You have a lot of preconceptions and, unfortunately, misconceptions about the sound of English.

在你十分了解英语之后开始进行发音训练的困难在于你对英语了解得太多。你有很多先入之见，但不幸的是它们都是对英语发音的误解。

## A Child Can Learn Any Language
## 儿童能学会任何语言

Every sound of every language is within every child. So, what happens with adults? People learn their native language and stop listening for the sounds that they never hear; then they lose the ability to hear those sounds. Later, when you study a foreign language, you learn a lot of spelling rules that take you still further away from the real sound of that language—in this case, English.

每一种语言的每一个发音都在每个儿童的掌握之中。那么，成年人到底是怎么了？人们学习母语，而不再注意听他们从未听到过的声音；于是他们丧失了听那些声音的能力。后来，当你学习一门外语时，你学了许多拼写规则，这使你更加远离那门语言的实际发音——比如说英语。

What we are going to do here is teach you to *hear* again. So many times, you've heard what a native speaker said, translated it into your own accent, and repeated it with your accent. Why? Because you "knew" how to say it.

在这里我们要做的是教你再次"听到"那些声音。很多次，你听到一个说母语的人讲的话之后，会把它转化为你的发音，并用你的发音将它复述出来。为什么呢？因为你"知道"怎么去说它。

## Exercise 8-1: Tell Me Wədai Say — Track 128

*The first thing you're going to do is write down exactly what I say. It will be nonsense to you for two reasons: First, because I will be saying* **sound units**, *not* **word units**. *Second, because I will be starting at the* **end** *of the sentence instead of the* **beginning**. *Listen carefully and write down exactly what you hear, regardless of meaning. The first sound is given to you—***kit**.

_____ _____´ kit

▸ *Once you have written it down, check with the version below.*

*äi **lie** kit*

▸ *Read it out loud to yourself and try to hear what the regular English is. Don't look ahead until you've figured out the sense of it.*

*I **like** it.*

## Exercise 8-2: Listening for Pure Sounds — Track 129

*Again, listen carefully and write the sounds you hear. Start at the end and fill in the blanks right to left, then read them back left to right. Write whichever symbols are easiest for you to read back. The answers are below.*

1. _____ _____ dəp´ .

2. _____ _____ dæout´ .

3. _____ _____ _____´ .

4. _____ _____ _____ _____´ .

## Exercise 8-3: Extended Listening Practice — Track 130

*Let's do a few more pure sound exercises to fine-tune your ear. Remember, start at the end and fill in the blanks right to left, then read them back left to right. You will only need five non-alphabet symbols:* **æ, ä, ə, ü,** *and* **ɛ**. *There are clues sprinkled around for you.*

1. _____´ _____ !

2. thæng´ _____ .

3. _____ _____´ ____´ _____ _____ _____´ _____ !

4. wə \_\_\_\_\_ \_\_\_\_\_ \_\_\_\_\_ ´ ?

5. kwee \_\_\_\_\_ \_\_\_\_\_ \_\_\_\_\_ \_\_\_\_\_ ?

6. \_\_\_\_\_ \_\_\_\_\_ \_\_\_\_\_ \_\_\_\_\_ \_\_\_\_\_ ´ \_\_\_\_\_ \_\_\_\_\_ \_\_\_\_\_ \_\_\_\_\_ ?

7. \_\_\_\_\_ \_\_\_\_\_ \_\_\_\_\_ \_\_\_\_\_ ´ \_\_\_\_\_ \_\_\_\_\_ \_\_\_\_\_ bæou \_\_\_\_\_ .

8. \_\_\_\_\_ \_\_\_\_\_ \_\_\_\_\_ ´ \_\_\_\_\_ \_\_\_\_\_ !

9. \_\_\_\_\_ \_\_\_\_\_ \_\_\_\_\_ \_\_\_\_\_ \_\_\_\_\_ ´ \_\_\_\_\_ wən.

10. wyn \_\_\_\_\_ \_\_\_\_\_ \_\_\_\_\_ \_\_\_\_\_ ´ ?

11. \_\_\_\_\_ \_\_\_\_\_ \_\_\_\_\_ ´ \_\_\_\_\_ \_\_\_\_\_ frə \_\_\_\_\_ ?

| | | | |
|---|---|---|---|
| 1. Yoo zih **dəp**. | 2. Wɛ rih **dæout**. | 3. May kit **doo**. | 4. Orr doo with **æout**. |
| Use it up. | Wear it out. | Make it do. | Or do without. |

# Chapter 9

> Even in complex sentences,
> stress the noun
> (unless there is contrast).
>
> 即使在复杂句中，也要重读名词
> （除非存在对比）。

# Grammar in a Nutshell
## 语法概述

## Everything You Ever Wanted to Know About Grammar... But Were Afraid to Use

**Track 131**

你曾经想了解但又害怕使用的有关语法的一切……

English is a chronological language. We just love to know when something happened, and this is indicated by the range and depth of our verb tenses.

英语是一种有时间顺序的语言。我们只是想知道某事是何时发生的，而这些信息可以通过动词时态的调域和音高显示出来。

*I **had** already **seen** it by the time she **brought** it in.*

As you probably learned in your grammar studies, "the past perfect is an action in the past that occurred before a separate action in the past." Whew! Not all languages do this. For example, Japanese is fairly casual about when things happened, but being a hierarchical language, it is very important to know what *relationship* the two people involved had. A high-level person with a low-level one, two peers, a man and a woman, all these things show up in Japanese grammar. Grammatically speaking, English is democratic.

像你可能在语法学习中学到的那样，"过去完成时是过去的动作，且这一动作发生在过去另外一个动作之前。"哟！并非所有的语言都是这样。比如，日语并不注重事情什么时候发生，但作为等级体系语言，日语很重视所涉及的两个人之间的关系。一个高层人士和一个低层人士，两个同辈，一个男人和一个女人，所有这些关系都体现在日语的语法中。从语法上讲，英语是民主的。

The confusing part is that in English the verb tenses are very important, but instead of putting them up on the *peaks* of a sentence, we throw them all deep down in the *valleys*! Therefore, two sentences with strong intonation—such as, "**Dogs eat bones**" and "The **dogs**'ll've eaten the **bones**" sound amazingly similar. Why? Because it takes the same amount of time to say both sentences since they have the same number of stresses. The three original words and the rhythm stay the same in these sentences, but the meaning changes as you add more stressed words. Articles and verb tense changes are usually not stressed.

令人费解的是，动词的时态在英语中很重要，但我们并没有将它们放在句子的"高点"，而是把它们放在了句子的"谷底"！因而，带重音语调的两个句子——比如，"**Dogs eat bones**"和"The **dogs**'ll've eaten the **bones**"听起来极其相似。为什么呢？由于两个句子有相同数量的重音，因而读起来所花费的时间是相同的。在这两个句子中，三个原始单词和节奏是相同的，但随着你加入更多的重读单词，意思就发生变化了。冠词和动词时态的变化通常不用重读。

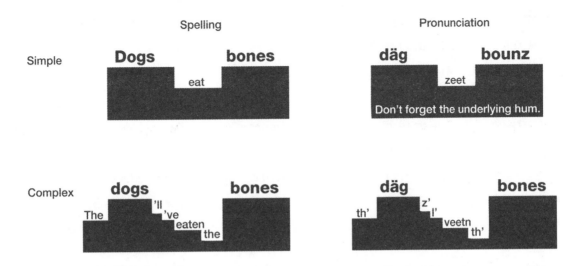

Now let's see how this works in the exercises that follow.

现在我们来看看在下面的练习中是不是这样的。

| **Exercise 9-1: Consistent Noun Stress in Changing Verb Tenses** | **Track 132** |

*This is a condensed exercise for you to practice simple intonation with a wide range of verb tenses. When you do the exercise the first time, go through stressing only the nouns:* **Dogs** *eat* **bones.** *Practice this until you are quite comfortable with the intonation. The pronunciation and word connections are on the right, and the full verb tenses are on the far left.*

| eat | 1. The **dogs** eat the **bones.** | the **däg** zeet the **bounz** |
| ate | 2. The **dogs** ate the **bones.** | the **däg** zɛit the **bounz** |
| are eating | 3. The **dogs**'re eating the **bones.** | the **däg** zr reeding the **bounz** |
| will eat | 4. The **dogs**'ll eat the **bones** (if) | the **däg** zə leet the **bounz** (if) |
| would eat | 5. The **dogs**'d eat the **bones** (if) | the **däg** zə deet the **bounz** (if) |
| would have eaten | 6. The **dogs**'d've eaten the **bones** (if) | the **däg** zədə veetn the **bounz** (if) |
| that have eaten | 7. The **dogs** that've eaten the **bones** (are) | the **däg** zədə veetn the **bounz** (are) |
| have eaten | 8. The **dogs**'ve eaten the **bones.** | the **däg** zə veetn the **bounz** |
| had eaten | 9. The **dogs**'d eaten the **bones.** | the **däg** zə deetn the **bounz** |
| will have eaten | 10. The **dogs**'ll've eaten the **bones.** | the **däg** zələ veetn the **bounz** |
| ought to eat | 11. The **dogs** ought to eat the **bones.** | the **däg** zädə eat the **bounz** |
| should eat | 12. The **dogs** should eat the **bones.** | the **dägz** sh'deet the **bounz** |
| should not eat | 13. The **dogs** shouldn't eat the **bones.** | the **dägz** sh'dn•neet the **bounz** |
| should have eaten | 14. The **dogs** should've eaten the **bones.** | the **dägz** sh'də veetn the **bounz** |
| should not have eaten | 15. The **dogs** shouldn't've eaten the **bones.** | the **dägz** sh'dn•nə veetn the **bounz** |
| could eat | 16. The **dogs** could eat the **bones.** | the **dägz** c'deet the **bounz** |

| could not eat | 17. The **dogs** couldn't eat the **bones**. | the **dägz** c'dn•neet the **bounz** |
|---|---|---|
| could have eaten | 18. The **dogs** could've eaten the **bones**. | the **dägz** c'də veetn the **bounz** |
| could not have eaten | 19. The **dogs** couldn't've eaten the **bones**. | the **dägz** c'dn•nə veetn the **bounz** |
| might eat | 20. The **dogs** might eat the **bones**. | the **dägz** mydeet the **bounz** |
| might have eaten | 21. The **dogs** might've eaten the **bones**. | the **dägz** mydəveetn the **bounz** |
| must eat | 22. The **dogs** must eat the **bones**. | the **dägz** məss deet the **bounz** |
| must have eaten | 23. The **dogs** must've eaten the **bones**. | the **dägz** məsdəveetn the **bounz** |
| can eat | 24. The **dogs** can eat the **bones**. | the **dägz** c'neet the **bounz** |
| can't eat | 25. The **dogs** can't eat the **bones**. | the **dägz** cæn$^{(d)}$eet the **bounz** |

## Exercise 9-2: Consistent Pronoun Stress in Changing Verb Tenses                 Track 133

*This is the same as the previous exercise, except you now stress the verbs: They **eat** them. Practice this until you are quite comfortable with the intonation. Notice that in fluent speech, the **th** of **them** is frequently dropped (as is the **h** in the other object pronouns, **him**, **her**). The pronunciation and word connections are on the right, and the tense name is on the far left.*

| present | 1. They **eat** them. | they**eed**'m |
|---|---|---|
| past | 2. They **ate** them. | they**ɛid**'m |
| continuous | 3. They're **eating** them. | there**eed**ing'm |
| future | 4. They'll **eat** them (if...) | the**leed**'m (if...) |
| present conditional | 5. They'd **eat** them (if...) | they **deed**'m (if...) |
| past conditional | 6. They'd've **eaten** them (if...) | they də**veet**n'm (if...) |
| relative pronoun | 7. The ones that've **eaten** them (are...) | the wənzədə**veet**n'm (are...) |
| present perfect | 8. They've **eaten** them (many times). | they **veet**n'm (many times) |
| past perfect | 9. They'd **eaten** them (before...) | they **deet**n'm (before...) |
| future perfect | 10. They'll have **eaten** them (by...) | they lə**veet**n'm (by...) |
| obligation | 11. They ought to **eat** them. | they ädə**eed**'m |
| obligation | 12. They should **eat** them. | they sh'**deed**'m |
| obligation | 13. They shouldn't **eat** them. | they sh'dn•**need**'m |
| obligation | 14. They should have **eaten** them. | they sh'də**veet**n'm |
| obligation | 15. They shouldn't've **eaten** them. | they sh'dn•nə**veet**n'm |
| possibility/ability | 16. They could **eat** them. | they c'**deed**'m |
| possibility/ability | 17. They couldn't **eat** them. | they c'dn•**need**'m |
| possibility/ability | 18. They could have **eaten** them. | they c'də **veet**n'm |
| possibility/ability | 19. They couldn't have **eaten** them. | they c'dn•nə **veet**n'm |
| possibility | 20. They might **eat** them. | they my**deed**'m |

| possibility | 21. | They might have **eaten** them. | they my də **veet**n'm |
|---|---|---|---|
| probability | 22. | They must **eat** them. | they məss **deed**'m |
| probability | 23. | They must have **eaten** them. | they məsdə**veet**n'm |
| ability | 24. | They can **eat** them. | they c'**need**'m |
| ability | 25. | They **can't eat** them. | they **cæn**⁽ᵈ⁾**eed**'m |

## Exercise 9-3: Writing Your Own Phonetics　　　　　Track 134

*In the blanks below, fill in the phonetic pronunciation, using the guidelines from Exercise 9-1. Remember, don't rely on spelling, and use the contracted forms whenever possible. Turn off the CD.*

| 1. | Bob | writes | a letter. |
|---|---|---|---|
|  | bä · | bry | · tsə ledder |
| 2. | Bob | wrote | a letter. |
|  | bä · | bro | · də ledder |
| 3. | Bob | is writing | a letter. |
|  | bä · | _____ | · _____ ledder |
| 4. | Bob | will write | a letter. |
|  | bä · | _____ | · _____ ledder |
| 5. | Bob | would write | a letter, if... |
|  | bä · | bədry | · də ledderif... |
| 6. | Bob | would have written | a letter. |
|  | bä · | _____ | · _____ ledder |
| 7. | The guy | that has written | a letter... |
|  | thə gäi · | _____ | · _____ ledder... |
| 8. | Bob | has written | a letter. |
|  | bä · | _____ | · _____ ledder |
| 9. | Bob | had written | a letter. |
|  | bä · | _____ | · _____ ledder |
| 10. | Bob | will have written | a letter. |
|  | bä · | _____ | · _____ ledder |

| 11. | Bob | ought to write | a letter. |
|-----|-----|----------------|-----------|
| | bä · | bädə ry | · də ledder |

| 12. | Bob | should write | a letter. |
|-----|-----|--------------|-----------|
| | bäb · | _____ | · _____ ledder |

| 13. | Bob | shouldn't write | a letter. |
|-----|-----|-----------------|-----------|
| | bäb · | _____ | · _____ ledder |

| 14. | Bob | should've written | a letter. |
|-----|-----|-------------------|-----------|
| | bäb · | _____ | · _____ ledder |

| 15. | Bob | shouldn't've written | a letter. |
|-----|-----|----------------------|-----------|
| | bäb · | shüdnə vri(t)n | · nə ledder |

| 16. | Bob | could write | a letter. |
|-----|-----|-------------|-----------|
| | bäb · | _____ | · _____ ledder |

| 17. | Bob | couldn't write | a letter. |
|-----|-----|----------------|-----------|
| | bäb · | _____ | · _____ ledder |

| 18. | Bob | could've written | a letter. |
|-----|-----|------------------|-----------|
| | bäb · | _____ | · _____ ledder |

| 19. | Bob | couldn't've written | a letter. |
|-----|-----|---------------------|-----------|
| | bäb · | _____ | · _____ ledder |

| 20. | Bob | might write | a letter. |
|-----|-----|-------------|-----------|
| | bäb · | _____ | · _____ ledder |

| 21. | Bob | might've written | a letter. |
|-----|-----|------------------|-----------|
| | bäb · | _____ | · _____ ledder |

| 22. | Bob | must write | a letter. |
|-----|-----|------------|-----------|
| | bäb · | _____ | · _____ ledder |

| 23. | Bob | must've written | a letter. |
|-----|-----|-----------------|-----------|
| | bäb | _____ | _____ ledder |

| 24. | Bob | can write | a letter. |
|-----|-----|-----------|-----------|
| | bäb | _____ | _____ ledder |

| 25. | Bob | can't write | a letter. |
|-----|-----|-------------|-----------|
| | bäb | _____ | _____ ledder |

**Exercise 9-4: Supporting Words**      **Track 135**

*For this next part of the intonation of grammatical elements, each sentence has a few extra words to help you get the meaning. Keep the same strong intonation that you used before and add the new stress where you see the boldface. Use your rubber band.*

| | | |
|---|---|---|
| 1. | The **dogs** eat the **bones** every **day**. | th' **däg** zeet th' **bounz**evree **day** |
| 2. | The **dogs** ate the **bones** last **week**. | th' **däg** zɛit th' **bounz**læss **dweek** |
| 3. | The **dogs**'re eating the **bones** right **now**. | th' **däg** zr reeding th' **bounz** räit **næo** |
| 4. | The **dogs**'ll eat the **bones** if they're **here**. | th' **däg** zə leet th' **bounz**if thɛr **hir** |
| 5. | The **dogs**'d eat the **bones** if they were **here**. | th' **däg** zə deet th' **bounz**if they wr **hir** |
| 6. | The **dogs**'d've eaten the **bones** if they'd **been** here. | th' **däg** zədə veetn th' **bounz**if theyd **bin** hir |
| 7. | The **dogs** that've eaten the **bones** are **sick**. | th' **däg** zədə veetn th' **bounz**r **sick** |
| 8. | The **dogs**'ve eaten the **bones** every **day**. | th' **däg** zə veetn th' **bounz**ɛvry **day** |
| 9. | The **dogs**'d eaten the **bones** by the time we **got** there. | th' **däg** zə deetn th' **bounz** by th' time we **gät** thɛr |
| 10. | The **dogs**'ll have eaten the **bones** by the time we **get** there. | th' **däg** zələ veetn th' **bounz** by th' time we **get** thɛr |

**Track 136**

English has a fixed word order that does not change with additional words.

| | auxiliary | negative | perfect auxiliary | adverb | passive | continuous | main verb |
|---|---|---|---|---|---|---|---|
| *Draw!* | | | | | | | Draw! |
| *He draws.* | | | | | | | |
| He | | | | | | | draws. |
| *He does draw.* | | | | | | | |
| He | does | | | | | | draw. |
| *He is drawing.* | | | | | | | |
| He | is | | | | | | drawing. |
| *He is not drawing.* | | | | | | | |
| He | is | not | | | | | drawing. |
| *He is not always drawing.* | | | | | | | |
| He | is | not | | always | | | drawing. |
| *He is not always being drawn.* | | | | | | | |
| He | is | not | | always | | being | drawn. |
| *He has not always been drawn.* | | | | | | | |
| He | has | not | | always | been | | drawn. |
| *He has not always been being drawn.* | | | | | | | |
| He | has | not | | always | been | being | drawn. |
| *He will not have always been being drawn.* | | | | | | | |
| He | will | not | have | always | been | being | drawn. |

## Exercise 9-5: Contrast Practice                                        Track 137

*Now, let's work with contrast. For example,* **The dogs'd eat the bones,** *and* **The dogs'd eaten the bones,** *are so close in sound, yet so far apart in meaning, that you need to make a special point of recognizing the difference by listening for content. Repeat each group of sentences using sound and intonation for contrast. (See also Chapter 4)*

| | | |
|---|---|---|
| would eat | The **dogs**'d eat the **bones**. | the **däg** zə deet the **bounz** |
| had eaten | The **dogs**'d eaten the **bones**. | the **däg** zə deetn the **bounz** |
| would have eaten | The **dogs**'d've eaten the **bones**. | the **däg** zədə veetn the **bounz** |
| that have eaten | The **dogs** that've eaten the **bones**. | the **däg** zədə veetn the **bounz** |
| will eat | The **dogs**'ll eat the **bones**. | the **däg** zə leet the **bounz** |
| would eat | The **dogs**'d eat the **bones**. | the **däg** zə deet the **bounz** |
| would have eaten | The **dogs**'d've eaten the **bones**. | the **däg** zədə veetn the **bounz** |
| have eaten | The **dogs**'ve eaten the **bones**. | the **däg** zə veetn the **bounz** |
| had eaten | The **dogs**'d eaten the **bones**. | the **däg** zə deetn the **bounz** |
| will have eaten | The **dogs**'ll have eaten the **bones**. | the **däg** zələ veetn the **bounz** |
| would eat | The **dogs**'d eat the **bones**. | the **däg** zə deet the **bounz** |
| ought to eat | The **dogs** ought to eat the **bones**. | the **däg** zädə eat the **bounz** |
| can eat | The **dogs** can eat the **bones**. | the **dägz** c'neet the **bounz** |
| can't eat | The dogs **can't eat** the **bones**. | the dägz **cæn**[(d)]**eet** the **bounz** |

## Exercise 9-6: Building an Intonation Sentence                          Track 138

*Repeat after me.*

1. I bought a **sand**wich.
2. I **said** I bought a **sand**wich.
3. I **said** I think I bought a **sand**wich.
4. I said I **really** think I bought a **sand**wich.
5. I said I **really** think I bought a chicken **sand**wich.
6. I said I **really** think I bought a **chicken** salad **sand**wich.
7. I said I **really** think I bought a **half** a chicken salad **sand**wich.
8. I said I **really** think I bought a **half** a chicken salad **sand**wich this after**noon**.
9. I **actually** said I **really** think I bought a **half** a chicken salad **sand**wich this after**noon**.
10. I **actually** said I **really** think I bought another **half** a chicken salad **sand**wich this after**noon**.
11. Can you **believe** I **actually** said I **really** think I bought another **half** a chicken salad **sand**wich this after**noon**?

1. I **did** it.
2. I did it **again**.
3. I already **did** it again.
4. I think I already **did** it again.
5. I **said** I think I already **did** it again.
6. I **said** I think I already did it again **yes**terday.
7. I **said** I think I already **did** it again the day before **yes**terday.

1. I want a **ball**.
2. I want a large **ball**.
3. I want a **large, red ball**.
4. I want a **large,** red, bouncy **ball**.
5. I want a **large,** red bouncy rubber **ball**.
6. I want a **large,** red bouncy rubber **basket**ball.

1. I want a **raise**.
2. I want a **big raise**.
3. I want a **big**, impressive raise.
4. I want a **big**, impressive, annual **raise**.
5. I want a **big**, impressive, annual cost of **living** raise.

---

**Exercise 9-7: Building Your Own Intonation Sentences**    **Track 139**

*Build your own sentence, using everyday words and phrases, such as* **think, hope, nice, really, actually, even, this afternoon, big, small, pretty,** *and so on.*

1. 
2. 
3. 
4. 
5. 
6. 
7. 
8. 
9. 
10.

## Breathing Exercises
呼吸练习

Different languages have different breathing patterns. Because Americans are a little louder than you may expect, in order to emulate this projection of the voice, you're going to have to take deeper breaths than you're accustomed to. Stand up straight, chest out, inhale deeply, and in a deep voice say, "Hi! How's it going?"

不同的语言有不同的呼吸方法。美国人可能比你想象中的声音更大些，所以为了模仿这种发音方法，你需要进行比通常更深的呼吸。站直，挺胸，深呼吸，用深沉的声音说："嗨！还好吗？"

As you saw with *Phrasing*, your breathing should be in sync with the phrasing and punctuation. If you're saying something short, you can get away with a more shallow inhale, but short panting breaths are interpreted as nervous or impatient, whereas long, deep exhalations of sound are considered calm and confident. Take deeper breaths than usual, and push the sound out from deep in your chest.

正如在断句部分所学到的，你的呼吸节奏应该与断句和标点一致。如果你的话很短，你用浅的呼吸就可以，但是经常喘气会让人觉得你紧张或不耐烦，而伴随长而深的吐气说出的话会让人感到平静和自信。用比平常更深的呼吸，把声音从你的胸腔深处推出来。

Pay particular attention that you do not push the air out through your nose, which would create a very unattractive nasal quality to your speech.

要特别注意不要把气流从鼻腔推出，那样会让你讲话的声音带有一种不招人喜欢的鼻音。

# Chapter 10
# 第10章

# Reduced Sounds
# 弱读

## The Down Side of Intonation
### 语调的低处

Reduced sounds are all those extra sounds created by an absence of lip, tongue, jaw, and throat movement. They are a principal function of intonation and are truly indicative of the American sound. (See also Chapter 4)

　　弱读音是由于缺乏唇部、舌部、颌部、喉部运动所产生的所有那些附加音。它们是语调的一项主要功能，并且是美音的真正代表。（也见第4章）

## Reduced Sounds Are "Valleys"
### 弱读音是"山谷"

American intonation is made up of peaks and valleys—tops of staircases and bottoms of staircases. To have strong *peaks,* you will have to develop deep *valleys.* These deep valleys should be filled with all kinds of reduced vowels, one in particular—the completely neutral *schwa.* Ignore spelling. Since you probably first became acquainted with English through the printed word, this is going to be quite a challenge. The position of a syllable is more important than spelling as an indication of correct pronunciation. For example, the words *photograph* and *photography* each have two **O**'s and an **A**. The first word is stressed on the first syllable so *photograph* sounds like *fod'græf*. The second word is stressed on the second syllable, *photography,* so the word comes out *f'tahgr'fee*. You can see here that their spelling doesn't tell you how they sound. Word stress or intonation will determine the pronunciation. Work on listening to words. Concentrate on hearing the pure sounds, not in trying to make the word fit a familiar spelling. Otherwise, you will be taking the long way around and giving yourself both a lot of extra work and an accent!

　　美语语调是由"山峰"和"山谷"（阶梯的顶部和底部）构成的。要登上雄浑的"山峰"，你就得形成深深的"山谷"。这些深深的山谷中应该充满各种各样的弱读元音，尤其是完全的非中央元音。忽略拼写。由于你可能首先是通过印刷文字来熟悉英语的，因而这将具有挑战性。作为正确发音的标示，音节的位置要比拼写更重要。例如单词photograph和photography中，每个单词都有两个O和一个A。第一个单词重读第一个音节，因而photograph听起来像**fod'græf**。第二个单词photography重读第二个音节，因而单词发音为f'**tah**gr'fee。在这里，你可以看出单词的拼写并不能告诉你它们的发音。单词的重音或语调将决定发音。努力听单词，集中精力听纯粹的发音，不要试图使单词和熟知的拼写对应。否则，你会绕很大的弯路，既费事又有口音。

Syllables that are perched atop a peak or a staircase are strong sounds; that is, they maintain their original pronunciation. On the other hand, syllables that fall in the valleys or on a lower stair step are weak sounds; thus they are reduced. Some vowels are reduced completely to schwas, a very relaxed sound, while others are only toned down. In the following exercises, we will be dealing with these "toned down" sounds.

停留在山峰或阶梯顶部的音节是强音；即音节保持了它们原本的发音。另一方面，降到山谷中或在较低阶梯上的音节是弱音；因而它们要弱读。有些元音完全弱读成了非中央元音，一种非常放松的音，而其他的音只是降低了音调。在以下练习中，我们将学习这些"音调降低"的音。

In the Introduction I talked about *overpronouncing.* This section will handle that overpronunciation. You're going to skim over words; you're going to dash through certain sounds. Your peaks are going to be quite strong, but your valleys, blurry—a very intuitive aspect of intonation that this practice will help you develop.

在前言中，我谈到过过于强调的发音。这部分将解决这个问题。你要略过单词，要快速发某些音。你的高音点会相当强，而你的低音点却是模糊的——这个练习将帮你形成对语调的直觉感。

Articles (such as *the, a*) are usually very reduced sounds. Before a consonant, *the* and *a* are both schwa sounds, which are reduced. Before a vowel, however, you'll notice a change—for example, the schwa of *the* turns into a long *e* plus a connecting (y)—*Th' book* changes to *thee*(y)*only book. A hat* becomes *a nugly hat:* The article *a* becomes *an.* Think of ə●nornj rather than *an orange;* ə●nop'ning, ə●neye; ə●nimaginary animal.

冠词（像the，a）通常是非常弱读的音。在辅音前，the和a都是非中央元音，需要弱读。然而，在元音前，你会注意到一个变化——the中的非中央元音变成长音e加上连音(y)——Th'book变为thee(y) only book；a hat成了a nugly hat：冠词a变成了an。想一想，是ə●nornj而不是an orange；ə●nop'ning，ə●neye，ə●nimaginary animal。

---

**Exercise 10-1: Reducing Articles**                    **Track 142**

| **Consonants** | | **Vowels** | |
|---|---|---|---|
| the man | a girl | thee(y)apple | an orange | ə●nornj |
| the best | a banana | thee(y)egg | an opening | ə●nop'ning |
| the last one | a computer | thee(y)easy way | an interview | ə●ninerview |

**Track 143**

When you used the rubber band with *Däg zeet bounz* and when you built your own sentence, you saw that intonation reduces the unstressed words. Intonation is the peak and reduced sounds are the valleys. In the beginning, you should make extra-high peaks and long, deep valleys. When you are not sure, reduce. In the following exercise, work with this idea. Small words such as articles, prepositions, pronouns, conjunctions, relative pronouns, and auxiliary verbs are lightly skimmed over and almost not pronounced.

当你利用橡皮筋来发**Däg** zeet **bounz**，还有当你自己造句子时，你发现语调弱化了非重读的单词。语调是"山峰"，而弱读音是"山谷"。刚开始，你应该形成超高的"山峰"和深长的"山谷"。当你不确定时，弱读。在下面的练习中，按照这个原则来练习。对于像冠词、介词、代词、连词、关系代词、助动词这些不重要的词要轻轻略过，几乎不发音。

You have seen how intonation changes the meaning in words and sentences. Inside a one-syllable word, it distinguishes between a final voiced or unvoiced consonant *be-ed* and *bet.* Inside a longer word, *éunuch* vs. *unique,* the pronunciation and meaning change in terms of vocabulary. In a sentence (He seems **nice**; He **seems** nice.), the meaning changes in terms of intent.

你已经明了语调是如何在单词和句子中改变意义的。在单音节单词中，语调能区分末尾辅音是浊辅音还是清辅音，如be-ed和bet。在长一些的单词中，比如éunuch和unique，两者的发音和意义由于是不同的词汇而发生变化。在句子（He seems **nice**; He **seems** nice）中，意义由于不同的强调目的而发生变化。

In a sentence, intonation can also make a clear vowel sound disappear. When a vowel is *stressed,* it has a certain sound; when it is *not stressed,* it usually sounds like *uh,* pronounced ə. Small words like *to, at,* or *as* are not usually stressed, so the vowel disappears.

在句子中，语调也能使清晰的元音发音消失。当一个元音被重读时，它发某个音；当它不被重读时，往往听起来像uh，发音为ə。像to，at或as这些不重要的单词通常不重读，因而元音也听不到。

| Exercise 10-2: Reduced Sounds | Track 144 |
| --- | --- |

*Read aloud from the right-hand column. The intonation is marked for you.*

| To | Looks Like... | Sounds Like... |
| --- | --- | --- |
| The preposition **to** usually reduces so much that it's like dropping the vowel. | today | t'**day** |
| | tonight | t'**night** |
| | tomorrow | t'**märou** |
| | to work | t' **wrk** |
| | to school | t' **school** |
| | to the store | t' th' **store** |
| Use a **t'** or **tə** sound to replace **to**. | We have to go now. | we hæftə **go** næo |
| | He went to work. | he wentə **work** |
| | They hope to find it. | they houptə **fine** dit |
| | I can't wait to find out. | äi **cæn**[(t)]wai[(t)]tə fine **dæot** |
| | We don't know what to do. | we dont know w'[(t)]t' **do** |
| | Don't jump to conclusions. | dont j'm t' c'n**cloo**zh'nz |
| | To be or not to be... | t' **bee**[(y)]r **nät** t' bee |
| | He didn't get to go. | he din ge[(t)]tə **gou** |
| If that same **to** follows a vowel sound, it will become **d'** or **də**. | He told me to help. | he told meedə **help** |
| | She told you to get it. | she tol joodə **ged**dit |
| | I go to work. | ai goudə **wrk** |
| | at a quarter to two | ædə kworder də **two** |
| | The only way to get it is... | thee[(y)]**ounly** waydə **ged**didiz |
| | You've got to pay to get it. | yoov gäddə paydə **ged**dit |
| | We plan to do it. | we plæn də **do** it |
| | Let's go to lunch. | lets goudə **lunch** |
| | The score was 4–6. | th' score w'z for də **six** |

**Exercise 10-2: Reduced Sounds** *continued*                                    **Track 144**

| To | Looks Like... | Sounds Like... |
|---|---|---|
| | It's the only way to do it. | its thee⁽ʸ⁾**ounly** weidə **do**⁽ʷ⁾'t |
| | So to speak... | soda **speak** |
| | I don't know how to say it. | äi don⁽ᵗ⁾know hæwdə **say**⁽ʸ⁾it |
| | Go to page 8. | goudə pay **jate** |
| | Show me how to get it. | shou me hæodə **ged**dit |
| | You need to know when to do it. | you nee⁽ᵈ⁾də nou wendə **do**⁽ʷ⁾it |
| | Who's to blame? | hooz də **blame** |
| | | |

| At | | |
|---|---|---|
| **At** is just the opposite of **to**. It's a small grunt followed by a reduced **t**. | We're at home. | wirᵊt **home** |
| | I'll see you at lunch. | äiyəl see you⁽ʷ⁾ət **lunch** |
| | Dinner's at five. | d'nnerzᵊ⁽ᵗ⁾ **five** |
| | Leave them at the door. | leevᵊmᵊ⁽ᵗ⁾thᵊ **door** |
| | The meeting's at one. | th' meeding z't **w'n** |
| | He's at the post office. | heezᵊ⁽ᵗ⁾th' **pouss**däffᵊs |
| | They're at the bank. | thɛrᵊ⁽ᵗ⁾th' **bænk** |
| | I'm at school. | äimᵊ⁽ᵗ⁾**school** |
| | | |

| | | |
|---|---|---|
| If **at** is followed by a vowel sound, it will become **'d** or **əd**. | I'll see you at eleven. | äiyəl see you⁽ʷ⁾ədə **lɛv'n** |
| | He's at a meeting. | heez'ə də **meeding** |
| | She laughed at his idea. | she **læf** dədi zy **deeyə** |
| | One at a time. | wənədə **time** |
| | We got it at an auction. | we gädidədə **näk**sh'n |
| | The show started at eight. | th' **show** stardədə **date** |
| | The dog jumped out at us. | th' däg jump **dæo** dədəs |
| | I was at a friend's house. | äi w'z'd' **frenz** hæos |
| | | |

| It | | |
|---|---|---|
| **It** and **at** sound the same in context—**'t**. | Can you do it? | k'niu **do**⁽ʷ⁾'t |
| | Give it to me. | g'v'⁽ᵗ⁾t' me |
| | Buy it tomorrow. | bäi⁽ʸ⁾ᵊ⁽ᵗ⁾t' **märrow** |
| | It can wait. | 't c'n **wait** |
| | Read it twice. | ree d'⁽ᵗ⁾**twice** |
| | Forget about it! | frgedd' **bæodit** |
| | | |

| | | |
|---|---|---|
| ...and they both turn to **'d** or **əd** between vowels or voiced consonants. | Give it a try. | gividə **try** |
| | Let it alone. | ledidə **lone** |
| | Take it away. | tay kida **way** |
| | I got it in London. | äi gädidin **l'nd'n** |
| | What is it about? | w'd'z'd'**bæot** |
| | Let's try it again. | lets try'd' **gen** |
| | Look! There it is! | **lük** there'd'**z** |

| For | Looks Like... | Sounds Like... | |
|---|---|---|---|
| | This is for you. | th's'z fr **you** | |
| | It's for my friend. | ts fr my **friend** | |
| | A table for four, please. | ə table fr **four**, pleeze | |
| | We planned it for later. | we **plan** dit fr **layd'r** | |
| | For example, for instance | fregg **zæmple frin** st'nss | |
| | What is this for? | w'd'z **this** for | *(for is not reduced at* |
| | What did you do it for? | w'j' **do**(w)it for | *the end of a sentence)* |
| | Who did you get it for? | hoojya **ged**dit for | |

| From | | | |
|---|---|---|---|
| | It's from the IRS. | ts frm thee(y)äi(y)ä **ress** | |
| | I'm from Arkansas. | äim fr'm **ärk'** nsä | |
| | There's a letter from Bob. | therzə **ledder** fr'm **Bäb** | |
| | This letter's from Alaska! | this **ledderz** frəmə **læskə** | |
| | Who's it from? | hoozit **frəm** | |
| | Where are you from? | wher'r you **frəm** | |

| In | | | |
|---|---|---|---|
| | It's in the bag. | tsin thə **bæg** | |
| | What's in it? | w'**ts**'n't | |
| | I'll be back in a minute. | äiyəl be **bæk**'nə **m'n't** | |
| | This movie? Who's in it? | this **movie**...hooz**'n't** | |
| | Come in. | c'**min** | |
| | He's in America. | heez'ən **mɛrəkə** | |

| An | | | |
|---|---|---|---|
| | He's an American. | heez'ən **mɛrəkən** | |
| | I got an A in English. | äi gäddə **nay** ih **nin**glish | |
| | He got an F in Algebra. | hee gäddə **neffinæl** jəbrə | |
| | He had an accident. | he hædə **næk**səd'nt | |
| | We want an orange. | we want'n **nornj** | |
| | He didn't have an excuse. | he didnt hævə neks **kyooss** | |
| | I'll be there in an instant. | äiyəl be there inə **nin**stnt | |
| | It's an easy mistake to make. | itsə **nee**zee m' stake t' **make** | |

| And | | | |
|---|---|---|---|
| | ham and eggs | hæmə **neggz** | |
| | bread and butter | bredn **buddr** | |
| | Coffee? With cream and sugar? | **käffee**...with creem'n **sh'g'r** | |
| | No, lemon and sugar. | **nou**...lem'n'n sh'g'r | |
| | ...And some more cookies? | 'n s'more **cükeez** | |
| | They kept going back and forth. | they kep going bækn **forth** | |
| | We watched it again and again. | we **wäch** didə **gen**'n' **gen** | |
| | He did it over and over. | he di di **dov**erə **no**ver | |
| | We learned by trial and error. | we lrnd by tryələ**ner**ər | |

| **Exercise 10-2: Reduced Sounds** *continued* | **Track 144** |

| Or | **Looks Like...** | **Sounds Like...** |
|----|-------------------|---------------------|
| | Soup or salad? | super **salad** |
| | now or later | næ^(w)r **lay**dr |
| | more or less | **mor**'r less |
| | left or right | **left**er **right** |
| | For here or to go? | f'r **hir**'r d'**go** |
| | Are you going up or down? | are you going **úp**per **dówn** |

*This is an **either** / **or** question: **Up**? **Down**?*
*Notice how the intonation is different from "Cream and **sugar**?", which is a **yes** / **no** question.*

| Are | | |
|-----|-------------------|---------------------|
| | What are you doing? | w'dr you **do**ing |
| | Where are you going? | wer'r you **go**ing |
| | What're you planning on doing? | w'dr yü planning än **do**ing |
| | How are you? | hæwr **you** |
| | Those are no good. | thozer no **good** |
| | How are you doing? | hæwer you **do**ing |
| | The kids are still asleep. | the **kid**zer stillə **sleep** |

| Your | | |
|------|-------------------|---------------------|
| | How's your family? | hæozhier **fæm**lee |
| | Where're your keys? | wher'r y'r **keez** |
| | You're American, aren't you? | yrə **mer**'k'n, arn choo |
| | Tell me when you're ready. | tell me wen yr **red**dy |
| | Is this your car? | izzis y'r **cär** |
| | You're late again, Bob. | yer lay də **gen**, Bäb |

| One | | |
|-----|-------------------|---------------------|
| | Which one is yours? | which w'n'z **y'rz** |
| | Which one is better? | which w'n'z **bed**der |
| | One of them is broken. | w'n'v'm'z **brok**'n |
| | I'll use the other one. | æl yuz thee^(y)**əther** w'n |
| | I like the red one, Edwin. | äi like the **red**w'n, edw'n |
| | That's the last one. | thæts th' lass **dw'n** |
| | The next one'll be better. | the **necks** dw'n'll be **bedd'r** |
| | Here's one for you. | **hir** zw'n f'r **you** |
| | Let them go one by one. | led'm gou **w'n** by **w'n** |

| The | | |
|-----|-------------------|---------------------|
| | It's the best. | ts th' **best** |
| | What's the matter? | w'ts th' **mad**der |
| | What's the problem? | w'tsə **präbl**'m |
| | I have to go to the bathroom. | äi hæf t' go d' th' **bæth**room |
| | Who's the boss around here? | hoozə **bäss** særæond hir |
| | Give it to the dog. | g'v'^(t)tə th' **däg** |
| | Put it in the drawer. | püdidin th' **dror** |

**Exercise 10-2: Reduced Sounds** *continued*                                    **Track 144**

| | Looks Like... | Sounds Like... |
|---|---|---|
| **A** | It's a present. | tsə **pre**znt |
| | You need a break. | you needə **bray-eek** |
| | Give him a chance. | g'v'mə **chæns** |
| | Let's get a new pair of shoes. | lets geddə new perə **shooz** |
| | Can I have a Coke, please? | c'nai hævə **kouk**, pleez |
| | Is that a computer? | izzædə k'm**pyoo**dr |
| | Where's a public telephone? | wherzə pəblic **tel**əfoun |
| | | |
| **Of** | It's the top of the line. | tsə täp'v th' **line** |
| | It's a state of the art printer. | tsə **stay** də thee<sup>(y)</sup>ärt **prin**ner |
| | As a matter of fact, ... | z'mæddərə **fækt**... |
| | Get out of here. | gedd**æow** də hir |
| | Practice all of the time. | **præk**t'säll'v th' **time** |
| | Today's the first of May. | t'**dayz** th' frss d'v **May** |
| | What's the name of that movie? | w'ts th' **nay** m'v thæt **movie** |
| | That's the best of all! | **thæts** th' bess d'**väll** |
| | some of them | **sə**məvəm |
| | all of them | **äll**əvəm |
| | most of them | **mos**dəvəm |
| | none of them | **nə**nəvəm |
| | any of them | **enn**yəvəm |
| | the rest of them | th' **res**dəvəm |
| | | |
| **Can** | Can you speak English? | k'new spee **king**lish |
| | I can only do it on Wednesday. | äi k'**noun**ly du<sup>(w)</sup>idän **wen**zday |
| | A can opener can open cans. | ə **kæn**op'ner k'nopen **kænz** |
| | Can I help you? | k'näi **hel** piu |
| | Can you do it? | k'niu **do**<sup>(w)</sup>'t |
| | We can try it later. | we k'n **try** it **layder** |
| | I hope you can sell it. | äi **hou** piu k'n **sell**'t |
| | No one can fix it. | nou w'n k'n **fick** sit |
| | Let me know if you can find it. | lemme no<sup>(w)</sup>'few k'n **fine** dit |
| | | |
| **Had** | Jack had had enough. | jæk'd hæd' **n'f** |
| | Bill had forgotten again. | bil'd frga<sup>(t)</sup>n nə **gen** |
| | What had he done to deserve it? | w'd'dee d'nd'd' **zr** vit |
| | We'd already seen it. | weedäl reddy **see** nit |
| | He'd never been there. | heed never **bin** there |
| | Had you ever had one? | h'jou<sup>(w)</sup>ever **hæd**w'n |
| | Where had he hidden it? | wer dee **hid**n●nit |
| | Bob said he'd looked into it. | bäb sedeed lük**din** tu<sup>(w)</sup>it |

## Exercise 10-2: Reduced Sounds *continued* — Track 144

**Would**

| Looks Like... | Sounds Like... |
| --- | --- |
| He would have helped, if... | he wüda **help** dif... |
| Would he like one? | woody **lye** kw'n |
| Do you think he'd do it? | dyiu thing keed **du**(w)'t |
| Why would I tell her? | why wüdäi **teller** |
| We'd see it again, if... | weed see(y)idəgen, if... |
| He'd never be there on time. | heed never **be** therän tyme |
| Would you ever have one? | w'jou(w)ever **hæv**w'n |

**Was**

| | |
| --- | --- |
| He was only trying to help. | he w'zounly trying də **help** |
| Mark was American. | **mär** kw'z'**mer**'k'n |
| Where was it? | wer **w'z**'t |
| How was it? | hæo**w'z**'t |
| That was great! | thæt w'z **great** |
| Who was with you? | hoow'z **with** you |
| She was very clear. | she w'z very **clear** |
| When was the war of 1812? | wen w'z th' **wor**'v ei(t)teen **twelv** |

**What**

| | |
| --- | --- |
| What time is it? | w't **tye** m'z't |
| What's up? | w'ts**'p** |
| What's on your agenda? | w'tsänyrə **jen**də |
| What do you mean? | w'd'y' **mean** |
| What did you mean? | w'j'**mean** |
| What did you do about it? | w'j' **du**(w)əbæodit |
| What took so long? | w't **tük** so läng |
| What do you think of this? | w'ddyə thing k'v **this** |
| What did you do then? | w'jiu do **then** |
| I don't know what he wants. | I dont know wədee **wänts** |

**Some**

| | |
| --- | --- |
| Some are better than others. | **s'm**r beddr thənətherz |
| There are some leftovers. | ther'r s'm **lef** doverz |
| Let's buy some ice cream. | let spy s' **mice** creem |
| Could we get some other ones? | kwee get s' **mother** w'nz |
| Take some of mine. | **take** səməv **mine** |
| Would you like some more? | w' joo like s'**more** |
| (or very casually) | jlike s'**more** |
| Do you have some ice? | dyü hæv sə**mice** |
| Do you have some mice? | dyü hæv sə**mice** |

"You can fool some of the people some of the time, but you can't fool all of the people all of the time."

yuk'n **fool səmə** thə peep°l **səmə** thə time, b'choo **kænt fool äll**əthə peep°l **äll**əthə time

**Exercise 10-3: Intonation and Pronunciation of "That"** | **Track 145**

*That is a special case because it serves three different grammatical functions. The **relative pronoun** and the **conjunction** are reducible. The **demonstrative pronoun** cannot be reduced to a schwa sound. It must stay **æ**.*

| Relative Pronoun | The car that she ordered is red. | th' **car** th't she order diz **red** |
|---|---|---|
| Conjunction | He said that he liked it. | he sed the dee **läik**dit. |
| Demonstrative | Why did you do that? | why dijoo **do** thæt? |
| Combination | I know that he'll read that book that I told you about. | äi **know** the dill read thæt **bük** the dai **tol**joo[(w)]' bæot |

**Exercise 10-4: Crossing Out Reduced Sounds** | **Track 146**

*Pause the CD and cross out any sound that is not clearly pronounced, including* **to**, **for**, **and**, **that**, **than**, **the**, **a**, *the* **soft i**, *and unstressed syllables that do not have strong vowel sounds.*

Hello, **my** name is_____. I'm taking American **Accent** Training. There's a **lot** to **learn**, but I **hope** to make it as en**joy**able as possible. I should pick **up** on the American into**na**tion pattern pretty **easily**, although the **only** way to **get** it is to **practice** all of the time. I use the **up** and down, or **peaks** and valleys, intonation more than I **used** to. I've been paying attention to **pitch**, **too**. It's like **walk**ing down a **stair**case. I've been **talk**ing to a lot of **Americans** lately, and they tell me that I'm **ea**sier to under**stand**. **Any**way, I could go **on** and on, but the im**port**ant thing is to **listen** well and sound **good**. **Well**, what do you **think**? **Do** I?

**Exercise 10-5: Reading Reduced Sounds** | **Track 147**

*Repeat the paragraph after me. Although you're getting rid of the vowel sounds, you want to maintain a strong intonation and let the sounds flow together. For the first reading of this paragraph, it is helpful to keep your teeth clenched together to reduce excess jaw and lip movement. Let's begin.*

Hello, **my** name'z_____. I'm taking 'mer'k'n **Acc**'nt Train'ng. Therez' **lot** t̆ **learn**, b't I **hope** t̆ make 't̆z 'n**joy**'bl'z poss'bl. I sh'd p'ck **'p** on the 'mer'k'n '**n**t̆nash'n pattern pretty **eas**'ly, although the **on**ly way t̆ **get** 't 'z t̆ **prac**t̆s all 'v th' time. I use the **'p**'n down, or **peaks** 'n valleys, 'nt̆nash'n more th'n I **used** to. Ive b'n pay'ng 'ttensh'n t̆ **p'ch**, **too**. 'Ts like **walk**'ng down' **stair**case. Ive b'n **talk**'ng to' lot 'v'**mer**'k'ns lately, 'n they tell me th't Im **ea**sier to 'nder**stand**. **Any**way, I k'd go **on** 'n on, b't the '**mport**nt th'ng 'z t̆ **l's**'n wel'n sound **g'd**. **W'll**, wh' d'y' **th'nk**? **Do** I?

Run your words together.

把单词连起来读。

# Chapter 11
# 第11章

# Word Connections
# 词的连续

**Track 148**

As mentioned in the previous chapter, in American English, words are not pronounced one by one. Usually, the end of one word attaches to the beginning of the next word. This is also true for initials, numbers, and spelling. Part of the glue that connects sentences is an underlying hum or drone that only breaks when you come to a period, and sometimes not even then. You have this underlying hum in your own language, and it helps a great deal toward making you sound like a native speaker.

如前所述，在美语中，单词不是逐个发音的。通常，一个单词的词尾连接下个单词的词首。这也适用于缩写、数字和拼写。连接句子的部分黏合剂是潜在的哼哼声或低沉单调的声音，这些声音在你到达句号处时中断，有时甚至到达句号处也不中断。在你说英语时带有这种潜在的哼哼声，将十分有助于使你听起来像说母语的人。

Once you have a strong intonation, you need to connect all those stair steps together so that each sentence sounds like one long word. This chapter is going to introduce you to the idea of liaisons, the connections between words, which allow us to speak in sound groups rather than in individual words. Just as we went over where to put intonation, here you're going to learn how to connect words. Once you understand and learn to use this technique, you can make the important leap from this practice book to other materials and your own conversation.

一旦你用了强语调，就需要将所有音阶连接起来，从而使一个句子听起来像一个长单词。本章将向你介绍连音（也就是单词连读）的概念，它使我们以音群的形式说话，而非一个单词一个单词地说。就像我们学习了在哪里使用语调一样，在这里你将学习怎样去连读单词。一旦你理解并学会运用这一技巧，你就会实现从这本练习书到其他材料以及你自己会话的重要飞跃。

To make it easier for you to read, liaisons are written like this: **They tell me the dai measier.** (You've already encountered some liaisons in Exercises 8-1, 9-1, 10-2.) It could also be written **theytellmethedaimeasier**, but it would be too hard to read. (See also Chapters 1 and 7)

为了更便于你阅读，连音这样书写：They tell me the dai measier。（你在练习8-1、9-1、10-2中已见过一些连音。）它也可以写成theytellmethedaimeasier，但这会难以阅读。（也见第1章和第7章）

*Read the following sentences. The last two sentences should be pronounced exactly the same, no matter how they are written. It is the* **sound** *that is important, not the spelling.*

> The dime.
> The dime easier.
> They tell me the dime easier.
> They tell me **the dime** easier to understand.
> They tell me **that I'm** easier to understand.

***Words are connected in four main situations:***

单词在以下四种情况下连读：

1. Consonant / Vowel

   辅音/元音

2. Consonant / Consonant

   辅音/辅音

3. Vowel / Vowel

   元音/元音

4. T, D, S, or Z + Y

   T，D，S或Z+Y

# Liaison Rule 1: Consonant / Vowel     **Track 150**

连音规则1：辅音 / 元音

Words are connected when a word ends in a consonant sound and the next word starts with a vowel sound, including the semivowels **W**, **Y**, and **R**.

当一个单词以辅音结尾，而下一个单词以元音开头，包括半元音W，Y和R，单词之间要连读。

| My name is... | my nay●miz |
| --- | --- |
| because I've | b'k'zäiv |
| pick up on the American intonation | pi●kə pän the⁽ʸ⁾əmer'kə ninətənashən |

In the preceding example, the word *name* ends in a consonant sound **m** (the *e* is silent and doesn't count), and *is* starts with a vowel sound *i*, so *naymiz* just naturally flows together. In *because I've,* the **z** sound at the end of *because* and the **äi** sound of *I* blend together smoothly. When you say the last line *pi●kəpän the⁽ʸ⁾amer'kəninətənashən,* you can feel each sound pushing into the next.

在第一个例子中，单词name以辅音m结尾（e不发音，所以不算在内），is以元音i开头，因而naymiz正好自然地交融在一起。在because I've中，because末尾的z音和I的äi音自然地融合在一起。当你说最后一行的pi●kəpän the⁽ʸ⁾əmer'kə ninətənashən时，你会感觉到每一个音都滑向下一个音。

**Exercise 11-3: Spelling and Number Connections**　　　　　　Track 152

*You also use liaisons in spelling and numbers. (See also Chapter 4)*

| LA (Los Angeles) | eh●lay |
| 902-5050 | nai●no●too fai●vo●fai●vo |

## What's the Difference Between a Vowel and a Consonant?
元音和辅音之间的区别是什么

In pronunciation, a consonant touches at some point in the mouth. Try saying **p** with your mouth open—you can't do it because your lips must come together to make the **p** sound. A vowel, on the other hand, doesn't touch anywhere. You can easily say **e** without any part of the mouth, tongue, or lips coming into contact with any other part. This is why we are calling **W**, **Y**, and **R** semivowels, or glides.

　　发辅音时会触及口腔某处。试着张开口说p——你做不到，因为你的双唇必须相互接触才能发出p音。而另一方面，发元音时不触及口腔任何部位。没有口腔中的任何部位、舌部或唇部与任何其他部位的接触，你就能毫不费力地说出e音。这就是为什么我们把W，Y和R叫做半元音或滑音的原因。

**Exercise 11-4: Consonant / Vowel Liaison Practice**　　　　　　Track 153

*Pause the CD and reconnect the following words. On personal pronouns, it is common to drop the H. Repeat.*

| hold on | hol don |
| turn over | tur nover |
| tell her I miss her | tellerl misser |

1. read only
2. fall off
3. follow up on
4. come in
5. call him
6. sell it
7. take out
8. fade away
9. 6–0
10. MA

## Liaison Rule 2: Consonant / Consonant

连音规则2: 辅音 / 辅音

Words are connected when a word ends in a consonant sound and the next one starts with a consonant that is in a similar position. What is a similar position? Let's find out.

当一个单词以辅音结尾，而下一个单词以发音部位相似的辅音开头，单词间要连读。什么是相似部位呢？我们一起来弄清楚。

| **Exercise 11-5: Consonant / Consonant Liaisons** | **Track 155** |
| --- | --- |

*Say the sound of each group of letters out loud (the sound of the letter, not the name: **b** is **buh** not **bee**). There are three general locations—the lips, behind the teeth, or in the throat. If a word ends with a sound created in the throat and the next word starts with a sound from that same general location, these words are going to be linked together. The same with the other two locations. Repeat after me.*

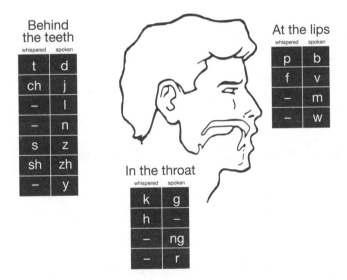

| **Exercise 11-6: Consonant / Consonant Liaisons** | **Track 156** |
| --- | --- |

| I just didn't get the chance. | I●jusdidn't●ge⁽ᵗ⁾the●chance. |
| --- | --- |
| I've been late twice. | I'vbinla⁽ᵗ⁾twice. |

In the preceding examples you can see that because the ending **st** *of just* and the beginning **d** of *didn't* are so near each other in the mouth, it's not worth the effort to start the sound all over again, so they just flow into each other. You don't say *I justǝ didn'tǝ getǝ the chance* but do say *I jusdidn't ge⁽ᵗ⁾the chance.* In the same way, it's too much work to say *I'vǝ beenǝ latǝ twice,* so you say it almost as if it were a single word, *I'vbinla⁽ᵗ⁾twice.*

在第一个例子中，你会发现由于just的尾音st和didn't的首音d在口腔中的发音位置十分相近，没有必要重新开始发音，因而它们就相互融合了。不说I justǝ didn'tǝ getǝ the chance，而说I jusdidn't ge⁽ᵗ⁾the chance。同样的，说I'vǝ beenǝ latǝ twice就太费事了，所以要像说一个单词一样地说这句话：I'vbinla⁽ᵗ⁾twice。

The sound of **TH** is a special case. It is a floater between areas. The sound is sometimes created by the tongue popping out from between the teeth and other times on the back of the top teeth, combining with various letters to form a new composite sound. For instance, **s** moves forward and the **th** moves back to meet at the midpoint between the two.

TH的发音是个特殊的例子。它在不同的发音部位间移动。有时候，它可以通过把舌尖伸出放在齿间产生，而其他时候，它可以在上齿背处和不同的字母结合形成新的合成音。例如：将s音前移，th音后移，在两者的中间位置发出这个音。

**Note** *Each of the categories in the drawing contains two labels—voiced and unvoiced. What does that mean? Put your thumb and index fingers on your throat and say z; you should feel a vibration from your throat in your fingers. If you whisper that same sound, you end up with s and you feel that your fingers don't vibrate. So, z is a voiced sound, s, unvoiced. The consonants in the two left columns are paired like that. (See also Chapters 17, 19, 21, 24, and 25)*

注意：下图中的两个列表中分别包含两个标记——浊音和清音。这是什么意思呢？把你的拇指和食指放在喉部，然后发z音；你的手指应该能感觉到来自喉部的振动。如果你轻声发相同的音，而以s音结束，你就感觉不到手指的振动。所以，z是浊音，s是清音。下图中左侧列表的两行辅音就是像那样成对排列的。（也见第17、19、21、24和25章）

## Consonants

| Voiced | Unvoiced |
|--------|----------|
| b | p |
| d | t |
| v | f |
| g | k |
| j | ch |
| z | s |
| th | th |
| zh | sh |

| Voiced | Unvoiced |
|--------|----------|
| — | h |
| l | — |
| r | — |
| m | — |
| n | — |
| ng | — |
| y | — |
| w | |

---

**Exercise 11-7: Liaisons with TH Combination**                    Track 157

*When the **TH** combination connects with certain sounds, the two sounds blend together to form a composite sound. In the following examples, see how the **TH** moves back and the **L** moves forward, to meet in a new middle position. Repeat after me. (See also Chapter 13)*

| th | + | l | with lemon | th | + | ch | both charges |
|----|---|---|------------|----|---|----|--------------| 
| th | + | n | with nachos | th | + | j | with juice |
| th | + | t | both times | | | | |
| th | + | d | with delivery | n | + | th | in the |
| th | + | s | both sizes | z | + | th | was that |
| th | + | z | with zeal | d | + | th | hid those |

**Exercise 11-8: Consonant / Consonant Liaison Practice**　　　　**Track 158**

*Pause the CD and reconnect the following words as shown in the models. Repeat.*

| hard times | hardtimes |
|---|---|
| with luck | withluck |

1. business deal
2. credit check
3. the top file
4. sell nine new cars
5. sit down
6. some plans need luck
7. check cashing
8. let them make conditions
9. had the
10. both days

## Liaison Rule 3: Vowel / Vowel　　　　**Track 159**
连音规则3：元音 / 元音

When a word ending in a *vowel* sound is next to one beginning with a *vowel* sound, they are connected with a glide between the two vowels. A glide is either a slight **y** sound or a slight **w** sound. How do you know which one to use? This will take care of itself—the position your lips are in will dictate either **y** or **w**.

当一个以元音结尾的单词紧邻着一个以元音开头的单词时，它们由两个元音之间的一个滑音连接起来。滑音要么是轻y音，要么是轻w音。你怎么知道使用哪一个呢？这个你不用担心——你双唇的位置将告诉你是y音还是w音。

| Go away. | Go⁽ʷ⁾away. |
|---|---|
| I also need the other one. | I⁽ʸ⁾also need the⁽ʸ⁾other one. |

For example, if a word ends in **o** your lips are going to be in the forward position, so a **w** quite naturally leads into the next vowel sound—*Go⁽ʷ⁾away*. You don't want to say: *Go...away* and break the undercurrent of your voice. Run it all together: *Go⁽ʷ⁾away*.

例如，如果一个单词以o结尾，你的双唇将向前伸，这样就会产生一个w音，它将十分自然地连向下一个元音——Go⁽ʷ⁾away。你肯定不想说Go...away，这样会中断你潜在的声音流动。所以将它们连起来读：Go⁽ʷ⁾away。

After a long ē sound, your lips will be pulled back far enough to create a **y** glide or liaison: *I⁽ʸ⁾also need the⁽ʸ⁾other one.* Don't force this sound too much, though. It's not a strong pushing sound. *I(y) also need the(y)other one* would sound really weird.

在长音 ē 后，你的双唇要足够向后缩来产生滑音y或连音：I(y)also need the(y)other one。但也不要使这个音太强。它不是一个强推音。如果说成I(y) also need the(y) other one，听起来会很怪异。

---

**Exercise 11-9: Vowel / Vowel Liaison Practice**　　　　　　　　　　**Track 160**

*Pause the CD and reconnect the following words as shown in the models. Add a (y) glide after an **e** sound, and a (w) glide after a **u** sound. Don't forget that the sound of the American **O** is really **ou**.*

| she isn't | she⁽ʸ⁾isn't |
|-----------|-------------|
| who is | who⁽ʷ⁾iz |

1. go anywhere
2. so honest
3. through our
4. you are
5. he is
6. do I?
7. I asked
8. to open
9. she always
10. too often

## Liaison Rule 4: T, D, S, or Z + Y　　　　　　　　　**Track 161**
连音规则4: T, D, S或Z + Y

When the letter or sound of **T, D, S,** or **Z** is followed by a word that starts with **Y**, or its sound, both sounds are connected. These letters and sounds connect not only with **y**, but they do so as well with the initial unwritten **y**. (See also Chapter 21)

当字母T，D，S，Z或发音为T，D，S或Z的音后面紧跟着以字母Y或Y音开头的单词时，两个音之间要连读。这些字母或发音与y连读，也与未写出的首音y连读。（也见第21章）

---

**Exercise 11-10: T, D, S, or Z + Y Liaisons**　　　　　　　　**Track 162**

*Repeat the following.*

| **T + Y = CH** | What's your **name**? | wǝcher **name** |
|----------------|------------------------|------------------|
| | Can't you **do** it? | kænt chew **do**⁽ʷ⁾it |
| | **Act**ually | **æk**·chully |
| | Don't you **like** it? | dont chew **lye** kit |

| | | |
|---|---|---|
| | **Wouldn't** you? | **wood**en chew |
| | **Haven't** you? No, not **yet**. | **hæv**en chew? nou, nä **chet** |
| | I'll let you **know**. | I'll letcha **know** |
| | Can I get you a **drink**? | k'näi getchewə **drink** |
| | We thought you weren't **coming**. | we thä chew wrnt **kəm**ing |
| | I'll bet you **ten** bucks he forgot. | æl betcha **ten** buxee frgät |
| | Is **that** your final **answer**? | is **thæ**chr fin'**læn** sr |
| | **na**tural | **næch**rəl |
| | per**pe**tual | per**pech**ə(w)əl |
| | **vir**tual | **vr**chə(w)əl |
| **D + Y = J** | Did you **see** it? | didjə **see**(y)it |
| | How did you **like** it? | hæo•jə **lye** kit |
| | Could you **tell**? | küjə **tell** |
| | Where did you send your **check**? | wɛrjə senjer **check** |
| | What did your **fam**ily think? | wəjer **fæm**lee think |
| | Did you find your **keys**? | didjə fine jer **keez** |
| | We followed your **instructions**. | we fallow jerin **strɔc**shunz |
| | Congratu**la**tions! | k'ngræj'**la**shunz |
| | edu**ca**tion | edjə•**ca**shun |
| | indi**vid**ual | ində**vij**ə(w)əl |
| | gradu**a**tion | græjə(w)**a**shun |
| | **gra**dual | **græ**jə(w)əl |
| **S + Y = SH** | **Yes**, you are. | **yesh**u are |
| | In**sur**ance | in**shu**rance |
| | **Bless** you! | **bless**hue |
| | Press your **hands** together. | pressure **hanz** d'gethr |
| | Can you **dress** yourself? | c 'new **dresh**ier self |
| | You can pass your **exams** this year. | yuk'n pæsher eg**zæmz** thisheer |
| | I'll try to guess your **age**. | æl trydə geshie**rage** |
| | Let him gas your **car** for you. | leddim gæshier **cär** fr you |
| **Z + Y = ZH** | How's your **family**? | hæozhier **fæm**lee |
| | How was your **trip**? | hæo•wəzhier **trip** |
| | Who's your **friend**? | hoozhier **frend** |
| | Where's your **mom**? | wɛrzh'r **mäm** |
| | When's your **birthday**? | wɛnzh'r **brth**day |
| | She says you're **OK**. | she sɛzhierou **kay** |
| | Who does your **hair**? | hoo dəzhier **hɛr** |
| | **ca**sual | **kæ**•zhyə(w)əl |

| | |
|---|---|
| **vi**sual | **vi**•zhyə$^{(w)}$əl |
| **u**sual | **yu**•zhyə$^{(w)}$əl |
| **ver**sion | **vr**zh'n |
| **vi**sion | **vi**zh'n |

## Exercise 11-11: T, D, S, or Z + Y Liaison Practice — Track 163

*Reconnect or rewrite the following words. Remember that there may be a **y** sound that is not written. Repeat.*

| | |
|---|---|
| put your | pücher |
| gradual | gradjyə$^{(w)}$l |

1. did you
2. who's your
3. just your
4. gesture
5. miss you
6. tissue
7. got your
8. where's your
9. congratulations
10. had your

This word exchange really happened.

Now that you have the idea of how to link words, let's do some liaison work.

既然你已经知道怎样来连读单词，让我们来做一些连音练习。

**Exercise 11-12: Finding Liaisons and Glides**      **Track 164**

*In the following paragraph connect as many of the words as possible. Mark your liaisons as we have done in the first two sentences. Add the (y) and (w) glides between the words.*

**Hello, my** name is_____. I'm taking American **Accent** Training. There's a **lot** to **learn,** but I **hope** to make it as **enjoyable** as possible. I should pick **up** on the American **intonation** pattern pretty **easily,** although the⁽ʸ⁾**only** way to **get** it is to **practice** all of the time. I use the **up** and down, or **peaks** and valleys, **intonation** more than I **used** to. I've been paying attention to **pitch, too.** It's like **walking** down a **stair**case. I've been **talking** to⁽ʷ⁾a lot of **Americans** lately, and they tell me that I'm **easier** to under**stand. Any**way, I could go **on** and on, but the **important** thing is to **listen** well and sound **good. Well,** what do you **think? Do** I?

▶ Practice reading the paragraph three times, focusing on running your words together.

◀ Turn the CD back on and repeat after me as I read. I'm going to exaggerate the linking of the words, drawing it out much longer than would be natural.

**Exercise 11-13: Practicing Liaisons**      **Track 165**

*Back up the CD to the last paragraph just read and repeat again. This time, however, read from the paragraph below. The intonation is marked for you in boldface. Use your rubber band on every stressed word.*

**Hello, my** nay miz _____. I'm takingə merica **næccent**(t)raining. There zə **lätt**ə learn, bə däi **hope** t́ ma ki desen **joy**ablez pässible. I shüd pi kəpän the⁽ʸ⁾əmerica nintənash'n pæddern pridy⁽ʸ⁾**ezily,** although thee⁽ʸ⁾**ounly** waydə **ge**ddidiz t́ **præk**ti sälləv th' time. I⁽ʸ⁾use thee⁽ʸ⁾**up**'n down, or **peak** s'n valley zintənashən more thə näi **used** to. Ivbn payingə tenshən t́ **pitch, too.** Itsläi **kwäl**king dow nə **stair**case. Ivbn **täl**king to⁽ʷ⁾ə läddəvə **mer**ican zla⁽ᵗ⁾ely, 'n they tell me the däi**mee**zier to⁽ʷ⁾under**stænd. Any**way, I could go⁽ʷ⁾**ä** nə nän, bu⁽ᵗ⁾thee⁽ʸ⁾im**port**ant thingiz t́ **lis**ənwellən soun⁽ᵈ⁾**good. Well,** whəddyü **think? Do**⁽ʷ⁾I?

When a clock is hungry...

It goes back four seconds.

**Exercise 11-14: Additional Liaison Practice** Track 166

▸ Use these techniques on texts of your own and in conversation.
(1) Take some written material and mark the *intonation,* then the *word groups,* and finally the *liaisons.*
(2) Practice saying it out loud.
(3) Record yourself and listen back.

▸ In conversation, think which word you want to make stand out, and change your pitch on that word. Then, run the in-between words together in the valleys. Listen carefully to how Americans do it and copy the sound.

**Exercise 11-15: Colloquial Reductions and Liaisons** Track 167

*In order for you to recognize these sounds when used by native speakers, they are presented here, but I don't recommend that you go out of your way to use them yourself. If, at some point, they come quite naturally of their own accord in casual conversation, you don't need to resist, but please don't force yourself to talk this way. Repeat. (See also Chapter 1)*

| | |
|---|---|
| I have got to **go**. | I've gotta **go**. |
| I have got a **book**. | I've gotta **book**. |
| Do you want to **dance**? | Wanna **dance**? |
| Do you want a **banana**? | Wanna **banana**? |
| Let me **in**. | Lemme **in**. |
| Let me **go**. | Lemme **go**. |
| I'll let you **know**. | I'll letcha **know**. |
| Did you **do** it? | Dija **do** it? |
| Not **yet**. | Nä **chet**. |
| I'll meet you **later**. | I'll meechu **lay**der. |
| What do you **think**? | Whaddyu **think**? |
| What did you **do** with it? | Whajoo **do** with it? |
| How did you **like** it? | Howja **like** it? |
| When did you **get** it? | When ju **ge**ddit? |
| Why did you **take** it? | Whyju **tay** kit? |
| Why don't you **try** it? | Why don chu **try** it? |
| What are you **waiting** for? | Whaddya **wait**in' for? |
| What are you **doing**? | Whatcha **do**in'? |
| How is it **going**? | Howzit **go**ing? |
| Where's the **what**-you-may-call-it? | Where's the **what**chamacallit? |
| Where's **what**-is-his-name? | Where's **what**sizname? |
| How **about** it? | How **'bout** it? |
| He has got to **hurry** because he is **late**. | He's gotta **hurry** 'cuz he's **late**. |
| I could've been a **contender**. | I coulda bina con**ten**der. |

| | |
|---|---|
| Could you speed it **up**, please? | Couldjoo spee di **dup**, pleez? |
| Would you mind if I **tried** it? | Would joo mindifai **try** dit? |
| Aren't you Bob **Barker**? | Arnchoo Bäb **Bar**ker? |
| Can't you see it **my** way for a change? | Kænchoo see it **my** way for a change? |
| Don't you **get** it? | Doancha **ged**dit? |
| I should have **told** you. | I shoulda **tol**joo. |
| Tell her (that) I **miss** her. | Teller I **mis**ser. |
| Tell him (that) I **miss** him. | Tellim I **mis**sim. |

### Extreme reductions

| | |
|---|---|
| Did you **eat**? | **Jeet**? |
| No, did **you**? | No, **joo**? |
| Why don't you **get a job**? | Whyncha **getta job**? |
| I don't know, **it's** too **hard**. | I dunno, stoo **härd**. |
| Could **we go**? | Kwee **gou**? |
| Let's **go**! | **Sko**! |
| I'm **going** to | **äi**mana |

## Spoon or Sboon?

Track 168

Spoon还是sboon?

An interesting thing about liaisons is that so much of it has to do with whether a consonant is voiced or not. The key thing to remember is that the vocal cords don't like switching around at the midpoint. If the first consonant is voiced, the next one will be as well. If the first one is unvoiced, the second one will sound unvoiced, no matter what you do. For example, say the word *spoon*. Now, say the word *sboon*. Hear how they sound the same? This is why I'd like you to always convert the preposition *to* to **də** when you're speaking English, no matter what comes before it. In the beginning, to get you used to the concept, we made a distinction between **tə** and **də**, but now that your schwa is in place, use a single **d'** sound everywhere, except at the very beginning of a sentence.

  关于连音的一个有趣现象是它与一个辅音是否是浊音有很大关系。记住重要的一点：声带不喜欢在中间点变换位置。如果第一个辅音是浊音，那么下一个音也会是浊音。如果第一个辅音是清音，无论怎样，第二个辅音也会发清音。比如，先说单词spoon，然后再说单词sboon。听出它们的相同之处了吗？这是为什么我让你在说英语时无论介词to前是什么音总是将其转换为də的原因。刚开始，为了让你熟悉这个概念，我们区分tə和də，但既然你的非中央元音在适当的位置上，那么除了在句首以外，都使用单音d'。

| After a voiced sound: | He had to **do** it. | he hæ(d)d' **du**(w)'t |
|---|---|---|
| After an unvoiced sound: | He got to **do** it. | he gä(t)d' **du**(w)'t |
| At the beginning of a sentence: | To **be** or **not** to be. | t' **bee**(y)r **nä**(t)d'bee |

```
A  =  æ
O  =  ä
U  =  ə
```

# Chapter 12
# 第12章

# Cat? Caught? Cut?
# Cat, Caught和Cut的发音区别

**Track 169**

After laying our foundation with intonation and liaisons, here we finally begin to refine your pronunciation! We are now going to work on the differences between æ, ä, and ə, as well as ō, ā, and ɛ. Let's start out with the æ sound. (See also page vii, Chapters 3, 18, 20, and the Nationality Guide)

在打下语调和连读的基础后，现在我们终于可以开始精炼你的发音了！我们现在要来区分æ，ä，ə音，以及ō，ā和ɛ音。我们从æ音开始学习。（也见第vii页，第3、18、20章以及"汉语发音与美音的对比"部分）

## The æ Sound
æ音

Although not a common sound, æ is very distinctive to the ear and is typically American. In the practice paragraph in Exercise 12-2 this sound occurs five times. As its phonetic symbol indicates, æ is a combination of ä + ɛ. To pronounce it, drop your jaw down as if you were going to say ä; but then from that position, try to say ɛ. The final sound is not two separate vowels but rather the end result of the combination. It is very close to the sound that a goat makes: *ma-a-a-a*!

æ音虽然不是一个常见音，但听起来很特别而且是典型的美音。在练习12-2的练习段落中，这个音出现了五次。像它的音标所表示的那样，æ音是ä音和ɛ音的结合。要发æ音，先把下颚向下拉，就好像你要发ä音；然后从那个位置尽力发ɛ音。最后形成的音不是两个独立的元音，而是它们结合的结果。发音很接近山羊的叫声：ma-a-a-a!

▶ Try it a few times now: **ä** ▶ **æ**

If you find yourself getting too nasal with æ, pinch your nose as you say it. If **kæt** turns into **kɛæt**, you need to pull the sound out of your nose and down into your throat.

如果你发现自己发æ音时鼻音太重，那么当你发这个音时，捏住鼻子。如果kæt变成了kɛæt，你需要把音从鼻腔中挤出，直接进入喉部。

**Note** *As you look for the æ sound you might think that words like **down** or **sound** have an æ in them. For this diphthong, try æ + **oh**, or **æo**. This way, **down** would be written **dæon**. Because it is a combined sound, however, it's not included in the Cat? category.*

注意：当你在寻找æ音时，你或许认为像down或sound这样的单词中有一个æ音。对于这类双元音，试着发æ+oh或æo。这样，down将被写成dæon。但是，因为它是一个复合音，所以它不包括在Cat? 发音的分类中。

## The ä Sound
ä音

The **ä** sound occurs a little more frequently; you will find ten such sounds in the exercise. To pronounce **ä**, relax your tongue and drop your jaw as far down as it will go. As a matter of fact, put your hand under your chin and say **mä, pä, tä, sä**. Your hand should be pushed down by your jaw as it opens. Remember, it's the sound that you make when the doctor wants to see your throat, so open it up and ***dräp** your **jäw***.

ä音出现得更频繁一些；你会在练习中找到十个这样的发音。发ä音时，放松你的舌部，尽力将下颚向下拉。事实上，把手放在你的下颚处，然后发mä，pä，tä，sä。当嘴巴张开时，你的手会被下颚往下推。记着，这个音就是当医生要看你的喉咙时，让你发出的那个音。所以张开嘴，向下拉下颚。

## The Schwa ə Sound
非中央元音ə音

Last is the schwa ə, the *most common* sound in American English. When you work on Exercise 12-2, depending on how fast you speak, how smoothly you make liaisons, how strong your intonation is, and how much you relax your sounds, you will find from 50 to 75 schwas. Spelling doesn't help identify it, because it can appear as any one of the vowels, or a combination of them. It is a neutral vowel sound, *uh*. It is usually in an unstressed syllable, though it can be stressed as well. Whenever you find a vowel that can be crossed out and its absence wouldn't change the pronunciation of the word, you have probably found a schwa: *photography* **ph'togr'phy** (the two apostrophes show the location of the neutral vowel sounds).

最后是非中央元音ə，它是美语中最常见的音。当你进行12-2的练习时，依据你说话的速度、连音流畅的程度、语调的强度，以及发音放松的程度，你会发现50到75个非中央元音。拼写无法帮助识别这个音，因为它可以以任何一个元音或元音的组合形式出现。它是一种中性元音发音，uh。虽然也可以被重读，但它通常出现在非重读音节中。每当你发现一个元音可以被删除，而且它的空缺不会改变单词的发音时，你可能就找到了一个非中央元音：photography **ph'togr'phy**（这两个撇号显示了中性元音的发音位置）。

Because it is so common, however, the wrong pronunciation of this one little sound can leave your speech strongly accented, even if you Americanized everything else.

因为ə音太常见了，因而这个小音的错误发音会让你听起来带有浓重的口音，即使你将其他的音都美语化了。

**Note** *Some dictionaries use two different written symbols, ə and ʌ, but for simplicity we are only going to use the first one.*

注意：一些词典使用两种不同的书写体，ə和ʌ，来表示非中央元音。为了简便，我们只使用第一种写法。

## Silent or Neutral?
### 不发音还是中性音？

A schwa is neutral, but it is not silent. By comparison, the silent **e** at the end of a word is a signal for pronunciation, but it is not pronounced itself: *code* is **kōd**. The **e** tells you to say an **o**. If you leave the **e** off, you have *cod,* **käd**. The schwa, on the other hand, is neutral, but it is an actual sound—*uh.* For example, you could also write *photography* as *phuh•tah•gruh•fee.*

非中央元音是中性音，但并不是不发音。相比之下，处于单词末尾不发音的字母e是发音的一个标志，但它本身不发音：code读作kōd音。字母e告诉你要发o音。如果你省去了字母e，那就是cod，读作käd。另一方面，非中央元音是中性的，但它有实际的发音——uh。例如：你也可以将photography写成phuh•tah•gruh•fee。

Because it's a neutral sound, the schwa doesn't have any distinctive characteristics, yet it is *the most common sound in the English language.*

非中央元音是中性的音，因而没有任何显著特征，但它是英语中最常见的音。

To make the ə sound, put your hand on your diaphragm and push until a grunt escapes. Don't move your jaw, tongue, or lips; just allow the sound to flow past your vocal cords. It should sound like *uh.*

要发ə音，把你的手放在膈肌上并向下按，直到发出哼哼声。不要移动下颚、舌头或双唇；让声音流过你的声带。它应该听起来像uh音。

Once you master this sound, you will have an even easier time with pronouncing *can* and *can't.* In a sentence, *can't* sounds like **kæn(t)**, but *can* becomes **kən**, unless it is stressed, when it is **kæn**.

一旦你掌握了这个音，发can和can't的音就会更加容易。在一个句子当中，can't听起来像kæn(t)，而can则成了kən，除非can被重读，那时它发kæn音。

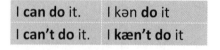

| I **can do** it. | I kən **do** it |
| --- | --- |
| I **can't do** it. | I **kæn't do** it |

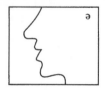

## Vowel Chart
元音表

In the vowel chart that follows, the four corners represent the four most extreme positions of the mouth. The center box represents the least extreme position—the neutral schwa. For these four positions, only move your lips and jaw. Your tongue should stay in the same place—with the tip resting behind the bottom teeth.

在下面的元音表中，四个角代表口腔中的四个极限位置。中间部分代表最不极限的位置——中性非中央元音。对于这四个极限位置，只需移动你的双唇和下颚。你的舌头应保持在同一位置——舌尖停留在下齿后部。

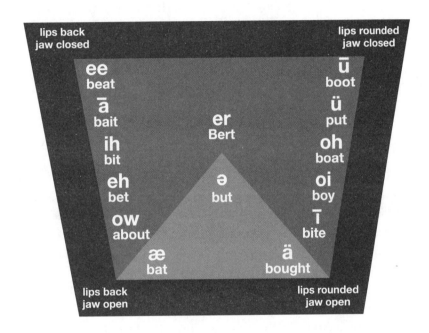

1. To pronounce *beat,* your lips should be drawn back, but your teeth should be close together. Your mouth should form the shape of a *banana.*

   要发beat的音，双唇应后缩，而牙齿应近于全合。嘴应呈香蕉的形状。

2. To pronounce *boot,* your lips should be fully rounded, and your teeth should be close together. Your mouth should form the shape of a *Cheerio.*

   要发boot的音，双唇应完全收圆，且牙齿应近于全合。嘴应呈麦片圈的形状。

3. To pronounce *bought,* drop your jaw straight down from the *boot* position. Your mouth should form the shape of an *egg.*

   要发bought的音，把下颚从boot的位置直线向下拉。嘴应呈鸡蛋的形状。

4. To pronounce *bat,* keep your jaw down, pull your lips back, and try to simultaneously say **ä** and **ɛ**. Your mouth should form the shape of a *box.*

   要发bat的音，保持下颚向下拉，将双唇向后缩，并且努力同时发ä音和ɛ音。嘴应呈盒子的形状。

**Note** *Word-by-word pronunciation will be different than individual sounds within a sentence. **That, than, as, at, and, have, had, can**, and so on, are æ sounds when they stand alone, but they are weak words that reduce quickly in speech.*

注意：在句子中，将单词与单词连起来发音与每个音单独发时是不同的。That，than，as，at，and，have，had，can等词，当它们单独发音时，是æ音，但它们在话语中时，音调降得很快，是弱读单词。

---

**Exercise 12-1: Word-by-Word and in a Sentence**                    **Track 170**

| Stressed | | Unstressed | | |
|---|---|---|---|---|
| that | thæt | th't | thət | He said th't it's OK. |
| than | thæn | th'n | thən | It's bigger th'n before. |
| as | æz | 'z | əz | 'z soon 'z he gets here |
| at | æt | 't | ət | Look 't the time! |
| and | ænd | 'n | ən | ham 'n eggs |
| have | hæv | h'v | həv | Where h'v you been? |
| had | hæd | h'd | həd | He h'd been at home. |
| can | cæn | c'n | cən | C'n you do it? |

---

**Exercise 12-2: Finding æ, ä, and ə Sounds**                    **Track 171**

*Underscore them in pen or pencil. (There are five **æ**, ten **ä**, and more than 50 **ə** sounds in the following paragraph. The first one of each sound is marked for you.)*

**He**llo, **my** name is_____. I'm taking əmerəcən **æ**ccent Training. There's a l**ä**t to **learn**, but I **hope** to make it as **enjoyable** as possible. I should pick **up** on the American **intonation** pattern pretty **easily**, although the **only** way to **get** it is to **practice** all of the time. I use the **up** and down, or **peaks** and valleys, **intonation** more than I **used** to. I've been paying attention to **pitch**, **too**. It's like **walking** down a **stair**case. I've been **talking** to a lot of **Americans** lately, and they tell me that I'm **easier** to under**stand**. **Any**way, I could go **on** and on, but the **important** thing is to **listen** well and sound **good**. **Well**, what do you **think**? **Do** I?

▸ Next, check your answers with the Answer Key. Finally, take your markers and give a color to each sound. For example, mark æ green, ä blue, and ə yellow.

✗ Turn off your CD and read the paragraph three times on your own.

**Note** *It sounds regional to end a sentence with **ustə**. In the middle of a sentence, however, it is more standard: I **ustə** live there.*

注意：用ustə结束一个句子时，听起来是有地方口音的。然而，当ustə用在句子中间时听起来就更标准了：I ustə live there。

## Exercise 12-3: Vowel-Sound Differentiation — Track 172

*Here we will read down from 1 to 24, then we will read one through four across. Give the **ā** sound a clear double sound **ɛ + ee**. Also, the **o** is a longer sound than you might be expecting. Add the full **ooh** sound after each "o."*

| | æ | ä | ə | ou | ā | ɛ |
|---|---|---|---|---|---|---|
| 1. | Ann | on | un- | own | ain't | end |
| 2. | ban | bond | bun | bone | bane | Ben |
| 3. | can | con | come | cone | cane | Ken |
| 4. | cat | caught/cot | cut | coat | Kate | ketch |
| 5. | Dan | Don/dawn | done | don't | Dane | den |
| 6. | fan | fawn | fun | phone | feign | fend |
| 7. | gap | gone | gun | goat | gain | again |
| 8. | hat | hot | hut | hotel | hate | het up |
| 9. | Jan | John | jump | Joan | Jane | Jenny |
| 10. | lamp | lawn | lump | loan | lane | Len |
| 11. | man | monster | Monday | moan | main | men |
| 12. | matter | motto | mutter | motor | made her | met her |
| 13. | Nan | non- | none/nun | known | name | nemesis |
| 14. | gnat | not/knot | nut | note | Nate | net |
| 15. | pan | pawn | pun | pony | pain/pane | pen |
| 16. | ran | Ron | run | roan | rain/reign | wren |
| 17. | sand | sawn | sun | sewn/sown | sane | send |
| 18. | shall | Sean | shut | show | Shane | Shen |
| 19. | chance | chalk | chuck | choke | change | check |
| 20. | tack | talk | tuck | token | take | tech |
| 21. | van | Von | vug | vogue | vague | vent |
| 22. | wax | want | won/one | won't | wane | when |
| 23. | yam | yawn | young | yo! | yea! | yen |
| 24. | zap | czar | result | zone | zany | zen |

| | single | double |
|---|---|---|
| ä | dock | dog |
| ə | duck | dug |

## Exercise 12-4: Reading the æ Sound

### The Tæn Mæn

A fashionably tan man sat casually at the bat stand, lashing a handful of practice bats. The manager, a crabby old bag of bones, passed by and laughed, "You're about average, Jack. Can't you lash faster than that?" Jack had had enough, so he clambered to his feet and lashed bats faster than any man had ever lashed bats. As a matter of fact, he lashed bats so fast that he seemed to dance. The manager was aghast. "Jack, you're a master bat lasher!" he gasped. Satisfied at last, Jack sat back and never lashed another bat.

✘ Pause the CD and read *The Tæn Mæn* aloud. Turn it back on to continue.

## Exercise 12-5: Reading the ä Sound

### A Lät of Läng, Hät Wälks in the Gärden

John was not sorry when the boss called off the walks in the garden. Obviously, to him, it was awfully hot, and the walks were far too long. He had not thought that walking would have caught on the way it did, and he fought the policy from the onset. At first, he thought he could talk it over at the law office and have it quashed, but a small obstacle* halted that thought. The top lawyers always bought coffee at the shop across the lawn and they didn't want to stop on John's account. John's problem was not office politics, but office policy. He resolved the problem by bombing the garden.

* *lobster • a small lobster • lobstacle • a small obstacle*

✘ Pause the CD and read *A Lät of Läng, Hät Wälks in the Gärden* aloud.

## Exercise 12-6: Reading the ə Sound

*When you read the following schwa paragraph, try clenching your teeth the first time. It won't sound completely natural, but it will get rid of all of the excess lip and jaw movement and force your tongue to work harder than usual. Remember that in speaking American English we don't move our lips much, and we talk through our teeth from far back in our throats. I'm going to read with my teeth clenched together and you follow along, holding your teeth together.*

### What Must the Sun Above Wonder About?

Some pundits proposed that the sun wonders unnecessarily about sundry and assorted conundrums. One cannot but speculate what can come of their proposal. It wasn't enough to trouble us,* but it was done so underhandedly that hundreds of sun lovers rushed to the defense of their beloved sun. None of this was relevant on Monday, however, when the sun burned up the entire country. *ət wəzənənəf tə trəbələs

✘ Pause the CD and read *What Must the Sun Above Wonder About?* twice. Try it once with your teeth clenched the first time and normally the second time.

# Chapter 13

Th is popped sound.
The tongue tip is pressed
firmly against the top teeth.

Th是一个爆破音。发音时，舌尖
紧紧抵住上齿背。

# Tee Aitch
# "Th" 的发音

## Exercise 13-1: Targeting the Th Sound — Track 176

*In order to target the **Th** sound, first, hold a mirror in front of you and read our familiar paragraph silently, moving only your tongue. It should be visible in the mirror each time you come to a **Th**. Second, find all of the **Th**s, both voiced and unvoiced. Remember, a voiced sound makes your throat vibrate, and you can feel that vibration by placing your fingers on your throat. There are ten voiced and two unvoiced **Th**s here. You can mark them by underscoring the former and drawing a circle around the latter. Or, if you prefer, use two of your color markers. Pause the CD to mark the **Th** sounds. Don't forget to check your answers against the Answer Key. (See also Chapter 3 and Chapters 14 and 17 for related sounds)*

**H**ello, **my** name is_____. I'm taking American **Accent** Training. There's a **lot** to **learn**, but I **hope** to make it as **enjoyable** as possible. I should pick **up** on the American **intonation** pattern pretty **easily**, although the **only** way to **get** it is to **practice** all of the time. I **use** the **up** and down, or **peaks** and valleys, **intonation** more than I **used** to. I've been paying attention to **pitch, too**. It's like **walking** down a staircase. I've been **talking** to a lot of **Americans** lately, and they tell me that I'm **easier** to under**stand**. Anyway, I could go **on** and on, but the **important** thing is to **listen** well and sound **good. Well,** what do you **think**? **Do** I?

## Exercise 13-2: The Thuringian Thermometers — Track 177

*I'm going to read the following paragraph once straight through, so that you can hear that no matter how fast I read it, all the **Th**s are still there. It is a distinctive sound, but, when you repeat it, don't put too much effort into it. Listen to my reading.*

The throng of thermometers from the Thuringian Thermometer Folks arrived on Thursday. There were a thousand thirty-three thick thermometers, though, instead of a thousand thirty-six thin thermometers, which was three thermometers fewer than the thousand thirty-six we were expecting, not to mention that they were thick ones rather than thin ones. We thoroughly thought that we had ordered a thousand thirty-six, not a thousand thirty-three, thermometers, and asked the Thuringian Thermometer Folks to reship the thermometers; thin, not thick. They apologized for sending only a thousand thirty-three thermometers rather than a thousand thirty-six and promised to replace the thick thermometers with thin thermometers.

th = voiced (17)
th = unvoiced (44)

## Exercise 13-3: Tongue Twisters                            Track 178

*Feeling confident? Good! Try the following tongue twisters and have some fun.*

1. The sixth sick Sheik's sixth thick sheep.

2. This is a zither. Is this a zither?

3. I thought a **thought**. But the thought I **thought** wasn't the thought I **thought** I thought. If the thought I **thought** I thought had been the thought I **thought**, I wouldn't have **thought** so much.

## Exercise 13-4: Mr. Thingamajig

*Sometimes, Americans have little mental pauses, where something's right on the tip of our tongue, but we can't think of the exact word—or when we want to euphemize unseemly speech. Fortunately, there's a way around this. We use substitution words that can mean anything and everything.*

I was rooting willy-nilly through a buncha stuff, looking every whichway for the dinky little what-chamacallit to fix the goldong thingamajig, but good ol' whatsizname had put it in the hoozi-whatsit, as usual! Boy oh boy, what a load of hooey. Always the same old rigamarole with that cockamamie bozo. He's such a pipsqueak! If I found it, ka-ching, I'd be rich, which would be just jim dandy! I'd be totally discombobulated. You-know-who had done you-know-what with the goofy little gadget again, so whaddyaknow...there was something-or-other wrong with it. What a snafu!

I had a heck of a time getting ahold of whatsername to come over and take care of it with her special little doohickey that she keeps there in the thingamabob. For the gazillionth time, the flightly little flibbertigibbit said alrighty, she wouldn't shilly shally, she'd schlep over with her widget fixer and whatnot to do a bodaciously whizbang job on the whole shebang. That's right, the whole kit 'n caboodle, no ifs, ands, or buts about it...no malarkey. Okee dokey, but she was a skosh busy right then, yada, yada, yada. Yessirreebob, we usually have gadgets galore, but what with the this-and-that, and all the hooplah, it's all topsy turvy today, 'cuz that humungous nincompoop is still in the whatsit acting like everything's just hunky dory.

That's just a bunch, gobbledeegook. Pure gibberish. He's such an old rapscallion. Jeeminy Christmas, the shenanigans of that old fogey. Yackety schmackety, blah, blah, blah! Shucks, I wanted to find it on my own, and not be penalized for it—I'm just so darned tired of gimme's and gotcha's by a lotta has-been nosybones out hobnobbing with hoity toity wannabes.

The real nitty gritty is that, young and old, they're just a buncha happy-go-lucky whippersnappers and cantankerous old fuddyduddies who don't know diddly. I poked among the gewgaws, tchotchkes, gimcracks, and knickknacks, there in the doodad, but I found zilch, zero, zippo, nil, nada and null. So-and-so told me such-and-such about the deeleebob, but I just don't know where that little gizmo is. Sheesh! It's a big whoopdedoo when you can't even remember where the gosh diddly darned whaddyacallit is!

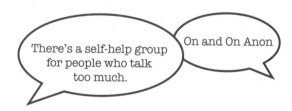

# Chapter 14
# 第14章

# The American T
# 美音中的 "T"

**Track 179**

The American **T** is influenced very strongly by intonation and its position in a word or phrase. At the *top* of a staircase, T is pronounced **T**, as in *Ted* or *Italian*; a **T** in the *middle* of a staircase is pronounced as **D**, *Beddy*, *Idaly*; whereas a **T** at the *bottom* of a staircase isn't pronounced at all, *ho*[(t)]. Look at *Italian* and *Italy* in the examples below. The **tæl** of *Italian* is at the top of the staircase and is strong: *Italian.* The **də** of *Italy* is in the middle and is weak: *Italy.* (See also Chapter 21)

美音中的T深受语调和它在单词或短语中的位置的影响。在音阶阶梯的顶部时，T的发音像在Ted或Italian中一样，发T；在音阶阶梯的中部时，T的发音像在Beddy和Idaly中一样，发D；然而，在音阶阶梯的底部时，T不发音，如ho[(t)]。看下面例子中的Italian和Italy。Italian中的tæl在音阶阶梯的顶部，因而重读：Italian。Italy中的də在音阶阶梯的中部，因而弱读：Italy。(也见第21章)

## Exercise 14-1: Stressed and Unstressed T Track 180

*Repeat after me.*

| | |
|---|---|
| Italian | Italy |
| attack | attic |
| atomic | atom |
| photography | photograph |

| **tael** | **I** |
|---|---|
| I      y'n | d' lee |

## Exercise 14-2: Betty Bought a Bit of Better Butter Track 181

*In the sentence **Betty bought a bit of better butter**, all the Ts are in weak positions, so they all sound like soft **D**s. Repeat the sentence slowly, word by word: **Beddy...badə...bidə...bedder...budder.** Feel the tip of your tongue flick across that area behind your top teeth. Think of the music of a cello again when you say, **Betty bought a bit of better butter.***

## Betty Bought a Bit of Better Butter

| | |
|---|---|
| Betty bought a bit of better butter. | Beddy bädə bihda bedder budder. |
| But, said she, | Bu(t), said she, |
| This butter's bitter. | This budder'z bidder. |
| If I put it in my batter, | If I püdi din my bædder, |
| It'll make my batter bitter. | Id'll make my bædder bidder. |

Along with liaisons, the American **T** contributes a great deal to the smooth, relaxed sound of English. When you say a word like *atom,* imagine that you've been to the dentist and you're a little numb, or that you've had a couple of drinks, or maybe that you're very sleepy. You won't be wanting to use a lot of energy saying **æ•tom,** so just relax everything and say **adəm,** like the masculine name, **Adam.** It's a very smooth, fluid sound. Rather than saying *BeTTy boughT a biT of beTTer buTTer,* which is physically more demanding, try *Beddy bada bidda bedder budder.* It's easy because you really don't need much muscle tension to say it this way.

美音中的T音以及连音大大促进了英语流畅、放松的发音。当你说一个单词，比如atom时，想象着你去看了牙医，且麻药还使你感觉有点迟钝，或者你已喝了几杯酒，或者也许你很困倦。你不想用很大的力气来说æ•tom，所以全身彻底放松地说出adəm，就像是男名Adam。它是非常平滑流畅的音。不要说BeTTy boughT a biT of beTTer buTTer，这需要更多的体力，而要试着说Beddy bada bidda bedder budder。这很简单，因为用这种方式发音，你真的不需要使肌肉太紧张。

The staircase concept will help clarify the various **T** sounds. The American **T** can be a little tricky if you base your pronunciation on spelling. Here are six rules to guide you.

阶梯概念将有助于分清不同种类的T音。如果你依据拼写进行发音，美音中的T音会有些难以捉摸。这里有6条规则来指导你。

1. **T is T** at the beginning of a word or in a stressed syllable.

   在单词的开头或在重读音节中，T发T音。

2. **T is D** in the middle of a word.

   在单词的中间，T发D音。

3. **T is Held** at the end of a word.

   在单词的末尾，T音被抑制。

4. **T is Held before N** in *-tain* and *-ten* endings.

   在以-tain和-ten结尾的单词中，T音在N音前被抑制。

5. **T is Silent after N** with lax vowels.

   在带有松元音的N音后，T不发音。

6. **T is Held** before glottal consonants **w, r, k, g** and **y**.

   在声门音w, r, k, g和y前，T音被抑制。

## Exercise 14-3: Rule 1—Top of the Staircase　　　　　Track 182

*When a **T** or a **D** is at the top of a staircase, in a stressed position, it should be a clear popped sound.*

1. In the beginning of a word, **T** is **t**.

   在单词的开头，T发t音。

*Ted took ten tomatoes.*

2. With a stressed **T** and **ST**, **TS**, **TR**, **CT**, and **LT**, and sometimes **NT** combinations, **T** is **t**.

   当T或ST，TS，TR，CT，LT，NT中的T被重读时，T发t音。

*He was content with the contract.*

T replaces **D** in the past tense, after an unvoiced consonant sound—**f, k, p, s, ch, sh, th**—(except **T**).

在过去式中，位于清辅音f，k，p，s，ch，sh，th后的ed发T音。

*T: laughed* **læft***, picked* **pikt***, hoped* **houpt***, raced* **rast***, watched* **wächt***, washed* **wäsht***, unearthed* **uneartht**

*D: halved* **hævd***, rigged* **rigd***, nabbed* **næbd***, raised* **razd***, judged* **j'jd***, garaged* **garazhd***, smoothed* **smoothd**

***Exceptions:*** *wicked/***wikəd***, naked/***nakəd***, crooked/***krükəd***, etc.*

| Exercise 14-4: Rule 1—Top of the Staircase Practice | Track 183 |
|---|---|

*Read the following sentences out loud. Make sure that the blue (stressed) Ts are sharp and clear.*

1. It took Tim ten times to try the telephone.
2. Stop touching Ted's toes.
3. Turn toward Stella and study her contract together.
4. Control your tears.
5. It's Tommy's turn to tell the teacher the truth.

| Exercise 14-5: Rule 2—Middle of the Staircase | Track 184 |
|---|---|

*An unstressed T in the middle of a staircase between two vowel sounds should be pronounced as a soft D.*

| Betty bought a bit of better butter. | Beddy bädə bida bedder budder |
|---|---|
| Pat ought to sit on a lap. | pædädə sidänə læp |

*Read the following sentences out loud. Make sure that the blue (unstressed) Ts sound like a soft D.*

| 1. | What a good **idea**. | wədə gudai **dee**yə |
|---|---|---|
| 2. | Put it in a **bottle**. | püdidinə **bädd**l |
| 3. | Write it in a **letter**. | räididinə **ledd**r |
| 4. | Set it on the metal **gutter**. | sedidän thə medl **gədd**r |
| 5. | Put all the **data** in the **computer**. | püdäl the **dei**də in the c'm**pyud**r |
| 6. | Insert **a quarter** in the **meter**. | inserdə **kwor**der in the **mee**dr |
| 7. | Get a better **water** heater. | gedə beddr **wäd**r heedr |
| 8. | Let her put a **sweater** on. | ledr püdə **swe**der än |
| 9. | **Betty**'s at a **meeting**. | **beddy**'s ædə **mee**ding |
| 10. | It's getting hotter and **hotter**. | its gedding häddr•rən **hädd**r |
| 11. | **Patty** ought to write a better **letter**. | **pæddy**(ᵛ)ädə ride a beddr **ledd**r |
| 12. | **Frida** had a **little** metal **bottle**. | **free**də hædə **lidd**l medl **bädd**l |

## Exercise 14-6: Rule 3—Bottom of the Staircase — Track 185

*T at the bottom of a staircase is in the held position. By held, I mean that the tongue is in the T position, but the air isn't released. To compare, when you say T as in **Tom**, there's a sharp burst of air over the tip of the tongue, and when you say **Betty**, there's a soft puff of air over the tip of the tongue. When you hold a T, as in **hot**, your teech is in the position for T, but you keep the air in.*

1. She hit the hot **hut** with her **hat**.
2. We went to that 'Net site to get what we **needed.**
3. **Pat** was quite **right, wasn't** she?
4. **What**? Put my **hat** back!
5. hot, late, fat, goat, hit, put, not, hurt, what, set, paint,
   wait, sit, dirt, note, fit, lot, light, suit, point, incident, tight

## Exercise 14-7: Rule 4—"Held T" Before N — Track 186

*The "held T" is, strictly speaking, not really a T at all. Remember t and n are very close in the mouth (see Liaisons, Exercise 11-5). If you have an N immediately after a T, you don't pop the T—the tongue is in the T position—but you release the air with the N, **not** the T. There is no t and no ə. Make a special point of not letting your tongue release from the top of your mouth before you drop into the **n**; otherwise, **bu(tt)on** would sound like two words: **but-ton**. An unstressed T or TT followed by N is held. Read the following words and sentences out loud. Make sure that the blue Ts are held. Remember, there is no **uh** sound before the **n**.*

**Note** *Another point to remember is that you need a sharp upward sliding intonation up to the "held T," then a quick drop for the **N**. Just go to the T position and hum: writt•nnnn.*

注意：记住另一点，你需要用急剧上升的滑动语调到达"被抑制的T音"，然后快速下降到N音。你只需要到达T音的位置，然后发出哼哼声：writt•nnnn。

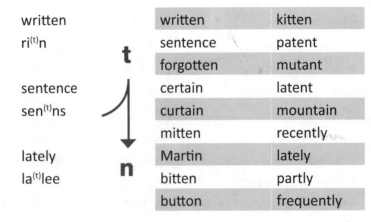

written
ri⁽ᵗ⁾n

sentence
sen⁽ᵗ⁾ns

lately
la⁽ᵗ⁾lee

| written | kitten |
|---------|--------|
| sentence | patent |
| forgotten | mutant |
| certain | latent |
| curtain | mountain |
| mitten | recently |
| Martin | lately |
| bitten | partly |
| button | frequently |

1. He's **forgotten** the **carton** of satin **mittens**.
2. She's **certain** that he has **written** it.
3. The cotton **curtain** is not in the **fountain**.
4. The **hikers** went in the **mountains**.
5. **Martin** has gotten a **kitten**.
6. **Students** study **Latin** in **Britain**.
7. **Whitney** has **a patent** on those **sentences**.
8. He has not **forgotten** what was **written** about the **mutant** on the **mountain**.
9. It's not **certain** that it was gotten from the **fountain**.
10. You need to put an **orange** cotton **curtain** on that **window**.
11. We like that certain **satin** better than the **carton** of cotton **curtains**.
12. The intercontinental **hotel** is in **Seattle**.
13. The frightened **witness** had forgotten the **important** written **message**.
14. The child wasn't **beaten** because he had **bitten** the **button**.

| **Exercise 14-8: Rule 5—The Silent T** | **Track 187** |
|---|---|

*T and N are so close in the mouth that the **t** can simply disappear. Repeat.*

| | | |
|---|---|---|
| 1. | **in**terview | **inn**erview |
| 2. | **in**terface | **inn**erface |
| 3. | **In**ternet | **inn**ernet |
| 4. | **in**terstate | **inn**erstate |
| 5. | inter**rupt** | inner**rupt** |
| 6. | inter**fere** | inner**fere** |
| 7. | inter**act**ive | inner**act**ive |
| 8. | inter**nat**ional | inner**nat**ional |
| 9. | ad**van**tage | əd**væn**'j |
| 10. | per**cen**tage | per**cen**'j |
| 11. | **twen**ty | **twen**ny |
| 12. | **print**out | **prin**nout or **prin**ᵈout |
| 13. | **print**er | **prin**ner or **prin**ᵈer |
| 14. | **win**ter | **win**ner or **win**ᵈer |
| 15. | **en**ter | **en**ner or **en**ᵈer |
| 16. | **pen**tagon | **pen**nagon |

| **Exercise 14-9: Rule 5—The Silent T** | **Track 188** |
|---|---|

*Read the following sentences out loud. Make sure that the underlined **T**s are silent.*

| | | |
|---|---|---|
| 1. | He had a great **int**erview. | he hædə gray ᵈ**inn**erview |
| 2. | Try to en**t**er the infor**ma**tion. | trydə enner the infr**ma**tion |
| 3. | Turn the **print**er on. | trn thə **prin**nerän |
| 4. | Finish the **print**ing. | f 'n'sh thə **prin**ning |
| 5. | She's at the int**er**national cent**er**. | sheez' ⁽ᵗ⁾the⁽ʸ⁾**inn**er**nat**ional senner |
| 6. | It's twen**t**y de**grees** in Toron**t**o. | 'ts twenny d'**gree**zin **trä**nno |

| | | |
|---|---|---|
| 7. | I don't under**stand** it. | I doe nənder **stæn** d't |
| 8. | She in**vent**ed it in Santa **Mo**nica. | she⁽ʸ⁾in**ven**əd'din sænə **män**əkə |
| 9. | He can't even **do** it. | he kæneevən **du**⁽ʷ⁾'t |
| 10. | They don't even **want** it. | they doe neevən **wän**'t |
| 11. | They won't ever **try**. | they woe never **try** |
| 12. | What's the **point** of it? | w'ts the **poi** n'v't |
| 13. | She's the intercont**inent**al repre**sent**ative. | shez thee⁽ʸ⁾innercän⁽ᵗ⁾n•**nen**l repr'**zen**'d'v |
| 14. | **Has**n't he? | **hæz**ə nee |
| 15. | **Is**n't he? | **iz**ə nee |
| 16. | **Aren**'t I? | **är** näi |
| 17. | **Won**'t he? | **woe** nee |
| 18. | **Does**n't he? | **dəz**ənee |
| 19. | **Would**n't it? | **wüd**ənit |
| 20. | **Did**n't I? | **did**n•näi |

## Exercise 14-10: Rule 6—"Held T" Before Glottal Consonants — Track 189

*Before a throat consonant, **T** is held by the back of the tongue. Repeat the following phrases.*

| | | | | |
|---|---|---|---|---|
| 1. | bright white | | 11. | it can |
| 2. | white car | | 12. | it runs |
| 3. | rent control | | 13. | that we |
| 4. | quit claim | | 14. | what we |
| 5. | get one | | 15. | that one |
| 6. | what was | | 16. | heat wave |
| 7. | that when | | 17. | net worth |
| 8. | it will | | 18. | but, yeah |
| 9. | not really | | 19. | what could |
| 10. | not good | | 20. | what would |

Sometimes Americans will hear the expression **quit claim** as **quick claim**.

有时美国人会把quit claim听成quick claim。

## Exercise 14-11: Karina's T Connections — Track 190

*Here are some extremely common middle **T** combinations. Repeat after me:*

| | What | But | That |
|---|---|---|---|
| **a** | wədə | bədə | thədə |
| **I** | wədäi | bədäi | thədäi |
| **I'm** | wədäim | bədäim | thədäim |
| **I've** | wədäiv | bədäiv | thədäiv |
| **if** | wədif | bədif | thədif |

| it | wədit | bədit | thədit |
|---|---|---|---|
| **it's** | wədits | bədits | thədits |
| **is** | wədiz | bədiz | thədiz |
| **isn't** | wədizn^t | bədizn^t | thədizn^t |
| **are** | wədr | bədr | thədr |
| **aren't** | wədärn^t | bədärn^t | thədärn^t |
| **he** | wədee | bədee | thədee |
| **he's** | wədeez | bədeez | thədeez |
| **her** | wədr | bədr | thədr |
| **you** | wəchew | bəchew | thəchew |
| **you'll** | wəchül | bəchül | thəchül |
| **you've** | wəchoov | bəchoov | thəchoov |
| **you're** | wəchr | bəchr | thəchr |

## Exercise 14-12: Combinations in Context — Track 191

*Repeat the following sentences.*

| | | |
|---|---|---|
| 1. | I don't know what it **means**. | I don^(t)know wədit **meenz** |
| 2. | But it **look**s like what I **need**. | bədi^(t)**lük** sly kwədäi **need** |
| 3. | But you **said** that you **wouldn't**. | bəchew **sed** thəchew **wüdnt** |
| 4. | I **know** what you **think**. | I **know** wəchew **think** |
| 5. | But I don't **think** that he **will**. | bədäi don^(t)**think** thədee **will** |
| 6. | He said that if we can **do** it, he'll **help**. | he sed the diff we k'n **do**^(w)it, hill **help** |
| 7. | But isn't it **easier** this **way**? | bədizni **dee**zier thi **sway**? |
| 8. | We **want** something that isn't **here**. | we **wänt** something thədizn^t **here** |
| 9. | You'll **like** it, but you'll **regret** it later. | yül **lye** kit, bəchül r'**gre** dit **laydr** |
| 10. | But he's not **right** for what I **want**. | bədeez nät **right** fr wədäi **wänt** |
| 11. | It's **amazing** what you've **accomplished**. | its amazing wəchoovəc**cäm**plisht |
| 12. | What if he **forgets**? | wədifee fr**gets** |
| 13. | **OK**, but aren't you **missing** something? | OK, bədärn^t chew **miss**ing səmthing |
| 14. | I think that he's **OK** now. | I think thədeez OK næo |
| 15. | She **wanted** to, but her **car** broke down. | She **wän**əd to, bədr **cär** broke dæon |
| 16. | We **think** that you're taking a **chance**. | We **think** thəchr taking a **chænce** |
| 17. | They don't know what it's **about**. | They doe noe wədit sə**bæot** |

## Exercise 14-13: Voiced and Unvoiced Sounds with T — Track 192

*This exercise is for the practice of the difference between words that end in either a vowel or a voiced consonant, which means that the vowel is lengthened or doubled. Therefore, these words are on a much larger, longer stairstep. Words that end in an unvoiced consonant are on a smaller, shorter stairstep. This occurs whether the vowel in question is tense or lax.*

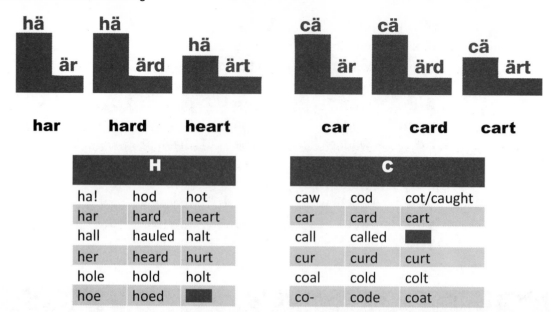

|        | H       |       |
|--------|---------|-------|
| ha!    | hod     | hot   |
| har    | hard    | heart |
| hall   | hauled  | halt  |
| her    | heard   | hurt  |
| hole   | hold    | holt  |
| hoe    | hoed    |       |

|        | C       |           |
|--------|---------|-----------|
| caw    | cod     | cot/caught|
| car    | card    | cart      |
| call   | called  |           |
| cur    | curd    | curt      |
| coal   | cold    | colt      |
| co-    | code    | coat      |

---

**Exercise 14-14: Finding American T Sounds**                    **Track 193**

---

*Once again, go over the following familiar paragraph. First, find all the T's that are pronounced D (there are nine to thirteen here). Second, find all the held Ts (there are seven). The first one of each is marked for you. Pause the CD to do this and don't forget to check your answers with the Answer Key when you finish.*

**He**llo, **my** name is_____. I'm taking American **Accen(t)** Training. There's a **lo(t)** to **learn**, but<sup>d</sup> I **hope** to make it as **enjoyable** as possible. I should pick **up** on the American **intonation** pattern pretty **easily**, although the **only** way to **get** it is to **practice** all of the time. I use the **up** and down, or **peaks** and valleys, **intonation** more than I **used** to. I've been paying attention to **pitch, too**. It's like **walking** down a **stair**case. I've been **talking** to a lot of **Americans** lately, and they tell me that I'm **easier** to understand. **Any**way, I could go **on** and on, but the **important** thing is to **listen** well and sound **good**. **Well**, what do you **think**? **Do I**?

## Voiced Consonants and Reduced Vowels                    **Track 194**
浊辅音和弱读元音

The strong intonation in American English creates certain tendencies in your spoken language. Here are four consistent conditions that are a result of intonation's tense peaks and relaxed valleys:

美式英语的强语调形成了你口语中的某些倾向。这里有四个一致条件，它们是语调的紧张"高峰"和放松"低谷"作用的结果。

## 1. Reduced vowels
弱读元音

You were introduced to reduced vowels in Chapter 1. They appear in the valleys that are formed by the strong peaks of intonation. The more you reduce the words in the valleys, the smoother and more natural your speech will sound. A characteristic of reduced vowels is that your throat muscles should be very relaxed. This will allow the unstressed vowels to reduce toward the schwa. Neutral vowels take less energy and muscularity to produce than tense vowels. For example, the word *unbelievable* should only have one hard vowel: **ənbəlēvəbəl**.

第1章已经介绍了弱读元音。它们出现在由语调的强"高峰"形成的"山谷"中。在"山谷"中，你越是弱读那些单词，你的语言听起来就越流畅、自然。弱读元音的一个特征就是你的喉部肌肉应该非常地放松。这会使非重读元音弱读为非中央元音。中性元音所消耗的能量以及调动的肌肉运动比紧元音要少。例如，单词unbelievable中应该只有一个紧元音：ənbəlēvəbəl。

## 2. Voiced consonants
浊辅音

The mouth muscles are relaxed to create a voiced sound like **z** or **d**. For unvoiced consonants, such as **s** or **t**, they are sharp and tense. Relaxing your muscles will simultaneously reduce your vowels and voice your consonants. Think of *voiced consonants* as *reduced consonants.* Both reduced consonants and reduced vowels are unconsciously preferred by a native speaker of American English. This explains why **T** so frequently becomes **D** and **S** becomes **Z**: *Get it is to...***gedidizdə**.

要发出像z或d那样的浊音，口腔肌肉需要放松。而发像s或t那样的清辅音时，口腔肌肉是敏捷、紧张的。放松肌肉能够同时弱读元音和浊化辅音。把浊辅音想象为弱读辅音。以美语为母语的人更喜欢弱读辅音和弱读元音，而他们自己并没有意识到这一点。这就解释了为什么T音总是会变成D音，S音总是会变成Z音：Get it is to...gedidizdə。

## 3. Like sound with like sound
相似音和相似音相连接

It's not easy to change horses midstream, so when you have a voiced consonant; let the consonant that follows it be voiced as well. In the verb *used*, **yuzd**, for example, the **S** is really a **Z**, so it is followed by **D**. The phrase *used to*, **yus tu**, on the other hand, has a real **S**, so it is followed by **T**. Vowels are, by definition, voiced. So when one is followed by a common, reducible word, it will change that word's first sound—like the preposition *to,* which will change to **də**.

河中换马不容易，所以当你碰到一个浊辅音时，让它后面的辅音也变成浊音。比如，在动词used（读作yuzd）中，S实际上发Z音，所以它后面跟的是D音。然而，短语used to（读作yus tu）具有一个真正的S音，所以它后面跟的是T音。按照定义，元音是浊音。所以当元音后紧跟一个常见的可弱读单词时，它会改变那个单词的首音——就像介词to会变成də一样。

> The only way to get it is to practice all of the time.
> They only wei•də•geddidiz•də•practice all of the time.

Again, this will take time. In the beginning, work on recognizing these patterns when you hear them. When you are confident that you understand the structure beneath these sounds and you can intuit where they belong, you can start to try them out. It's not advisable to memorize one reduced word and stick it into an otherwise overpronounced sentence. It would sound strange.

当然，这一切也需要时间。在刚开始，当你听到这样的发音时，努力去识别它们。当你相信自己理解了这些音的内在结构，并且能够凭直觉知道它们属于哪一类时，就可以开始试着说出它们了。记住一个弱读单词，并将它用在其他过于强调的句子中，这是不明智的。因为那样听起来会很怪异。

## 4. R'læææææææææx
### 放轻松

You've probably noticed that the preceding three conditions, as well as other areas that we've covered, such as liaisons and the schwa, have one thing in common—the idea that *it's physically easier this way.* This is one of the most remarkable characteristics of American English. You need to relax your mouth and throat muscles (except for æ, ä, and other tense vowels) and let the sounds flow smoothly out. If you find yourself tensing up, pursing your lips, or tightening your throat, you are going to strangle and lose the sound you are pursuing. Relax, relax, relax.

你可能已经注意到，前面的三个条件和我们之前讲过的其他方面，比如连音和非中央元音，有一个共同之处，就是这样做更加节省体力。这是美式英语最显著的特点之一。你需要放松口腔和喉部的肌肉（除了æ，ä和其他紧元音），让音平滑地流出。如果你发现自己紧张起来，缩拢了双唇，或者绷紧了喉咙，你就会抑制并且发不出你要发的音。所以放松，放松，再放松。

# Chapter 15

> The tongue doesn't touch anywhere.
> Growl out the **R** in the throat.
>
> 舌头不触碰任何地方。
> 从喉咙处发出R音。

# The American R
# 美音中的"R"

**Track 195**

American English, today—although continually changing—is made up of the sounds of the various people who have come to settle here from many countries. All of them have put in their linguistic two cents, the end result being that the easiest way to pronounce things has almost always been adopted as the most American. **R** is an exception, along with **L** and the sounds of **æ** and **th**, is one of the most troublesome sounds for people to acquire. Not only is it difficult for adults learning the language but also for American children, who pronounce it like a **W** or skip over it altogether and only pick it up after they've learned all the other sounds. (See also Chapters 1, 3, and the Nationality Guide)

今天的美语——虽然不断变化——是由从许多国家来美定居的人的声音构成的。他们都加入了自己的语言观点，最终的结果就是，最简单的发音方式几乎通常被认为是最美国化的。R音除外，它和L音、æ音和th音是最难发的几个音。对于进行美音学习的成人是这样，对于美国小孩也是这样。很多小孩把R音发成W音或直接跳过，然后在学完了其他所有音之后再重新学习。（也见第1章、第3章以及"汉语发音与美音的对比"）

## The Invisible R
看不见的R音

The trouble is you can't see an **R** from the outside. With a **P**, for instance, you can see when people put their lips together and pop out a little puff. With **R**, however, everything takes place behind almost closed lips—back down in the throat—and who can tell what the tongue is doing? It is really hard to tell what's going on if, when someone speaks, you can only hear the *err* sound, especially if you're used to making an **R** by touching your tongue to the ridge behind your teeth. So, what should your tongue be doing? This technique can help you visualize the correct tongue movements in pronouncing the **R**.

麻烦的是，你无法看到R音是如何发出的。比如，发P音时，你能看到人们什么时候合拢双唇，什么时候爆发出一些气流。然而，对于R音，一切都发生在几乎紧闭的双唇之后——向后至喉部——所以谁能知道舌头在做些什么呢？当有人说话时，真的很难知道到底发生了什么，你只能听到err音，尤其是如果你习惯用舌头触及齿龈来发R音的话。那么，你的舌头应该在做些什么呢？下面这个技巧能帮助你想象出在R音的发音过程中正确的舌部运动。

1. Hold your hand out flat, with the palm up, slightly dropping the back end of it. That's basically the position your tongue is in when you say *ah*, **ä**, so your flat hand will represent this sound.

   伸出你的手，放平，掌心向上，微微降低手掌后部。那是当你发ah，也就是ä音时，你的舌头基本所在的位置，所以你摊开的手将代表这个音。

2.  Now, to go from *ah* to the *er,* take your fingers and curl them into a tight fist. Again, your tongue should follow that action. The sides of your tongue should come up a bit, too. When the air passes over that hollow in the middle of your tongue, that's what creates the *er* sound.

现在，从ah音过渡到er音，运用你的手指并将它们紧握成拳。你的舌头还是应该跟随这个动作。舌的两侧也应轻微抬起。当气流通过舌头中间的中空地带时，就产生了er音。

Try it using both your hand and tongue simultaneously. Say *ah,* with your throat open (and your hand flat), then curl your tongue up (and your fingers) and say *errr.* The tip of the tongue should be aimed at a middle position in the mouth, but never touching, and your throat should relax and expand. **R**, like **L**, has a slight schwa in it. This is what pulls the *er* down so far back in your throat.

试着同时运用你的手和舌头来练习。发ah音时，喉咙打开（手摊平），然后卷起舌头（弯曲手指），再发errr。舌尖应该对准口腔的中间位置，但是不接触口腔，并且你的喉咙应该放松并打开。R音，像L音一样，含有微弱的非中央元音。正是非中央元音将er音拉低至你的喉咙深处。

Another way to get to *er* is to put a spoon on your tongue, and go from the *ee* sound and slide your tongue straight back like a collapsing accordion, letting the two sides of your tongue touch the insides of your molars; the tip of the tongue, however, again, should not touch anything. Now from *ee,* pull your tongue back toward the center of your throat, and pull the sound down into your throat:

另一种发er音的方法是在舌头上放一把汤匙，从ee音开始，直接向后滑动舌头，就像是折叠的风琴褶，让舌的两侧触及磨牙内部；然而，舌尖还是不应该触及任何部位。现在从ee音开始，将你的舌头卷向喉咙的中心，并且将音拉低至喉部：

> ee ▶ ee ▶ eeeer

Since the **R** is produced in the throat, let's link it with other throat sounds.

由于R音在喉部产生，我们将它和其他的喉音联系起来学习。

---

### Exercise 15-1: R Location Practice      Track 196

*Repeat after me.*

g, gr, greek, green, grass, grow, crow, core, cork, coral, cur, curl, girl, gorilla, her, erg, error, mirror, were, war, gore, wrong, wringer, church, pearl

While you're perfecting your **R**, you might want to rush to it, and in doing so, neglect the preceding vowel. There are certain vowels that you can neglect, but there are others that demand their full sound. We're going to practice the ones that require you to keep that clear sound before you add an **R**.

在完善R的发音时，你可能会急于求成，这样做就会忽略它前部的元音。有一些元音，你可以忽略，但有些元音，则需要你发出完整的音。我们将练习那些在你加入R音前需要保持清晰发音的元音。

*Refer to the subsequent lists of sounds and words as you work through each of the directions that follow them. Repeat each sound, first the vowel and then the ər, and each word in columns 1 to 3. We will read all the way across.*

| 1 | 2 | 3 |
|---|---|---|
| ä + er | hä•ərd | hard |
| e + ər | he•ər | here |
| ɛ + ər | shɛ•ər | share |
| o + ər | mo•ər | more |
| ər + ər | wər•ər | were |

We will next read column 3 only. Try to keep that doubled sound, but let the vowel flow smoothly into the **ər**; imagine a double stairstep that cannot be avoided. Don't make them two staccato sounds, though, like **ha•rd**. Instead, flow them smoothly over the double stairstep: *hard, here, share, more, were.*

下面，我们将只读第三竖行；努力保持双倍发音，但要让元音平滑地流动形成ər音；想象着一个无法避免的双层音阶阶梯。但不要使它们成为两个断音，像ha•rd，而要使它们在双层阶梯上平滑地流动：hard, here, share, more, were。

Of course, they're not *that* long; this is an exaggeration, and you're going to shorten them up once you get better at that sound. When you say the first one, *hard,* to get your jaw open for the **hä**, imagine that you are getting ready to bite into an apple: **hä**. Then for the *er* sound, you would bite into it: **hä•erd**, *hard.*

当然，它们的音没有那么长；这是一种夸张，一旦你能更好地发这个音，你将缩短它们的音长。当你发hard的第一个音阶时，要把嘴张开，想象着你正准备啃苹果：hä。然后，对于er音，你将啃住苹果：hä•erd，hard。

▶ Pause the CD to practice five times on your own.

From a spelling standpoint, the American **R** can be a little difficult to figure out. With words like *where*, **wɛər** and *were*, **wər**, it's confusing to know which one has two different vowel sounds *(where)* and which one has just the **ər** *(were)*. When there is a full vowel, you must make sure to give it its complete sound, and not chop it short, **wɛ + ər**.

从拼写的角度看，美音中的R可能有点难以理解。像where(wɛər)和were(wər)这样的单词，要知道哪个单词有两个不同的元音发音（where）而哪个单词只有ər音（were）是很难的。当有一个完全的元音时，你必须确保将它完整地发出，而不要将它的发音缩短成wɛ+ər。

For words with only the schwa + R **ər**, don't try to introduce another vowel sound before the **ər**, *regardless of spelling*. The following words, for example, don't have any other vowel sounds in them.

对于只有非中央元音+R（ər）的单词，无论拼写是怎样的都不要试图在ər音前插入另外的元音。例如，在以下单词中没有任何其他元音的发音。

| Looks like | Sounds like |
|:---:|:---:|
| word | wərd |
| hurt | hərt |
| girl | gərl |
| pearl | pərl |

The following exercise will further clarify this for you.

### Exercise 15-3: How to Pronounce Troublesome Rs                    Track 198

*The following seven **R** sounds, which are represented by the ten words, give people a lot of trouble, so we're going to work with them and make them easy for you. Repeat.*

| | | |
|:---|:---|:---|
| 1. | were | wər•ər |
| 2. | word/whirred | wər•ərd |
| 3. | whirl | wərrul |
| 4. | world/whirled | were rolled |
| 5. | wore/war | woər |
| 6. | whorl | worul |
| 7. | where/wear | wɛər |

1.  *Were* is pronounced with a doubled **ər**: **wər•ər**

    were的发音中有两个ər音：wər•ər。

2.  *Word* is also doubled, but after the second **ər**, you're going to put your tongue in place for the **D** and hold it there, keeping all the air in your mouth, opening your throat to give it that full-voiced quality (imagine yourself puffing your throat out like a bullfrog): **wərərd**, *word*. Not **wərd**, which is too short. Not **wordə**, which is too strong at the end. But **wər•ər^d**, *word*.

    word也有两个ər音，但在第二个ər音后，你要把舌头放在发D音的位置，并且保持在那里，让所有的气流都在口腔中，打开喉咙，完整发音（想象自己像只牛蛙，把喉咙鼓起）：wərərd，word。不是wərd，这个音太短了。也不是wordə，这个音的尾音太强了。而是wər•ər^d，word。

3.  In *whirl* the **R** is followed by **L**. The **R** is in the throat and the back of the tongue stays down because, as we've practiced, **L** starts with the schwa, but the tip of the tongue comes up for the **L**: **wər•rə•lə**, *whirl*.

    在单词whirl中，R音后紧跟着L音。R音在喉部，并且舌的后部压得很低，因为正如我们练习过的，L以非中央元音开始，但舌尖因为L音而抬起：wər•rə•lə，whirl。

4. *World/whirled* has two spellings (and two different meanings, of course). You're going to do the same thing as for *whirl*, but you're going to add that voiced **D** at the end, holding the air in: **wər•rəlᵈ**, *world/whirled*. It should sound almost like two words: *wére rolled.*

   单词world与whirled拼写不同（当然意思也不同）。你要先用发whirl的方式发音，但要在末尾加上浊音D抑制气流：wər•rəlᵈ，world/whirled。这个音应该听起来像两个单词的发音：wére rolled。

5. Here, you have an **o** sound in either spelling before the **ər**: **wo•ər**, *wore/war.*

   现在在ər音前有一个o音：wo•ər，wore/war。

6. For *whorl,* you're going to do the same thing as in 5, but you're going to add a schwa + **L** at the end: **wo•ərəl**, *whorl.*

   对于单词whorl，应像第5条一样发音，但末尾应加上一个非中央元音+L：wo•ərəl，whorl。

7. This sound is similar to 5, but you have **ɛ** before the **ər**: **wɛ•ər**, *where/wear.*

   这个音和第5条中的类似，但在ər音前有个ɛ音：wɛ•ər，where/wear。

**Track 199**

The following words are typical in that they are spelled one way and pronounced in another way. The *ar* combination frequently sounds like **ɛr**, as in *embarrass*, **embɛrəs**. This sound is particularly clear on the West Coast. On the East Coast, you may hear **embæras**.

下面的单词很典型，因为它们虽然拼写方式相同，但发音迥异。ar组合常常听起来像ɛr，例如在embarrass（读作embɛrəs）这个单词中。在美国西海岸人们把这个音发得特别清晰。而在美国东海岸，你可能会听到人们把这个词发成embæras。

## Exercise 15-4: Zbigniew's Epsilon List                    Track 200

*Repeat after me.*

| | | | Common Combinations |
|---|---|---|---|
| embarrass | stationary | Larry | |
| vocabulary | care | Sarah | |
| parent | carry | narrate | ar |
| parallel | carriage | guarantee | par |
| paragraph | marriage | larynx | bar |
| para- | maritime | laryngitis | mar |
| parrot | barrier | necessary | lar |
| apparent | baritone | itinerary | kar |
| parish | Barron's | said | war |
| Paris | library | says | har |
| area | character | transparency | sar |
| aware | Karen | dictionary | nar |
| compare | Harry | many | gar |
| imaginary | Mary | any | rar |

**Exercise 15-5: R Combinations**                                                        **Track 201**

*Don't think about spelling here. Just pronounce each column of words as the heading indicates.*

|     | ər     | är       | ɛr     | or     | eer    | æwr       |
|-----|--------|----------|--------|--------|--------|-----------|
| 1.  | earn   | art      | air    | or     | ear    | hour      |
| 2.  | hurt   | heart    | hair   | horse  | here   | how 're   |
| 3.  | heard  | hard     | haired | horde  | here's | ■         |
| 4.  | pert   | part     | pair   | pour   | peer   | power     |
| 5.  | word   | ■        | where  | war    | we're  | ■         |
| 6.  | a word | ■        | aware  | award  | a weird| ■         |
| 7.  | work   | ■        | wear   | warm   | weird  | ■         |
| 8.  | first  | far      | fair   | four   | fear   | flower    |
| 9.  | firm   | farm     | fairy  | form   | fierce | ■         |
| 10. | rather | cathartic| there  | Thor   | theory | 11th hour |
| 11. | murky  | mar      | mare   | more   | mere   | ■         |
| 12. | spur   | spar     | spare  | sport  | spear  | ■         |
| 13. | sure   | sharp    | share  | shore  | shear  | shower    |
| 14. | churn  | char     | chair  | chore  | cheer  | chowder   |
| 15. | gird   | guard    | scared | gored  | geared | Gower     |
| 16. | cur    | car      | care   | core   | kir    | cower     |
| 17. | turtle | tar      | tear   | tore   | tear   | tower     |
| 18. | dirt   | dark     | dare   | door   | dear   | dour      |
| 19. | stir   | star     | stair  | store  | steer  | ■         |
| 20. | sir    | sorry    | Sarah  | sore   | seer   | sour      |
| 21. | burn   | barn     | bear   | born   | beer   | bower     |

**Exercise 15-6: The Mirror Store**                                                      **Track 202**

*Repeat after me.*

The Hurly Burly Mirror Store at Vermont and Beverly featured hundreds of first-rate mirrors. There were several mirrors on the chest of drawers*, and the largest one was turned toward the door in order to make the room look bigger. One of the girls who worked there was concerned that a bird might get hurt by hurtling into its own reflection. She learned by trial and error** how to preserve both the mirrors and the birds. Her earnings were proportionately increased at the mirror store to reflect her contribution to the greater good. *chesta drorz **tryla nerr'r

✘ Pause the CD to practice reading out loud three times on your own.

## Exercise 15-7: Finding the R Sound                                    Track 203

*Pause the CD and go through our familiar paragraph and find all the **R** sounds. The first one is marked for you.*

Hello, **my** name is_____. I'm taking American **Accent** Training. There's a **lot** to **learn**, but I **hope** to make it as **enjoyable** as possible. I should pick **up** on the American **intonation** pattern pretty **easily**, although the **only** way to **get** it is to **practice** all of the time. I use the **up** and down, or **peaks** and valleys, **intonation** more than I **used** to. I've been paying attention to **pitch**, **too**. It's like **walking** down a **stair**case. I've been **talking** to a lot of **Americans** lately, and they tell me that I'm **easier** to unde**rstand**. **Any**way, I could go **on** and on, but the **important** thing is to **listen** well and sound **good**. **Well**, what do you **think**? **Do** I?

▸ Check the Answer Key.

> One of the best ways to get the **R** is to literally growl. Say **grrrr** as if you were a wild animal growling in the woods.

The tongue tip touches the ridge, even at the end of a word.

舌尖抵住牙槽骨，即使在词尾也是如此。

# Chapter 16
# 第16章

# The El
# 美音中的"El"

Track 204

This chapter discusses the sound of **L** (not to be confused with that of the American **R**, which was covered in the last chapter). We'll approach this sound first by touching on the difficulties it presents to foreign speakers of English, and next by comparing **L** to the related sounds of **T**, **D**, and **N**. (See also Chapter 21, and for related sounds see Chapters 14 and 24)

　　这一章讨论L的发音（不要和上一章涉及的美音R的发音相混淆）。我们首先看一下L音对说英语的外国人造成的困难，然后把L音和相关的T，D和N音进行比较。（也见第21章，相关音见第14章和第24章）

## L and Foreign Speakers of English
## L音和说英语的外国人

The English **L** is usually no problem at the beginning or in the middle of a word. The native language of some people, however, causes them to make their English **L** much too short. At the end of a word, the **L** is especially noticeable if it is either missing (Chinese) or too short (Spanish). In addition, most people consider the **L** as a simple consonant. This can also cause a lot of trouble. Thus, two things are at work here: location of language sounds in the mouth, and the complexity of the **L** sound.

　　L音在单词的开头或中间时，发音通常是没有问题的。然而，一些人的母语导致其英语的L音发音过短。在单词的末尾，如果L音消失（汉语）或过短（西班牙语），就尤其值得注意。此外，大多数人把L音当做一个简单的辅音，这也会导致很多问题。因而，这里要涉及两个方面：语言在口腔中的发音位置以及L音的复杂性。

### *Location of Language in the Mouth*
语言在口腔中的发音位置

The sounds of many Romance languages are generally located far forward in the mouth. My French teacher told me that if I couldn't see my lips when I spoke French—it wasn't French! Spanish is sometimes even called the smiling language. Chinese, on the other hand, is similar to American English in that it is mostly produced far back in the mouth.

The principal difference is that English also requires clear use of the tongue's tip, a large component of the sound of **L**.

很多浪漫语言的发音通常是从口腔十分靠前的部位发出的。我的法语老师告诉过我，在我说法语时，要是看不见自己的双唇——那就不是法语！西班牙语有时甚至被叫做微笑语言。汉语则和美语相似，因为其发音通常在口腔十分靠后的部位产生。英语与这些语言的主要区别在于需要明显地运用舌尖和大量的L音。

### *The Compound Sound of L*

L的合成音

The **L** is not a simple consonant; it is a compound made up of a vowel and a consonant. Like the **æ** sound discussed in Chapter 12, the sound of **L** is a combination of **ə** and **L**. The **ə**, being a reduced vowel sound, is created in the throat, but the **L** part requires a clear movement of the tongue. First, the tip must touch behind the teeth. (This part is simple enough.) But then, the back of the tongue must then drop down and back for the continuing schwa sound. Especially at the end of a word, Spanish-speaking people tend to leave out the schwa and shorten the **L**, and Chinese speakers usually leave it off entirely.

L音不是一个简单的辅音；它是由一个元音和一个辅音组成的合成音。就像第12章讨论的æ音一样，L的发音是ə音和L音的组合。ə音作为一个弱读元音，在喉部产生，而L音需要明显的舌部运动。首先，舌尖必须触及齿背。（这部分发音非常容易。）然后，舌后部必须接着下压后后移，来继续非中央元音的发音。尤其在一个单词的末尾时，说西班牙语的人常常省略非中央元音并缩短L音，而说汉语的人通常完全不发L的音。

One way to avoid the pronunciation difficulty of a final **L**, as in *call,* is to make a liaison when the next word begins with a vowel. For example, if you want to say *I have to call on my friend,* let the liaison do your work for you; say *I have to kälän my friend.*

有一种方法可以避免像在call之类的单词中词尾L的发音困难，那就是，当下一个单词以元音开头时，进行连读。例如，如果你想说I have to call on my friend，让连音来帮你的忙；说成I have to kälän my friend。

### *L Compared with T, D, and N*

**Track 205**

L音和T，D，N音的比较

When you learn to pronounce the **L** correctly, you will feel its similarity with **T**, **D**, and **N**. Actually, the tongue is positioned in the same place in the mouth for all four sounds—behind the teeth. The difference is in how and where the air comes out. (See the drawings in Example 16-1)

在你学习准确发L音时，你会感觉到它与T，D和N音有相似之处。事实上，发这四个音时，舌头在口腔中的位置是相同的——都处于齿背处。区别在于气流以什么方式出来，以及从哪里出来。（看练习16-1中的图片）

## T and D
### T音和D音

The sound of both **T** and **D** is produced by allowing a puff of air to come out over the tip of the tongue.

要发T音和D音，需要让一股气流从舌尖的上部流出。

## N
### N音

The sound of **N** is nasal. The tongue completely blocks all air from leaving through the mouth, allowing it to come out only through the nose. You should be able to feel the edges of your tongue touching your teeth as you say *nnn*.

N音是鼻音。舌头完全堵塞了口腔通道中的所有气流，让气流只从鼻腔中流出。当你发nnn音时，你应该能够感觉到舌头边缘触及牙齿。

## L
### L音

With **L**, the tip of the tongue is securely touching the roof of the mouth behind the teeth, but the sides of the tongue are dropped down and tensed. This is where **L** is different from **N**. With **N**, the tongue is relaxed and covers the entire area around the back of the teeth so that no air can come out. With **L**, the tongue is very tense, and the air comes out around its sides.

发L音时，舌尖牢牢地抵住牙齿后面的上颚，而舌头向下压，并且紧绷。这是L音和N音的不同之处。发N音时，舌头是放松的，并且覆盖齿背周围的所有地方，这样就没有气流能够流出。发L音时，舌头是非常紧绷的，气流从舌头两侧流出。

At the beginning it's helpful to exaggerate the position of the tongue. Look at yourself in the mirror as you stick out the tip of your tongue between your front teeth. With your tongue in this position say *el* several times. Then, try saying it with your tongue behind your teeth, el. This sounds complicated, but it is easier to do than to describe. You can practice this again later with Exercise 16-3. Our first exercise, however, must focus on differentiating the sounds.

刚开始发这个音时，舌头的位置夸张一些是有帮助的。当你从齿间伸出舌尖时，在镜中看着自己。舌头保持在这个位置，说几遍el。然后，把舌头放在齿背，再试着说el。这听起来很复杂，其实做起来比描述的要容易。你可以在随后的练习16-3中再进行练习。而我们的第一个练习必须重点区分这些音。

---

**Exercise 16-1: Sounds comparing L with T, D, and N**        **Track 206**

---

*For this exercise, concentrate on the different ways in which the air comes out of the mouth when producing each sound of **L**, **T**, **D**, and **N**. Look at the drawings, included here, to see the correct position of the tongue. Instructions for reading the groups of words listed next are given after the words.*

## T / D Plosive
T / D爆破音

A puff of air comes out over the tip of the tongue.
一股气流从舌尖的上面流出。

The tongue is somewhat tense.
舌头有些紧张。

## N
## Nasal
鼻音

Air comes out through the nose.
气流从鼻腔流出。

The tongue is completely relaxed.
舌部完全放松。

## L
## Lateral
侧音

Air flows around the sides of the tongue.
The tongue is very tense.
气流从舌头两侧流出，舌部非常紧张。

The lips are *not* rounded!
双唇不要收圆！

| **Exercise 16-2: Sounds Comparing L with T, D, and N** | **Track 207** |
| --- | --- |

*Repeat after me, first down and then across.*

| **1.** | **At the beginning of a word** | | |
| --- | --- | --- | --- |
| law | gnaw | taw | daw |
| low | know | toe | dough |
| lee | knee | tea | D |
| **2.** | **In the middle of a word** | | |
| belly | Benny | | Betty |
| caller | Conner | | cotter |
| alley | Annie's | | at ease |
| **3.** | **At the end of a word** | | |

| 3. | At the end of a word | | | |
|---|---|---|---|---|
| **A** | hole | hold | hone | hoed |
| | call | called | con | cod |
| **B** | fill | full | fool | fail |
| | fell | feel | fuel | furl |

▶ Look at group 3, B. This exercise has three functions:

1. Practice final *els.*
2. Review vowel sounds.
3. Review the same words with the staircase.

**Note** *Notice that each word has a tiny schwa after the* **el**. *This is to encourage your tongue to be in the right position to give your words a "finished" sound. Exaggerate the final* **el** *and its otherwise inaudible schwa.*

注意：每个单词在el后都有一个微弱的非中央元音。这能促使你把舌头放在正确的位置来发单词的尾音。夸大末尾的el和其他听不到的非中央元音。

▶ Repeat the last group of words.

Once you are comfortable with your tongue in this position, let it just languish there while you continue vocalizing, which is what a native speaker does.

　　一旦你感觉舌头放在这个位置很舒服，让它保持在那里，同时你继续发声。以英语为母语的人都是这样做的。

▶ Repeat again: filllll, fulllll, foolllll, failllll, feelllll, fuelllll, furlllll.

## What Are All Those Extra Sounds I'm Hearing?     Track 208
我听到的那些附加音是什么？

I hope that you're asking a question like this about now. Putting all of those short little words on a staircase will reveal exactly how many extra sounds you have to put in to make it "sound right." For example, if you were to pronounce *fail* as **fāl**, the sound is too abbreviated for the American ear—we need to hear the full **fāyəlᵊ**.

　　我希望你现在问这样的问题。将所有那些短小的单词放在音阶阶梯上，会确切地显示出你必须加进多少个附加音来使单词"听起来正确"。例如，如果你将fail发音为fāl，这个音在美国人听来就太简短了——我们需要听到完整的fāyəlᵊ。

## Exercise 16-3: Final El with Schwa
### Track 209

*Repeat after me.*

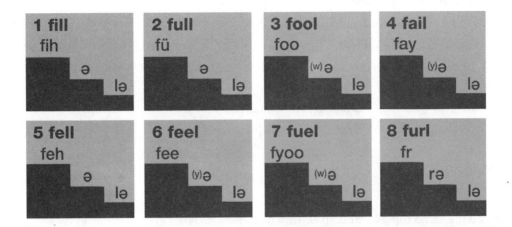

## Exercise 16-4: Many Final Els
### Track 210

*This time, simply hold the **L** sound extra long. Repeat after me.*

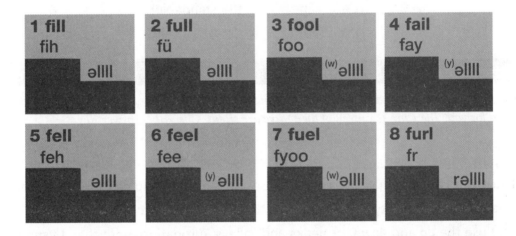

## Exercise 16-5: Liaise the Ls
### Track 211

*As you work with the following exercise, here are two points you should keep in mind. When a word ends with an **L** sound, either (a) connect it to the next word if you can, or (b) add a slight schwa for an exaggerated **lə** sound. For example:*

| | |
|---|---|
| (a) enjoyable as | enjoyəbələz |
| (b) possible | pasəbələ |

**Note** *Although (a) is really the way you want to say it, (b) is an interim measure to help you put your tongue in the right place. It would sound strange if you were to always add the slight schwa. Once you can feel where you want your tongue to be, hold it there while you continue to make the L sound. Here are three examples:*

注意：虽然（a）确实是你发音时想用的方式，但（b）是用来帮助你将舌头放在正确位置的临时措施。如果你总是加上微弱的非中央元音，就会听起来很怪异。一旦你能够感觉到你想使舌头处于口腔中的哪个位置时，当你继续发L音时，就把舌头保持在那个位置。这里有三个例子：

| **Call** | | |
|---|---|---|
| caw | kä | (incorrect) |
| call | cälə | (understandable) |
| call | källl | (correct) |

You can do the same thing to stop an **N** from becoming an **NG**.

| **Con** | | |
|---|---|---|
| cong | käng | (incorrect) |
| con | känə | (understandable) |
| con | kännn | (correct) |

## Exercise 16-6: Finding L Sounds                    Track 212

*Pause the CD, and find and mark all the L sounds in the familiar paragraph below; the first one is marked for you. There are seventeen of them; **five are silent**. Check the Answer Key.*

He**ll**o, **my** name is_____. I'm taking American **Accent** Training. There's a **lot** to **learn**, but I **hope** to make it as **enjoyable** as possible. I should pick **up** on the American **intonation** pattern pretty **easily**, although the **only** way to **get** it is to **practice** all of the time. **I use** the **up** and down, or **peaks** and valleys, **intonation** more than I **used** to. I've been paying attention to **pitch, too**. It's like **walking** down a **stair**case. I've been **talking** to a lot of **Americans** lately, and they tell me that I'm **easier** to under**stand**. **Any**way, I could go **on** and on, but the **important** thing is to **listen** well and sound **good**. **Well**, what do you **think**? Do I?

## Exercise 16-7: Silent Ls                    Track 213

*Once you've found all the L sounds, the good news is that very often you don't even have to pronounce them. Read the following list of words after me.*

| | | | |
|---|---|---|---|
| 1. | would | could | should |
| 2. | chalk | talk | walk |
| 3. | calm | palm | psalm |
| 4. | already | alright | almond |
| 5. | although | almost | always |
| 6. | salmon | alms | Albany |
| 7. | folk | caulk | polka |
| 8. | half | calf | behalf |
| 9. | yolk | colonel | Lincoln |

**Track 214**

Before reading about *Little Lola* in the next exercise, I'm going to get off the specific subject of **L** for the moment to talk about learning in general. Frequently, when you have some difficult task to do, you either avoid it or do it with dread. I'd like you to take the opposite point of view. For this exercise, you're going to completely focus on the thing that's most difficult: leaving your tongue attached to the top of your mouth. And rather than saying, "Oh, here comes an L, I've got to do something with my tongue," just leave your tongue attached *all through the entire paragraph!*

在读下个练习的"Little Lola"之前，我暂时不谈L的具体内容，而来大体上谈论一下学习。通常，当你有一些困难的工作要做时，你要么回避它，要么带着畏惧去做。我想让你持相反的观点。对于这个练习，你要将精力完全集中在最难的事情上：让你的舌头贴住上颚。不要说："哦，这是L音，我最好用舌头来发音"，你只需在整个段落中，保持舌头贴住上颚。

Remember our clenched-teeth reading of *What Must the Sun Above Wonder About?*, in Chapter 12? Well, it's time for us to make weird sounds again.

还记得在第12章，我们咬紧牙来读"What Must the Sun Above Wonder About?"吗？嗯，是我们再次发怪音的时候了。

---

### Exercise 16-8: Hold Your Tongue                                    Track 215

*You and I are going to read with our tongues firmly held at the roofs of our mouths. If you want, hold a clean dime there with the tongue's tip; the dime will let you know when you have dropped your tongue because it will fall out. (Do not use candy; it will hold itself there since wet candy is sticky.) If you prefer, you can read with your tongue between your teeth instead of the standard behind-the-teeth position, and use a small mirror. Remember that with this technique you can actually see your tongue disappear as you hear your **L** sounds drop off.*

*It's going to sound ridiculous, of course, and nobody would ever intentionally sound like this, but no one will hear you practice. You don't want to sound like this: llllllllll. Force your tongue to make all the various vowels in spite of its position. Let's go.*

**Leave a little for Lola!**

**Exercise 16-9: Little Lola**                                                    **Track 216**

*Now that we've done this, instead of **L** being a hard letter to pronounce, it's the easiest one because the tongue is stuck in that position. Pause the CD to practice the reading on your own, again, with your tongue stuck to the top of your mouth. Read the following paragraph after me with your tongue in the normal position. Use good, strong intonation. Follow my lead as I start dropping **h**'s here.*

**Little** Lola felt left out in life. She told herself that luck controlled her and she truly believed that only by loyally following an exalted leader could she be delivered from her solitude. Unfortunately, she learned a little late that her life was her own to deal with. When she realized it, she was already eligible for Social Security, and she had lent her lifelong earnings to a lowlife in Long Beach. She lay on her linoleum and slid along the floor in anguish. A little later, she leapt up and laughed. She no longer longed for a leader to tell her how to live her life. Little Lola was finally all well.

**Track 217**

In our next paragraph about *Thirty Little Turtles*, we deal with another aspect of **L**, namely, consonant clusters. When you have a *dl* combination, you need to apply what you learned about liaisons and the American **T** as well as the **L**.

在关于"Thirty Little Turtles"的下个段落里，我们将涉及L音的另一个方面，那就是辅音丛。当你碰到dl的结合音时，你需要运用你所了解的连音、美音T以及L音的知识。

Since the two sounds are located in a similar position in the mouth, you know that they are going to be connected, right? You also know that all of these middle **T**s are going to be pronounced **D**, and that you're going to leave the tongue stuck to the top of your mouth. That may leave you wondering: Where is the air to escape? The **L** sound is what determines that. For the **D**, you hold the air in, the same as for a final **D**; then for the **L**, you release it around the sides of the tongue. Let's go through the steps before proceeding to our next exercise.

因为这两个音在口腔中处于相似的位置，你知道它们会连读，是吧？你也知道所有这些处于中间位置的T音会发成D音，你要保持舌头抵住上颚。这可能让你感到纳闷：气流从哪里流出呢？这是由L音来决定的。在D音处，你抑制住气流，就像发尾音D一样；然后在L音处，把气流从舌的两侧释放。在继续下一个练习之前，让我们先复习一下步骤。

**Exercise 16-10: Dull versus -dle**                                              **Track 218**

*Repeat after me.*

**laid**      Don't pop the final **D** sound.
          不要爆破末尾的D音。

**ladle**     Segue gently from the **D** to the **L**, with a small schwa in between. Leave your tongue touching behind the teeth and just drop the sides to let the air pass out.
          从D音轻轻地滑入L音，中间带有微弱的非中央元音。让你的舌头触及齿背，并且只压低舌的两侧让气流流出。

**lay dull**     Here, your tongue can drop between the **D** and the **L**.

这时，你的舌头可以在D音和L音之间下压。

*To hear the difference between **dəl** and **dəᵊl**, contrast the sentences, Don't lay dull tiles and Don't ladle tiles.*

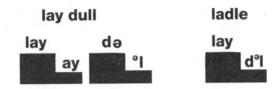

*Repeat the following lists.*

| | üll | äll | æwl | ell | ale | oll | eel | dl |
|---|---|---|---|---|---|---|---|---|
| 1. | bull | ball | bowel | bell | bale | bowl | Beal | bottle |
| 2. | ▇ | hall | howl | hell | hail | hole | heel | huddle |
| 3. | ▇ | hauled | howled | held | hailed | hold | healed | hurtle |
| 4. | pull | pall | Powell | pell | pail | pole | peel | poodle |
| 5. | wool | wall | ▇ | well | whale | whole | wheel | wheedle |
| 6. | full | fall | foul | fell | fail | foal | feel | fetal |
| 7. | Schultz | shawl | ▇ | shell | shale | shoal | she'll | shuttle |
| 8. | tulle | tall | towel | tell | tale | toll | teal | turtle |
| 9. | ▇ | vault | vowel | veldt | veil | vole | veal | vital |
| 10. | you'll | yawl | yowl | yell | Yale | ▇ | yield | yodel |
| 11. | ▇ | call | cowl | Kelly | kale | cold | keel | coddle |

*Repeat the following paragraph, focusing on the consonant + ᵊl combinations. (This paragraph was quoted in* The New York Times *by Pulitzer-Prize winning journalist, Thomas Friedman.)*

### Thrdee Liddəl Terdəl Zinə Bäddələ Bäddəl Dwäder

A bottle of bottled water held 30 little turtles. It didn't matter that each turtle had to rattle a metal ladle in order to get a little bit of noodles, a total turtle delicacy. The problem was that there were many turtle battles for the less than oodles of noodles. The littlest turtles always lost, because every time they thought about grappling with the haggler turtles, their little turtle minds boggled and they only caught a little bit of noodles.

## Exercise 16-13: Speed-reading                                          Track 221

*We've already practiced strong intonation, so now we'll just pick up the speed. First I'm going to read our familiar paragraph, as fast as I can. Subsequently, you'll practice on your own, and then we'll go over it together, sentence by sentence, to let you practice reading very fast, right after me. By then you will have more or less mastered the idea, so record yourself reading really fast and with very strong intonation. Listen back to see if you sound more fluent. Listen as I read.*

**He**llo, **my** name is_____. I'm taking American **Accent** Training. There's a **lot** to **learn**, but I **hope** to make it as **enjoyable** as possible. I should pick **up** on the American **intonation** pattern pretty **easily**, although the **only** way to **get** it is to **practice** all of the time. I use the **up** and down, or **peaks** and valleys, **intonation** more than I **used** to. I've been paying attention to **pitch, too**. It's like **walking** down a **stair**case. I've been **talking** to a lot of **Americans** lately, and they tell me that I'm **easier** to under**stand. Any**way, I could go **on** and on, but the **important** thing is to **listen** well and sound **good**. **Well**, what do you **think**? **Do** I?

▸ Pause the CD and practice speed-reading on your own five times.
▸ Repeat each sentence after me.
▸ Record yourself speed-reading with strong intonation.

## Exercise 16-14: Tandem Reading                                          Track 222

*The last reading that I'd like you to do is one along with me. Up to now, I have read first and you have repeated in the pause that followed. Now, however, I would like you to read along at exactly the same time that I read, so that we sound like one person reading. Read along with me.*

# Chapter 17

> S is hissed, Z is buzzed.
> Most S's are Z's.
>
> S是清音，Z是浊音。
> 大部分S's都发Z's。

# S or Z?
# 发S音还是Z音？

**Track 223**

The sound of the letter **S** is **s** only if it follows an unvoiced consonant. Otherwise, it becomes a **z** in disguise. When an **S** follows a vowel, a voiced consonant, or another **S**, it turns into a **z**. The following exercise will let you hear and practice **S** with its dual sound. There are many more **Z** sounds in English than **S** sounds. (See also Chapters 13 and 21 for related sounds)

字母S只有在清辅音后才发s音，在其他情况下都发z音。当S在元音、浊辅音，或另一个S后，发z音。下面的练习将让你听到并练习S的双重发音。在英语中，Z音比S音多得多。（相关音见第13章和第21章）

---

## Exercise 17-1: When S Becomes Z　　　　　　　　Track 224

*Under Contrast, in the list that follows, notice how the voiced word is drawn out and then repeat the word after me. Both voiced and unvoiced diphthongs have the underlying structure of the tone shift, or the double stair step, but the shift is much larger for the voiced ones.*

**Contrast**

| | **S** | **Z** | | prä äis | prä äiz |
|---|---|---|---|---|---|
| | | | **nouns** | books | waxes |
| 1. | price | prize | | maps | pencils |
| 2. | peace | peas | | months | dogs |
| 3. | place | plays | | hats | trains |
| 4. | ice | eyes | | pops | oranges |
| 5. | hiss | his | | bats | clothes |
| 6. | close | to close | | bikes | windows |
| 7. | use | to use | **verbs** | laughs | washes |
| 8. | rice | rise | | thanks | arrives |
| 9. | pace | pays | | eats | comes |
| 10. | lacey | lazy | | takes | goes |
| 11. | thirsty | Thursday | | speaks | lunches |
| 12. | bus | buzz | **contractions** | it's | there's |
| 13. | dust | does | | what's | he's |
| 14. | face | phase | | that's | she's |
| 15. | Sue | zoo | **possessives** | a cat's eye | a dog's ear |
| 16. | loose | lose | | | |

---

### Exercise 17-2: A Surly Sergeant Socked an Insolent Sailor     Track 225

*Repeat the S sounds in the paragraph below.*

Sam, a surly sergeant from Cisco, Texas, saw a sailor sit silently on a small seat reserved for youngsters. He stayed for several minutes, while tots swarmed around. Sam asked the sailor to cease and desist, but he sneered in his face. Sam was so incensed that he considered it sufficient incentive to sock the sailor. The sailor stood there for a second, astonished, and then strolled away. Sam was perplexed, but satisfied, and the tots scampered like ants over to the see saw.

---

### Exercise 17-3: Allz Well That Endz Well     Track 226

*Repeat the Z sounds in the paragraph below.*

A lazy Thursday at the zoo found the zebras grazing on zinnias, posing for pictures, and teasing the zookeeper, whose nose was bronzed by the sun. The biggest zebra's name was Zachary, but his friends called him Zack. Zack was a confusing zebra whose zeal for reason caused his cousins, who were naturally unreasoning, to pause in their conversations. While they browsed, he philosophized. As they grazed, he practiced zen. Because they were Zack's cousins, the zebras said nothing, but they wished he would muzzle himself at times.

---

       **Track 227**

As mentioned, like sounds follow naturally. If one consonant is voiced, chances are, the following **S** will be voiced as well (**dogz**). If it's unvoiced, the following sound will be as well (**cats**). In the past tense, **S** can be both voiced **z** and unvoiced **s** in some cases.

    如前面所提到的，相似音自然地融合在一起。如果一个辅音是浊音，后面跟随的复数S很有可能也会被浊化（如dogz）。如果它是清辅音，则后面的音也会是清音（如cats）。在过去时中，S既可以发成浊音z也可以发成清音s。

---

### Exercise 17-4: Voiced and Unvoiced Endings in the Past Tense     Track 228

*The following will explain the differences between four expressions that are similar in appearance but different in both meaning and pronunciation.*

| | Meaning | Example | Pronunciation |
|---|---|---|---|
| **S** | Past action | I used to eat rice. | yūst tu |
| | To be accustomed to | I am used to eating rice. | yūs tu |
| **Z** | Present passive verb | Chopsticks are used to eat rice. | yūzd tu |
| | Simple past | I used chopsticks to eat rice. | yūzd |

*Used to*, depending on its position in a sentence, will either take a tense **ū** or a schwa. At the end of a sentence, you need to say, ...*more than I used tooo;* in the middle of a sentence you can say, *He usta live there.*

used to根据它在句子中的位置，可以发成紧元音ū或者是非中央元音。在句子的末尾时，你需要说成...more than I used tooo；在句子的中间时，你可以说He usta live there。

Exercise 17-5: Finding S and Z Sounds      Track 229

*Go through the paragraph and underline all of the **s** sounds. The first, **æksent** is marked for you. Next, circle all of the **z** sounds, no matter how the word is written (is = iz, as = æz, and so on).*

Hello, **my** name iz _____. I'm taking American **æksent** Training. There's a **lot** to **learn**, but I **hope** to make it as **enjoyable** as possible. I should pick **up** on the American **intonation** pattern pretty **easily**, although the **only** way to **get** it is to **practice** all of the time. I use the **up** and down, or **peaks** and valleys, intonation more than I **used** to. I've been paying attention to **pitch, too**. It's like **walking** down a **stair**case. I've been **talking** to a lot of **Americans** lately, and they tell me that I'm **easier** to under**stand**. **Any**way, I could go **on** and on, but the **important** thing is to **listen** well and sound **good**. **Well,** what do you **think**? **Do** I?

▶ Practice reading the paragraph three times on your own, concentrating on strong **Z**s.

Exercise 17-6: Application Steps with S and Z      Track 230

*Build up the following sentence, adding each aspect one at a time.*

## Always be a little kinder than necessary.

### 1. Intonation
**Always** be a little **kinder** than **necessary**.

### 2. Word Groups
**Always** be a little kinder(pause) than necessary.

### 3. Liaisons
**Always** be(y)a little kinder tha(n)necessary.

### 4. æ, ä, ə
äweez be ə littʰl kinder thən nesəssary.

## 5. The American T
Always be a liddle kinder than necessary.

## 6. The American R
Always be a little kindər than necessɛry.

## 7. Combination of concepts 1 through 6
**äweez** be<sup>(y)</sup>ə liddəl **kindər**<sup>(pause)</sup> thə<sup>(n)</sup>necəssɛry.

| Exercise 17-7: Your Own Application Steps with S and Z | Track 231 |

*Write your own sentence, and then build it up, adding each aspect one at a time.*

1.  **Intonation**

2.  **Word Groups**

3.  **Liaisons**

4.  **æ, a, ə**

5.  **The American T**

6.  **The American R**

7.  **Combination of concepts 1 through 6**

I wanted to be sure and win the pun contest, so I submitted ten of them.

Unfortunately, no pun in ten did.

# Telephone Tutoring
# 电话指导

## Mid-Point Diagnostic Analysis
中期诊断分析

**Track 232**

After three to six months, you're ready for the follow-up analysis. If you are studying on your own, contact (800) 457-4255 or AmericanAccent.com for a referral to a qualified telephone analyst. The diagnostic analysis is designed to evaluate your current speech patterns to let you know where your accent is standard and nonstandard.

经过三个月到半年的学习，你已经为进一步的诊断分析做好了准备。如果你在自学本书，在中国大陆地区请拨打001-800-457-4255，在美国本土请拨打800-457-4255，或登录www.AmericanAccent.com，会有专业的分析师对你进行测评。诊断分析的目的在于评价你目前的言语特点，并让你知道自己的发音是否标准。

Think the United Auto Workers can beat Caterpillar, Inc. in their bitter contract battle? Before placing your bets, talk to Paul Branan, who can't wait to cross the picket line at Caterpillar's factory in East Peoria. Branan, recently laid off by a rubber-parts plant where he earned base pay of $6.30 an hour, lives one block from a heavily picketed gate at the Cat complex. Now he's applying to replace one of the 12,600 workers who have been on strike for the past five months. "Seventeen dollars an hour and they don't want to work?" asks Branan. "I don't want to take another guy's job, but I'm hurting, too."

| | | | |
|---|---|---|---|
| 1. saw, lost, cough | 5. shine, time, my | 9. some, dull, possible | 13. how, down, around |
| 2. can, Dan, last | 6. sit, silk, been | 10. tooth, two, blue | 14. appoint, avoid, boil |
| 3. same, say, rail | 7. seat, see, bean | 11. look, bull, should | |
| 4. yet, says, Paris | 8. word, girl, first | 12. don't, so, whole | |

| A | B | C | D | E | F |
|---|---|---|---|---|---|
| 1. parry | 1. bury | 1. apple | 1. able | 1. mop | 1. mob |
| 2. ferry | 2. very | 2. afraid | 2. avoid | 2. off | 2. of |
| 3. stew | 3. zoo | 3. races | 3. raises | 3. face | 3. phase |
| 4. sheer | 4. girl | 4. pressure | 4. pleasure | 4. crush | 4. garage |
| 5. two | 5. do | 5. petal | 5. pedal | 5. not | 5. nod |
| 6. choke | 6. joke | 6. gaucho | 6. gouger | 6. rich | 6. ridge |
| 7. think | 7. that | 7. ether | 7. either | 7. tooth | 7. smooth |
| 8. come | 8. gum | 8. bicker | 8. bigger | 8. pick | 8. pig |
| 9. yes | 9. rate | 9. accent | 9. exit | 9. tax | 9. tags |
| 10. wool | 10. grow | 10. player | 10. correct | 10. day | 10. tower |
| 11. his | 11. me | 11. shower | 11. carry | 11. now | 11. neater |
| 12. late | 12. next | 12. ahead | 12. swimmer | 12. towel | 12. same |
| 13. bleed | | 13. collect | 13. connect | 13. needle | 13. man |
| | | 14. Kelly | 14. finger | | 14. ring |

1. Who opened it?
2. We opened it.
3. Put it away.
4. Bob ate an orange.
5. Can it be done?

1. Who⁽ʷ⁾oup'n did?
2. We⁽ʸ⁾oup'n dit.
3. Pü di də way.
4. Bä bei d' nornj.
5. C'n't be dən?

1. Write a letter to Betty.

2. Ride a ledder d' Beddy.

| 3. tatter | tattoo |
|-----------|---------|
| 4. platter | platoon |
| 5. pattern | perturb |
| 6. critic | critique |
| 7. let | led |
| 8. written | ridden |

# Review and Expansion
# 复习和扩展

**Track 233**

In the first seventeen chapters of the American Accent Training program, we covered the concepts that form the basis of American speech—intonation, word groups, the staircase, and liaisons, or word connections. We also discussed some key sounds, such as **æ**, **ä**, and **ə** (Cat? Caught? Cut?), the **El**, the American **T**, and the American **R**. Let's briefly review each item.

在美语发音训练课程的前17章，我们涉及了构成美语发音基础的概念——语调、词群、音阶阶梯和连音（或词的连读）。我们也讨论了一些关键的音，比如æ，ä，ə（cat，caught，cut的发音区别），El，美音T和R。让我们逐项简单复习一下。

## Intonation
语调

You've learned some of the reasons for changing the pitch (or saying a word louder or even streeetching it out) of some words in a sentence.

你已经了解了改变一个句子中某些单词的音高（或大声说一个单词，甚至延长它的发音）的部分原因。

1. To introduce new information (nouns)
   为了引入新信息（名词）

2. To offer an opinion
   为了提出观点

3. To contrast two or more elements
   为了对比两个或更多的成分

4. To indicate the use of the negative contraction *can't*
   为了指出使用了否定缩略词can't

For example:

**New information**
He bought a **car**.
**Contrast**
**Timing** is more important than **technique**.

**Opinion**
It **feels** like mink, but I think it's **rabbit**.
**Can't**
He **can't do** it.

You've also learned how to change meaning by shifting intonation, without changing any of the actual words in a sentence.

你已经学习了在不改变句子中任何实际存在的单词的情况下，怎样通过改变语调来改变意义。

I applied for the job (not **you**!).
I **applied** for the job (but I don't think I'll **get** it).
I applied **for** the job (not I applied myself **to** the job).
I applied for **the** job (the **one** I've been dreaming about for **years**!)
I applied for the **job** (not the **life**style!).

## Miscellaneous Reminders of Intonation
### 各种各样的语调提示

When you have a verb/preposition combination, the stress usually goes on the preposition: *pick **up**, put **down**, fall **in**,* and so on. Otherwise, prepositions are placed in the valleys of your intonation: *It's f'r **you**., They're fr'm **LA**.*

当你碰到动词和介词搭配时，重音通常在介词上：pick **up**，put **down**，fall **in**等等。另外，介词放在你的语调的"低谷"中：It's f'r **you**，They're fr'm **LA**。

When you have initials, the stress goes on the last letter: IB**M**, P**O** Box, ASA**P**, IO**U**, and so on. (See also Chapters 4 and 6)

如果是缩写，重音在最后一个字母上：IB**M**，P**O** Box，ASA**P**，IO**U**等等。（也见第4章和第6章）

## Liaisons and Glides
### 连音和滑音

Through liaisons, you learned about *voiced* and *unvoiced consonants*—where they are located in the mouth and which sounds are likely to attach to a following one. You were also introduced to glides. (See also Chapter 7)

通过连音，你了解了浊辅音和清辅音——它们在口腔中的发音位置，以及它们中哪一个音倾向于和后面的音连读。此外，你还学习了滑音。（也见第7章）

| 1. | **Consonant and Vowel** | Put it *on*. | Pu•di•dan. |
|---|---|---|---|
| 2. | **Consonant and Consonant** | *race*track | ray•stræk |
| 3. | **Vowel and Vowel** | No *other* | No^(w)other |
| 4. | **T and Y** | Put you *on* | Puchü^(w)än |
| | **D and Y** | *Had* you? | Hæjoo? |
| | **S and Y** | *Yes*, you do. | Yeshu do. |
| | **Z and Y** | Is your *cat*? | Izher cat? |

## Cat? Caught? Cut?

Cat，Caught，Cut的区别

This lesson was an introduction to pronunciation, especially those highly characteristic sounds, æ, ä, and ə. (See also Chapter 12)

这节课是对发音的介绍，尤其是那些很有特点的音：æ音，ä音和ə音。（也见第12章）

æ  The jaw moves down and back while the back of the tongue pushes forward and the tip touches the back of the bottom teeth. Sometimes it almost sounds like there's a Y in there: *cat*, **kyæt**.

下巴向下、向后拉，同时舌的后部向前伸，并且舌尖触及下齿背。有时这个音听起来像有个Y音在里面：cat，kyæt。

ä  Relax the tongue, open the throat like you're letting the doctor see all the way to your toes: *aah.*

放松舌头，打开喉咙，就好像你让医生从你的喉咙口往下一直看到你的脚趾头一样：aah。

ə  This sound is the sound that would come out if you were pushed (lightly) in the stomach: *uh.* You don't need to put your mouth in any particular position at all. The sound is created when the air is forced out of the diaphragm and past the vocal cords.

这个音就是当你（轻轻地）按腹部时，会产生的那个音：uh。你一点也不需要做出特别的口形。当气流挤出膈肌并通过声带时，这个音就产生了。

## The American T

美音中的T

T is **T**, a clear popped sound, when it is at the **top** of the staircase.

当T在音阶阶梯的顶部时，它发T音，一个清晰的爆破音。

- at the beginning of a word, *table*
  在单词的开头，如table

- in a stressed syllable, *intend*
  在重读音节里，如intend

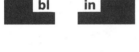

- in **ST**, **TS**, **TR**, **CT** clusters, *instruct*
  在ST，TS，TR，CT音丛中，如instruct

- replaces **D** after unvoiced consonants, *hoped*, **hopt**
  在清辅音后代替D，如hoped（读作hopt）

T is **D**, a softer sound, when it is in the **middle** of the staircase.

当T在音阶阶梯的中部时，发D音，一个比较轻柔的音。

- in an unstressed position between vowels, *cattle*, **caddle**
  在元音间非重读的位置，如cattle（读作caddle）

**T** and **D** are held (*not* pronounced with a sharp burst of air) when they are at the **bottom** of the staircase.

> 当位于音阶阶梯的底部时，T音或D音被抑制（发音时没有气流的剧烈爆破）。

- at the end of a word, *bought*, **bä**<sup>(t)</sup>

> 在单词的末尾，如bought（读作bä⁽ᵗ⁾）

**T** is held before **N**.

> 在N音前，T音被抑制。

- unstressed and followed by *-ten* or *-tain*, *written*, **wri(tt)en**

> 非重读，并且其后是-ten或-tain，如written（读作wri(tt)en）

**T** is swallowed by **N**.

> T音被N音吞没。

- *interview*, **innerview**

> 如interview（读作innerview）

(See also Chapter 14)

> （也见第14章）

## The EI
### 美音中的EI

The **EI** is closely connected with the schwa. Your tongue drops down in back as if it were going to say *uh*, but the tip curls up and attaches to the top of the mouth, which requires a strong movement of the tip of the tongue. The air comes out around the sides of the tongue, and the sound is held for slightly longer than you'd think. (See also Chapter 16)

> EI音和非中央元音紧密相连。压低舌头后部，就像要发uh音，但是舌尖卷起并抵住上颚，这需要舌尖的剧烈运动。气流从舌的两侧流出，这个音保持的时间比你以为的略长。（也见第16章）

## The American R
### 美音中的R

The main difference between a consonant and a vowel is that with a consonant there is contact at some point in your mouth. It might be the lips, **P**; the tongue tip, **N**; or the throat, **G**. Like a vowel, however, the **R** doesn't touch anywhere. It is similar to a schwa, but your tongue curls back in a retroflex movement and produces a sound deep in the throat. *The tongue doesn't touch the top of the mouth.* Another way to approach it is to put your tongue in the position for *ee*, and then slide straight back to *eeer*. Some people are more comfortable collapsing their tongue back, like an accordion instead of curling it. It doesn't make any difference in the sound, so do whichever you prefer. (See also Chapter 15)

> 辅音和元音之间的主要区别在于发辅音时会接触口腔中的某点：可能是双唇，如P；舌尖，如N；或是喉部，如G。然而，R音就像一个元音一样，发音时不触及任何部位。R音和非中央元音相似，

但舌头是向后卷的，进行卷舌运动，并且从喉咙深处发音。舌头不触及上颚。另一种发R音的方法是把舌头放在发ee的位置上，然后直接向后滑动到eeer。有些人觉得，相对于卷舌，把舌头向后折更舒适，就像是风琴褶。这两种发R音的方法在发音上不会产生任何区别，所以你可以选择自己喜欢的方法。（也见第15章）

## Application Exercises
### 应用练习

Now you need to use the exercises you've learned so far and make the transference to your everyday speech. In the beginning, the process is very slow and analytical, but as you do it over and over again, it becomes natural and unconscious. The exercises presented here will show you how. For example, take any phrase that may catch your ear during a conversation—because it is unfamiliar, or for whatever other reason—and work it through the practice sequence used in Review Exercise 1.

现在你需要将目前已学到的技巧运用到日常会话中去。起初，这个过程是十分缓慢且需要分析的，但当你反复练习后，就会变得自然而随性。这里的练习将指引你怎样去做。例如，挑选在会话中引起你注意的任何短语——可以是因为不熟悉它，也可以是任何其他的原因——并且用Review Exercise 1中使用的练习顺序来练习。

---

**Review Exercise 1: To have a friend, be a friend.**　　　　　　　**Track 234**

*Take the repeated phrase in the following application steps. Apply each concept indicated there, one at a time and in the sequence given. Read the sentence out loud two or three times, concentrating only on the one concept. This means that when you are working on liaisons, for instance, you don't have to pay much attention to intonation, just for that short time. First, read the phrase with no preparation and record yourself doing it.*

### To have a friend, be a friend.

---

**Review Exercise 2: To have a friend, be a friend.**　　　　　　　**Track 235**

*Pause the CD and go through each step using the following explanation as a guide.*

## 1. Intonation
### 语调

You want to figure out where the intonation belongs when you first encounter a phrase. In this example, **friend** is repeated, so a good reason for intonation would be the contrast that lies in the verbs *have* and *be*:

当你首次遇到一个短语时，你会想弄清楚应该使用什么样的语调。在这个例子中，friend是重复的，因而应该将语调放在形成对比的动词have和be上：

### To **have** a friend, **be** a friend.

## 2. Word groups
词群

The pause in this case is easy because it's a short sentence with a comma, so we put one there. With your own phrases, look for a logical break, or other hints, as when you have the verb *to be,* you usually pause very slightly just before it, because it means that you're introducing a definition:

在这个例子中，停顿很简单，因为这是一个带有逗号的短句，所以我们把停顿放在逗号处。表达自己的意思时，要寻找符合逻辑的停顿，或者其他的暗示，就像当你碰到系动词be，你通常会在它前面做个十分轻微的停顿，因为它意味着你将介绍定义：

**A** <sup>(pause)</sup> is **B**.

**Cows**<sup>(pause)</sup> are **ruminants**.

To **have** a friend,<sup>(pause)</sup> **be** a friend.

## 3. Liaisons
连音

Figure out which words you want to run together. Look for words that start with vowels and connect them to the previous word:

弄清楚你想把哪些单词连读在一起。寻找以元音开头的单词，并将它们和前一个单词连读。

To hava friend, be<sup>(y)</sup>a friend.

## 4. æ, ä, ə
æ, ä, ə

Label these common sounds in the sentence:

在句子中标记这些常见的发音。

Tə hævə friend, be ə friend.

## 5. The American T
美音中的T

Work with it, making it into a **D** or **CH**, holding it back or getting rid of it altogether, as appropriate. In this phrase, there are no **T**s, but the **D** is held:

练习美音T，把它发成D音或CH音，酌情抑制它的发音或完全去掉它的发音。在下面这个短句中，没有T音，而D音则被抑制：

To have a frien<sup>(d)</sup>, be a frien<sup>(d)</sup>.

## 6. The American R

美音中的R

Mark all the **R**s.

标记所有的R音。

To have a friend, be a friend.

## 7. Combination of concepts 1–6

概念1–6 的结合

Tə **hæ**və frɛn⁽ᵈ⁾, ⁽ᵖᵃᵘˢᵉ⁾ **be**⁽ʸ⁾ə frɛnd⁽ᵈ⁾.

▸ Practice the sequence of steps a couple of times and then record yourself again; place your second recording right after the first one on your tape. Play them both back and see if you hear a strong difference.

---

**Review Exercise 3: Get a Better Water Heater!**　　　　　　　　**Track 236**

*Pause the CD and go through the same steps with "Get a better water heater!"*

| | | |
|---|---|---|
| 1. | Intonation | **Get** a better **water** heater! |
| 2. | Word groups | Get a better water heater! ⁽ᵖᵃᵘˢᵉ⁾ |
| 3. | Liaisons | Geta better water heater! |
| 4. | æ, ä, ə | Getə better wäter heater! |
| 5. | The American T | Gedda bedder wadder heeder! |
| 6. | The American R | Get a better**rr** water**rr** heater**rr**! |
| 7. | Combination of Concepts 1–6 | **G**ɛdə bɛddrrr **wä**drrr heedrrr! |

---

**Review Exercise 4: Your Own Sentence**　　　　　　　　　　　　**Track 237**

*Pause the CD and apply the steps to your own sentences.*

| | |
|---|---|
| 1. | Intonation |
| 2. | Word groups |
| 3. | Liaisons |
| 4. | æ, ä, ə |
| 5. | The American T |
| 6. | The American R |
| 7. | Combination of Concepts 1–6 |

Are you shy? Does doing this embarrass you? Are you thinking that people will notice your new accent and criticize you for it? In the beginning, you may feel a little strange with these new sounds that you are using, but don't worry, it's like a new pair of shoes—they take awhile to break in and make comfortable. Nevertheless, I hope that you are enjoying this program. Adopting a new accent can become too personal and too emotional an issue, so don't take it too seriously. Relax. Have a good time. Play with the sounds that you are making. Whenever a word or phrase strikes your fancy, go somewhere private and comfortable and try out a couple of different approaches, styles, and attitudes with it—as you are going to do in the next exercise. If possible, record yourself on tape so you can decide which one suits you best.

　　你害羞吗？这样做让你尴尬吗？你是否在想，人们会注意到你的新口音并为此批评你？刚开始，对于你使用的这些新的音，你可能感到有点奇怪，但不必担心，这就像是一双新鞋——需要一段时间才能合脚，才能舒适。然而，我希望你能享受这个课程的乐趣。接受一个新的发音是非常私人和情绪化的事情，所以不必过于认真。放松，好好享受。以你正在发的音为乐。每当你喜欢上一个单词或短语，就去某个私人、舒适的地方，试着用几种不同的方式、风格或态度发出来——就像你在下个练习中要做的那样。如果有可能，用磁带录下自己的声音，这样你就能确定哪种发音最适合你。

## Review Exercise 5: Varying Emotions　　　　　　　　　　　　　　　**Track 239**

*Repeat the following statement and response expressing the various feelings or tone.*

| | | |
|---|---|---|
| **anger** | I told you it wouldn't work!! | I thought it would! |
| **excitement** | I told you it wouldn't work!! | I thought it would! |
| **disbelief** | I told you it wouldn't work? | And I thought it would? |
| **smugness** | I told you it wouldn't work. | I thought it would. *(I-told-you-so attitude)* |

| | | |
|---|---|---|
| **humor** | I told you it wouldn't work. | I thought it would. |
| **sadness** | I told you it wouldn't work. | I thought it would. |
| **relief** | I told you it wouldn't work. | Whew! I thought it would. |
| **resignation** | I told you it wouldn't work. | I thought it would. |

▶ Pause the CD and repeat the statement using three other tones that you'd like to try.

| | | |
|---|---|---|
| **Your choice** | I told you it wouldn't work. | I thought it would. |
| **Your choice** | I told you it wouldn't work. | I thought it would. |
| **Your choice** | I told you it wouldn't work. | I thought it would. |

Now that you've run through a couple of emotions and practiced speaking with both meaning and feeling, try having some two-word conversations. These are pretty common in day-to-day situations.

既然你已经练习了用几种不同的情绪来传情达意，那么试着说一些只有两个词的会话。这些会话在日常情景中很常见。

---

**Review Exercise 6: Really? Maybe!**                                      Track 240

*Repeat the following statements and responses expressing the various feelings.*

| | | | |
|---|---|---|---|
| 1. | Really? (general curiosity) | Maybe. | (general potential) |
| 2. | Really? (avid curiosity) | Maybe. | (suggestive possibility) |
| 3. | Really? (boredom) | Maybe | (equal boredom) |
| 4. | Really? (laughing with disbelief) | Maybe. | (slight possibility) |
| 5. | Really? (sarcasm) | Maybe. | (self-justification) |
| 6. | Really? (sadness) | Maybe. | (equal sadness) |
| 7. | Really? (relief) | Maybe. | (hope) |
| 8. | Really? (coy interrogation) | Maybe. | (coy confirmation) |
| 9. | Really? (seeking confirmation) | Rilly! | (confirmation) |

✗ *Pause the CD and try three on your own.*

| | | |
|---|---|---|
| 10. | Really? (your choice) | Maybe. (your choice) |
| 11. | Really? (your choice) | Maybe. (your choice) |
| 12. | Really? (your choice) | Maybe. (your choice) |

---

**Review Exercise 7: Who Did It? I Don't Know!**                          Track 241

*Repeat the following statements and responses expressing the various feelings.*

| | | |
|---|---|---|
| 1. | Who did it? (curiosity) | I don't know. (ignorance) |
| 2. | Who did it? (interrogation) | I don't know. (self-protection) |
| 3. | Who did it? (anger) | I don't know. (insistence) |
| 4. | Who did it? (repeating) | I don't know. (strong denial) |
| 5. | Who did it? (sarcasm) | I don't know. (self-justification) |
| 6. | Who did it? (sadness) | I don't know. (despair) |
| 7. | Who did it? (relief) | I sure don't know. (blithe ignorance) |
| 8. | Whooo did it? (coy interrogation) | I don't know. (singsong) |
| 9. | Who did it? (annoyance) | I don't know. (equal annoyance) |
| 10. | Who did it? (laughing with disbelief) | I don't know. (laughing ignorance) |
| 11. | Who did it? (surprise) | I dunno. (sullenness) |
| 12. | Who did it? (your choice) | I don't know. (your choice) |

**Review Exercise 8: Russian Rebellion**                                   **Track 242**

Rəshəz əfensəv əgɛnst rebəlz in thə brɛikəway reejənəv Chechnyə iz entering ə nyu fɛiz. än thə wən hænd, Rəshən forsəzr teiking fül kəntrol əv Gräzny, ənd Mäskæo sez thə wor seemz tə be trning in its feivr. än thee əthr hænd, thə rebəlz küd be reetreeding Gräzny jəst tə fight ənəthr day—enshring ə läng grrilə wor. Thə for-mənth känflikt täpt thee əjendə tədäy during Sɛkrətɛry əv State Mædəlin älbräit's täks with ækting Rəshən prezəd'nt Vlædəmir Putin, älbräit then left fr Kro⁽ʷ⁾ɛishə, əbæot which we will hear more shortly. Bət frst, we trn tə thə Wrldz Nenet Shevek in Mäskæo.

*"olbräit ɛn Pu-tin met feu l'nger thɛn plennd tədäy—feu nillee three äwɛz. äftə thɛə t'ks, olbrait k'ld thɛ meeting intens, bət plɛznt, ɛn 'feud this ɛsɛsmɛnt ɛf Rəshəz ɛkting prezidɛnt."*

"I fæond him ə very wellin formd persən. Heez äveeəslee ə Rəshən paytreeət ən älso səmwən who seeks a norməl pəzishən fr Rəshə within thə West—ən he strəck me əzə präbləm sälvr."

– ✦ –

Russia's offensive against rebels in the breakaway region of Chechnya is entering a new phase. On the one hand, Russian forces are taking full control of Grozny, and Moscow says the war seems to be turning in its favor. On the other hand, the rebels could be retreating Grozny just to fight another day—ensuring a long guerilla war. The four-month conflict topped the agenda today during Secretary of State Madeline Albright's talks with acting Russian president Vladimir Putin. Albright then left for Croatia, about which we'll hear more shortly. But first, we turn to the World's Nennet Shevek in Moscow.

*"Albright and Putin met for longer than planned today—for nearly three hours. After the talks, Albright called the meeting intense, but pleasant, and offered this assessment of Russia's acting president."*

"I found him a very well-informed person. He's obviously a Russian patriot and also someone who seeks a normal position for Russia within the West—and he struck me as a problem solver."

## Two-Word Phrases

二词短语

---

**Review Exercise A: Contrasting Descriptive and Set Phrases**          **Track 243**

---

*Here we are reprising the exercise from Exercises 6-1 to 6-14. To review, an adjective and a noun make a **descriptive phrase**, and the second word is stressed. Two nouns make a compound noun, or **set phrase**, and the first word is stressed. Repeat the following sentences. Copy your descriptive phrases and set phrases (from Exercise 6-8). You will continue using these word combinations throughout this series of exercises. (See also Chapter 6)*

| | **Descriptive Phrase** | **Set Phrase** |
|---|---|---|
| 1. | It's a short **nail**. | It's a **finger**nail. |
| 2. | It's a chocolate **cake**. | It's a **pan**cake. |
| 3. | It's a hot **bath**. | It's a **hot** tub. |
| 4. | It's a long **drive**. | It's a **hard** drive. |
| 5. | It's the back **door**. | It's the **back**bone. |
| 6. | There are four **cards**. | It's a **card** trick. |
| 7. | It's a small **spot**. | It's a **spot**light. |
| 8. | It's a good **book**. | It's a **phone** book. |
| 9. | It's a _____ | It's a _____ |
| 10. | It's a _____ | It's a _____ |
| 11. | It's a _____ | It's a _____ |

---

**Review Exercise B: Intonation Review Test**          **Track 244**

---

*Pause the CD and put an accent mark over the word that should be stressed.*

| | | | |
|---|---|---|---|
| 1. | They live in **Los Angeles**. | 11. | We like **everything**. |
| 2. | Give me a **paper bag**. | 12. | It's a **moving van**. |
| 3. | Is that your **lunch bag**? | 13. | It's a **new paper**. |
| 4. | 7-11 is a **convenience store**. | 14. | It's the **newspaper**. |
| 5. | Lucky's is a **convenient store**. | 15. | The doll has **glass eyes**. |
| 6. | Do your **homework**! | 16. | The doll has **eyeglasses**. |
| 7. | He's a **good writer**. | 17. | It's a **high chair**. |
| 8. | It's an **apple pie**. | 18. | It's a **high chair**. *(for babies)* |
| 9. | It's a **pineapple**. | 19. | It's a **baseball**. |
| 10. | We like **all things**. | 20. | It's a **blue ball**. |

# Three-Word Phrases

三词短语

**Review Exercise C: Modifying Descriptive Phrases**                    **Track 245**

*When you modify a **descriptive phrase** by adding an adjective or adverb, you maintain the original intonation pattern and simply add an additional stress point.*

| | **Descriptive Phrase** | **Modified Descriptive Phrase** |
|---|---|---|
| 1. | It's a short **nail**. | It's a **really** short **nail**. |
| 2. | It's a chocolate **cake**. | It's a **tasty** chocolate **cake**. |
| 3. | I took a hot **bath**. | I took a **long**, hot **bath**. |
| 4. | It's a hard **drive**. | It's a **long**, hard **drive**. |
| 5. | It's the **back door**. | It's the **only** back **door**. |
| 6. | There **are** four **cards**. | There **are four** slick **cards**. |
| 7. | It's a little **spot**. | It's a **little** black **spot**. |
| 8. | It's a good **book**. | It's a **really** good **book**. |
| 9. | It's a _____ | It's a _____ |
| 10. | It's a _____ | It's a _____ |
| 11. | It's a _____ | It's a _____ |

**Review Exercise D: Modifying Set Phrases**                    **Track 246**

*When you modify a **set phrase**, you maintain the same pattern, leaving the new adjective unstressed.*

| | **Set Phrase** | **Modified Set Phrase** |
|---|---|---|
| 1. | It's a **finger**nail. | It's a short **finger**nail. |
| 2. | It's a **pan**cake. | It's a delicious **pan**cake. |
| 3. | It's a **hot** tub. | It's a leaky **hot** tub. |
| 4. | It's a **hard** drive. | It's an expensive **hard** drive. |
| 5. | It's the **back**bone. | It's a long **back**bone. |
| 6. | It's a **card** trick. | It's a clever **card** trick. |
| 7. | It's a **spot**light. | It's a bright **spot**light. |
| 8. | It's a **phone** book. | It's the new **phone** book. |
| 9. | It's a _____ | It's a _____ |
| 10. | It's a _____ | It's a _____ |
| 11. | It's a _____ | It's a _____ |

**Review Exercise E: Two- and Three-Word Set Phrases**          **Track 247**

*You should be pretty familiar with the idea of a set phrase by now. The next step is when you have more components that link together to form a new thing—a three-word set phrase. Combine **three things**: finger + nail + clipper. Leave the stress on the first word: **finger**nail clipper. Although you are now using three words, they still mean **one new thing**. Write your own sentences, using the word combinations from the previous exercises.*

| | Two-Word Set Phrase | Three-Word Set Phrase |
|---|---|---|
| 1. | It's a **finger**nail. | It's a **finger**nail clipper. |
| 2. | It's a **pan**cake. | It's a **pan**cake shop. |
| 3. | It's a **hot** tub. | It's a **hot** tub maker. |
| 4. | It's a **hard** drive. | It's a **hard** drive holder. |
| 5. | It's the **back**bone. | It's a **back**bone massage. |
| 6. | It's a **playing** card. | It's a **playing** card rack. |
| 7. | It's a **spot**light. | It's a **spot**light stand. |
| 8. | It's a **phone** book. | It's a **phone** book listing. |
| 9. | It's a _____ | It's a _____ |
| 10. | It's a _____ | It's a _____ |
| 11. | It's a _____ | It's a _____ |

**Review Exercise F: Three-Word Phrase Summary**          **Track 248**

*Repeat the following sentences. Write your own sentences at the bottom, carrying over the same examples you used in the previous exercise.*

| Modified Description | Modified Set Phrase | 3-Word Set Phrase |
|---|---|---|
| 1. a **really** short **nail** | a long **finger**nail | a **finger**nail clipper |
| 2. a **big** chocolate **cake** | a thin **pan**cake | a **pan**cake shop |
| 3. a **long**, hot **bath** | a leaky **hot** tub | a **hot** tub maker |
| 4. a **long**, boring **drive** | a new **hard** drive | a **hard** drive holder |
| 5. a **broken** back **door** | a long **back**bone | a **back**bone massage |
| 6. **four** slick **cards** | a new **playing** card | a **playing** card rack |
| 7. a **small** black **spot** | a bright **spot**light | a **spot**light stand |
| 8. a **well**-written **book** | an open **phone** book | a **phone** book listing |
| 9. | a blind **sales**man | a **blind** salesman |
| | *(He can't see.)* | *(He sells blinds.)* |
| 10. | a light **house**keeper | a **light**house keeper |
| | *(She cleans the house.)* | *(She lives in a lighthouse.)* |
| 11. | a green **house**plant | a **green**house plant |
| | *(It's a healthy houseplant.)* | *(It's from a greenhouse.)* |

12. It's a _____ . It's a _____ . It's a _____ .
13. It's a _____ . It's a _____ . It's a _____ .
14. It's a _____ . It's a _____ . It's a _____ .

## Review Exercise G: Three-Word Phrase—The Three Little Pigs                    Track 249

*Notice where there are patterns, where the words change, but the rhythm stays the same (**straw**-cutting tools, **wood**cutting tools, **brick**laying tools). Read the story aloud.*

Once upon a time, there were **three** *little* **pigs**. They lived with their **kind** *old* **mother** near a **large**, *dark* **forest**. One day, they decided to build **their** *own* **houses**. *The* **first** *little* pig used straw. He took his **straw**-*cutting* **tools** and his *new* **lawn** mower and built a **little** straw **house**. The **second** *little* pig used sticks. He took his **wood**cutting **tools** and some *old* **paint**brushes and built a *small* **wooden** house. The **third** *little* pig, who was a **very** *hard* **worker**, used bricks. He took his **brick**laying **tools**, an *expensive* **mortar**board, and built a *large* **brick** house. In the forest, lived a **big** *bad* **wolf**. He wanted to eat the **three** *little* **pigs**, so he went to *the* **flimsy** *straw* **abode** and tried to blow it down. "Not by the hair of my **chinny** *chin* **chin**!" cried the **three** *little* **porkers**. But the house was **not** *very* **strong**, and the **big** *bad* **beast** blew it down. The **three** *little* **pigs** ran to the *rickety* **wooden** *structure*, but the **big** *bad* **wolf** blew it down, too. Quickly, the **three** *little* **piggies** ran to the *sturdy* **brick** *dwelling* and hid inside. The **big** *bad* **wolf** huffed and he puffed, but he couldn't blow the *strong* **brick** *house* down. The **three** *little* **pigs** laughed and danced and sang.

## Review Exercise H: Sentence Balance—Goldilocks                    Track 250

*One of the most fascinating things about spoken English is how the intonation prepares the listener for what is coming. As you know, the main job of intonation is to announce new information. However, there is a secondary function, and that is to alert the listener of changes down the road. Certain shifts will be dictated for the sake of **sentence balance**. Set phrases and contrast don't change, but the intonation of a **descriptive phrase** will move from the second word to the first, **without changing the meaning**. The stress change indicates that it's not the end of the sentence, but rather, there is more to come. This is why it is particularly important to speak in phrases, instead of word by word.*

*When we practiced* Goldilocks and the Three Bears *the first time, we had very short sentences so we didn't need sentence balance. All of the blue descriptive phrases would otherwise be stressed on the second word, if the shift weren't needed.*

There is a **little** *girl* called **Goldi**locks. She is **walking** *through* a *sunny* **forest** and sees a *small* **house**. She **knocks** *on* the door, but **no** *one* answers. She **goes** *inside* to see what's **there**. There are **three** *chairs* in the *large* **room**. **Goldilocks** sits on the **biggest** chair. It's **too** *high* for her to **sit** *on*. She sits on the **middle**-*sized* one, but it's is *too* **low**. She sits on the **small** *chair* and it is *just* **right**. On the table, there are **three** *bowls* of **porridge**. She tries the **first** *one*, but it is **too** *hot* to **swallow**. The **second** *one* is *too* **cold**, and the **third** *one* is *just* **right**, so she eats it all. **After** *that*, she **goes** *upstairs* to look **around**. There are **three** *beds* in the **bed**room.

She *sits* down on the **biggest** one. It's **too** hard to **sleep** on. The **middle**-*sized* bed is *too* **soft**. The **little** one is *just* **right,** so she **lies** down and falls **asleep.**

In the *meantime,* the family of *three* **bears** comes home—the **Papa** bear, the **Mama** bear, and the **Baby** bear. They **look** around and **say,** "Who's been sitting in our chairs and eating our porridge?" Then they **run** upstairs and **say,** "Who's been sleeping in our beds?" **Goldilocks wakes** up when she hears all the **noise** and is **so scared** that she **runs** out of the house and never *comes* **back.**

## Four-Word Phrases
四词短语

| Review Exercise I: Multiple Modifiers with Set Phrases | Track 251 |
|---|---|

*When you continue to modify a set phrase, you maintain the original intonation pattern and simply add an additional stress point.*

| | **Modified Set Phrase** | **Remodified Set Phrase** |
|---|---|---|
| 1. | It's a short **finger**nail. | It's a **really** short **finger**nail. |
| 2. | It's a banana **pan**cake. | It's a **tasty** banana **pan**cake. |
| 3. | It's a leaky **hot** tub. | It's a **leaky** old **hot** tub. |
| 4. | It's a new **hard** drive. | It's a **brand**-new **hard** drive. |
| 5. | It's a long **back**bone. | It's a **long,** hard **back**bone. |
| 6. | It's a wrinkled **playing** card. | It's a **wrinkled,** old **playing** card. |
| 7. | It's a bright **spot**light. | It's a **bright** white **spot**light. |
| 8. | It's the new **phone** book. | It's a **new**-age **phone** book. |
| 9. | It's a _____ | It's a _____ |
| 10. | It's a _____ | It's a _____ |
| 11. | It's a _____ | It's a _____ |

| Review Exercise J: Compound Intonation of Numbers | Track 252 |
|---|---|

*In short phrases (#1 and #2), **-teen** can be thought of as a separate word in terms of intonation. In longer phrases, the number + **-teen** becomes one word. Repeat after me.*

| 1. How **old** is he? | 2. How long has it **been?** | 3. How **old** is he? |
|---|---|---|
| He's four**teen.** (for**téen**) | **Fourteen years.** | He's **fourteen** years **old.** |
| He's **for**ty. (**fór**dy) | Forty **years.** | He's **forty** years **old.** |

**Review Exercise K: Modifying Three-Word Set Phrases**　　　　　**Track 253**

*When you continue to modify a set phrase, you maintain the original intonation pattern and simply add an unstressed modifier.*

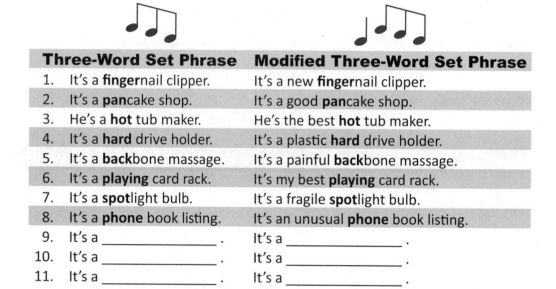

| | Three-Word Set Phrase | Modified Three-Word Set Phrase |
|---|---|---|
| 1. | It's a **finger**nail clipper. | It's a new **finger**nail clipper. |
| 2. | It's a **pan**cake shop. | It's a good **pan**cake shop. |
| 3. | He's a **hot** tub maker. | He's the best **hot** tub maker. |
| 4. | It's a **hard** drive holder. | It's a plastic **hard** drive holder. |
| 5. | It's a **back**bone massage. | It's a painful **back**bone massage. |
| 6. | It's a **playing** card rack. | It's my best **playing** card rack. |
| 7. | It's a **spot**light bulb. | It's a fragile **spot**light bulb. |
| 8. | It's a **phone** book listing. | It's an unusual **phone** book listing. |
| 9. | It's a _____ . | It's a _____ . |
| 10. | It's a _____ . | It's a _____ . |
| 11. | It's a _____ . | It's a _____ . |

**Rev. Exercise L: Four-Word Phrase Story—Little Red Riding Hood**　　　**Track 254**

*Repeat after me.*

Once upon a time, there was a ***cute** little **red**head* named ***Little** Red **Riding** Hood*. One day, she told her mother that she wanted to take a ***well**-stocked **picnic** basket* to her ***dear** old **grand**mother* on the other side of the ***dark**, scary Black **Forest***. Her mother warned her not to talk to strangers—especially the *dangerous **big** bad **wolf***. ***Little** Red **Riding** Hood* said she would be careful, and left. Halfway there, she saw a ***mild**-mannered **hitch**hiker*. She pulled over in her ***bright** red **sports** car* and offered him a ride. Just before they got to the ***free**way **turn**off* for her *old **grand**mother's house*, the ***heavily** bearded young **man*** jumped out and ran away. (Was he the wolf?) He hurried ahead to the *waiting **grand**mother's house*, let himself in, ate her, and jumped into her bed to wait for ***Little** Red **Riding** Hood*. When ***Little** Red **Riding** Hood* got to the house, she was surprised, "Grandmother, what big *eyes* you have!" The wolf replied, "The better to *see* you with, my dear..." "But Grandmother, what big *ears* you have!" "The better to *hear* you with, my dear..." "Oh, Grandmother, what big *teeth* you have!" "The better to *eat* you with!" And the wolf jumped out of the bed to eat ***Little** Red **Riding** Hood*. Fortunately for her, she was a ***recently** paid-up **member*** of the infamous *National **Rifle** Association* so she pulled out her ***brand**-new **shotgun*** and shot the wolf dead.

**Review Exercise M: Building Up to Five-Word Phrases**      **Track 255**

*Repeat after me, then pause the CD and write your own phrases, using the same order and form.*

| | | |
|---|---|---|
| 1. | It's a **pot**. | *noun* |
| 2. | It's **new**. | *adjective* |
| 3. | It's a new **pot**. | *descriptive phrase (noun)* |
| 4. | It's brand-**new**. | *descriptive phrase (adjective)* |
| 5. | It's a **brand**-new pot. | *modified descriptive phrase* |
| 6. | It's a **tea**pot. | *two-word set phrase* |
| 7. | It's a new **tea**pot. | *modified set phrase* |
| 8. | It's a **brand**-new **tea**pot. | *modified set phrase* |
| 9. | It's a **tea**pot lid. | *three-word set phrase* |
| 10. | It's a new **tea**pot lid. | *modified three-word set phrase* |
| 11. | It's a **brand**-new **tea**pot lid. | *modified three-word set phrase* |

| | | |
|---|---|---|
| 1. | _____ | *noun* |
| 2. | _____ | *adjective* |
| 3. | _____ | *descriptive phrase (noun)* |
| 4. | _____ | *descriptive phrase (adjective)* |
| 5. | _____ | *modified descriptive phrase* |
| 6. | _____ | *two-word set phrase* |
| 7. | _____ | *modified set phrase* |
| 8. | _____ | *modified set phrase* |
| 9. | _____ | *three-word set phrase* |
| 10. | _____ | *modified three-word set phrase* |
| 11. | _____ | *modified three-word set phrase* |

**Track 256**

Since so many people are familiar with the binary system, let's do a quick review of how complex intonation can be viewed with zeroes and ones.

既然很多人都很熟悉数学中的二进制，那么我们就来快速地复习一下综合语调怎样用0和1来表示。

| | |
|---|---|
| **pot** | 1 |
| **new** | 1 |
| new **pot** | 01 |
| brand-**new** | 01 |
| **brand**-new **pot** | 101 |
| **tea**pot | 10 |
| new **tea**pot | 010 |
| **brand**-new **tea**pot | 1010 |
| **tea**pot lid | 100 |
| new **tea**pot lid | 0100 |
| **brand**-new **tea**pot lid | 10100 |

Do a global **Search All** and **Replace** for these patterns.

对这些重读方式进行全面的"搜索"和"替换"。

| Review Exercise 9: Ignorance on Parade | Track 257 |
| --- | --- |

*Now, let's dissect a standard paragraph, including its title, as we did in Review Exercise 1. **First**—in the boxes in the first paragraph, decide which is a descriptive phrase, which is a set phrase, and where any additional stress might fall. Use one of your colored markers to indicate the stressed words. **Second**—go through the paragraph and mark the remaining stressed words. **Third**—put slash marks where you think a short pause is appropriate. Listen as I read the paragraph. (See also Chapters 4 and 11)*

✘ Pause the CD and do the written exercises including intonation; word groups; liaisons; **æ, ä, ə**; and the American **T**.

1.  ***Two-word phrases, intonation, and phrasing***
    二词短语、语调和断句

    **Ignorance on Parade**

    You say you don't know a proton from a crouton? Well, you're not the only one. A recent nationwide survey funded by the National Science Foundation shows that fewer than 6 percent of American adults can be called scientifically literate. The rest think that DNA is a food additive, Chernobyl is a ski resort, and radioactive milk can be made safe by boiling. *Judith Stone / 2109 Discover Publications*

2.  ***Word connections***
    词的连读

    **Ignoran sän Parade**

    You say you don't know a proton from a crouton? Well, you're not the only one. A recent nationwide survey funded by the National Science Foundation shows that fewer than 6 percent of American adults can be called scientifically literate. The rest think that DNA is a food additive, Chernobyl is a ski resort, and radioactive milk can be made safe by boiling.

3.  ***æ, ä, ə***
    æ, ä, ə

    **Ignərənce än Pərade**

    You say you don't know a proton from a crouton? Well, you're not the only one. A recent nationwide survey funded by the National Science Foundation shows that fewer than 6 percent of American adults can be called scientifically literate. The rest think that DNA is a food additive, Chernobyl is a ski resort, and radioactive milk can be made safe by boiling.

### 4. *The American T*
美音中的T

**Ignorants on Parade**

You say you don't know a proton from a crouton? Well, you're not the only one. A recent nationwide survey funded by the National Science Foundation shows that fewer than 6 percent of American adults can be called scientifically literate. The rest think that DNA is a food additive, Chernobyl is a ski resort, and radioactive milk can be made safe by boiling.

---

## Review Exercise 10: Ignorance on Parade Explanations

*Here, go over each topic, point by point.*

### 1. *Two-word phrases, intonation, and phrasing*
二词短语、语调和断句

a **proton** from a **crouton**? *(contrast)*
Well, **you're** not the **only** one. *(contrast)*
A **recent** nationwide **survey** *(modified descriptive phrase)*
National **Science** Foundation *(modified set phrase)*
**6** percent of American **adults** *(descriptive phrase with sentence balance)*
scientifically **literate** *(descriptive phrase)*
The **rest** think *(contrast)*
DN**A** *(acronym)*
**food** additive *(set phrase)*
**ski** resort *(set phrase)*
radioactive **milk** *(descriptive phrase)*

**Ig**norance on Pa**rade**(stop)
You say you don't know a **pro**ton from a **crou**ton? (pause) Well,(pause) you're not the **only** one.(pause) A **recent** nationwide **survey**(pause) funded by the National **Science** Foundation(pause) shows that fewer than **6** percent of American **adults**(pause) can be called scientifically **liter**ate.(stop) The **rest** think(pause) that DNA is a **food** additive,(pause) Cher**no**byl is a **ski** resort,(pause) and radioactive **milk**(pause) can be made **safe** by **boiling**.

### 2. *Word connections*
词的连读

**Ig**noran sän Pa**rade**

You sa(y)you don(t)knowa **pro**ton froma **crou**ton? Well, you're no(t)the(y)**only** one. A **re**cen(t)nationwide**sur**vey funded by the National**Sci**(y)ence Foundation showzthat fewer than**six** percen'v'merica na**dults** can be called scientifically **lit**erate. The **ress**think that Dee(y)ɛNA(y)iza **foo** daddittive, Cher**no**byliza **ski** resort, and radi(y)o(w)active **milk** can be made**safe** by **boiling**.

**3.** *æ, ä, ə*

æ, ä, ə

**Ign**ərənce **än** Pə**rade**

You say you dont know ə **pro**tän frəm ə **croo**tän? Well, yer nät thee⁽ʸ⁾**only** wən. ə **res**ənt nashənwide **srvey** fəndəd by thə Næshənəl **Sci**⁽ʸ⁾əns Fæondashən showz thət fewər thən **6** pr senəv əmerəcən **əd**əlts cən be cälld sci⁽ʸ⁾əntifəklee **lid**erət. Thə **rest** think thət Dee Yeh **Nay**⁽ʸ⁾izə **food** æddətv, Chrnobl izə **skee** rəzort, ən radee⁽ʸ⁾o⁽ʷ⁾ æctəv **milk** cən be made **safe** by **boil**ing.

**4.** *The American T*

美音中的T

**Ign**orants on Pa**rade**

You say you don⁽ᵗ⁾ know a **pro**Ton from a **crou**Ton? Well, you're nä⁽ᵗ⁾ the **only** one. A **recen**⁽ᵗ⁾ nationwide **sur**vey funded by the National **Sci**ence Foundation shows tha⁽ᵗ⁾ fewer than **6** percen of American a**dulT**s can be called scienTifically **lid**erə⁽ᵗ⁾. The **ress** think tha⁽ᵗ⁾ DNA is a **food** addidive, Cher**no**byl is a **ski** resor⁽ᵗ⁾, and radioakdiv **milk** can be made **safe** by **boil**ing.

**5.** *Combined*

结合

**Ign**ərən **sän** Pə**rade**

You sa⁽ʸ⁾you don⁽ᵗ⁾no wə **pro**tän frəmə **croo**tän?⁽ˢᵗᵒᵖ⁾Well,⁽ᵖᵃᵘˢᵉ⁾yer nät thee⁽ʸ⁾**only** wən. ⁽ᵖᵃᵘˢᵉ⁾ə **rees**ən⁽ᵗ⁾nāshənwide **srvey**⁽ᵖᵃᵘˢᵉ⁾fəndəd by thə Næshənəl **Sci**⁽ʸ⁾əns Fæondāshən⁽ᵖᵃᵘˢᵉ⁾shoz thə⁽ᵗ⁾ fewər thən **6** prcenə vəmerəcə nədəlts⁽ᵖᵃᵘˢᵉ⁾cən be cälld sci⁽ʸ⁾əntifəklee **lid**erət.⁽ˢᵗᵒᵖ⁾Thə **ress** think⁽ᵖᵃᵘˢᵉ⁾thə⁽ᵗ⁾ Dee Yeh **Nay**⁽ʸ⁾izə **foo** dæddədv,⁽ᵖᵃᵘˢᵉ⁾ Chrnobə lizə **skee** rəzort,⁽ᵖᵃᵘˢᵉ⁾ən raydee⁽ʸ⁾o⁽ʷ⁾æctəv **milk**⁽ᵖᵃᵘˢᵉ⁾cən be made **sāfe** by **boil**ing.

## More Reduced Sounds
## 更多的弱读音

**Track 258**

There are two sounds that look similar but sound quite different. One is the tense vowel **u**, pronounced *ooh*, and the other is the soft vowel **ü**, whose pronunciation is a combination of *ih* and *uh*. The **u** sound is located far forward in the mouth and requires you to round your lips. The **ü** is one of the four reduced vowel sounds that are made in the throat: the most tense, and highest in the throat is **ε**, next, slightly more relaxed is **i**, then **ü**, and deepest and most relaxed is the neutral schwa **ə**. For the reduced semivowel *schwa + R*, the throat is relaxed, but the tongue is tense. (See also Chapters 3, 12, 15, and 20)

有两个音，看起来相似，但听起来很不同。一个是紧元音u，发音为ooh，另一个是松元音ü，它的发音是ih和uh的结合。u音在口腔非常靠前的位置，发音时需要收圆嘴唇。ü音是四个弱读元音之一，在喉部产生：喉部产生的最紧、最高的音是ε音，其次放松一点的是i音，然后是ü音，最深、最放松的音是非中央元音ə音。发弱读半元音"非中央元音+R"时，喉部是放松的，但舌头是紧张的。（也见第3、12、15和20章）

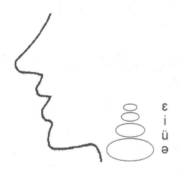

| Exercise 18-1: Comparing u and ü | Track 259 |
|---|---|

*Look at the chart that follows and repeat each word. We are contrasting the sound **u** (first and third columns)—a strong, nonreducible sound, **ooh**, that is made far forward in the mouth, with the lips fully rounded—with the reduced **ü** sound in the second and fourth columns.*

|  | u | ü |  | u | ü |
|---|---|---|---|---|---|
| 1. | booed | book | 11. | Luke | look |
| 2. | boo | bushel | 12. | nuke | nook |
| 3. | cooed | could | 13. | pool | pull |
| 4. | cool | cushion | 14. | pooch | put |
| 5. | food | foot | 15. | shoe | sugar |
| 6. | fool | full | 16. | suit | soot |
| 7. | gooed | good | 17. | shoot | should |
| 8. | who'd | hood | 18. | stewed | stood |
| 9. | kook | cook | 19. | toucan | took |
| 10. | crew | crook | 20. | wooed | would |

*OO,, OH,,*

*bük bük*

*No lips!*

For the **ooh** sound, round your lips like a fish. For the **ü** sound, think of a chicken. Chickens don't have lips, so they certainly can't round them. You have to say **ü** down in the back of your throat.

发ooh音时，像鱼一样收圆嘴唇。发ü音时，想象鸡的样子。鸡没有嘴唇，所以当然无法收圆嘴唇。你需要从喉咙的后部发出ü音。

---

## Exercise 18-2: Lax Vowels                                   Track 260

*The lax vowels are produced in the throat and are actually quite similar to each other. Let's practice some lax vowels. See also Chapter 20 to contrast with tense vowels. Remember to double the vowel when the word ends in a voiced consonant.*

|  | e | i | ü | ə | ər |
|---|---|---|---|---|---|
| 1. | end | it | ▇ | un- | earn |
| 2. | bet | bit | book | but | burn |
| 3. | kept | kid | could | cut | curt |
| 4. | check | chick | ▇ | chuck | church |
| 5. | debt | did | ▇ | does | dirt |
| 6. | fence | fit | foot | fun | first |
| 7. | fell | fill | full | ▇ | furl |
| 8. | get | guilt | good | gut | girl |
| 9. | help | hit | hook | hut | hurt |
| 10. | held | hill | hood | hull | hurl |
| 11. | gel | Jill | ▇ | jump | jerk |
| 12. | ked | kid | cook | cud | curd |
| 13. | crest | crypt | crook | crumb | ▇ |
| 14. | let | little | look | lump | lurk |
| 15. | men | milk | ▇ | muck | murmur |
| 16. | net | knit | nook | nut | nerd |
| 17. | pet | pit | put | putt | pert |

**Tense Vowels**

| Sound | Symbol | Spelling |
|---|---|---|
| ɛi | bāt | bait |
| ee | bēt | beat |
| äi | bīt | bite |
| ou | bō<sup>u</sup>t | boat |
| ooh | būt | boot |
| ah | bät | bought |
| ä + ɛ | bæt | bat |
| æ + o | bæot | bout |

**Lax Vowels**

| Sound | Symbol | Spelling |
|---|---|---|
| eh | bɛt | bet |
| ih | bit | bit |
| ih + uh | püt | put |
| uh | bət | but |
| er | bərt | Bert |

| 18. | pell | pill | pull | ▮ | pearl |
|---|---|---|---|---|---|
| 19. | red | rid | root | rut | rural |
| 20. | said | sit | soot | such | search |
| 21. | shed | shin | should | shut | sure |
| 22. | sled | slim | ▮ | slug | slur |
| 23. | stead | still | stood | stuff | stir |
| 24. | It's stewed. | It'd stick. | It stood. | It's done. | It's dirt. |
| 25. | stretch | string | ▮ | struck | ▮ |
| 26. | tell | tip | took | ton | turn |
| 27. | then | this | ▮ | thus | ▮ |
| 28. | ▮ | thing | | thug | third |
| 29. | vex | vim | ▮ | vug | verb |
| 30. | wet | wind | would | was | word |
| 31. | yet | yin | ▮ | young | yearn |
| 32. | zen | Zinfandel | ▮ | result | deserve |

Eh (Lax)

Eee (Tense)

---

**Exercise 18-3: Bit or Beat?**                                    **Track 261**

---

*We've discussed intonation in terms of new information, contrast, opinion, and negatives. Americans tend to stretch out certain one-syllable words...but which ones? The answer is simple—when a one syllable word ends in an unvoiced consonant, the vowel is on a* **single** *stairstep—short and sharp. When the word ends in a voiced consonant, or a vowel, the vowel is on a* **double** *stairstep. You can also think of this in terms of musical notes.*

*Here you are going to compare the four words* **bit**, **bid**, **beat**, *and* **bead**. *Once you can distinguish these four, all of the rest are easy. Repeat.*

|  | single | double |
|---|---|---|
| **tense** | beat | bead |
| **lax** | bit | bid |

**Note** *You may hear* **tense vowels** *called* **long vowels**, *but this can cause confusion when you are talking about the long, or doubled, vowel before a voiced consonant. Use the rubber band to distinguish: make a short, sharp snap for the single-note words (beat, bit) and a longer, stretched-out loop for the double-note words (bead, bid).*

注意：你可能听到过把紧元音叫做长元音，但当你说到浊辅音前的长元音或双元音时，这会引起混淆。用橡皮筋来区分：对于单音符单词（beat，bit），拉动橡皮筋形成短而急促的啪啪声；对于双音符单词（bead，bid），拉动橡皮筋形成伸长、延展的橡皮圈。

---

**Exercise 18-4: Bit or Beat? Bid or Bead?**                       **Track 262**

---

*Read each column down. Next, contrast the single and double tense vowels with each other and the single and double lax vowels with each other.*

| | Tense Vowels | | Lax Vowels | |
|---|---|---|---|---|
| 1. | beat | bead | bit | bid |
| 2. | seat | seed | sit | Sid |
| 3. | heat | he'd | hit | hid |
| 4. | Pete | impede | pit | rapid |
| 5. | feet | feed | fit | fin |
| 6. | niece | knees | miss | Ms. |
| 7. | geese | he's | hiss | his |
| 8. | deep | deed | disk | did |
| 9. | neat | need | knit | (nid) |
| 10. | leaf | leave | lift | live |

**Track 263**

*Finally, read all four across.*

**Note** *Bear in mind that the single/double intonation pattern is the same for all final voiced and unvoiced consonants, not just **T** and **D**.*

注意：记住，不仅仅是T和D，对于所有的末尾浊辅音和清辅音，单音符/双音符单词的语调模式都是相同的。

---

**Exercise 18-5: Tense and Lax Vowel Exercise**                                    **Track 264**

*Let's practice tense and lax vowels in context. The intonation is marked for you. When in doubt, try to leave out the lax vowel rather than run the risk of overpronouncing it: **l'p** in place of **lip**, so it doesn't sound like **leap**. Repeat.*

| | Tense | Lax | |
|---|---|---|---|
| 1. | eat | it | I **eat** it. |
| 2. | beat | bit | The **beat** is a bit strong. |
| 3. | keys | kiss | Give me a **kiss** for the keys. |
| 4. | cheek | chick | The chick's **cheek** is soft. |
| 5. | deed | did | He **did** the **deed**. |
| 6. | feet | fit | These **shoes** fit my **feet**. |
| 7. | feel | fill | Do you feel that we should **fill** it? |
| 8. | green | grin | The Martian's **grin** was **green**. |
| 9. | heat | hit | Last **summer**, the **heat** hit **hard**. |
| 10. | heel | hill | Put your **heel** on the **hill**. |
| 11. | jeep | Jill | Jill's **jeep** is here. |
| 12. | creep | crypt | Let's **creep** near the **crypt**. |
| 13. | leap | lip | He bumped his **lip** when he **leaped**. |
| 14. | meal | mill | She had a **meal** at the **mill**. |
| 15. | neat | knit | He can **knit** neatly. |

| 16. | peel | pill | Don't **peel** that **pill**! |
|-----|------|------|------------------------------|
| 17. | reed | rid | Get **rid** of the **reed**. |
| 18. | seek | sick | We seek the **sixth** sick sheik's **sheep**. |
| 19. | sheep | ship | There are **sheep** on the **ship**. |
| 20. | sleep | slip | The girl **sleeps** in a **slip**. |
| 21. | steal | still | He still **steals**. |
| 22. | Streep | strip | Meryl **Streep** is in a **comic** strip. |
| 23. | team | Tim | **Tim** is on the **team**. |
| 24. | these | this | **These** are better than **this** one. |
| 25. | thief | thing | The **thief** took my **thing**. |
| 26. | weep | whip | Who **weeps** from the **whips**? |

**Track 265**

In the time you have taken to reach this point in the program, you will have made a lot of decisions about your own individual speech style. Pronunciation of reduced sounds is more subjective and depends on how quickly you speak, how you prefer to express yourself, the range of your intonation, how much you want to reduce certain vowels, and so on.

学到课程的这个地方，你已经做了很多有关自己个人语言风格的决定。弱读音的发音更加主观，并且取决于你说话的速度，你喜欢的表达自己的方式，你的语调调域以及你想将某个元音弱读的程度等。

## Exercise 18-6: The Middle "I" List                    Track 266

*The letter I in the unstressed position devolves consistently into a schwa. Repeat.*

| | | | | |
|--------|--------|-------------|-------------|----------------|
| -ity | ədee | **chemi**stry | hos**ti**lity | oppor**tu**nity |
| -ify | əfái | chrono**lo**gical | hu**ma**nity | organi**za**tion |
| -ited | əd'd | **cla**rity | hu**mi**dity | par**tia**lity |
| -ible | əb°l | com**mo**dity | hu**mi**lity | **phy**sical |
| -ical | əc°l | com**mu**nity | i**den**tity | **pi**tiful |
| -imal | əm°l | communi**ca**tion | imi**ta**tion | **po**litics |
| -ization | əzāsh'n | com**plex**ity | imma**tu**rity | **po**sitive |
| -ication | əcāsh'n | **con**fident | immi**gra**tion | **po**ssible |
| -ination | ənāsh'n | confidenti**a**lity | im**mu**nity | possi**bi**lity |
| -ifaction | əfæksh'n | contri**bu**tion | **in**cident | **pre**sident |
| -itation | ətāsh'n | crea**ti**vity | individu**a**lity | **prin**ciple |
| | | **cre**dit | in**fi**nity | pri**o**rity |
| ability | | **cri**tical | inse**cu**rity | psycho**lo**gical |
| **acci**dent | | **cu**bicle | insta**bi**lity | pub**li**city |
| accounta**bi**lity | | **cu**riosity | **in**stitute | **qua**lify |
| ac**ti**vity | | **dif**ficult | investi**ga**tion | **qua**lity |

| | | | |
|---|---|---|---|
| ad**ver**si ty | **dig**ni ty | in**vis**i ble | **quan**ti ty |
| A**mer**i ca | di**spar**i ty | in vi**ta**tion | **rad**i cal |
| ana**lyt**i cal | di**ver**si ty | **jan**i tor | re**al**i ty |
| **an**i mal | **Ed**i son | **Jen**ni fer | **rec**ti fy |
| **ap**pli cant | **ed**i tor | legali**za**tion | **res**i dent |
| appli**ca**tion | elec**tric**i ty | lia**bil**i ty | responsi**bil**i ty |
| **ar**ti cle | eli gi **bil**i ty | **Mad**i son | **sac**ri fice |
| astro**nom**i cal | e**lim**i nated | ma**tur**i ty | **san**i ty |
| **au**di ble | engi**neer** | **med**i cine | se**cur**i ty |
| **au**di tor | **ep**i sode | men**tal**i ty | **sem**i nar |
| au**thor**i ty | e**qual**i ty | ma**jor**i ty | sen**ior**i ty |
| a**vail**a bili ty | **ev**i dence | **max**i mum | se**ver**i ty |
| **beau**ti ful | ex**per**i ment | **Mich**i gan | sen**si**ti vi ty |
| bru**tal**i ty | fa**cil**i ty | **min**i mum | **sim**i lar |
| ca**lam**i ty | famili**ar**i ty | mi**nor**i ty | **skep**ti cal |
| Cali**for**ni a | feasi**bil**i ty | **mod**i fy | super**ior**i ty |
| **can**di date | flexi**bil**i ty | **Mon**i ca | **tech**ni cal |
| ca**pac**i ty | **Flor**i da | **mon**i tor | **tes**ti fy |
| ce**leb**ri ty | **for**eign er | munici**pal**i ty | **typ**i cal |
| **char**i ty | for**mal**i ty | nation**al**i ty | **uni**form |
| Christi**an**i ty | fra**ter**ni ty | naturali**za**tion | **uni**ty |
| **clin**i cal | **grav**i ty | ne**ces**si ty | uni**ver**si ty |
| **cler**i cal | he**red**i ty | **neg**a ti ve | va**lid**i ty |
| **chem**i cal | hospi**tal**i ty | nomi**na**tion | **vis**i tor |

---

**Exercise 18-7: Reduction Options**      **Track 267**

*In the following example, you will see how you can fully sound out a word (such as* to*), replace it slightly, or do away with it altogether.*

1. ...easier tŭ⁽ʷ⁾ənderstand.
2. ...easier tü⁽ʷ⁾ənderstand.
3. ...easier tə ənderstand.
4. ...easier tənderstand.
5. ...easier dənderstand.

Each of the preceding examples is correct and appropriate when said well. If you have a good understanding of intonation, you might be best understood if you used the last example.

上述每个例子，当说得恰当时，都是正确、合适的。如果你对语调理解得透彻，那么使用最后一个例子或许最易被别人理解。

How would this work with the rest of our familiar paragraph, you ask? Let's see.

你或许会问，对于我们熟悉的段落的其他部分，弱读音是怎样发音的呢？我们一起来看一下。

**Exercise 18-8: Finding Reduced Sounds**  Track 268

*Go through the paragraph that follows and find the three **ü**'s and the five to seven **u**'s. Remember that your own speech style can increase the possibilities. With "**to**" before a vowel, you have a choice of a strong **u**, a soft **ü**, a **schwa**, or to telescope the two words and eliminate the vowel entirely. Pause the CD to mark the **ü** and **u** sounds. The first one is marked for you.*

**Hello, my** name is_____. I'm taking American **Accent** Training. There's a **lot** to **learn**, but I **hope** to make it as **enjoyable** as possible. I shüd pick **up** on the American **intonation** pattern pretty **easily**, although the **only** way to **get** it is to **practice** all of the time. I ūse the **up** and down, or **peaks** and valleys, **intonation** more than I **used** to. I've been paying attention to **pitch, too.** It's like **walking** down a **stair**case. I've been **talking** to a lot of **Americans** lately, and they tell me that I'm **easier** to under**stand. Any**way, I could go **on** and on, but the **important** thing is to **listen** well and sound **good. Well,** what do you **think? Do** I?

Track 269

## All Prefixes Have a Schwa

| | | | | | | |
|---|---|---|---|---|---|---|
| **a-** | avert | attend | appellate | attract | apportion | adduce |
| **con/com-** | convert | contend | compel | contract | comport | conduct |
| **di/dis/de-** | divert | distend | dispel | distract | deport | deduct/deduce |
| **e/ex-** | evert | extend | expel | extract | export | educate |
| **in/im-** | invert | intend | impel | intractable | import | induce |
| **pro/pre/per-** | pervert | pretend | propel | protract | proportion | produce |
| **re-** | revert | retain | repel | retract | report | reduce |

**Exercise 18-9: How Much Wood Would a Woodchuck Chuck?**  Track 270

*How fast can you say:*

| | |
|---|---|
| How much wood | hæo məch wüd |
| would a woodchuck chuck, | wüdə wüdchək chək |
| if a woodchuck | ifə wüdchəck |
| could chuck | cüd chəck |
| wood? | wüd |

| | |
|---|---|
| How many cookies | hæo meny cükeez |
| could a good cook cook, | cüdə güd cük cük |
| if a good cook | ifə güd cük |
| could cook | cüd cük |
| cookies? | cükeez |

In the following two exercises, we will practice the two vowel sounds separately.
在下面这两个练习中，我们将分别练习这两个元音。

## Exercise 18-10: Büker Wülsey's Cükbük                    Track 271

*Repeat after me.*

Booker Woolsey was a good cook. One day, he took a good look at his full schedule and decided that he could write a good cookbook. He knew that he could and thought that he should, but he wasn't sure that he ever would. Once he had made up his mind, he stood up, pulled up a table, took a cushion, and put it on a bushel basket of sugar in the kitchen nook. He shook out his writing hand and put his mind to creating a good, good cookbook.

## Exercise 18-11: A True Fool                              Track 272

*Repeat after me.*

A true fool will choose to drool in a pool to stay cool. Who knew that such fools were in the schools, used tools, and flew balloons? Lou knew and now you do, too.

Track 273

People often ask if **Tuesday** and **newspaper** are pronounced **Tiuzday** and **niuzpaper** or **Toozday** and **noozpaper**. Most Americans tend toward the latter, but you can go either way. On some words, however, you cannot add that extra **i** sound, as with **shoes** or **cool**.

人们总会问Tuesday和newspaper是发音为Tiuzday和niuzpaper还是Toozday和noozpaper。大部分的美国人倾向于后者，但是两种发音方式都可以。但是，对于一些单词来说，你不能增加那个i音，如shoes和cool。

# Chapter 19
# 第19章

# "V" as in Victory
# "V" 的发音

**Track 274**

When pronounced correctly, **V** shouldn't stand out too much. Its sound, although noticeable, is small. As a result, people, depending on their native language, sometimes confuse **V** with **B** (Spanish, Japanese), with **F** (German), or with **W** (Chinese, Hindi). These four sounds are not at all interchangeable.

在正确发音时，V音不会特别突兀。V的发音虽然显著，但是比较轻微。结果，受母语的影响，人们有时将V音和B音混淆（西班牙语、日语），有时和F音混淆（德语），有时和W音混淆（汉语、印地语）。这四个音根本不可互换。

The **W** is a semivowel, and there is no friction or contact. The **B**, like **P**, uses both lips and has a slight pop. Americans tend to have a strong, popping **P**. You can check your pronunciation by holding a match, a sheet of paper, or just your hand in front of your mouth. If the flame goes out, the paper wavers, or you feel a distinct puff of air on your hand, you've said **P** not **B**. **B** is the voiced pair of **P**.

W音是个半元音，发音时没有口腔摩擦或接触。B音和P音一样，运用双唇并有轻微的爆破。美国人发P音时往往喜欢强烈爆破。你可以拿一根火柴、一张纸，或只将你的手放在嘴的前方来检验你的发音。如果火苗熄灭，纸片颤动，或者你的手感到一股明显的气流，你发的就是P音，而不是B音。B音是与P音相对应的浊音。

Although **F** and **V** are in exactly the same position, **F** is a hiss and **V** is a buzz. The **V** is the voiced pair of **F**, as you saw in Chapter 11. When you say **F**, it is as if you are *whispering*. So, for **V**, say **F** and simply add some voice to it, which is the whole difference between *fairy* and *very,* as you will hear in our next exercise.

尽管F音和V音的发音位置完全相同，但F是清辅音，V是浊辅音。V是与F相对应的浊音，就像你在第11章见到的那样。当你发F音时就好像在低语。所以，对于V音，发F音并且简单地加上一些声音，fairy和very之间的区别仅在于此，就像在我们的下个练习中你将听到的那样。

**Note** In speaking, *of* is reduced to əv.

注意：在口语中，of弱读为əv。

## Exercise 19-1: Mind Your Vees

**Track 275**

*Repeat the following words and sounds after me.*

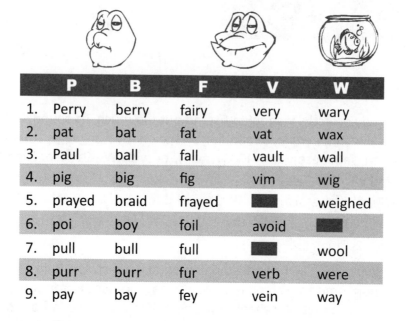

| | P | B | F | V | W |
|---|---|---|---|---|---|
| 1. | Perry | berry | fairy | very | wary |
| 2. | pat | bat | fat | vat | wax |
| 3. | Paul | ball | fall | vault | wall |
| 4. | pig | big | fig | vim | wig |
| 5. | prayed | braid | frayed | ▮ | weighed |
| 6. | poi | boy | foil | avoid | ▮ |
| 7. | pull | bull | full | ▮ | wool |
| 8. | purr | burr | fur | verb | were |
| 9. | pay | bay | fey | vein | way |

## Exercise 19-2: The Vile VIP

**Track 276**

*Repeat after me, focusing on **V** and **W**. **Of** is pronounced **əv**.*

**W**hen re**v**ising his **v**isitor's **v**ersion o**f** a plan for a **v**ery **w**ell-pa**v**ed a**v**enue, the **V**IP **w**as ad**v**ised to re**v**eal none o**f** his moti**v**es. E**v**entually, ho**w**e**v**er, the hapless **v**isitor disco**v**ered his kna**v**ish **v**iews and confided that it **w**as **v**ital to re**v**iew the plans together to a**v**oid a conflict. The **V**IP **w**as not con**v**inced and a**v**erred that he **w**ould ha**v**e it **v**etoed by the **v**ice president. This quite **v**exed the **v**isitor, who then **v**o**w**ed to in**v**ent an indestructible pa**v**ing compound in order to a**v**enge his good name. The **V**IP found himself on the **v**erge of a ci**v**il **w**ar **w**ith a **v**isitor **w**ith whom he had pre**v**iously con**v**ersed easily. It **w**as only due to his insufferable **v**anity that the ine**v**itable di**v**ision arri**v**ed as soon as it did. Ne**v**er again did the **v**isitor con**v**erse **w**ith the **v**ain **V**IP and they remained di**v**ided forever.

## Exercise 19-3: Finding V Sounds

**Track 277**

*Underline the five **V** sounds in this paragraph. The first one is marked for you. Don't forget "of."*

**Hello, my** name is_____. I'm taking American **Accent** Training. There's a **lot** to **learn**, but I **hope** to make it as **enjoyable** as possible. I should pick **up** on the American **intonation** pattern pretty **easily**, although the **only** way to **get** it is to **practice** all o<u>f</u> the time. I use the **up** and down, or **peaks** and valleys, **intonation** more than I **used** to. I've been paying attention to **pitch, too**. It's like **walking** down a **stair**case. I've been **talking** to a lot of **Americans** lately, and they tell me that I'm **easier** to under**stand**. **Any**way, I could go **on** and on, but the **important** thing is to **listen** well and sound **good**. **Well**, what do you **think**? **Do** I?

| Exercise 19-4: W, V & F | Track 278 |
|---|---|

*Repeat the following sentences, focusing on the targeted sounds. Notice that **one** starts with a **W** sound and **of** ends with a **V** sound.*

**W**here were we in World War One? On one wonderful Wednesday, we were wandering in Westwood with a wonderful woman from Wisconsin, whose name was Wanda Wilkerson. We had been with Wanda for weeks, and we were wondering when we would wear out our welcome. "Don't worry," warbled Wanda, waving wildly, "I've been waiting since winter!"

**Track 279**

**V**ictor Vickerson voted to review the very vilest version of the veto to avoid a controversy. Even Evan reviewed Virginia's available provisions for the vacation as inevitably devoid of value. Evan eventually arrived at the village and saved the day with vast amounts of venison and veal.

**Track 280**

**F**red fried five flat fish on Friday afternoon at four.

Track 281

|  | A | B | C | D | E | F | G | H | I | J | K | L | M | N | O |
|---|---|---|---|---|---|---|---|---|---|---|---|---|---|---|---|
|  | æ | æo | u | i | ee | ü | ε | a | ə | ä | r | är | o | i | oi |
| 1. | back | bow | booed | Bic | beak | book | beck | bake | buck | Bach | Burke | bark | boat | bite | point |
| 2. | black | blouse | blued | bliss | bleed | books | bled | blade | blood | block | blurred | blarney | bloat | blight | boy |
| 3. | brad | browse | brood | brick | breed | brook | bread | break | brother | brought | fir | far | broke | bright | broil |
| 4. | pat | about | boot | pit | peak | put | pet | paid | putt | pot | pert | part | post | pike | boil |
| 5. | cat | couch | coot | kit | parakeet | cookie | kept | Kate | cut | caught | curt | cart | coat | kite | coin |
| 6. | cad | cowed | cooed | kid | keyed | could | Keds | okayed | cud | cod | curd | card | code | cried | coil |
| 7. | fat | found | food | fit | feet | foot | fed | fade | fun | fog | first | farm | phone | fight | Foyt |
| 8. | flack | flower | fluke | flick | fleet | put | fleck | flake | flood | father | flurry | far | flow | flight | Floyd |
| 9. | fragile | frown | fruit | frill | free | fructose | French | afraid | from | frog | further | farther | fro | fright | Freud |
| 10. | fallow | foul | fool | fill | feel | full | fell | fail | fuss | fall | furl | Carl | photo | file | foil |
| 11. | gas | gout | gooed | give | geek | good | get | gate | gun | gone | gird | guard | goad | guide | goiter |
| 12. | catch | couch | cool | kick | key | cook | ketch | cake | come | calm | Kirk | carp | coal | kind | coy |
| 13. | lack | loud | Luke | lick | leak | look | lecture | lake | luck | lock | lurk | lark | local | like | lawyer |
| 14. | mallet | mound | mood | mill | meal | wooden | men | main | mother | mom | murmur | march | mobile | mile | Des Moines |
| 15. | pal | Powell | pool | pill | peel | pull | pell | pail | puck | pock | pearl | park | pole | pile | poison |
| 16. | sand | sound | soon | sin | seen | soot | send | same | some | sawn | sir | sorry | sewn | sign | soil |
| 17. | satin | mountain | gluten | mitten | eaten | wouldn't | retina | latent | button | gotten | certain | carton | potent | tighten | ointment |
| 18. | shad | shout | shoed | Schick | sheet | should | shed | shade | shun | shop | insured | sharp | show | shy | ▓ |
| 19. | shack | shower | shooed | shiver | chic | shook | chef | shake | shuck | shock | shirt | shark | shows | shyster | ▓ |
| 20. | shallow | showers | shoot | shift | sheep | sugar | shell | shale | shut | shot | sure | shard | shown | shine | ▓ |
| 21. | chance | chowder | choose | chin | cheek | ▓ | chest | change | chuck | chalk | churn | charge | chose | child | choice |
| 22. | tack | towel | two | tick | teak | took | tech | take | tuck | talk | turkey | tarp | toke | tyke | toy |
| 23. | that | thousand | through | this | these | would | then | they | the | thought | third | cathartic | though | thigh | thyroid |
| 24. | had | how'd | who'd | hid | he'd | hood | hen | hate | hug | hod | heard | hard | hoed | hide | hoi polloi |
| 25. | hat | about | hoot | hit | heat | foot | heck | Hague | hut | hot | hurt | heart | hotel | height | Hoyle |
| 26. | value | vow | review | villain | reveal | ▓ | vegetable | vague | vug | von | verve | varnish | vote | vile | avoid |
| 27. | whack | wow | wooed | wick | weak | would | wed | weighed | what | walk | word | harm | woke | white | woi |

# Chapter 20

# Tense and Lax Vowels
## 紧元音和松元音

**Move your lips for tense vowels.**
**Don't move your lips for lax vowels.**

发紧元音时，移动双唇；
发松元音时，不要移动双唇。

**Track 282**

In this chapter, we tackle tense and lax vowels. This is the difference between **ā**, *tense* and **ɛ**, *lax;* **ē**, *tense* and **i**, *lax.* We will start with tense vowels. (See also Chapters 3, 12, and 18)

在本章中，我们来看紧元音和松元音。本章将讲解紧音ā和松音ɛ，紧音ē和松音i之间的区别。我们将从紧元音开始。（也见第3、12和18章）

| | Exercise 20-1: Tense Vowels | | | | | | Track 283 |

*Don't pay attention to spelling or meaning. Just remember that if you are in the **ä** column, they all have the same **ah** sound. Repeat.*

| | æ | æo | ä | i | ā | ē | ū | ōū |
|---|------|----------|--------|--------|-------|-------|--------|-------|
| 1. | at | out | ought | I'd | ate | eat | ooze | own |
| 2. | bat | about | bought | bite | bait | beat | boot | boat |
| 3. | cat | couch | caught | kite | cane | keys | cool | coat |
| 4. | chat | chowder | chalk | child | chair | cheer | choose | chose |
| 5. | dad | doubt | dot | dial | date | deed | do | don't |
| 6. | fat | found | fought | fight | fate | feet | food | phone |
| 7. | fallow | fountain | fall | file | fail | feel | fool | foal |
| 8. | gas | gown | got | kite | gate | gear | ghoul | go |
| 9. | hat | how | hot | height | hate | heat | hoot | hope |
| 10. | Hal | howl | hall | heil | hail | heel | who'll | hole |
| 11. | Jack | jowl | jock | giant | jail | jeep | jewel | Joel |
| 12. | crab | crowd | crawl | crime | crate | creep | cruel | crow |
| 13. | last | loud | lost | line | late | Lee | Lou | low |
| 14. | mat | mountain | mop | might | mate | mean | moon | moan |
| 15. | gnat | now | not | night | Nate | neat | noon | note |
| 16. | pal | pound | Paul | pile | pail | peel | pool | pole |
| 17. | rat | round | rot | right | rate | real | rule | role |
| 18. | sat | sound | soft | sight | sale | seal | Sue | soul |
| 19. | shall | shower | shawl | shine | shade | she | shoe | show |

| | æ | æo | ä | i | ā | ē | ū | ōū |
|---|---|---|---|---|---|---|---|---|
| 20. | slap | slouch | slop | slide | slade | sleep | slew | slow |
| 21. | stag | stout | stop | style | stale | steal | stool | stole |
| 22. | strap | Stroud | straw | stride | straight | stream | strew | stroll |
| 23. | tap | town | top | type | tape | team | tool | told |
| 24. | that | thou | thar | thine | they | these | ▮ | though |
| 25. | thang | thousand | thought | thigh | thane | thief | ▮ | throw |
| 26. | van | vow | volume | viper | vain | veal | voodoo | vote |
| 27. | wax | Wow! | wash | wipe | wane | wheel | woo | woe |
| 28. | yank | Yow! | yawn | yikes | Yale | year | you | yo |
| 29. | zap | Zowie! | zombie | xylophone | zany | zebra | zoo | Zoe |

---

### Exercise 20-2: Tense Vowels Practice Paragraph — Track 284

*Go through the subsequent paragraph and mark all the tense vowels, starting with ā (there are 12 here). The first one is **name** (nɛim, not nɛm). The first ē sound is **the American**. The same five æ sounds can be found as in Exercise 12-2, plus the æo of **sound** ànd **down**. Pause the CD to do the marking.*

Hello, **my** nāme is_____. I'm taking American **æccent** Training. There's a **lot** to **learn**, but I **hope** to make it as **enjoyable** as possible. I should pick **up** on thē American **intonation** pattern pretty **easily**, although the **only** way to **get** it is to **practice** all of the time. I use the **up** and down, or **peaks** and valleys, **intonation** more than I **used** to. I've been paying attention to **pitch, too**. It's like **walking** down a **stair**case. I've been **talking** to a lot of **Americans** lately, and they tell me that I'm **easier** to under**stand**. **Any**way, I could go **on** and on, but the **important** thing is to **listen** well and sound **good**. **Well**, what do you **think**? **Do** I?

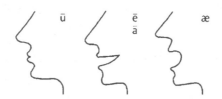

*Tense vowels use the lips and jaw muscles.*
紧元音运用双唇和下巴的肌肉。

## Exercise 20-3: Lax Vowels — Track 285

*As we saw in Chapter 18, these are the lax vowels.*

|     | e     | i     | ü     | ə     | ər    |
|-----|-------|-------|-------|-------|-------|
| 1.  | end   | it    |       | un-   | earn  |
| 2.  | bet   | bit   | book  | but   | burn  |
| 3.  | kept  | kiss  | could | cut   | curt  |
| 4.  | check | chick |       | chuck | church|
| 5.  | debt  | did   |       | does  | dirt  |
| 6.  | fence | fit   | foot  | fun   | first |
| 7.  | fell  | fill  | full  |       | furl  |
| 8.  | get   | gill  | good  | gut   | girl  |
| 9.  | help  | hit   | hook  | hut   | hurt  |
| 10. | held  | hill  | hood  | hull  | hurl  |

Soft vowels are subtle variations of sound using the throat muscles.

松元音运用喉部肌肉，发音轻微变化。

e slightly tense: **bet**
i more relaxed: **bit**
ü even more relaxed: **put**
ə throat is completely relaxed: **but**

## Exercise 20-4: Lax Vowels Practice Paragraph — Track 286

*Again, go over this paragraph and mark the lax vowels, starting with ɛ. The first one (of about 12 possible) is in* **hello** *or* **American**. *The first i sound (of about 21 possible) may be found in* **i̱s**. *(The numbers are approximations because you may have already reduced the ɛ of* **hello** *and the i of* **is** *into schwas.) Pause the CD to do the marking. Check your answer in the Answer Key.*

He**llo**, **my** name is_____. I'm taking American **Accent** Training. There's a **lot** to learn, but I **hope** to make it as **enjoyable** as possible. I should pick **up** on the American **intonation** pattern pretty **easily**, although the **only** way to **get** it is to **practice** all of the time. I use the **up** and down, or **peaks** and valleys, **intonation** more than I **used** to. I've been paying attention to **pitch, too**. It's like **walking** down a **stair**case. I've been **talking** to a lot of **Americans** lately, and they tell me that I'm **easier** to under**stand**. **Any**way, I could go **on** and on, but the **important** thing is to **listen** well and sound **good. Well**, what do you **think**? **Do** I?

**Exercise 20-5: Take a High-Tech Tack**　　　　　　　　　　　　　　**Track 287**

*Repeat the following paragraph and words after me.*

Sāy, Rāy, tāke a tack. A high-tack tack? No, Rāy, a high-tech tack, **e**ight high-tech tacks, tāke them. Then find a wāy to māke a plāce for the tacks on the dāy bed. H**e**y, you lāy the tacks on the pāper plāce mat on the tāble, not on the dāy bed, Rāy. At your āge, why do you always māke the sāme mistākes?

**Track 288**

| late | lack | let | tāke | tack | tech | mate | mat | met |
|------|------|-----|------|------|------|------|-----|-----|
| hāil | Hal  | hell | fāte | fat | fetch | cane | can | Ken |

**Exercise 20-6: Pick a Peak**　　　　　　　　　　　　　　　　　　**Track 289**

*Repeat the following paragraph and words after me. Boldfaced elements represent the ē sound. The **i** is only marked with underscoring.*

**Pe**ople who p**i**ck p**ea**ks w**ee**kly s**ee**m to n**ee**d to app**ea**r d**ee**p **i**n order to be dist**i**ngu**i**shed from m**e**re p**ea** p**i**ckers. P**e**ter, a champ**io**n p**ea**k p**i**cker, thought he'd b**e** **e**ven n**ea**ter **i**f he were the d**ee**pest p**ea**k p**i**cker **i**n P**e**or**i**a, Ph**oe**nix, and New Z**ea**land. On his p**ea**k p**ea**k-p**i**ck**i**ng w**ee**k, though, P**e**ter, a p**ea**k p**i**cker's p**ea**k p**i**cker, r**ea**lized that h**e** was not d**ee**p. Th**i**s **i**s not **e**asy for a p**ea**k p**i**cker to adm**i**t, and **i**t p**i**tched P**e**ter **i**nto a p**i**t of p**ea**k-p**i**ck**i**ng d**e**spair. H**e** was p**i**tiful for three w**ee**ks and then l**i**fted h**i**mself to h**i**therto unrev**ea**led personal p**ea**ks.

**Track 290**

| eat / it | sheep / ship | seat / sit | neat / nit | feet / fit | sleep / slip |
|----------|--------------|------------|------------|------------|--------------|

# Chapter 21

# The Ridge
# 牙槽骨

The tongue tip touches the ridge in a variety of ways.
舌尖以各种方式碰触牙槽骨。

## Those Bumps at the Top of Your Mouth
口腔上方的突起

**Track 291**

Those bumps at the top of your mouth form the alveolar ridge, and it's the location of a lot of activity, including **S**, **Z**, **T**, **D**, **N**, **L**, **Sh**, **Zh**, **Ch** and **J**! (See also the Nationality Guide)

口腔上方的突起就是牙槽骨，很多音都从这里发出，包括S，Z，T，D，N，L，Sh，Zh，Ch 和J！（也见"汉语发音与美音的对比"部分）

### Exercise 21-1: It's So Sad
**Track 292**

*Repeat the following paragraph.*

It's so sad, Sally stole Sammy's snakeskin suit and sold it to a salesman from Sonoma. Sid, the salesman, suggested that Sally stop stealing, but Sally simply said, "So!" Sid sighed sadly and stomped off to search for a more suitable subject.

### Exercise 21-2: Allz Well That Endz Well
**Track 293**

*Repeat the following paragraph.*

Zero Zippers is a zillion-dollar organization near the Osgood zoo in Zimbabwe. It zigzagged through an embezzlement scandal and zipped past all reasonable expectations. Zero was in the most desirable zip code in the business zone, but the end result was zilch. As the founder's motto was "Easy come, easy go!", no one resented the bizarre disaster.

**Track 294**

Make your **T**s crisper (when they are **T**s and not the middle **D**). If the tip of your tongue is even a bit too far forward, it flattens the rest of the tongue. Make sure it's planted right there on the alveolar ridge and that it's clearly popped.

（当T发T音而非D音时）把它发得清脆一些。如果你的舌尖伸得太靠前，就会使舌头的其余部分变平。确保舌尖牢牢地抵在牙槽骨的位置，并且清晰地爆破出来。

## Exercise 21-3: Ted Took Ten Tasty Tacos                               Track 295

*Repeat the following paragraph. Put your hand in front of your mouth when you say the following. You should feel distinct puffs of air against your palm.*

Ted took ten tasty tacos from the tidy taco truck on Tuesday at two. It's a tried-and-true test of temperament to try resisting tasty tacos. Take the taco-tasting test ten times to determine your type.

## Exercise 21-4: Trudy Tried to Trill in Trinidad                       Track 296

*Repeat the following paragraph. Once you've got your tongue tapping on the alveolar ridge, for this next one, you're going to drop away from the ridge. Remember, in American English, the **R** acts more like a vowel because no two points of the mouth come into contact. With your **T** tensely poised on the ridge, it's going to release plosively from there, and the back of your tongue will form the **R**. You'll still feel the puffs of air.*

Trudy tried to trill on Trevor's Trail in Trinidad, but tripped up and got off track.

## Exercise 21-5: Eddie Oughtta Wait a Little Longer                      Track 297

*Repeat the following sentence.*

Eddie ought to try to wait a little longer. (Eddie oughtta tryda way da little longer.)

## Exercise 21-6: Little League in Little Italy                           Track 298

*Repeat the following sentence, focusing on the **L** sounds.*

Little Lola played Little League with a little old lady in Little Italy.

## Exercise 21-7: No! No! Not Nine!                                       Track 299

*Repeat the following paragraph.*

No! Not nine new novels! Nine'll never be enough!

## Exercise 21-8: Chester's Chocolate Cherries                            Track 300

*Repeat the following paragraph.*

Chuck Richards charged Chester a surcharge on the chewy chocolates. Chester chafed and kvetched but fetched Chuck a chest of riches for his chocolate cherries.

## Exercise 21-9: She Should Share Sherman's Shoes

*Repeat the following paragraph.*

**Sh**elly and **Sh**erman **sh**are a **sh**adowy pa**ss**ion for **sh**oes. Lu**sh**, plu**sh sh**oes in **sh**ocking **sh**ades of **ch**artreuse. Go**sh**, why won't **sh**e **sh**are her **sh**oes with **Sh**erman?

## Exercise 21-10: George Judged Jenny's Jewelry

*Repeat the following paragraph.*

**G**eorge ju**dg**ed **J**enny's **j**ewelry as **j**ust a**g**e. **J**ewelry is **J**enny's life. En**j**oying a**g**eless **g**ems and **j**ewels ca**dg**ed from Ro**g**ers of **J**acksonville, **J**enny a**dj**usted **G**eorge's **j**ud**g**ement of her **j**ewelry, as it was not **j**ust avera**g**e—it was a **g**em **j**ubilee!

## Exercise 21-11: Was Your Usual Menage in the Beige Garage?

*Repeat the following paragraph.*

It was a beige, beige garage and a vision of precision. The revision of the usual menage's decision was a collision of collusion and illusion.

It was a bei**zh**, bei**zh** gara**zh** and a vi**zh**'n of preci**zh**'n. The revi**zh**'n of the u**zh**ual mena**zh**'s deci**zh**'n was a colli**zh**'n of collu**zh**'n and illu**zh**'n.

> **Ch** and **J** are almost the same sound. The tongue position is the same, and they both **pop**. There's one little difference. **Ch** is **whispered** and **J** is **spoken**.
>
> Ch音和J音发音几乎相同。它们舌头的位置相同，也都是爆破音。唯一的一点小小的不同是，Ch是清音，而J是浊音。
>
> **Sh** and **Zh** are almost the same. The tongue position is the same, and they both **slide** out. The difference: **Sh** is **whispered** and **Zh** is **spoken**.
>
> Sh音和Zh音发音几乎相同。它们舌头的位置相同，也都是滑音。不同之处是，Sh是清音，而Zh是浊音。

In order to make a clear **Ch**, you need to start with a **T** sound, so it sounds like **tch** not **shhh**. The invisible **T** before the **Ch** blocks the air momentarily, before the rest of the sound comes out. With the **Sh**, the air flows freely. For **J**, start with a **D**, so **judge** sounds like **djudge**.

为了发出清晰的Ch音，你需要先发T音，这样它听起来就像是tch而不是shhh。在其他音发出来之前，Ch前面无形的T音暂时地挡住了气流。而Sh音中的气流是自由地流出的。对于J音，是先发D音，所以judge听起来像是djudge。

| Unvoiced | Voiced | Unvoiced | Voiced |
|----------|--------|----------|--------|
| **Ch** | **J** | **Sh** | **Zh** |
| cheese | jeans | she's | Jaque's |
| in charge | enjoy | insure | usual |
| much | judge | mush | garage |
| watch | lodge | wash | rouge |
| watcher | lodger | washer | was your |
| patch | page | bash | beige |
| patches | pages | bashes | beiges |
| ritual | vigil | vicious | visual |
| rich | ridge | wish | menage |
| hatcher | had your | hasher | has your |

# Chapter 22

Even with complex grammar,
use the basic rules of intonation.

即使在复杂的语法中，
也使用最基本的语调规则。

# Grammar in a Bigger Nutshell
# 语法扩展

**Track 306**

In Chapter 9, we studied compound nouns and complex verb tenses. Now, we are going to put them together and practice the intonation of some complicated sentences.

在第9章，我们学习了复合名词和复杂的动词时态。现在，我们将把它们放在一起，练习一些复杂句子的语调。

| Exercise 22-1: Compound Nouns and Complex Verbs | Track 307 |
|---|---|

*No matter how complex the verb gets, remember to follow the basic* **Dogs** *eat* **bones** *intonation, where you stress the nouns. For the noun intonation, stick with the basic* **set phrase or description** *rule. Let's build up one complex noun for the subject and another one for the object, starting with* **The millionaires were impressed by the equipment.**

| Subject | Object |
|---|---|
| The **millionaires** | the **equipment**. |
| The elderly **millionaires** | **eaves**dropping equipment. |
| The elderly Texas **millionaires** | electronic **eaves**dropping equipment. |
| The two **elderly** Texas **millionaires**...**sophisticated** electronic **eaves**dropping equipment. |
| The two **elderly** Texas **millionaires** were impressed by the **sophisticated** electronic **eaves**dropping equipment. |

The two elderly Teksəs millyənair zwerim presst by the
səfistəkaydədəlektränik ēvzdräppiŋə kwipmənt.

*zərim prest*                                                                 **Track 308**

1. The two **elderly** Texas **millionaires**'re impressed by the **sophisticated** electronic **eaves**dropping equipment.

*zwərim prest*

2. The two **elderly** Texas **millionaires** were impressed by the **sophisticated** electronic **eaves**dropping equipment.

*zər beeyingim prest*

3. At the moment, the two **elderly** Texas **millionaires**'re being impressed by the **sophis**ticated electronic **eaves**dropping equipment.

*zəl beeyim prest*

4. The two **elderly** Texas **millionaires**'ll be impressed by the **sophisticated** electronic **eaves**dropping equipment.

*zəd beeyim prest*

5. The two **elderly** Texas **millionaires**'d be impressed by the **sophisticated** electronic **eaves**dropping equipment if there were more practical applications for it.

*zədəv binim prest*

6. The two **elderly** Texas **millionaires**'d've been impressed by the **sophisticated** electronic **eaves**dropping equipment if there had been more practical applications for it.

*zədəv bin so im prest*

7. The two **elderly** Texas **millionaires** that've been so impressed by the **sophisticated** electronic **eaves**dropping equipment are now researching a new program.

*zəv binim prest*

8. The two **elderly** Texas **millionaires**'ve been impressed by the **sophisticated** electronic **eaves**dropping equipment for a long time now.

*zəd binim prest*

9. The two **elderly** Texas **millionaires**'d been impressed by the **sophisticated** electronic **eaves**dropping equipment long before the burglary was thwarted.

*zələv bin thərə lee⁽ʸ⁾im prest*

10. The two **elderly** Texas **millionaires**'ll've been thoroughly impressed by the **sophisticated** electronic **eaves**dropping equipment by the time I've done my presentation.

*zädə bee⁽ʸ⁾im prest*

11. The two **elderly** Texas **millionaires** ought to be impressed by the **sophisticated** electronic **eaves**dropping equipment.

*shüd bee⁽ʸ⁾im prest*

12. The two **elderly** Texas **millionaires** should be impressed by the **sophisticated** electronic **eaves**dropping equipment.

*shüd•n beetoo⁽ʷ⁾im prest*

13. The two **elderly** Texas **millionaires** shouldn't be too impressed by the **sophisticated** electronic **eaves**dropping equipment.

*shüdəv binim prest*

14. The two **elderly** Texas **millionaires** should've been impressed by the **sophisticated** electronic **eaves**dropping equipment.

*shüdn•nəv bin thæ dim prest*

15. Given the circumstances, the two **elderly** Texas **millionaires** shouldn't've been that impressed by the **sophisticated** electronic **eaves**dropping equipment.

*cüdee zəlee bee⁽ʸ⁾im prest*

16. We think that the two **elderly** Texas **millionaires** could easily be impressed by the **sophisticated** electronic **eaves**dropping equipment.

*cüd•n bee⁽ʸ⁾im prest*

17. No matter what we did, the two **elderly** Texas **millionaires** couldn't be impressed by even the most **sophisticated** electronic **eaves**dropping equipment.

*cüdəv binim prest*

18. The two **elderly** Texas **millionaires** could've been impressed by the **sophisticated** electronic **eaves**dropping equipment, but we're not sure.

*cüdn•nəv binim prest*

19. The two **elderly** Texas **millionaires** couldn't've been impressed by the **sophisticated** electronic **eaves**dropping equipment, because they left after five minutes.

*myt bee⁽ʸ⁾im prest*

20. The two **elderly** Texas **millionaires** might be impressed by the **sophisticated** electronic **eaves**dropping equipment this time around.

*mydəv binim prest*

21. The two **elderly** Texas **millionaires** might've been impressed by the **sophisticated** electronic **eaves**dropping equipment, but they gave no indication one way or the other.

*məss bee⁽ʸ⁾im prest*

22. The two **elderly** Texas **millionaires** must be impressed by the **sophisticated** electronic **eaves**dropping equipment because they are considering a huge order.

*məsdəv binim prest*

23. The two **elderly** Texas **millionaires** must have been impressed by the **sophisticated** electronic **eaves**dropping equipment because they ordered so much of it.

*cən bee⁽ʸ⁾im prest*

24. The two **elderly** Texas **millionaires** can be impressed by the **sophisticated** electronic **eaves**dropping equipment because they don't know much about surveillance.

*cæn⁽ᵗ⁾ bee⁽ʸ⁾im prest*

25. The two **elderly** Texas **millionaires** can't be impressed by the **sophisticated** electronic **eaves**dropping equipment because they invented most of the state-of-the-art technology currently available.

| **Exercise 22-2: Your Own Compound Nouns** | **Track 309** |
|---|---|

*Pause the CD and build up your own compound nouns, both subject and object.*

| **Subject** | **Object** |
|---|---|
| _____ | _____ |
| _____ | _____ |
| _____ | _____ |
| _____ | _____ |
| _____ | _____ |

## The Verb Map                                                      Track 310
动词地图

This is a handy overview of the various verb tenses and verb forms. (The **T formation** in each box indicates the more commonly used tenses. The single symbols indicate a completed action, whereas the double symbols indicate two related events. The white symbols are *contrary to fact* and didn't, don't, or won't take place.)

　　这是个很方便查看的各种动词时态和形式的概图。（每个框中由浅蓝色构成的T形表示更加常用的时态。单个的符号表示一个完整的动作，两个符号表示两个相关的事件。白色的符号代表与事实相反，表示过去、现在或将来没有或不会发生的事情。）

## Active

| | Past | Present | Future |
|---|---|---|---|
| Simple | I did it. ◄ | I do it. ● | I will do it. ► |
| Real Duo | I'd done A before I did B. ◄ ◄ | I've done it. ◄ ● | I'll have done A before I do B. ► ► |
| Unreal Duo | If I had done A I would've done B. ◄ ◄ | If I did A I would do B. ◄ ● | If I do A I'll do B. ► ► |

## To Be

| | Past | Present | Future |
|---|---|---|---|
| Simple | I was there. ◄ | I am here. ● | I will be there. ► |
| Real Duo | I'd been there (before then). ◄ ◄ | I've been here (before now). ◄ ● | I'll have been there for an hour (by then). ► ► |
| Unreal Duo | If I had been there, I'd have done it. ◄ ◄ | If I were there, I would do it. ◄ ● | If I am there, I'll do it. ► ► |

## Negative

| | Past | Present | Future |
|---|---|---|---|
| Simple | I didn't do it. | I don't do it. | I won't do it. |
| Real Duo | I hadn't done A until I did B. | I haven't done it. | I won't have done A before I do B. |
| Unreal Duo | If I hadn't done A I wouldn't have done B. | If I didn't do A I wouldn't do B. | If I don't do A I won't do B. |

## Continuous

| | Past | Present | Future |
|---|---|---|---|
| Simple | I was doing it. | I'm doing it. | I'll be doing it. |
| Real Duo | I had been doing A before I did B. | I've been doing A for a long time. | I'll have been doing A for a while, when I start B. |
| Unreal Duo | If I'd been doing A, I wouldn've been doing B. | If I were doing A, I'd be doing B. | If I'm doing A I'm doing B. |

## Questions

| | Past | Present | Future |
|---|---|---|---|
| Simple | Did I do it? | Do I do it? | Will I do it? |
| Real Duo | Had I done A before I did B? | Have I done A? | Will I have done A before I do B? |
| Unreal Duo | If I had done A would I have done B? | If I did A would I do B? | If I do A will I do B? |

## Helping Verbs

| | Past | Present | Future |
|---|---|---|---|
| Simple | I had to do it. | I have to do it. | I'll have to do it. |
| Real Duo | I had had to do A before I had to do B. | I've had many times. | I'll have had to do A before I have to do B. |
| Unreal Duo | If I had had to do A, I would have had to do B. | If I had to do A, I would have to do B. | If I have to do A, I will have to do B. |

## Causative

| | Past | Present | Future |
|---|---|---|---|
| Simple | I had it done. | I have it done. | I will have it done. |
| Real Duo | I'd had done A before I had B done. | I've had A done many times. | I'll have had A done by the time I have B done. |
| Unreal Duo | If I had had A done, I would've had B done. | If I had A done, I would have B done. | If I have A done, I'll have B done. |

## Passive

| | Past | Present | Future |
|---|---|---|---|
| Simple | It was done. | It is done. | It will be done. |
| Real Duo | A had been done before B was done. | A has been done many times. | A will be done before B is done. |
| Unreal Duo | If A had been done B would have been done. | If A were done B would be done. | If A is done B will be done. |

**Exercise 22-3: Your Compound Nouns and Complex Verbs**  **Track 311**

*Using your compound nouns from Exercise 22-2, choose a verb and put it through all the changes. Remember that it helps to have a verb that starts with a vowel. Add explanatory words to round out the sentence, complete the thought, and support the verb.*

| | |
|---|---|
| do | 1. |
| did | 2. |
| are doing | 3. |
| will do | 4. |
| would do | 5. |
| would've done | 6. |
| that have done | 7. |
| have done | 8. |
| had done | 9. |
| will've done | 10. |
| ought to do | 11. |
| should do | 12. |
| shouldn't do | 13. |
| should've done | 14. |
| shouldn't have done | 15. |
| could do | 16. |
| couldn't do | 17. |
| could've done | 18. |
| couldn't have done | 19. |
| might do | 20. |
| might've done | 21. |
| must do | 22. |
| must've done | 23. |
| can do | 24. |
| can't do | 25. |

> Take everything you've learned
> and use it.
>
> 将所学的所有内容加以运用。

# Chapter 23
# 第23章

# Practical Application
# 实际应用

---

**Exercise 23-1: Practical Application—U.S./Japan Trade Friction**　　　　Track 312

*Listen to the following excerpt and compare the two versions.*

Forty years after the end of World War II, Japan and the U.S. are again engaged in conflict. Trade frictions, which began as minor irritants in an otherwise smooth relationship in the 1960s, have gradually escalated over the years.

The conflict is more dangerous than it appears because its real nature is partially hidden. It masquerades as a banal and sometimes grubby dispute over widgets with the stakes being whether American or Japanese big business makes more money.

In truth, the issue is strategic and geopolitical in nature. Japan is once again challenging the U.S., only this time the issue is not China or the Pacific but world industrial and technological leadership and the military and economic powers, which have always been its corollaries.

*By permission of *U.S. News and World Report*

**For**dee yir **zæf**tr⁽ᵖᵃᵘˢᵉ⁾thee⁽ʸ⁾end'v wrl dwor **too**,⁽ᵖᵃᵘˢᵉ⁾J'**pæn**'n thə yoo⁽ʷ⁾**ess**⁽ᵖᵃᵘˢᵉ⁾ärə **ge**nin gɛij din⁽ᵖᵃᵘˢᵉ⁾**cän**fl'ct.⁽ˢᵗᵒᵖ⁾**Trəid** fr'ksh'nz,⁽ᵖᵃᵘˢᵉ⁾w'ch b'gæn'z mynr **rir**rət'nts⁽ᵖᵃᵘˢᵉ⁾in'n ətherwise⁽ᵖᵃᵘˢᵉ⁾ smooth r'**lɛi**sh'nship in the näinteen **siks**deez⁽ᵖᵃᵘˢᵉ⁾h'v græjəlee⁽ʸ⁾**ɛs**cəladəd⁽ᵖᵃᵘˢᵉ⁾dover thə **yirz**.

Thə **känf**l'k d'z mor **dɛi**njer's thəni dəpirz b'kəzəts **ree**⁽ʸ⁾əl nɛichyr'z pärshəlee **h'dd**'n. It mæske**rɛid** zəzə bənälən səmtäimz **grə**bee d'spyu dover **wij**'ts withthə **stɛiks** be⁽ʸ⁾ing wɛthərə **mɛr**əkəner Jæpəneez big **biz**n's mɛiks mor **man**ee.

In **truth**, thee⁽ʸ⁾**ishu**⁽ʷ⁾iz strə**tee**jəkən jee⁽ʸ⁾o**pəli**dəkələn nɛichyer. Jə**pæn**əz wən səgɛn **chæl**ənjing thə you⁽ʷ⁾**ess**, only **this** täim, thee⁽ʸ⁾**ishu**⁽ʷ⁾iz nät **Chäi**nə or thə **Pəs'f**ək bət wr rolld'in **dəss**tree⁽ʸ⁾l'n tɛknə**läj**əkəl **lee**dershipən the **mil**ətɛree⁽ʸ⁾ənɛkə**näm**ək pæwrz, w'ch h'**vä**weez bi n'ts **kor**əlɛreez.

## The Letter A　　　　Track 313
字母A

You've seen many examples of illogical spelling by now, and the letter **A** is a major contributor. **A** can be:

到目前为止，你已经见到了许多不符合逻辑的拼写例子，其中字母A是一个重要的因素。A可以发音为：

| æ cat | ä part | ā make | ə final | ɛ parallel | o war |

**Note** People who speak Chinese frequently pronounce **a**, **æ**, and **ɛ** the same. The common denominator of the three sounds is **ɛ**. When a Chinese speaker says *mate, mat, met,* it can sound like *met, met, met.* If this happens to be your case, in order to say common words like *make* and *man* correctly, first practice putting them on the stairsteps and drawing them out. Don't be afraid to exaggerate. You can even draw them out with a final unvoiced consonant.

注意：说汉语的人常把a，æ和ɛ发成相同的音。这三个音的共同特征是ɛ。当中国人说mate，mat，met时，听起来可能就像met，met，met。如果你恰巧也有这个问题，为了正确地发出像make和man这样的常用单词，首先练习将单词放在音阶阶梯上，然后拖出它们的发音。不要害怕过于夸张。你甚至可以带着末尾的清辅音拖出它们的发音。

**make**      **man**

| Exercise 23-2: Presidential Candidates' Debate | Track 314 |
| --- | --- |

Thə prezədənt təmärrou näidiz əxpectədiniz stɛidəv thə yoonyən mesəj tə prəpouz fedrəl səbzədeez tə help lou⁽ʷ⁾inkəm fæmleez ouvrkəm thə sou-käld dijədəl dəväid. Izidə nəpropree⁽ʸ⁾ət yusəv gəvrmnt fənz tə hændæot kəmpyudrz ən prəväid Innernet ækses tə thouz hu cæn⁽ᵈ⁾əford it; ənd if nät, why nät? Will bəgin with Mr. Keez.

"I think this iz ənəthər keis whɛer pälətishənz try də jəmpän thə bændwægən əv səmthing thæts going än in thee⁽ʸ⁾əcänəmee, sou evreebədeez gənnə think thət they ækchəlee hæv səmthing tə do with thə rəzəlt when they dont. Thɛrz nou need fr this. Wiräl reddy seeing æot thɛr prəpouzəlz fr thə distrəbyushən əv free PeeCees, nät beis dän səm pälətishən meiking ə judgment ən spending tæxpeiyer mənee, bət beis dän thə self-intrst əv thouz hu⁽ʷ⁾är involvd inə nyu world, ə nyu world ən which p'rtisəpeishən iz thə kee də präfit—ənd in which thɛr iz ækchəlee ə sträng insentiv əməng thouz hu prtisəpɛidin thə präivət sektər tə giv æksɛss tə indəvijəls sou thət they c'n impruv their äpərtyunədeez fr präfit, fr infərmeishn shɛring. Thæts whəts älredee bin going än—it will kəntinyu. Thɛr iz nou need fr thə gəvərmənt tə prətend thæt it needs tə teik leedership hir. I think thæts jəst pəlidəkəl päsjuring."

Senədər Mə⁽ᵏ⁾kein.

I bəleev th't wee du hæv ə präbləm. æn thædiz thət thɛrizə growing gæp bətween thə hævz ənd hæv-näts in əmɛrəkə, thouz thədr ɛibl də tɛik pärdin this infərmeishn teknäləjee ən thouz th't hævnt. Wee took ə mɛijər step forwərd when wee dəsaidəd də wäi⁽ʸ⁾r evree skool ən lybrɛree in əmɛrəkə tə thee⁽ʸ⁾Innərnet. Thætsə güd prougrəm. Wee hæf tə hæv step tu, three, ən for, which meenz güd əkwipmənt, güd teechərz, ənd güd clæssroomz. No, I wüdn du⁽ʷ⁾it d'rektlee. Bət thɛrz läts əv weiz th'chyu kən inkerəj korpəreishnz, who in their own self-intrest, wüd wänt tə prəvaid...wüd rəseev tæks benəfits, wüd rəseev kredit, ənd mɛny əthər weiz fr beeing invölvd in thə skoolz, in əpgreiding thə kwälədee əv əkwipmənt th't thei hæv, thə kwälədee əv thə styudənts ənd thɛrby prəvaiding ə məch-needed well-treind wərkfors.

Thæng kyu. Mr. Forbz.

*The president tomorrow night is expected in his State of the Union message to propose federal subsidies to help low-income families overcome the so-called digital divide. Is it an appropriate use of government funds to hand out computers and provide Internet access to those who can't afford it, and if not, why not? We'll begin with Mr. Keyes.*

"I think this is another case where politicians try to jump on the bandwagon of something that's going on in the economy, so everybody's gonna think that they actually have something to do with the result when they don't. There's no need for this. We're already seeing out there proposals for the distribution of free PCs, not based on some politician making a judgment and spending taxpayer money, but based on the self-interest of those who are involved in a new world, a new world in which participation is the key to profit—and in which there is actually a strong incentive among those who participate in the private sector to give access to individuals so that they can improve their opportunities for profit, for information sharing. That's what's already been going on—it will continue. There is no need for the government to pretend that it needs to take leadership here. I think that's just political posturing."

*Senator McCain.*

"I believe that we do have a problem. And that is that there is a growing gap between the *haves* and *have-nots* in America, those that are able to take part in this information technology and those that haven't. We took a major step forward when we decided to wire every school and library in America to the Internet. That's a good program. We have to have step two, three, and four, which means good equipment, good teachers, and good classrooms. No, I wouldn't do it directly. But there's lots of ways that you can encourage corporations, who in their own self-interest, would want to provide...would receive tax benefits, would receive credit, and many other ways for being involved in the schools, in upgrading the quality of equipment that they have, the quality of the students, and thereby providing a much-needed well-trained workforce."

*Thank you. Mr. Forbes.*

An Australlian tourist steps into the road and a traffic cop yells at him, "Did you come here to die?!"

"Nah, mate. I came here yesterdie!"

Block the air with your tongue and release it through your nose.

用舌头阻塞住气流，将它从鼻腔释放。

# Chapter 24
# 第24章

# Nasal Consonants
# 鼻辅音

**Track 315**

We now turn to the three consonants whose sound comes out through the nose—**M**, **N**, and the **NG** combination. They each have one thing in common—their sound is blocked in the mouth in one of three locations. Two of them, **N** and **NG**, you can't even see, as with **R**, so they're hard to pick up on. (See also Chapters 3, 16, 21, and the Nationality Guide)

我们现在来学习三个从鼻腔中发出的辅音——M，N和NG。三个音有一个共同点——它们都在口腔中的三个位置中的一处被阻塞。它们中的两个音，N音和NG音，就像是R音，你甚至看不到发音部位，因而难以理解它们的发音方法。（也见第3、16、21章和"汉语发音与美音的对比"）

**m** is the easiest and most obvious. Like **b**, the lips come together; the air can't get out, so it has to come out through the nose.

m音是最简单、最明显的音。和b音相似，发m音时双唇合拢；气流无法通过，所以不得不从鼻腔流出。

**n** is in a position similar to **t**, but it can't be at all tense. It has to be completely relaxed, filling the whole mouth, touching the insides of all the teeth, leaving no room for the air to escape, except by the nose.

n音的发音位置和t音相似，但一点也不紧张。发n音时舌头必须完全放松，阻塞整个口腔，并且触及所有牙齿内侧，让气流除了通过鼻腔没有其他空间可以流出。

**ng** is back in the throat with **g**. The back of the tongue presses back, and again, the air comes out through the nose.

ng音和g音的发音位置相似，都在喉咙的后部。发ng音时，舌的后部向后压，然后气流从鼻腔流出。

## Exercise 24-1: Nasal Consonants — Track 316

*We are going to contrast nasals with regular consonant sounds. Repeat after me.*

|  | **Initial** | | **Middle** | | **Final** | |
|---|---|---|---|---|---|---|
| **m/b** | me | bee | llama | lobber | ROM | rob |
| **n/d** | knees | deals | Lana | lauder | Ron | rod |
| **ng/g** | long eels | geese | longer | logger | wrong | log |

## Exercise 24-2: Ending Nasal Consonants — Track 317

*Here we will focus on the final sounds. Repeat after me.*

| M | N | NG |
|---|---|---|
| rumª | runª | rungª |
| sum/some | sun/son | sung |
| bum | bun | bung |
| turn | ton | tongue |
| dumb | done | dung |
| psalm | sawn | song |

## Exercise 24-3: Reading Nasal Consonant Sounds — Track 318

*We will read the following paragraph. Repeat after me.*

The young King Kong can sing along on anything in the kingdom, as long as he can bring a strong ringing to the changing songs. He can only train on June mornings when there is a full moon, but June lends itself to singing like nothing else. Ding Dong, on the other hand, is not a singer; he cannot sing for anything. He is a man often seen on the green lawn on the Boston Open, where no one ever, ever sings.

## Exercise 24-4: Finding n and ng Sounds — Track 319

*Find and mark the final **n** and **ng** sounds.*

**Hello, my** name is_____. I'm taking American **Accent** Training. There's a **lot** to **learn**, but I **hope** to make it as **enjoyable** as possible. I should pick **up** on the American **intonation** pattern pretty **easily**, although the **only** way to **get** it is to **practice** all of the time. I use the **up** and down, or **peaks** and valleys, **intonation** more than I **used** to. I've been paying attention to **pitch, too**. It's like **walking** down a **stair**case. I've been **talking** to a lot of **Americans** lately, and they tell me that I'm **easier** to under**stand**. **Any**way, I could go **on** and on, but the **important** thing is to **listen** well and sound **good**. **Well**, what do you **think**? **Do** I?

# Chapter 25

> Throat sounds are formed with the back of the tongue.
>
> 喉辅音通过舌头后部形成。

# Throaty Consonants
# 喉辅音

**Track 320**

There are five consonant sounds that are produced in the throat: **h**, **k**, **g**, **ng**, **er**. Because **R** can be considered a consonant, its sound is included here. For pronunciation purposes, however, elsewhere this book treats it as a semivowel. (See also Chapters 15, 24, and the Nationality Guide)

有五个辅音的发音位置在喉部：h，k，g，ng和er。因为R可以被当做辅音，所以这里也将其包括在内。然而，出于发音的目的，这本书其他的地方把R当做半元音来讲解。（也见第15章、第24章和"汉语发音与美音的对比"）

---

**Exercise 25-1: Throaty Consonants** Track 321

*Here we will read across the lists of initial, middle, and final consonants.*

|      | Initial       | Middle    | Final     |
|------|---------------|-----------|-----------|
| **h**  | haw           | reheat    |           |
|      | hood          | in half   |           |
|      | he'll         | unhinge   |           |
|      | hat           | unheard of|           |
| **k**  | caw           | accident  | rink      |
|      | could         | accent    | rack      |
|      | keel          | include   | cork      |
|      | cat           | actor     | block     |
| **g**  | gaw           | regale    | rug       |
|      | good          | ingrate   | hog       |
|      | geese         | agree     | big       |
|      | gat           | organ     | log       |
| **ng** | Long Island   | Bronx     | wrong     |
|      | a long wait   | inky      | daring    |
|      | Dang you!     | larynx    | averaging |
|      | being honest  | English   | clung     |
| **r**  | raw           | error     | rare      |
|      | roof          | arrow     | air       |
|      | real          | mirror    | injure    |
|      | rat           | carbon    | prefer    |

## Exercise 25-2: The Letter X      Track 322

*The letter **X** can sound like either **KS** or **GZ**, depending on the letter that follows the **X** and where the stress falls.*

| **ks** | | |
|---|---|---|
| *Followed by the letter **C** or other **unvoiced consonants*** | excite | ɛk**säit** |
| | extra | **ɛk**strə |
| | exercise | **ɛk**sersiz |
| | experience | ɛks**piree**⁽ʸ⁾əns |
| | except | əks**ɛpt** |
| | execute | **ɛk**sekyut |
| | excellent | **ɛk**sələnt |
| **gz** | example | əg**zæmp**əl |
| *Followed by a **vowel** and usually stressed on the second syllable* | exist | əg**zist** |
| | exam | əg**zæm** |
| | exert | əg**zrt** |
| | examine | əg**zæm**ən |
| | executive | əg**zɛk**yudəv |
| | exit | **ɛg**zit |
| | exactly | əg**zæk**lee |

## Exercise 25-3: Reading the H, K, G, NG, and R Sounds      Track 323

*Repeat after me.*

### H

"**H**elp!" **h**issed the **h**arried intern. "We **h**ave to **h**urry! The **h**alf-wit w**h**o was **h**ired to **h**elp **h**er **h**ome **h**it **h**er **h**ard with the **H**onda. She didn't **h**ave a **h**elmet on **h**er **h**ead to protect **h**er, so she **h**as to **h**ave a checkup a**h**ead of the others."

**Track 324**

### K

The **c**omputer **c**ursor **c**areened a**c**ross the s**c**reen, erasing **k**ey **c**haracters as it s**c**rolled past. The te**c**hnician was e**q**ually **c**onfused by the **c**omputer te**c**hnology and the **c**ompli**c**ated **k**eyboard, so he **c**li**c**ked off the **c**omputer, **c**leaned off his desk, a**c**cepted his payche**c**k, and **c**aught a taxi**c**ab for the airport, destination **C**ara**c**as.

**G**

### The Wizard of Og

| | |
|---|---|
| There was a man named... | Og |
| Who was his best friend? | Dog |
| Where did he live? | Bog |
| What was his house made of? | Log |
| Who was his neighbor? | Frog |
| What did he drink? | Eggnog |
| What did he do for fun? | Jog |
| What is the weather in his swamp? | Fog |

**NG**

The stunning woman would not have a fling with the strong young flamingo trainer until she had a ring on her finger. He was angry because he longed for her. She inquired if he were hungry, but he hung his head in a funk. The flamingo trainer banged his fist on the fish tank and sang out, "Dang it, I'm sunk without you, Punkin!" She took in a long, slow lungful of air and sighed.

**R**

War is horrible. During any war, terrible things occur. The result is painful memories and disfiguring scars for the very people needed to rebuild a war-torn country. The leaders of every country must learn that wars are never won, lives are always lost, and history is doomed to repeat itself unless we all decide to live in harmony with our brothers and sisters.

---

| **Exercise 25-4: Glottal Consonant Practice Paragraph** | Track 328 |
|---|---|

*Pause the CD and go through the paragraph and mark the **h**, **k**, **g**, **ng**, and **r** sounds.*

Hello, **my** name is_____. I'm taking American **Accent** Training. There's a **lot** to **learn**, but I **hope** to make it as **enjoyable** as possible. I should pick **up** on the American **intonation** pattern pretty **easily**, although the **only** way to **get** it is to **practice** all of the time. I use the **up** and down, or **peaks** and valleys, **intonation** more than I **used** to. I've been paying attention to **pitch, too**. It's like **walking** down a **stair**case. I've been **talking** to a lot of **Americans** lately, and they tell me that I'm **easier** to under**stand. Any**way, I could go **on** and on, but the **important** thing is to **listen** well and sound **good. Well**, what do you **think**? **Do** I?

# Telephone Tutoring
# 电话指导

## Final Diagnostic Analysis
最终诊断分析

After a year, you're ready for the final analysis. If you're studying on your own, please contact (800) 457-4255 or AmericanAccent.com for a referral to a qualified telephone analyst. The diagnostic analysis is designed to evaluate your current speech patterns to let you know where your accent is standard and nonstandard.

经过一年的学习，相信你已经准备好做最终的诊断分析。如果你在自学本书，在中国大陆地区请拨打001-800-457-4255，在美国本土请拨打800-457-4255，或登录www.AmericanAccent.com，会有专业的分析师对你的语音进行诊断。诊断分析的目的在于评价你目前的语言特点，并让你知道自己的发音是否标准。

The Nasdaq composite index on Monday suffered its biggest loss in three weeks after a wave of selling slammed Internet and other tech shares in Asia and Europe overnight—suggesting many investors are increasingly nervous about tech shares' current heights. The Nasdaq index ended down 141.38 points, or 2.8%, at 4,907.24, though it recovered from a morning sell-off that took it down as much as 209 points from Friday's record high. Biotechnology stocks were particularly hard hit. The broader market was also lower, though the Dow Jones industrial average managed to inch up 18.31 points to 9,37.13.

| | | | |
|---|---|---|---|
| 1. law, job, collar | 5. China, dime, fly | 9. won, color, Florida | 13. about, now, down |
| 2. class, chance, last | 6. if, is, been | 10. new, blue, through | 14. joy, royal, deploy |
| 3. name, date, way | 7. eve, ease, bean | 11. good, put, could | |
| 4. ten, many, says | 8. worm, third, hard | 12. won't, know, go | |

| A | B | C | D | E | F |
|---|---|---|---|---|---|
| 1. pat | 1. bat | 1. apparition | 1. abolition | 1. lap | 1. lab |
| 2. fat | 2. vat | 2. a rifle | 2. arrival | 2. life | 2. live |
| 3. stink | 3. zinc | 3. graces | 3. grazes | 3. dice | 3. dies |
| 4. sheer | 4. girl | 4. mesher | 4. measure | 4. dish | 4. deluge |
| 5. ten | 5. den | 5. latter | 5. ladder | 5. ought | 5. odd |
| 6. cheer | 6. jeer | 6. nature | 6. major | 6. etch | 6. edge |
| 7. thing | 7. the | 7. author | 7. other | 7. breath | 7. breathe |
| 8. core | 8. gore | 8. lacking | 8. lagging | 8. snack | 8. snag |
| 9. yet | 9. rice | 9. access | 9. example | 9. box | 9. bogs |
| 10. wolf | 10. prance | 10. association | 10. refract | 10. way | 10. bar |
| 11. her | 11. my | 11. actual | 11. arrive | 11. down | 11. mutter |
| 12. lice | 12. not | 12. behind | 12. climber | 12. ball | 12. name |
| 13. plants | | 13. reflect | 13. innate | 13. muddle | 13. ran |
| | | 14. alive | 14. singer | | 14. wrong |

1. Sue arranged it.

2. She organized her office.

3. Get your report done.

4. Where did you put it?

5. She's your usual television star.

1. Soo⁽ʷ⁾ərɛinj dit.

2. Shee⁽ʸ⁾orgənizdr räfəs.

3. Gɛcher r'port dən.

4. Wɛrjə püd't?

5. Shezhier yuzhəwᵊl tɛləvizhən stär.

1. Get a better water heater.

2. Gedda bedder wädr heedr.

| 3. alter | later |
|----------|-------|
| 4. intern | enter |
| 5. data | deter |
| 6. metal | metallic |

| 7. bet | bed |
|--------|-----|

# Nationality Guide
## 汉语发音与美音的对比

No matter what language you speak, you will have different sounds and rhythms from a native speaker of American English. The Nationality Guide will give you a head start on what to listen for in American English from the perspective of your own native language. In order to specifically identify what you need to work on, this section can be used in conjunction with the *diagnostic analysis.* The analysis provides an objective rendering of the sounds and rhythms based on how you currently speak, as well as specific guidelines for how to standardize your English; call (800) 457-4255 for a private consultation.

不论你说哪种语言，你的发音和节奏都会和以美语为母语的人的不一样。"汉语发音与美音的对比"会让你的学习有个好的开端，使你从自己的母语的角度来了解应该注意听美语的哪些部分。为了明确你需要学习的内容，本部分可以和"诊断分析"一起使用。诊断分析可以基于你目前的口语水平，向你提供对发音和节奏的客观描述以及如何让你的英语更标准的具体指南；你可以拨打001-800-457-4255（中国大陆）或800-457-4255（美国本地）来进行个人咨询。

This section will cover *intonation*, *word connections*, *pronunciation*, *location of the language in the mouth*, as well as particular difficulties to work through, and solutions to common misperceptions.

这部分将包括语调、连读、发音、语言在口腔中的发音位置，以及需要克服的特殊困难和一些常见误解的解答。

Most adult students rely too heavily on spelling. It's now your job to listen for pure sound, and reconcile that to spelling—not the other way around. This is the same path that a native speaker follows.

大部分成年的学习者都太过于依赖拼写。现在你要做的就是只注意听纯粹的发音，然后使拼写和这个发音相吻合——而不是采取相反的做法。这就是说母语的人学习的方法。

As you become familiar with the major characteristics and tendencies in American English, you will start using that information in your everyday speech. One of the goals of the diagnostic analysis is to show you what you already know, so you can use the information and skills in English as *transfer skills,* rather than *newly learned skills.* You will learn more readily, more quickly, and more pleasantly—and you will retain the information and use the accent with less resistance.

一旦你熟悉了美语的主要特点和趋向，你将开始在日常会话中使用这些信息。诊断分析的目的之一就是向你展示你已经知道的内容，从而让你在英语中使用这些被称之为"可转移性技巧"的信息和技巧，而不是"刚学到的技巧"。你的学习将会变得更容易、更快速、更愉快——并且你将掌握这些信息，在使用这些发音时也会带有更少的抵触情绪。

Read the Nationality Guide—you never know when you'll pick up something useful for yourself.

仔细阅读"汉语发音与美音的对比"部分的所有内容——你很难预料什么时候就学到了对自己有用的东西。

# Intonation
语调

**Important Point**
**要点**

*In English, a pitch change indicates the speaker's intention. In Chinese, a pitch change indicates a different word.*
在英语中，音高变化表示说话人的意图。在汉语中，音高变化表示不同的汉字。

There are several immediately evident characteristics of a Chinese accent. The most notable is the lack of speech music, or the musical intonation of English. This is a problem because, in the English language, *intonation* indicates meaning, new information, contrast, or emotion. Another aspect of speech music is *phrasing,* which tells if it is a statement, a question, a yes/no option, a list of items, or where the speaker is in the sentence (introductory phrase, end of the sentence, etc.). In Chinese, however, a change in tone indicates a different vocabulary word. (See also Chapter 4)

汉语发音有几个显而易见的特征。最显著的特征是缺乏语言韵律，或是英语的音乐语调。这是个问题，因为在英语语言中，语调表示意义、新信息、对比或情绪。语言韵律的另一个方面是断句，它表明句子是否是陈述句、疑问句、选择、列举，或说话人在句中的位置（起始短语，句子的末尾等）。然而，在汉语中，声调的变化表示的是不同的汉字。（也见第4章）

In English, Chinese speakers have a tendency to increase the *volume* on stressed words but otherwise give equal value to each word. This atonal volume increase will sound aggressive, angry, or abrupt to a native speaker. When this is added to the tendency to lop off the end of each word, and almost no word connections at all, the result ranges from choppy to unintelligible.

中国人说英语时常常提高重读单词的音量，但却分配相同的音量值给其他的每个单词。这种非调性的音量增加在说母语的人听来是挑衅、愤怒，或是唐突的。除此之外，再加上对单词尾音的省略，以及连音的几乎完全缺失，结果是突兀甚至难以理解的。

*The four "ma" tones of Mandarin Chinese*
汉语普通话中 "ma" 的四个声调

ma¹ —
ma² ╱
ma³ ⌄
ma⁴ ╲

In spite of this unpromising beginning, Chinese learners have a tremendous advantage. Here is an amazingly effective technique that radically changes how you sound. Given the highly developed tonal qualities of the Chinese language, you are truly a "pitch master." In order for you to appreciate your strength in this area, try the four *ma* tones of Mandarin Chinese. These four tones sound identical to Americans— *ma, ma, ma, ma.*

虽然开始并不乐观，但中国学习者还是有极大的优势的。这里有个非常有效的技巧，能快速改变你的发音。你被赋予了高度发达的汉语语言的声调特征，是真正的 "音高大师"。为了让你体会到这方面的优势，试着用普通话发ma的四个声调。这四个声调在美国人听来是相同的——ma，ma，ma，ma。

Take the first sentence in Exercise 4-5, *It sounds like **rain,*** and replace *rain* with *ma*¹. Say *It sounds like ma*¹. This will sound strangely flat, so then try *It sounds like ma*². This isn't it either, so go on to *It sound like ma*³ and *It sounds like ma*⁴. One of the last two will sound pretty good, usually *ma*³. You may need to come up with a combination of

*1. Say the four **ma**'s.*
发ma的四声。

*2. Write them out
with the appropriate
arrows.*
用恰当的箭头将它们
写出。

*3. Replace the
stressed word in a
sentence with each
of the four **ma**'s.*
用ma的四声分别代替句
子中的重读单词。

*4. Decide which one
sounds best.*
找出哪个音听起来最好。

*5. Put the stressed
word back in the
sentence, keeping
the tone.*
将重读单词放回句中，
保持声调。

ma³ and ma⁴, but once you have the idea of what to listen for, it's really easy. When you have that part clear, put *rain* back in the sentence, keeping the tone:

以练习4-5中的第一个句子It sounds like **rain**为例，用一声ma代替rain，说It sounds like ma¹。这听起来异常地平，那么试着说It sounds like ma²。这听起来也不对，那么接着说It sounds like ma³ 以及it sounds like ma⁴。最后两个句子中的一个听起来很纯正，通常是ma³。你可能需要把ma³和ma⁴结合起来，然而一旦你知道了你要用心听什么，这就很简单了。当你弄清楚了这一点，把rain放回句中，并保持那个声调：

It sounds like *ma*³.

It sounds like *rain*³.

**If it sounds a little short *(It sounds like ren)*, double** the sound:

如果rain的发音听起来有点短（听起来像"ren"），把发音延长一倍：

It sounds like

When this exercise is successful, go to the second sentence, *It **sounds** like rain* and do the same thing:

当这个练习成功了，继续第二个句子，It **sounds** like rain，用相同的方法来做：

It *ma*³ like rain.

It *sounds*³ like rain.

Then, contrast the two:

然后，对比这两个句子：

It sounds like *rain*³.

It *sounds*³ like rain.

From this point on, you only need to periodically listen for the appropriate *ma*, substituting it in for words or syllables. You don't even need to use the rubber band since your tonal sophistication is so high.

从现在开始，你只需常常用心去听适当的ma，并用单词或音节来代替它。你甚至无需使用橡皮圈，因为你的声调很复杂。

**Goal**
目标

*To get you to use
your excellent tone
control in English.*
让你在英语中运用自己
极强的音调控制能力。

The main point of this exercise is to get you listening for the tone shifts in English, which are very similar to the tone shifts in Chinese. The main difference is that Americans use them to indicate stress, whereas in Chinese, they are fully different words when the tone changes.

这个练习的要点是让你用心去听英语中的音调变化，这和汉语中的声调变化很相似。其主要区别在于，美国人用音调变化来表示重音，而在汉语中，声调变化表示完全不同的汉字。

A simple way to practice intonation is with the sound that American children use when they make a mistake—*uh-oh.* This quick note shift is completely typical of the pattern, and once you have mastered this double note, you can go on to more complex patterns. Because Chinese grammar is fairly similar to English grammar, you don't have to worry too much about word order.

一个练习语调的简单方法是用**uh**-oh来练习，这个音是美国小孩做错了事时会发出的。这种快速的音符变化是非常典型的模式，一旦你掌握了这种双音符，就可以继续练习更加复杂的模式。因为汉语语法和英语语法十分相似，所以你不必过于担心词序。

## Liaisons
## 连音

All of the advantages that you have from *intonation* are more than counterbalanced by your lack of *word connections.* The reason for this is that Chinese characters (words or parts of words) start with consonants and end with either a vowel or a nasalized consonant, *n* or *ng.* There is no such thing as a final *t, l,* or *b* in Chinese. This leads to several difficulties:

单词连音的缺乏大大抵消了你在语调上具有的所有优势。原因在于汉字（即英文中的单词或单词的组成部分）以辅音开头，以元音或鼻辅音n或ng结尾。在汉语中，没有以t，l，或b结尾的音。这就带来了几点困难：

*Chinese characters start with consonants and end with either a vowel or a nasalized consonant (n or ng).*
中国汉字以辅音开头，以元音或鼻辅音（n或ng）结尾。

- No word endings
  没有单词尾音

- No word connections
  没有单词连读

- No distinction between final voiced or unvoiced consonants
  没有末尾浊辅音和清辅音的区别

It takes time and a great deal of concentration, but the lack of word endings and word connections can be remedied. Rather than force the issue of adding on sounds that will be uncomfortable for you, which will result in overpronunciation, go with your strengths—notice how in *speech,* but not *spelling,* Americans end their words with vowel sounds and start them with consonants, just as in Chinese! It's really a question of rewriting the English script in your head that you read from when you speak. (See also Chapter 11)

这要花费时间和大量的精力，但是，缺少单词尾音和单词连读是可以纠正的。不要强行加上让你不自在的音，这会令你显得太做作，而要发挥你的优势——注意怎样发音，而不是怎样拼写。美国人以元音结束单词，以辅音开始单词，正好和汉语一样。这实际上是在你的大脑中将说话时读出的文字重新写了一遍。（也见第11章）

**Goal**

目标

*To get you to rewrite your English script and to speak with sound units rather than word units.*

令你重新书写你的英语文字，并且用音群而非用词群说话。

*Liaisons* or *word connections* will force the final syllable to be pronounced by pushing it over to the beginning of the next word, where Chinese speakers have no trouble—not even with **L**.

连音或单词的连读会通过将最后一个音节挤向下一个单词的开头来迫使其发音，在这方面说汉语的人没有任何困难——甚至对于L音也一样没问题。

| Written English | Chinese Accent | American (with Liaisons) |
|---|---|---|
| Tell him | teo him | tellim |
| Pull it out | puw ih aw | pü li dout |

Because you are now using a natural and comfortable technique, you will sound smooth and fluid when you speak, instead of that forced, exaggerated speech of people who are doing what they consider unnatural. It takes a lot of correction to get this process to sink in, but it's well worth the effort. Periodically, when you speak, write down the exact sounds that you made, then write it in regular spelling, so you can *see* the Chinese accent and the effect it has on meaning *(puw ih aw* has no meaning in English). Then convert the written English to spoken American *(pull it out* changes to *pü li dout)* to help yourself rewrite your English script.

因为现在你在使用自然而舒适的技巧，所以当你说话时，听起来会平滑而流畅，而不像人们在发他们认为奇怪的音时那样强迫而夸张。要了解这个过程，需要进行大量的纠正，但这一切努力都是值得的。定期写下你说话时发出的确切的音，然后用常规的拼写方式写下来，这样，你就能明白地看出自己说英语时的汉语口音，以及汉语口音对意义产生的影响（puw ih aw在英语中没有意义）。然后，将书面英语转化为美语口语（pull it out变成了pull li dout），来帮助你自己重新书写英语文字。

When you don't use liaisons, you also lose the underlying hum that connects sentences together. This *co-assonance* is like the highway, and the words are the cars that carry the listener along.

当你不使用连音时，你也就失去了把句子连接起来的不明显的哼哼声。这种声音就像是条大道，而单词就像是载着听者的汽车。

The last point of intonation is that Chinese speakers don't differentiate between voiced and unvoiced final consonants—*cap* and *cab* sound exactly the same. For this, you will need to go back to the staircase. When a final consonant is voiced, the vowel is lengthened or doubled. When a final consonant is unvoiced, the vowel is short or single.

语调的最后一点，就是说汉语的人不区别末尾辅音是浊音还是清音——cap和cab听起来完全相同。为此，你需要回到音阶阶梯理论。当末尾辅音是浊音时，元音的发音延长且在两个音阶阶梯上。当末尾辅音是清音时，元音的发音缩短且在一个音阶阶梯上。

Additionally, the long *a* before an *m* is generally shortened to a short ε. This is why the words *same* and *name* are particularly difficult, usually being pronounced *sem* and *nem.* You have to add in the second half of the sound. You need *nay + eem* to get *name.* Doubled vowels are explained on page 38.

此外，说汉语的人总是将m前的长音a缩短为短音ε。这是为什么难以正确发出same和name，而通常将其发为sem和nem的原因。你必须在第二个音的中间加音。你需要通过nay+eem来发出name的音。对于"两个音阶阶梯上的元音"的解释在第38页。

## Pronunciation
发音

**Goal**
**目标**

*For you to hear the actual vowel and consonant sounds of English, rather than a Chinese perception of them.*
让你听到英语元音和辅音的实际发音，而非对它们中国式的理解。

The most noticeable nonstandard pronunciation is the lack of final **L**. This can be corrected by either liaisons, or by adding a tiny schwa after it (l^(uh) or l^(ə)) in order to position your tongue correctly. This is the same solution for *n* and *ng.* Like most other nationalities, Chinese learners need to work on *th* and *r,* but fortunately, there are no special problems here. The remaining major area is ā, **ε**, and **æ**, which sound the same. *Mate, met, mat* sound like *met, met, met.* The **ε** is the natural sound for the Chinese, so working from there, you need to concentrate on Chapters 3, 12, and 20. In the word *mate,* you are hearing only the first half of the **εi** combination, so double the vowel with a clear *eet* sound at the end (even before an unvoiced final consonant). Otherwise, you will keep saying *meh-eht* or *may-eht.*

最明显的不标准发音就是缺乏尾音L。这可以通过连音来纠正，或者在l后加上微弱的非中央元音（l^(uh) 或 l^(ə)），从而将你的舌头放在正确的位置。这与n和ng的发音纠正方法相同。和大多数其他国家的人一样，中国学习者也需要努力练习th和r音，但幸运的是在这方面没有特别大的问题。剩下的主要问题是ā，ε和æ的发音，中国人发这几个音时听起来是一样的。Mate，met，mat听起来像met，met，met。ε音对中国人来说是自然的发音，所以从ε音开始练习，你需要认真学习第3、12和20章。在单词mate中，你听到的只是εi合成音的前半部分，所以把元音放在两个音阶阶梯上，在词尾加上清晰的eet音（即使末尾是清辅音也这样做）。否则，你会一直发成meh-eht或may-eht。

made
**ā**
long A

China

long i

It frequently helps to know exactly how something would look in your own language—and in Chinese, this entails characters. The characters on the left are the sounds needed for a Chinese person to say both the long *i* as in *China* and the long *ā* as in *made* or *same.* Read the character, and then put letters in front and in back of it so you are reading half alphabet, half character. An **m** in front and a **d** in back of the first character will let you read *made.* A *ch* in front and **na** in back of the second character will produce *China.* It's odd, but it works. (See also Chapter 12)

确切地了解一些音在你的母语中是怎样发的通常是很有益的——在汉语中，这要借助汉字。左边的两个汉字是中国人发长音i（比如在China中）和长音ā（比如在made或same中）所需要的音。先读汉字，然后把字母放在汉字的前后，这样你就在读一半的字母和一半的汉字。m在第一个汉字前，d在第一个汉字后，这会让你读出made。ch在第二个汉字前，na在第二个汉字后，这会产生China的发音。这种方法虽然怪异，但很有效。（也见第12章）

fay
**l**
yə
eˡ
fail

A word that ends in *-ail* is particularly difficult for Chinese speakers since it contains both the hard **εi** combination and a final **l** (Chapter 5). It usually sounds something like *feh-o.* You need to *say fail* as if it had three full syllables —*fay-yə-lº.* (See also Chapter 16)

以-ail结尾的单词对说汉语的人尤其困难，因为它包含了难发的εi组合音和末尾的l音（第5章）。它常常会被发成像feh-o之类的音。当你发fail的音时，需要发成fay-yə-lº，就像它有三个完全的音节。（也见第16章）

**u, v,**
**f, w**

Another difficulty may be **u, v, f,** and **w.** The point to remember here is that **u** and **w** can both be considered *vowels* (i.e., they don't touch anywhere in the mouth), whereas **v** and **f** are *consonants* (your upper teeth touch your lower lip). **ū**, as in *too* or *use* should be no problem. Similar to **ū**, but with a little push of slightly rounded lips is **w,** as in *what* or *white.* The letters **f** and **v** have basically the same sound, but **f** is unvoiced and **v** is voiced. Your lower lip should come up a little to meet your top teeth. You are not biting down on the outside of your lip here; the sound is created using the inside of your lower lip. Leave your mouth in the same position and make the two sounds, both voiced and unvoiced. Practice words such as *fairy, very,* and *wary.* (See also Chapter 19)

另一个困难可能是u，v，f和w的发音。需要记住一点，u和w都可以被当做元音（即发音时不触及口腔中的任何部位），而v和f是辅音（发音时你的上齿接触下唇）。ū音，如在too或use中的发音，应该没有问题。和ū音相似，但将略微收圆的双唇轻微向前突就是w音，如在what或white中的发音。字母f和v从根本上讲是同一个音，但f是清辅音，而v是浊辅音。你的下嘴唇要略微向上抬，并触及上齿。在这里，不要咬到唇的外侧；这个音要靠下嘴唇内侧产生。让嘴放在相同的位置，发这两个音，一个浊音一个清音。练习像fairy，very和wary之类的单词的发音。（也见第19章）

There is another small point that may affect people from southern mainland China who use *l* and *n* interchangeably. This can be corrected by working with *l* words and pinching the nose shut. If you are trying to say *late* and it comes out *Nate,* hold your nose closed and the air will be forced out through your mouth. (See also Chapter 16)

另外一个小问题可能会影响到来自中国大陆南方的人，他们将l音和n音互换使用。这可以通过练习含字母l的单词，并且捏紧鼻子来纠正。如果你想说late，但发成了nate，那么捏紧鼻子，气流将被迫从你的口腔流出。（也见第16章）

**æ** The **æ** sound doesn't exist in Chinese, so it usually comes out as *ä* or *ɛ*, so *last* sounds like *lost* or *name* sounds like *nem.* You need to work on Chapter 12, which drills this distinctively American vowel. (See also Chapters 12, 18, and 20)

æ音在汉语中不存在，所以它总是被错发为ä或ɛ，因而last听起来像lost，name听起来像nem。你需要学习第12章，这章对这个具有美音特色的元音进行了训练。（也见第12、18和20章）

**ä** Because of spelling, the *ä* sound can easily be misplaced. The *ä* sound exists in Chinese, but when you see an *o,* you might want to say *ō,* so *hot* sounds like *hōht* instead of *häht.* Remember, most of the time, the letter *o* is pronounced *ah.* This will give you a good reference point for whenever you want to say *ä* instead of *ō: astronomy, call, long, progress,* etc. (See also Chapters 12, 18, and 20)

因为拼写的缘故，ä音很容易被发错。ä音在汉语中存在，但当你看到一个字母o，你可能想发成ō音，所以hot听起来像hōht，而不是häht。记住，大多数时候，字母o都发成ɑh音。无论何时你想用ä来替代ō，这都会给你一个很好的参照，比如astronomy，call，long，progress等。（也见第12、18和20章）

**o** Conversely, you may pronounce the letter *o* as *ä* or *ə* when it should be an *o,* as in *only, most, both.* Make sure that the American *o* sounds like *ou: ounly, moust, bouth.* (See also Chapters 12, 18, and 20)

相反地，当字母o应当发o音时，你可能会把它发得像ä或ə音，比如在only，most，both中。请确保美音o听起来像ou：ounly，moust，bouth。（也见第12、18和20章）

**ə** The schwa is typically overpronounced based on spelling. Work on Chapter 4, American Intonation, and Chapter 12, Cat? Caught? Cut?. If your intonation peaks are strong and clear enough, then your valleys will be sufficiently reduced as well. Concentrate on smoothing out and reducing the valleys and *ignore spelling!* (See also Chapters 12, 18, and 20)

由于拼写的原因，非中央元音的发音总是被过于强调。学习第4章"美音语调"，以及第12章"Cat，Caught和Cut的发音区别"。如果你的语调"顶峰"足够强烈和清晰，那么你的语调"低谷"也会足够降低。集中精力于平滑地发出并弱读语调"低谷"的音，忽略拼写。（也见第12、18和20章）

**ü**

The ü sound is generally overpronounced to *ooh.* Again, spelling is the culprit. Words such as *smooth, choose,* and *too* are spelled with two o's and are pronounced with a long *ū* sound, but other words such as *took* and *good* are spelled with two o's but are pronounced halfway between *ih* and *uh;* **tük** and **güd.** (See also Chapters 18 and 20)

ü音通常被过于强调地发成ooh。拼写又一次成为了"罪魁祸首"。像smooth，choose和too这些单词，拼写中有两个o，发音是长音ū，而其他的单词，比如took和good，它们的拼写中也有两个o，但发音居于ih和uh的中间；应发成tük和güd。（也见第18章和20章）

**i**

In most Chinese dictionaries, the distinction between *i* and *ē* is not made. The *ē* is generally indicated by *i:,* which causes problems with final consonants, and the *ih* sound is overpronounced to *eee.* Practice these four sounds, remembering that *tense vowels* indicate that you tense your lips or tongue, while *lax vowels* mean that your lips and tongue are relaxed and the sound is produced in your throat. *Unvoiced* final consonants (*t, s, k, p, ch, f*) mean that the vowel is short and sharp; *voiced* final consonants (*d, z, g, b, j, v*) mean that the vowel is doubled. Work on *Bit or Beat? Bid or Bead?* in Chapter 18. (See also Chapter 20)

在中国的大多数英文词典中，不区分i和ē的发音。ē音通常被表示为i:，这会给末尾辅音带来问题；同时i音被过于强调，发成了eee。练习这四个音，记住，紧元音表明你的双唇和舌部要紧绷，而松元音意味着你的双唇或舌部要放松，并且发音在喉部产生。末尾是清辅音（t，s，k，p，ch，f）意味着元音又短又急促；末尾是浊辅音（d，z，g，b，j，v）意味着元音发音要两倍长。练习第18章中的"Bit还是Beat? Bid还是Bead?"（也见第20章）

**r**

Chinese speakers usually pronounce American *r* as *ä* at the end of a word (*car* sounds like *kaaah*) or almost a *w* in the beginning or middle (*grow* sounds like *gwow*). The tongue should be curled back more, and the *r* produced deep in the throat. (See also Chapter 15)

说汉语的人常常把词尾的美音r发成ä（car听起来像kaaah），或把词首或词中的r发成w(grow听起来像gwow)。舌头应该更加向后卷，使r音在喉咙深处产生。（也见第15章）

**th**

If you pronounce *th* as *t* or *d* (depending if it's voiced or unvoiced), then you should allow your tongue tip to move about a quarter of an inch forward, so the very tip is just barely between your teeth. Then, from this position you make a sound similar to *t* or *d.* (See also Chapter 13)

如果你把th发得像t或d（取决于它是浊音还是清音），那么你应该让你的舌尖向前伸大约1/4英寸，这样舌尖恰好位于齿间。然后，从这个位置，发类似t或d的音。（也见第13章）

**n**

Chinese will frequently interchange final *n* and *ng.* The solution is to add a little schwa at the end, just like you do with the *el*: **men**ᵊ, **thing**ᵊ, **call**ᵊ. This will make the tongue position more apparent, as you can see on page 147. (See also Chapter 25)

中国人常常会互换尾音n和ng。解决的方法是在末尾加上一个微弱的非中央元音，就像你发el那样：menᵊ，thingᵊ，callᵊ。这样会使舌头的位置更加明显，就像你在147页看到的那样。（也见第25章）

**sh**   Some people pronounce the *sh* in a particularly Chinese-sounding way. It seems that the tongue is too curled back, which changes the sound. Make sure that the tongue is flat, the tongue tip is just at the ridge behind the top teeth, and that only a thin stream of air is allowed to escape. (See also Chapter 21)

一些人用特别中国化的方式来发sh的音。舌头似乎卷得太靠后，这就改变了发音。请确保舌头是平的，舌尖恰好放在上齿后的牙槽骨上，并且只允许微弱的气流流出。（也见第21章）

**t**   American English has a peculiar characteristic in that the *t* sound is, in many cases, pronounced as a *d*. (See also Chapter 14)

美式英语有一个奇怪的特征，那就是在很多情况下，t音发得像d音。（也见第14章）

**Final Consonants** One of the defining characteristics of Chinese speech is that the final consonants are left off *(hold* sounds like *ho)*. Whenever possible, make a liaison with the following word. For example, *hold* is difficult to say, so try *hold on = hol dän.* Pay particular attention to Chapter 11.

汉语的特征之一，就是末尾的辅音被省略（hold听起来像ho）。所以只要有可能，就和下一个单词连读。例如，发hold的音是困难的，所以试着说hold on = hol dän。要特别注意第11章的内容。

## Location of the Language
语言的位置

Chinese, like American English, is located in the *back of the throat.* The major difference between the two languages is that English requires that the speaker use the *tongue tip* a great deal: th and final *t, d, n, l.* Chapter 21, The Ridge, will help a great deal with this.

汉语和美式英语的发音位置都在喉咙的深处。这两种语言的主要区别在于，英语要求说话者经常使用舌尖，如th以及末尾的t，d，n，l。第21章"牙槽骨"会讲到很多相关知识。

# Answer Key
# 参考答案

**Exercise 1-4: Sounds of Empathy**

| | | | | | | |
|---|---|---|---|---|---|---|
| 1. B | 4. A | 7. C | 10. A | 13. A | 16. B | 19. C |
| 2. B | 5. B | 8. C | 11. C | 14. C | 17. A | 20. B |
| 3. B | 6. A | 9. B | 12. A | 15. B | 18. A | 21. B |

**Exercise 3-5: Regular English**

1. Bob lost his job.
2. Scott taught a lot.
3. Don bought a bike.

**Exercise 3-7: Rhyme Time**

| | | | | |
|---|---|---|---|---|
| 1. No | 11. No | 21. Yes | 31. Yes | 41. Yes |
| 2. No | 12. No | 22. No | 32. Yes | 42. Yes |
| 3. Yes | 13. Yes | 23. Yes | 33. Yes | 43. Yes |
| 4. Yes | 14. Yes | 24. No | 34. No | 44. Yes |
| 5. No | 15. No | 25. Yes | 35. No | 45. Yes |
| 6. Yes | 16. No | 26. No | 36. Yes | 46. Yes |
| 7. No | 17. Yes | 27. No | 37. No | 47. Yes |
| 8. No | 18. No | 28. Yes | 38. No | 48. No |
| 9. No | 19. No | 29. No | 39. Yes | 49. Yes |
| 10. No | 20. Yes | 30. No | 40. No | 50. Yes |

**Exercise 4-4: Sentence Intonation Test**

1. **Sam** sees **Bill**.
2. She **wants** one.
3. **Betty** likes **English**.
4. They **play** with them.
5. **Children** play with **toys**.
6. **Bob** and I call you and **Bill**.
7. You and **Bill** read the news.
8. It **tells** one.
9. **Bernard** works in a restaurant.
10. He **works** in one.
11. He **sees** him.
12. **Mary** wants a **car**.
13. She **likes** it.
14. They **eat** some.
15. **Len** and **Joe** eat some **pizza**.
16. We **call** you.
17. You **read** it.
18. The **news** tells a **story**.
19. **Mark** lived in **France**.
20. He **lived** there.

**Exercise 4-17: Can or Can't Quiz**

| | | |
|---|---|---|
| 1. A | 4. D | 7. C |
| 2. B | 5. A | 8. B |
| 3. C | 6. D | 9. A |

**Exercise 4-18: Application of Stress**

Hello, **my** name is_____. I'm taking American **Accent** Training. There's a **lot** to **learn**, but I **hope** to make it as **enjoyable** as possible. I should pick **up** on the American **intonation** pattern pretty **easily**, although the **only** way to **get** it is to **practice** all of the time. I use the **up** and down, or **peaks** and valleys, **intonation** more than I **used** to. I've been paying attention to **pitch, too**. It's like **walking** down a **stair**case. I've been **talking** to a lot of **Americans** lately, and they tell me that I'm **easier** to under**stand**. **Any**way, I could go **on** and on, but the **important** thing is to **listen** well and sound **good**. **Well,** what do you **think**? **Do** I?

**Exercise 4-26: Regular Transitions of Adj. and Verbs**

1. You need to in**sert** a paragraph here on this newspaper **insert**.
2. How can you ob**ject** to this **object**?
3. I'd like to pre**sent** you with this **present**.
4. Would you care to ela**bor**eit on his **elabor**'t explanation?
5. The manufacturer couldn't re**call** if there'd been a **recall**.
6. The religious **con**vert wanted to con**vert** the world.
7. The political **re**bels wanted to re**bel** against the world.
8. The mogul wanted to re**cord** a new **record** for his latest artist.
9. If you per**fect** your intonation, your accent will be **perfect**.
10. Due to the drought, the fields didn't pro**duce** much **produce** this year.
11. Unfortunately, City Hall wouldn't per**mit** them to get a **permit**.
12. Have you heard that your asso**ci**'t is known to asso**ciet** with gangsters?

13. How much do you **estim**eit that the **estim**'t will be?
14. The facilitator wanted to **separe**it the general topic into **sepr**'t categories.

**Exercise 6-6: Making Set Phrases**

| | | |
|---|---|---|
| 1. a **chair**man | 8. the **Bullet** train | 15. a **dump** truck |
| 2. a **phone** book | 9. a **race** car | 16. a **jelly**fish |
| 3. a **house** key | 10. a **coffee** cup | 17. a **love** letter |
| 4. a **base**ball | 11. a **wrist**watch | 18. a **thumb**tack |
| 5. a **door**bell | 12. a **beer** bottle | 19. a **lightning** bolt |
| 6. the **White** House | 13. a **high** chair | 20. a **pad**lock |
| 7. a **movie** star | 14. a **hunting** knife | |

**Exercise 6-12: Contrast of Compound Nouns**

| | | |
|---|---|---|
| 1. The **White** House | 21. **convenience** store | 41. a **door**knob |
| 2. a white **house** | 22. convenient **store** | 42. a glass **door** |
| 3. a **dark**room | 23. to pick **up** | 43. a locked **door** |
| 4. a dark **room** | 24. a **pickup** truck | 44. **ice** cream |
| 5. Fifth **Avenue** | 25. six years **old** | 45. I **scream**. |
| 6. **Main** Street | 26. a **six**-year-old | 46. elementary |
| 7. a main **street** | 27. six and a **half** | 47. a **lémon** tree |
| 8. a hot **dog** | 28. a **sugar** bowl | 48. **Water**gate |
| 9. a **hotdog** | 29. a wooden **bowl** | 49. the back **gate** |
| 10. a **baby** blanket | 30. a large **bowl** | 50. the final **year** |
| 11. a baby's **blanket** | 31. a **mixing** bowl | 51. a **year**book |
| 12. a baby **bird** | 32. a **top** hat | 52. United **States** |
| 13. a **black**bird | 33. a nice **hat** | 53. New **York** |
| 14. a black **bird** | 34. a straw **hat** | 54. **Long** Beach |
| 15. a **green**house | 35. a **chair**person | 55. Central **Park** |
| 16. a green **house** | 36. Ph.**D**. | 56. a raw **deal** |
| 17. a green **thumb** | 37. **IBM** | 57. a **deal** breaker |
| 18. a **parking** ticket | 38. **MIT** | 58. the bottom **line** |
| 19. a one-way **ticket** | 39. **USA** | 59. a **bottom** feeder |
| 20. an unpaid **ticket** | 40. **ASAP** | 60. a new **low** |

**Exercise 6-13: Description and Set Phrase Test**

1. He's a **nice guy**.
2. He's an **American guy** from San **Francisco**.
3. The **cheer leader** needs a **rubber band** to hold her **pony tail**.
4. The **executive asst**. needs a **paper clip** for the **final report**.
5. The **law student** took an **English test** in a **foreign country**.
6. The **police man** saw a **red car** on the **free way** in Los **Angeles**.
7. My **old dog** has **long ears** and a **flea problem**.
8. The **new teacher** broke his **coffee cup** on the **first day**.
9. His **best friend** has a **broken cup** in his **other office**.
10. Let's play **foot ball** on the **week end** in New **York**.
11. "**Jingle Bells**" is a **nice song**.
12. Where are my **new shoes**?
13. Where are my **tennis shoes**?
14. I have a **head ache** from the **heat wave** in South **Carolina**.
15. The **newly weds** took a **long walk** in **Long Beach**.
16. The **little dog** was sitting on the **side walk**.
17. The **famous athlete** changed clothes in the **locker room**.
18. The **art exhibit** was held in an **empty room**.
19. There was a **class reunion** at the **high school**.
20. The **head lines** indicated a **new policy**.
21. We got **on line** and went to American **Accent dot com**.
22. The **stock options** were listed in the **company directory**.
23. All the **second -graders** were out on the **play ground**.

**Exercise 7-4: Punctuation & Phrasing**

| | | | |
|---|---|---|---|
| 1. D | 2. A | 3. C | 4. B |

### Exercise 7-5: Tag Endings

| | | | |
|---|---|---|---|
| 1. isn't he | 8. will you | 15. hadn't we | 22. did I |
| 2. can't he | 9. doesn't he | 16. wouldn't we | 23. will I |
| 3. does she | 10. don't we | 17. hasn't it | 24. don't you |
| 4. didn't they | 11. haven't we | 18. could you | 25. aren't I |
| 5. do you | 12. didn't we | 19. won't you | 26. didn't you |
| 6. is it | 13. didn't we | 20. shouldn't we | 27. did you |
| 7. aren't I | 14. hadn't we | 21. shouldn't he | 28. isn't it |

### Exercise 8-3: Extended Listening Practice

1. Take it! tay•kit
2. Thank you. thæng•kiu
3. I need a cup of coffee. äi•nee•də•kə•pə•kä•fee
4. What did he do? wə•di•dee•doo
5. Can we go get it now? kwee•go•geh•dit•næo
6. Where did you learn to speak English so well?
   where•jə•lrrn•də•spee•king•glish•so•well
7. I'm going to have to think about it.
   äi•mə•nə•hæf•tə•thing•kə•bæou•dit
8. I'm a little late. äi•mə•li•də•late
9. Try to get another one. try•də•ge•də•nə•thr•wən
10. Why don't you turn it on? wyn•chə•tr•ni•dän
11. Could/Can you hold on to this for a sec?
    kyu•hol•dän•də•this•frə•sec

### Exercise 9-3: Writing Your Own Phonetics

1. bä bry tsa ledder
2. bä bro də ledder
3. bä bi zrydi ngə ledder
4. bä bəl ry də ledder
5. bä bədry də ledderif
6. bä bə də ri(t)n nə ledder
7. thə gäi thə dəz ri(t)n nə ledder
8. bä bə zri(t)n nə ledder
9. bä bə dri(t)n nə ledder
10. bä bə lə vri(t)n nə ledder
11. bä bädə ry də ledder
12. bäb shüdry də ledder
13. bäb shüdn ry də ledder
14. bäb shüdə vri(t)n nə ledder
15. bäb shüdnə vri(t)n nə ledder
16. bäb cüdry də ledder
17. bäb cüdn dry də ledder
18. bäb cüdə vri(t)n nə ledder
19. bäb cüdn nəvri(t)n nə ledder
20. bäb my(t) ry də ledder
21. bäb my də vri(t)n nə ledder
22. bäb məs dry də ledder
23. bäb məs də vri(t)n nə ledder
24. bäb cən ry də ledder
25. bäb cæn(t) ry də ledder

### Exercise 11-4: Consonant/Vowel Liaison Practice

| | |
|---|---|
| 1. ree donly | 6. se lit |
| 2. fä läff | 7. ta kout |
| 3. fällo wə pän | 8. fa də way |
| 4. cə min | 9. sik so |
| 5. cä lim | 10. eh may |

### Exercise 11-8: Consonant/Consonant Liaison Practice

| | |
|---|---|
| 1. businessteal | 6. someplan znee dluck |
| 2. credi(t)check | 7. che(ck)cashing |
| 3. the topfile | 8. let(t)themma(k)conditions |
| 4. sellnine newcars | 9. hadthe |
| 5. sitdown | 10. bothdays |

### Exercise 11-9: Vowel/Vowel Liaison Practice

| | |
|---|---|
| 1. go(w)ɛnywhere | 6. do(w)äi |
| 2. so(w)änest | 7. I(y)æskt |
| 3. through(w)är | 8. to(w)open |
| 4. you(w)är | 9. she(y)äweez |
| 5. he(y)iz | 10. too(w)äffen |

### Exercise 11-11: T, D, S, or Z + Y Liaison Practice

| | |
|---|---|
| 1. dijoo | 6. tisshue |
| 2. hoozhier | 7. gächer |
| 3. jesjer | 8. wherzhier |
| 4. jesjer | 9. c'ngræjəläshunz |
| 5. misshue | 10. hæjer |

### Exercise 11-12: Finding Liaisons and Glides

Hello, **my** name-is _____. I'm taking-American-Accent-Training. There's-a **lot**-to **learn**, but-I **hope** to make-it-as-enjoyable-as possible. I should pick-**up**-on-the(y)American-into**na**tion pattern pretty(y)**ea**sily, although the(y)**only** way-də **get**-it-is-to **practice**-all-of the time. I(y)use the(y)**up**-and-down, or **peaks**-and valleys,-intonation more than-I(y)**used**-to. I've-been paying-attention-to **pitch**,-**too**. It's-like-**walk**ing down-a **stair**case. I've-been-**talk**ing to(w)a lot-of-A**mer**icans-lately, and-they tell me that-I'm-**eas**ier to(w) under**stand**. **Any**way,-I could go(w) **on**-and-on, but-the(y)im**port**ant-thing-is-to **listen**-well-and-sound **good**. **Well**, what-do-you **think**? **Do**(w)I?

### Exercise 12-2: Finding æ, ä, and ə Sounds

Həllo, **my** name is _____. I'm taking əmerəcən **æc**sənt Training. There's ə **lät** tə **learn**, bət I **hope** tə make ət əs ənjoyəbələs pässəbəl. I should pick əp än the əmerəcən əntənashən pættern pretty eəsəly, ä°lthough the **only** way tə **get** ət əs tə **præc**təss ä°ll əv the time. I use the **əp** ənd down, ər **peaks** ənd vælleys, intənashən more thən I **used** to. I've been paying əttenshən tə **pitch, too**. It's like **wälk**ing down ə **stair**case. I've been **tälk**ing to ə **lät** əf **əmer**əcəns lately, ənd they tell me thət I'm **eas**ier tə əndər**stænd**. **Any**way, I could go **än** ənd än, bət the im**port**ant thing əs tə **lissən** we°ll ənd sound **good**. **We°ll**, whət də yə **think**? **Do** I?

### Exercise 13-1: Targeting the Th Sound

Hello, **my** name is _____. I'm taking American **Accent** Training. <u>Th</u>ere's a **lot** to **learn**, but I **hope** to make it as en**joy**able as possible. I should pick **up** on <u>th</u>e American into**na**tion pattern pretty **ea**sily, al<u>th</u>ough <u>th</u>e **only** way to **get** it is to **prac**tice all of <u>th</u>e time. I use <u>th</u>e **up** and down, or **peaks** and valleys, **into**nation more <u>th</u>an I **used** to. I've been paying attention to **pitch, too**. It's like **walk**ing down a **stair**case. I've been **talk**ing to a lot of A**mer**icans lately, and <u>th</u>ey tell me <u>th</u>at I'm **eas**ier to under**stand**. **Any**way, I could go **on** and on, but <u>th</u>e im**port**ant <u>th</u>ing is to **lis**ten well and sound **good**. **Well**, what do you <u>**think**</u>? **Do** I?

### Exercise 13-4: Mr. Thingamajig

I was looking randomly through my belongings for the little unnamed object to fix the darned other little thing, but some guy had put it in the unnamed place, as usual! How annoying. Always the same nonsense with that guy. He's such a small insignificant person! If I found it, (sound of cash register), I'd be rich, which would be just great. I'd be totally confused! That unnamed person had misplaced the unnamed thing again, so surprise, surprise! There was something wrong with it. What a confused situation!

I had a hard time getting in touch with some girl to come over and take care of it with her special little contraption, that she keeps in the unspecified location. For the hundredth time, the silly girl said OK, she wouldn't waste time—she'd come over with her mechanical device fixer and everything to do a great job on the whole project. That's right, the whole repair project, no excuses and no nonsense. Yes, but she was a little busy right then, etc. Yes, we usually do have many devices, but with all the activity and excitement, it's all out of control because that big fool is still in the unnamed location, acting like everything's fine.

That's a lot of nonsense! He's such an old fashioned person. The antics of that guy! Well, I wanted to find it on my own, and not be penalized for it—I'm so tired of requests and catches by curious people who are past their prime, and out associating with snobbish people who used to be famous. The truth is that young and old, they're just a group of cheerful lightweights and crabby old people who don't know anything. I looked through the trinkets, decorative objects, cheap and showy ornaments and small worthless objects, there in the back of the unspecified place, but I couldn't find anything at all. Some guy gave me information about the unnamed thing, but I don't know where it is. It's a big problem when you can't even remember where the darned thing is!

### Exercise 14-14: Finding American T Sounds

Hello, **my** name is _____. I'm taking American **Accen**[(t)] Training. There's a **lo**[(t)] to **learn**, bud I **hope** to make id as en**joy**able as possible. I should pick **up** on the American into**na**tion paddern priddy **ea**sily, although the **only** way də **ged**didis də **prac**tice all of the time. I use the **up** and down, or **peaks** and valleys, into**na**tion more than I **use**[(t)]to. I've been paying attention to **pitch, too.** It's like **walk**ing down a **stair**case. I've been **talk**ing to a **läd**dəv **Amer**icans la[(t)]ely, and they tell me the dime **ea**sier də under**stand. Any**way, I could go **on** and on, bu[(t)] the im**por**[(t)]n[(t)] thing is də **lis**sen well and sound **good. Well,** wha[(d)] do you **think? Do** I?

### Exercise 15-7: Finding the R Sound

Hello, **my** name is _____. I'm taking Ame**ri**can **Accent** Training. There's a **lot** to **learn**, but I **hope** to make it as en**joy**able as possible. I should pick **up** on the Ame**ri**can into**na**tion **pat**tern pretty **ea**sily, although the **only** way to **get** it is to **prac**tice all of the time. I use the **up** and down, o**r** peaks and valleys, **intona**tion mo**re** than I **used** to. I've been paying attention to **pitch, too.** It's like **walk**ing down a **stair**case. I've been **talk**ing to a lot of Ame**ri**cans lately, and they tell me that I'm **ea**sier to unde**rstand. Any**way, I could go **on** and on, but the im**por**tant thing is to **lis**ten well and sound **good. Well,** what do you **think? Do** I?

### Exercise 16-6: Finding L Sounds

He**llo, my** name is _____. I'm taking American **Accent** Training. There's a **lot** to **learn**, but I **hope** to make it as en**joy**ab**le** as possible. I should pick **up** on the American into**na**tion pattern pretty **ea**si**ly,** a**l**though the **on**ly way to **get** it is to **practice** a**ll** of the time. I **use** the **up** and down, or **peaks** and va**lleys, **intona**tion more than I **used** to. I've been paying attention to **pitch, too.** It's **like **walk**ing down a **stair**case. I've been **talk**ing to a **lot** of Americans **lately,** and they te**ll** me that I'm **ea**sier to understand. Any**way, I could go **on** and on, but the im**por**tant thing is to **lis**ten we**ll** and sound **good. We**ll, what do you **think? Do** I?

### Exercise 17-5: Finding S and Z Sounds

Hello, **my** name **iz** _____. I'm taking American **Ac**sent Training. There'**z** a **lot** to **learn**, but I **hope** to make it a**z** en**joy**able a**z** po**ss**ible. I should pick **up** on the American into**na**tion pattern pretty **ea**zily, although the **only** way to **get** it i**z** to **prac**ti**se** all of the time. I u**ze** the **up** and down, or **peak**s and valley**z, **intona**tion more than I **used** to. I've been paying attention to **pitch, too.** It'**s** like **walk**ing down a **stair**ca**se.** I've been **talk**ing to a lot of American**z** lately, and they tell me that I'm **ea**zier to under**stand. Any**way, I could go **on** and on, but the im**por**tant thing i**z** to **lis**ten well and **s**ound **good. Well,** what do you **think? Do** I?

### Review Exercise B: Intonation Review Test

| | | | |
|---|---|---|---|
| 1. | Los **Angeles** | 11. | **every**thing |
| 2. | paper **bag** | 12. | **moving** van |
| 3. | **lunch** bag | 13. | new **paper** |
| 4. | **convenience** store | 14. | **news**paper |
| 5. | convenient **store** | 15. | glass **eyes** |
| 6. | **home**work | 16. | **eye**glasses |
| 7. | good **writer** | 17. | high **chair** |
| 8. | apple **pie** | 18. | **high**chair |
| 9. | **pine**apple | 19. | **base**ball |
| 10. | all **things** | 20. | blue **ball** |

### Exercise 18-8: Finding Reduced Sounds

Hello, **my** name is _____. I'm taking American **Accent**

Training. There's a **lot** to **learn**, but I **hope** to make it as en**joy**able as possible. I **shüd** pick **up** on the American into**na**tion pattern pretty **ea**sily, although the **only** way to **get** it is to practice all of the time. I **üse** the up and down, or **peaks** and valleys, intonation more than I **used tü.** I've been paying attention to **pitch, tü.** It's like **walk**ing down a **stair**case. I've been **talk**ing **tü** a lot of Americans lately, and they tell me that I'm **ea**sier **tü** under**stand. Any**way, I **cüd** go **on** and on, but the im**por**tant thing is to **lis**ten well and sound **güd. Well,** what do you **think? Dü** I?

### Exercise 19-3: Finding V Sounds

Hello, **my** name is _____. I'm taking American **Accent** Training. There's a **lot** to **learn**, but I **hope** to make it as en**joy**able as possible. I should pick **up** on the American into**na**tion pattern pretty **ea**sily, although the **only** way to **get** it is to **prac**tice all o**f** the time. I use the **up** and down, or **peaks** and **v**alleys, intonation more than I **used** to. I'**ve** been paying attention to **pitch, too.** It's like **walk**ing down a **stair**case. I'**ve** been **talk**ing to a lot o**f** Americans lately, and they tell me that I'm **ea**sier to understand. Any**way, I could go **on** and on, but the im**por**tant thing is to **lis**ten well and sound **good. Well,** what do you **think? Do** I?

### Exercise 20-2: Tense Vowels Practice Paragraph

Hello, **my** n**a**me is_____. I'm t**a**king American **æk**sent Tr**a**ining. Th**e**re's a **lot** to learn, but I **hope** to m**a**ke it as en**joy**able as possible. I should pick **up** on th**e** American into**na**tion p**æ**ttern prett**y** **ea**sily, although th**e** only w**a**y to **get** it is to **præc**tice all of the time. I use th**e** **up** an d**æ**on, or **peaks** and v**æ**lleys, into**na**tion more than I **used** to. I've been p**a**ying attention to **pitch, too.** It's like **walk**ing d**æ**on a **stair**c**a**se. I've been **talk**ing to a lot of Americans l**a**tely, and th**a**y tell m**e** that I'm **ea**sier to understænd. Any**wa**y, I could go **on** and on, but th**e** import'nt thing is to **lis**ten well and s**æ**ond **good. Well,** what d' you **think? Do** I?

### Exercise 20-4: Lax Vowels Practice Paragraph

Hello, **my** name is_____. I'm taking əm**e**rəcən **Acc**ənt Training. Th**e**re's ə **lot** tə learn, bət I **hope** tə make it əs ɛn**joy**əb°l əs possəbəl. I should pick **ə**p on the əm**e**rəcən intənashən pattern pritty **ea**səly, although the only way tə **get** it is tə **prac**təs all əv thə time. I use the **up** ən down, or **peaks** ən valleys, intənashən more than I **used** to. I've bin paying əttɛnshən tə **pitch, too.** It's like **walk**ing down ə st**e**rcase. I've bin **talk**ing to ə lot əv əm**e**rəcəns lately, ənd they tell me thət I'm **ea**sier to əndərstand. ɛny**way, I could go **on** ənd on, bət the import'nt thing is to **lis**tən well ənd sound **good. Well,** whət d' you **think? Do** I?

### Exercise 24-4: Finding n and ng Sounds

Hello, **my** n̲ame is _____. I'm taki**n**g America**n** **Accent** Trai**n**i**n**g. There's a **lot** to **learn**, but I **hope** to make it as e**n**joyable as possible. I should pick **up** o**n** the American i**n**to**n**ation pattern pretty **ea**sily, although the **on**ly way to **get** it is to **prac**tice all of the time. I use the **up** a**n**d dow**n**, or **peaks** a**n**d valleys, i**n**to**n**ation more tha**n** I **used** to. I've bee**n** paying atte**n**tio**n** to **pitch, too.** It's like **walk**ing dow**n** a staircase. I've bee**n** **talk**ing to a lot of America**n**s lately, a**n**d they tell me that I'm **ea**sier to u**n**der**stand.** Any**way, I could go **on** a**n**d on, but the im**por**tant thing is to **lis**ten well a**n**d sou**n**d **good. Well,** what do you **thin**gk? Do I?

### Exercise 25-4: Glottal Consonant Practice Paragraph

Hello, **my** name is _____. I'm taki**n**g Ameri̱kan A̱kcent Training. There's a **lot** to **learn**, but I **hope** to make it as en**joy**able as possible. I should pick **up** on the Ameri̱kan into**na**tion pattern pretty **ea**sily, although the **only** way to **get** it is to **prak**tice all of the time. I use the **up** and down, or **peaks** and valleys, intonation mo̱re than I **used** to. I've been payi̱ng attention to **pitch, too.** It's like **walk**ing down a stair̲case. I've been **talk**ing to a lot of Ameri̱kans lately, and they tell me that I'm **ea**sier to under**stand.** Any**way, I kould go **on** and on, but the im**por**tant thing is to **lis**ten well and sound **good. Well,** what do you **think? Do** I?

# Teacher's Guide
# 教师指导

This is a very practical, step-by-step guide to working with foreign-born adults. If you go through all the exercises, giving strong feedback, you should have results similar to the one you heard on CD.

这部分对于不在美国出生的成年人来说，是一个非常实用的、循序渐进的指导。如果你把所有的练习从头到尾做了一遍，并且给出了强烈的回应，那么你取得的结果应该会跟CD中听到的一样。

## Chapter 1: The American Sound

**Intonation**, **voice quality, liaisons** and **pronunciation** are the four pillars of the American Accent Training method. It's the way that children learn their native language, and they are the main elements that are unfortunately missing when adults study a foreign language. Without intonation and voice quality, a student is simply using English words in a non-English format. It is your task to make sure that the voice is properly placed and that the rhythm patterns become ingrained. Voice quality is a combination of vocal placement and cadence, which means a throaty sound and a stairstep intonation. Intonation is the pitch-change patterns used by native speakers. Within a word, a phrase, or a sentence, certain syllables are given more stress (accorded a higher pitch) than others. How this stress changes the meaning of a sentence, how it can move around in a sentence and how it can reflect the speaker's intent—or even personality—is what you need to convey to your students. Use the Nationality Guide to let the students see the correlation between their intonation and pronunciation; where it's similar and where it's different. Also point out that every language has intonation, but it's most likely that they won't have realized that about their own language.

语调、音质、连读和发音是美语发音训练方法的四大支柱。这是孩子们学习母语的方法，同时也是成年人学习外语时不幸漏掉的几大要素。如果没有语调和音质，学生就只是在用非英语的方式使用英语单词。你的任务是确保学生的发音位置正确，让语调成为他们的一部分。音质是发声位置和韵律的结合，也就是喉音和阶梯状语调的结合。语调是以英语为母语者的音高变化模式。在一个单词、短语或句子中，有些音节要比其他音节读得重（用了高音调）。这个重读音是如何改变句子的意思，如何在一个句子中移动，如何反映出说话者的意图——或者甚至是性格——是你需要教给学生的。通过"汉语发音与美音的对比"部分使学生看到他们的语调和发音之间的关系；它们在什么地方相似，在什么地方有区别。也要告诉学生每种语言都有语调，他们很可能没有意识到自己的语言也是如此。

### Asking Questions
### 提问

In America, students are encouraged to ask questions; Asian students are not. Your students need to realize that not only are questions welcomed, they **must** ask them. ESL teachers tend to talk too much. Limit yourself to 10% of the talking, and have your students do the other 90%. This means you only talk for six minutes in a one-hour class. Make the students do the work, not you.

在美国，学生们被鼓励提问题；但亚洲的学生却并非如此。你需要让学生意识到，你不仅欢迎他们提问，而且还要求他们"必须"提问。英语作为第二语言教学的老师往往讲解得过多。要限制自己只占用10%的说话时间，让你的学生在其余90%的时间说话。这意味着在一个小时的课时中，你只说6分钟的话。要让学生说话，而不是你自己。

## The American Sound
美音

The first step is to get the student to generate his voice from the correct place. It's not up in the head or forward in the mouth, but in the back of the throat with the air projected from the diaphragm. While working on the airflow and sound production, have the student start correlating the phonetic symbols with the actual spelling. One of the main goals is to get visual students oriented to the auditory aspects of English.

第一步是让学生从正确的部位发音。不是从头部或口腔的前部发音，而是使用膈肌发出的气流，从喉咙的后部发音。在学习控制气流和如何发音的过程中，让学生把音标和实际的拼写联系起来。其中最主要的目的之一是让视觉型学习者适应英语的听觉方面。

As you heard on Track 004, Eddie Izzard demonstrates moving his voice back and down to imitate the American sound. This essential throaty quality—*rhoticity*—is that solid R as in **hard** and **far**.

正如你在Track 004中所听到的，埃迪·伊泽德展示了如何通过把声音后移和下压来模仿美语发音。这种重要的喉音音质——卷舌化——就是hard和far里清晰可辨的R音。

With a slight detour to the general pronunciation introduction in Chapter 3, the first third of this program deals with voice quality and intonation. Even as you work through word connections and pronunciation, you'll find yourself coming back to vocal placement and cadence as the most important determinants of a standard accent.

稍微绕到第3章的一般发音的介绍部分，这本教程的前三分之一都在讲音质和语调。即便当你学习词的连读和发音时，你也会发现自己又回到了发声位置和韵律，它们是决定发音是否纯正的最为重要的因素。

Most intermediate to advanced students have studied a lot of grammar and have sufficient vocabularies. They need to understand, however, that their accent is actually more important than perfect grammar or an extensive vocabulary—after all, if the listener can't understand, what's the point of a mastery of the pluperfect subjunctive? It's interesting to know that 25% of what we say consists of just nine words: *and, be, have, it, of, the, to, will, you* and they are almost always unstressed. Of the hundreds of thousands of words that exist in English, the daily usage is about 1000. Get your students to focus on high-frequency vocabulary.

大多数中到高级水平的学生已经学到了许多语法知识，也有充足的词汇量。但是，他们需要明白，他们的发音实际上比完美的语法或丰富的词汇重要——毕竟，如果听话者无法理解，那掌握了过去完成时的虚拟语气又有什么用呢？有趣的是，我们说的25%的内容仅仅是由9个单词组成的：and, be, have, it, of, the, to, will, you，而且它们几乎从来不重读。在成千上万个英语单词中，日常使用的大约有1000个。让你的学生把注意力集中在高频词汇上。

Explain the difference between the intonation or rhythm of a sentence—the music or tonality—and the actual sounds of the individual words or pronunciation and demonstrate that rhythm has more to do with "sounding American" than the individual words do. Make the sound that Americans make when they say, **I don't know** (one step beyond **I dunno**) without enunciating the words. In this case, rhythm alone is communication. (See page 40)

解释某个句子的语调或节奏的区别——韵律或音调——以及每个单词或发音的实际读音，说明与"听起来像美国人"更有关系的是节奏而不是每个单词。发出美国人在说I don't know时所发的音（比 I dunno 更夸张一点），不要发出每个单词的音。在这种情况下，节奏本身就是交流。（见第40页）

## Getting Started
开始学习

During the diagnostic analysis on page xv, ask why the student is taking an accent class. You can call us for advice at 800-457-4255. In order to get students into the zone and to find out what they think their potential is, ask what they think they can achieve on a scale of 1 to 10. Make a note of the number. Ask where they think they are now and note that number as well. It's usually pretty accurate.

在第xv页的诊断分析过程中，问问学生为什么要上发音课。你可以拨打001-800-457-4255（中国大陆地区）或800-457-4255（美国本地）咨询我们。为了让学生入门，找出他们认为自己所具备的潜力，问他们认为在1到10的等级中自己可以达到哪个级别。记下这个数字。问他们认为自己现在处于哪个级别，也记下那个数字。通常来说，这个数字是非常准确的。

In order to give them confidence in what you will be doing, explain that they will be recorded at the beginning and at the end of the course, as well as intermittently throughout, and that after they have gone through the steps, they can't help but sound more American. If the students haven't had a diagnostic analysis, mention you will be integrating all four components of the accent (voice quality, intonation, liaisons, pronunciation), and you will be covering it all in detail. Things like **tense** and **lax vowels**, **voiced** and **unvoiced consonants** can all be dealt with as they come up in their respective chapters. If you are asked directly, of course, go ahead and answer. Start right in on the American speech music and get the student to have the proper vocal placement. In the second exercise, you'll be approaching the American sound via nonsense syllables. This will circumvent the student's inclination to fall back on old habits and misconceptions. Have the student write down the five syllables, **bä bee bä də bäik**. It doesn't have to be phonetically accurate and don't insist on the symbols. If they write **bah bi bah duh byk**, that's just fine. Have the student say it out loud as a regular sentence and they will get bits and pieces before figuring out, **Bobby bought a bike**. The major take-aways are that the letter **O** sounds like **ah** and that the **T** between vowels turns into a **D**. This is the first step in guiding a student from spelling-based pronunciation to a phonetic understanding of pure sound. Next, have the student work on perfecting a go-to phrase, including vocal placement and facial position, to get into the American zone. Along these same lines, work on active listening, with the student responding to your scenarios with the various options on page 8. This segues directly into the non-verbal intonation exercise and the sounds of empathy. For Exercise 1-4, you can either work from Track 018 or, if you're confident, you can create the sounds yourself.

为了让学生对你将要做的事情有信心，告诉学生在课程的开始和结束他们会被录音，并且在学习的整个过程中也会被间断性地录音，在他们学完了整个课程后，会不自觉地听起来更像美国人。如果学生还没有接受诊断分析，告诉他们你会在课程中融入发音的四个组成部分（音质、语调、连读和发音），并且你会仔细地讲解它们。像紧元音和松元音、浊辅音和清辅音这些内容，当它们出现在各个章节时，你们也会进行学习。如果你被直接提问，当然就直接回答。直接从美语韵律部分开始，让学生用正确的部位发音。在第二个练习中，你会通过一些看起来无意义的音节来练习美语发音。这样可以防止学生有退回到原来的习惯和错误想法的倾向。让学生写下这5个音节：bä bee bä də bäik。音标不一定要准确，不要过分在意这些音标符号。如果他们写下了bah bi bah duh byk，也是可以的。让学生们像读一个正常的句子一样大声读出来，他们会慢慢地发现这个句子是Bobby bought a bike。这个句子的发音重点是字母O的发音像ah，元音之间的T发成了D。这是引导学生从基于拼写的发音向真实发音的语音理解进行转变的第一步。接下来，为了进入美语发音领域，让学生把go-to短语练熟，包括发声和面部的位置。除了上面所说的这些，还要练习积极听力，让学生用第8页上的不同方式来回应你所设置的情境。这样会直接进入到"非语言语调练习"和"同感发音"的练习。对于练习1-4，你可以学习Track 018中的内容，或者，如果你足够自信，可以自己创造出发音。

## Chapter 2: Psycholinguistics

Have the student listen to the before/after audio on Track 021. The purpose of this is to get them in the frame of mind that *it's just an accent*. To find out if your students are all-at-oncers or step-by-steppers, play Track 024, **Please call Stella**, and have them mimic the sound. If they sound pretty much like they already do, or fixate on what the actual words are, you've got *steppers*. If they capture the essence of the sound, you've got *oncers*. Follow up on this with Exercise 2-2 to see how they respond. This is actually a quick triage to see who is flexible and who might be more stubborn and resistant to change. Follow up on the Stella mimicry by having the student imitate you saying, **There was a time when people really had a way with words**. Their mimicry should include the vocal quality, rhythm, and as much pronunciation as possible. (These words were chosen because they are very high frequency.) Circling back to pure sound in Exercise 2-4, have the student read **gäddit**. Make sure the **ä** is clear and open and that it's a quick, flicked **D** in the middle. Stress the first syllable. Have the student repeat at least ten times or until it sounds just right. As you correlate in Exercise 2-5, you may notice some backsliding with the **O** in **got** rounding up a little. In that case, go back to the phonetics and make sure that the vowel is nice and open and the lips aren't at all rounded. The next step is super important, particularly for the empiricists in your class. They need to actually go out and use this phrase with actual Americans. They can use it as either a statement: **Got it**, an exclamation: **Got it**! or a query: **Got it**? Have them bring back the real-life experience of how it turned out. This is an important discussion and will lead to a better understanding of how to interact with Americans while applying the techniques.

让学生听Track 021中的前后对比的音频。这样做是为了让他们进入到"它只是一种发音而已"的心境中。为了弄清楚你的学生是"一步到位型"还是"循序渐进型"的学习者，播放Track 024：Please call Stella，让他们模仿发音。如果他们的发音听起来跟之前没有什么区别，或者还是只集中注意力于实际的单词，那么他们就是"循序渐进型"的。如果他们能抓住发音的精髓，那么他们就是"一步到位型"的。使用练习2-2继续看看他们如何回答。实际上，这能够帮你快速辨别出哪些人灵活，哪些人可能更加固执、不愿改变。继续模仿Stella这句话，让学生模仿你说There was a time when people really had a way with words。他们的模仿应该包括音质、节奏，以及尽可能多的发音。（这些单词被选中的原因是它们出现的频率很高。）回到练习2-4中的纯粹的发音，让学生读gäddit。确保ä音是清楚的、打开的，中间有一个快速的、轻弹的D音。重读第一个音节。让学生至少重复十遍，或者直到听起来是正确的。如果与练习2-5联系起来，你可能会注意到got中的O有些回缩，有些收圆了。如果是这样，再返回到音标部分，确保元音的发音很漂亮，是打开的，并且双唇没有收圆。接下来这一步非常重要，尤其是对于你班上的经验主义者而言。他们需要走出去，对真正的美国人说这个短语。他们既可以把它当成陈述：Got it，也可以当成感叹：Got it! 或是疑问：Got it? 让他们向你反馈真实生活中的体验结果如何。这是一次非常重要的实践，会让学生对如何在与美国人的互动中使用这些技巧有一个更好的理解。

Ask your students how many times a day they have to repeat themselves and make of note of this as their What Factor. The goal is, of course, to get it down to zero.

问你的学生，他们每天需要重复几次自己说过的话，并把这记录下来，作为他们的"What因素"。毋庸置疑，你的目的是让他们把次数降为零。

## Chapter 3: General Pronunciation

Here, you're diving straight into pronunciation, starting with an incredibly easy sound, **mmm**, which everyone can do. Have the student observe how and where the air comes out, the point of contact, and the vocality. This pre-answers a lot of questions that tend to come up, such as *What is a consonant?, What do you mean by voiced?, What's a nasal?* In Exercise 3-2, you'll have them take the baby step of adding the **ah** sound and some other bilabials, for a nice, clear **mah**, **pah**, **bah**. Repeat this several times, making sure that the **pah** and **bah** are sufficiently popped. You can have them hold their hand in front of their mouth to feel the air. Next, you're going to start combining pronunciation and rhythm with Exercise 3-3, using the physicality of snapping, slapping, or pulling. We'll delve more deeply into the different ways of making intonation in Chapter 4, page 39, but for the moment, just make sure they are using **pitch** and not **volume**. Encourage them to lengthen the vowel duration a bit when the second syllable is stressed.

在这部分，你将直接开始学习发音，先从一个非常简单的音mmm开始。这个音每个人都会发。让学生观察气流如何流出、从哪个部位流出、接触点在哪里以及是否发声。这就提前回答了许多即将出现的问题，比如"什么是辅音？""你说的浊音是什么意思？""什么是鼻音？"在练习3-2中，你要让他们像婴儿学发音一样，把ah音和其他双唇音连读，完美而清楚地说出mah，pah，bah。重复几次，确保pah和bah有充分的爆破。你可以让他们把手放在嘴巴前面来感受气流。接着，在练习3-3中，你要开始把发音和节奏结合起来，使用拍、打、拉这样的肢体动作。我们将会在第4章的第39页更加深入地探究各种语调的发音方式，但是现在，只要确保他们使用的是"音高"而不是"音量"就行。当第二个音节是重音时，鼓励他们稍微拉长元音的音长。

In Exercise 3-4, you'll circle back for the third time to pure sound. The reason we approach this from so many directions is that students are *very* invested in maintaining the correlation between spelling and pronunciation. We've even heard people pronounce the **L** in **would** and **half**! Have the student read the three sentences and focus on pronouncing it exactly the way it's written. Quite often, they'll get very distracted trying to figure what the meaning is, but keep them laser focused on the sounds. In Exercise 3-5, they get to put it into regular English and in Exercise 3-6 to create the sounds while knowing what the meaning is. Your job is to make sure they maintain the **bä bläs diz jäb, skät tä də lät, dän bä də bäik** pronunciation.

在练习3-4中，你会第三次回到纯粹的发音部分。我们从这么多不同的角度来学习它的原因是，学生总习惯于把拼写和发音联系在一起。我们甚至听到有人发出了would和half中的L音！让学生读这三个句子，注意发音要和书写方式完全一致。通常情况下，因为想要弄明白句子的意思，他们的注意力会分散，但是要让他们把注意力集中在发音上。在练习3-5中，他们要看着普通的英语来发音。在练习3-6中，他们需要在知道句意的情况下发出音来。你要做的就是确保他们一直发的是bä bläs diz jäb, skät tä də lät, dän bä də bäik的音。

Exercise 3-7 is a great reality check and students are amazed at what rhymes and what doesn't. Exercise 3-8 is a very soothing exercise, almost like chanting the sounds in sequence. The first column should be 95% easy, with just a few predictable hiccups on **rä** and **thä**. Based on the nationality, you'll also need to work on **bä/vä** (Spanish), **fä** (Japanese), **dä** (Spanish), **pä/bä** (Arabic), **lä/nä** (Southern China), **vä/wä** (India/Pakistan), **fä/vä/wä** (German), **sä/zä** (Spanish). Make sure that the vowel is clear and open, and you may need to have them double the vowel–**mä-ah**–to catch the musicality and the proper vowel duration.

练习3-7是个很棒的现实检验，学生会惊叹于哪些单词押韵，哪些单词不押韵。练习3-8会让你轻松一些，几乎像是按顺序哼唱出这些发音。第一列中的95%都很简单，预计只有在发rä和thä音时会有停顿。根据不同的国籍，你可能还需要学习bä/vä（西班牙人），fä（日本人），dä（西班牙人），pä/bä（阿拉伯人），lä/nä（中国南方人），vä/wä（印度人/巴基斯坦人），fä/vä/wä（德国人），sä/zä（西班牙人）。确保元音的发音是清楚的、打开的，你可能需要让他们发出双倍的元音——mä-ah——来把握韵律以及适当的元音音长。

The second column is a bit more problematic, both because **æ** doesn't exist in other languages and it's a rather unlovely sound. It's so distinctly American, though, that you need to have them get comfortable with it early on. The third column is as easy as **ä** because everyone has an **eh** sound. Other universal sounds are **eeh**, **ooh**, and the **long A** and **long I**. It's quite a task to get students to distinguish **ih / eeh** and **ü / ooh**. The latter pair can be illustrated with the chicken (**ü**) and the fish (**ooh**) in Chapter 20, *Tense & Lax Vowels*. Actually, **ih / ü** are very similar, as in **kick / cook**. The key is that should be no lip rounding with **ü**. The long vowels **A** and **I** are actually diphthongs and the task is to get students to produce both halves, **eh-ee** and **ah-ee**. This brings us to the neutral vowel, the schwa (**ə**), which students have a heck of a time distinguishing from **ä**. You need to contrast the two columns, side by side, **bä / bə, chä / chə, dah / duh**, etc.

第二列出现的问题会稍多一些，既是因为æ音在其他语言中不存在，也是因为它是一个相当不讨人喜欢的音。但是，它是如此典型的美音，所以你需要让学生尽早适应这个音。第三列和ä列一样简单，因为每个人都会发eh音。其他普遍存在的音包括eeh，ooh，以及长元音A和长元音I。要让学生区分ih/eeh和ü/ooh是很艰巨的任务。后一组可以用第20章"紧元音&松元音"中的鸡（ü）和鱼（ooh）来说明。实际上，ih/ü非常相似，就像在kick/cook中一样。关键在于，发ü音时，嘴唇不能收圆。长元音A和I都是双元音，关键是让学生把两部分的音都发好，即eh-ee和ah-ee。接着我们就要开始学习中性元音，也就是非中央元音（ə），学生需要花很长时间才能把它和ä区分开来。你需要一个挨一个地对比这两列，bä/bə, chä/chə, dah/duh等。

Exercise 3-9 is important in that it helps with the lateral transfer of information. Rather than creating a sound from scratch, they can work from a nearby one in their own language. Chances are, when they read their character set, the vowels will be shorter than you want, so have them double them up. This is a good time to direct them to the Nationality Guide in the back of the book.

练习3-9的重要性在于，它有助于信息的平行转移。与其重新学会一个新的音，不如从他们自己语言中近似的发音出发进行学习。不过当他们在读自己的文字时，元音可能会比你所期望的短，所以要让他们把元音拉长到原来的两倍。这是一个指导他们学习本书后面的"汉语发音与美音的对比"部分的良机。

Exercise 3-10 is similar to Exercise 3-6 in that they will be transitioning from pure sound over to spelling again. Make sure to hold them strictly accountable for each sound, in particular **the**, as it's the most commonly used word in English. Exercise 3-10 will give you a head start on the **Th** (more detailed in Chapter 13). The main point is that although it's tempting to teach a breathy **Th**, it's actually popped in natural speech.

练习3-10和练习3-6的相似点在于它们会让学生再次从纯粹的发音过渡到拼写。确保学生非常准确地发出了每个音，特别是the的发音，因为它是英语里最常用的单词。练习3-10会让你提早接触Th音（详见第13章）。关键之处在于，虽然Th常常被当做气息音来教，但在自然的语言中它其实是爆破的。

## Chapter 4: American Intonation

You've already introduced intonation in Chapters 1 and 3, and now you're going to introduce the concept of musicality and tone shift that can be visually represented by the staircase. One of the most important things that students know intuitively in their own language is the importance of pitch change and the effect of shortening a word. For some reason, however, that information does not transfer in the second language. Students tend to shorten their words, which makes them sound *curt*, *clipped*, or *abrupt*. Literally, each of these words just means short, but figuratively (and that's what accent is all about) they sound rude.

你已经在第1章和第3章中介绍了语调，现在你将介绍可用音阶阶梯进行视觉呈现的韵律和声调变化的概念。学生本能地从他们自己的语言中知道的最重要的事情之一，就是音高变化和缩短某个单词发音的效果的重要性。但是，由于某种原因，这个信息并没有转移到第二语言中。学生倾向于缩短单词的发音，这让他们听起来很curt（草率）、clipped（短促）、abrupt（唐突）。从字面上来看，这些单词的意思都是"短的"，但是从比喻意义上来看（这就是发音的重要之处），它们听起来很粗鲁。

Let the students know that they are to use this book and CD on their own and that your role is to listen and give them feedback. They also need to know that they will not be losing their accent—they will be learning a new one. This is an important psychological point since people are nervous about the effects of such a change. As they learn the accent, they will make it their own, and their thinking won't change as a consequence; it's just a skill like a new dance step. It comforts students to hear that even among Americans there are misunderstandings due to intonation and meaning. Once a student can accurately hear and use the difference between a compound noun and a description, a large part of the intonation work is done.

让学生明白，他们将自己使用这本书和CD，而你的角色就是聆听，并且给出反馈。他们也需要知道自己不会丢弃原来的发音——而只是学了一种新的发音。这从心理上来说是很重要的一点，因为人们很担心做出如此改变的效果。在学习一种发音的过程中，他们会把这种发音变成自己的一部分，但他们的思维不会因此发生变化；它仅仅是一种技能，就像是一种新的舞步。让学生知道，即便是美国人也会因为语调和含意而产生误会，这会让他们感到一丝安慰。一旦学生可以准确地听懂并区分出复合名词和描述性短语的不同用法，那么语调学习的很大一部分内容就完成了。

## Three Ways to Make Intonation
### 构成语调的三种方式

Once they have the sounds in place, you're ready to get more specific with the intonation. Demonstrate all three ways, and then have the student focus on **pitch**, rather than **volume**. Vowel duration is an extremely important component of intonation and it is covered throughout the text.

一旦他们的发音到位了，你就要准备好让他们更详细地学习语调。展示所有的三种方式，接着让学生将注意力集中在"音高"而不是"音量"上。元音的音长是语调的极其重要的组成部分，全书都会涉及这个问题。

## Nonsense Syllables
### 无意义的音节

Exercise 4-1 is extremely important. Students can disassociate from grammar, content, meaning and vocabulary, and simply focus on the pure sound and rhythm of English. Some students are staccato, some heavy on volume, some monotone, some misplace the stress points, and some sound like they're singing rather than talking. You know what it should sound like—keep modifying until the student sounds like you. Female teachers should deepen their voices a bit with male students.

练习4-1非常重要。学生可以脱离语法、内容、意义和词汇，仅仅将注意力集中于英语的纯粹的发音和节奏。有些学生会出现断音，有些学生的音量很高，有些学生没有音调，有些学生会放错重音的位置，有些学生甚至听起来像是在唱歌而不是说话。你知道正确的发音应该是什么——不断地修正学生的发音，直到跟你的发音一样。女教师在教男学生时，需要使自己的声音稍微深沉一些。

In Exercise 4-1, there are two groups—one of purely nonsense syllables and a second of the transition from nonsense to sense. In the first group, have the student read each row across (A–D) for the same pattern with different sounds, then down (1–4) for the same sound with different patterns. The main point here is to capture both the musicality and the vocal placement. If the student is able to sound American saying **duh-duh-duh**, everything else can follow from there.

在练习4-1中有两组内容——第一组是毫无意义的音节，第二组是从无意义到有意义的转化。在第一组的练习中，让学生先读每个横排的发音（A–D），它们有相同的模式，但发音不同；接着读竖排的发音（1–4），它们发音相同，模式不同。这里需要注意的是，要同时把握韵律和发声位置。如果学生能像美国人一样说duh-duh-duh，那么其他音也可以以此类推进行学习。

In the second group, have the student read column A (1–4). Make sure that **duh-duh-duh** and **ABC, 123, Dogs eat bones** all sound the same, in terms of voice placement, cadence and musicality. Then go on to columns B, C, and D.

在第二组中，让学生先读A列（1–4）。确保duh-duh-duh，ABC，123，Dogs eat bones在发音位置、节奏和韵律上听起来都一致。然后再练习B、C和D列。

## Staircase Intonation
阶梯状语调

The staircase is simply a visual metaphor to help students understand pitch. It is the same as a stress point, the musical notes or an accent mark. The primary rule of stress in English is that, given no counter indicators, such as contrast, nouns are stressed. Have the student read Exercise 4-2, giving a slight lift to each noun. In Exercise 4-3, have the student read side to side, contrasting the noun stress with the verb stress. This makes the test in Exercise 4-4 extremely simple.

阶梯状语调仅仅是为了帮助学生们理解音高的一种视觉上的比喻。它和重音标志、音符以及重音符号一样。英语中重音的主要规则是，如果没有反义指示词，比如表示对比，那么名词是重读的。让学生朗读练习4-2，读到名词时，稍微提高音高。在练习4-3中，让学生把两列对照着读，对比一下名词和动词的重音。这会让练习4-4变得十分简单。

## Shifting the Stress Points
改变重音

Intonation is the mainstay of the American Accent Training method. It is the way that children learn their native language, and it is the main element that is usually missing when adults study a foreign language. Intonation is the pitch change pattern used by native speakers. Within a word, a phrase or a sentence, certain syllables are given more stress (accorded a higher pitch) than others. How this stress changes the meaning of a sentence, how it can move around in a sentence and how is can reflect the speakers intent or even personality is what you need to convey to your students.

语调是美语发音训练方法的支柱。它是孩子们学习母语的方法，也是成年人学习外语时通常会忽略的一大要素。语调是以英语为母语者的音高变化形式。在一个单词、短语或句子中，某些音节与其他音节相比被赋予了重音（伴随着较高的音高）。这个重音如何改变句子的意思，如何在一个句子中变化位置以及如何反映出作者的意图或者甚至是性格，这是你需要传达给学生的知识。

## Duh-Duh-Duh
Duh-Duh-Duh

One of the first steps in the transition from the printed word to the sound of spoken English is to have students start applying an unmistakable intonation to all sorts of different expressions. Even when you walk the student through the importance of the American up & down, people will still want to underemphasize.

从印刷体到英语口语发音转变的第一步，就是让学生们开始在不同种类的表达中使用准确的语调。即使你让学生了解了美语阶梯语调的重要性，他们仍然对它不够重视。

To get around this, after the student reads the **New Information** sentence **It sounds like rain** and it sounds flat and unmusical, have them replace most of the words with **duh-duh-duh**. Stress **RAIN** very heavily. **duh-duh-duh RAIN**. If **rain** is stressed loudly but unmusically, have them put it on two tone levels: **ray-een**.

为了解决这个问题，在学生把"新信息"句子It sounds like rain读得很平淡、没有韵律之后，让他们把大部分的单词用duh-duh-duh代替。重重地强调RAIN。duh-duh-duh RAIN。如果他们只是把rain读得声音很大而没有韵律，那就让他们把它放在两个音调阶梯上：ray-een。

This tone shift will help students with the idea of the staircase. Have them read the four sentences, and every time they lose the intonation and start stressing each word **(It. Sounds.Like.Rain)**, go back to **duh-duh-duh**. Every time they lose the musicality, break the key word into two parts, put it on a little stair step and make the pitch higher on the first step.

这种声调变化可以帮助学生理解音阶阶梯的概念。让他们读下面这四个句子，每当他们找不到语调并开始重读每个单词时（It.Sounds.Like.Rain），就回到duh-duh-duh。每当他们找不到韵律，就把关键词分成两部分，把它放在一个小台阶上，让第一个台阶上的音高更高一些。

| | |
|---|---|
| It sounds like **rain**. | duh-duh-duh **rain** |
| It **sounds** like rain. | duh-duh-duh **sounds** duh-duh-duh |
| He **likes** rain, but he **hates** snow. | duh-duh-duh **likes** duh-duh-duh, |
| | duh-duh-duh **hates** duh-duh-duh |
| The rain **didn't affect** his plans. | duh-duh-duh **didn't affect** duh-duh-duh |

**Translation**
翻译

The next part of the intonation exercise is a translation. This again is twofold. In many English classes, native languages are implicitly or explicitly forbidden. Since language is such an integral part of an individual, it feels as if part of him or her is being denied or shut out. I think it is much preferable to use what you can of each language to show the student where his or her natural advantages lie. Let your students know what their strengths are, and you will have much more confident and teachable students.

语调练习的下一阶段是翻译。这也有双重意义。在许多英语课堂上，学生或含蓄或明确地被禁止说母语。由于语言是每个人不可分割的一部分，这样会让他或她感觉到自己的一部分被否定或排斥在外。我认为更好的方式是尽你所能地利用每种语言向学生展示他们自身的优势所在。让你的学生们知道自己的长处，你将会有更加自信的和可教的学生。

**Translation Summary**
翻译总结

1. Translate the sentence.
   翻译句子。

2. Write it out on the board, phonetically or otherwise.
   用音标或其他方式在黑板上写出来。

3. Students read them with their normal accents.
   让学生用他们平时的发音读句子。

4. You read the sentences in an American accent.
   你用美语发音读句子。

5. Students imitate your accent.

   让学生模仿你的发音。

6. Students read it in a native accent, emphasizing a word.

   让学生用自己的母语读句子，强调其中一个词。

7. Other students guess which sound was stressed.

   让其他学生猜哪个音被重读了。

8. Explain the similarities or differences in intonations in different languages, such as the American staircase, the Indian upward glide, or the Swiss up-and-down.

   解释不同语言在语调上的相同点或不同点，例如美语的阶梯状语调，印度语上扬的滑音，或瑞士式发音中上下起伏的腔调。

9. Briefly discuss how this strong intonation feels to them.

   简要地讨论一下，这些浓重的语调让他们感觉如何。

### Maybe in English, but in my dialect...
可能在英语里可以，但是在我的方言里……

Have the students translate the sentence **I didn't say he stole the money** into their own language or dialect. Have them say it at a regular speed and intonation so you can hear how different it is from English. Then, jot down the translation, phonetically or by normal ABC's, and read it back with an average American accent. It's a hugely important exercise to have the student imitate you, saying their own language with an American accent. They should feel like they're talking and chewing gum. For them to speak their own language sounding like an American is funny and unnerving, but it definitely improves their American accent in English.

　　让学生把句子I didn't say he stole the money翻译成自己的母语或方言。让他们用正常的速度和语调说出来，使你可以听出来它和英语有多大的区别。接着，用音标或是正常的字母简单地记下翻译后的句子发音，然后用普通美语发音读出来。让学生模仿你，用美语发音来说他们自己的语言，这是个非常重要的练习。他们应该感觉到自己像是在边嚼口香糖边说话。让他们把自己的母语说得像是美国人说的，对于他们来说有点好笑，也有点不知所措，但这绝对可以提高他们说英语时的美语发音水平。

Next, have the student read the sentence with a natural, native accent, but jumping heavily on a stressed word while you identify which word stood out. It may take a couple of tries here, but it is important to get them to realize that it is only the sound you are looking for, not the meaning of the sound.

　　接着，让学生用自然的、母语的发音来读句子，但是需要把你指出的突出的单词特别地重读。这可能需要试好几次，但是重要的是让学生们意识到你期待的只是发音，而不是发音的意思。

After they can move the intonation around freely in their own sentences, ask if this is it similar to his or her native language?; does it feel natural to do it?; how did it feel? You will get a wonderful variety of answers as they start thinking about how they actually do it. At this point, students realize that they do the same thing in their own language and it is just a question of applying concepts that they already know and use, to English.

当他们可以在自己所说的句子中自如地移动语调时，问他们：这和他们的母语是不是很相似？这样做感觉自然吗？之前的感觉是怎样的？当他们开始思考自己是如何做到的时，你会得到各式各样很棒的回答。这时候，学生会意识到，他们在自己的语言中也做同样的事情，现在要做的只是把他们已经知道和使用的概念运用到英语中去。

## Chapter 5: Syllable Stress

This is a dense and important section, where you'll be working on making sure that the student's pitch is appropriate, in terms of placement, pitch range and vowel duration. The one-syllable patterns contrast the single stairstep of the vowel in a word ending in a whispered consonant (unvoiced) with the double stairstep of a word ending in a voiced consonant. In the two-syllable patterns, you start to get into descriptions (stressing the second word—white house) and set phrases or compound nouns (stressing the first word—White House). Students often feel the need to have a set list of rules for syllable stress, but this is not typically a big problem. To assuage them, however, there is a Syllable Rules section on page 64. You will notice that Indians stress the first word in beginning and component, and the French like to stress the last syllable of just about everything, but this is minor compared with the rest of the intonation problems.

这一章的信息量比较大，也比较重要。在这部分的学习中，你需要确保学生的音高是合适的，涉及发音位置、音高范围和元音音长。在单音节单词的部分，对于以不发音的辅音（清辅音）结尾的单词中其元音位于一个音阶上的情况和以浊辅音结尾的单词中其元音位于两个音阶上的情况进行了对比。在双音节部分，将学习描述性短语（重读第二个单词——white **house** 白色的房子），以及固定短语或复合名词（重读第一个单词——**White** House 白宫）。学生常常觉得他们应该有一个音节重音的列表，但这不算什么典型的大问题。然而，为了满足他们的需求，在第64页有音节规则的讲解。你会发现印度人会重读开头和组成部分的第一个单词，法国人喜欢重读几乎所有单词的最后一个音节，但是这跟其余的语调问题相比，是较次要的问题。

## Chapter 6: Complex Intonation

This chapter starts getting to the heart of the rhythm patterns and you'll need to review it, both in exercises and in context while they are speaking. You'll notice that the sentences are fairly short in **Goldilocks**, and there are two reasons for this. The first is that they need to master the basics, and the second is that this will be contrasted with *sentence balance* later on.

本章开始进入节奏模式学习的中心部分，你需要不断地回顾它，不论是在练习中还是在学生说话的语境中都是如此。你会发现Goldilocks这篇文章中的句子非常短，原因有两点：第一是他们需要掌握这些基本单词的发音，第二是它会与之后的"句子平衡"部分进行对比。

## Chapter 7: Phrasing

Phrasing is pretty straightforward in that punctuation is such a strong guide. Tag endings are included on page 83 because students tend to underuse them. They should practice with tags as both a query and an affirmation.

断句很简单，因为标点符号是很直观的标志。第83页包含了反意疑问句，因为学生们常常会使用不当。他们应该练习这些附加语作为疑问句以及肯定句的用法。

## Chapter 8: The Miracle Technique

**Reverse Phonetics**
反向语音学

The purpose of this exercise is to get your students away from the impression that they can't do it—"it" being to produce native-sounding speech. Stated or not, conscious or not, students have resistance to changing their pronunciation either from their native accent or from how they think the spelling indicates. You need to hone their skill in hearing and reproducing pure sound, in or out of context, and they need to abandon the spelling crutch.

这个练习的目的是让你的学生脱离"他们无法做到它"的印象——"它"指的是像说母语一样说话。不论学生们是否承认或者是否意识到，他们都抗拒改变自己的发音，不论是改变他们的母语口音还是改变他们对拼写的刻板印象。你需要磨练他们的听力技能，并让他们无论是否在语境中都可以重新发出纯粹的音，而他们需要抛弃对拼写的依赖。

In Exercise 8-1, you're introducing the concepts of pure sound, of ignoring spelling, of using any phonetic system. Let them know that they are going to write backwards, but just two little sounds. Say **lie** and listen for the students to say back what they heard. They can write it **lie**, **ly**, **lye** or **läi**. Then, have them repeat it after you, making sure they get both the **ah** and the **eeh** sounds. When both sounds are in place, have them read it back themselves and decipher what it says: **I like it**. Read the sentence using the rubber band or tapping on the stressed word (**like**) until everyone sounds quick and fluent. After you've finished Exercises 8-2 and 8-3, have the students create their own sentences, broken up into pieces. They should give you the pieces, back to front, and you then decipher. Interestingly, in the beginning, as you read back, you'll have their accent. As they come to understand the rules, you'll sound more and more standard.

在练习8-1中，你要介绍这些概念：纯粹的发音、对拼写的忽略以及任何音标体系的使用。让他们知道要把发音写出来，但是只有两个小发音。你说lie，让学生向你反馈他们所听到的。他们可以写成lie，ly，lye或läi。接着，让他们跟着你读，确保他们的ah音和eeh音都发得正确。当两个音都发到位了，让学生自己读，并破译出它的意思：I like it。在读这个句子的时候，使用橡皮筋或者在读重读单词（like）时敲打，直到每个人的发音都快速而流畅。在完成了练习8-2和8-3之后，让学生自己造句，并拆分成几个部分。他们从后往前地把这些单词读给你，你来破译。有趣的是，一开始你读给他们听时，会带有他们的口音。随着他们对发音规则的掌握，你说出来的也会越来越标准。

## Chapter 9: Grammar in a Nutshell

Along with the Miracle Techique, this is a Desert Island exercise. If all you had was a sheet of paper with these two exercises, you could get a lot of English teaching done. It covers intonation, voice quality, linking, pronunciation, phrasing, and grammar. The only tricky part is when the students write their own sentences. To have as much linking as possible, follow the rules in Exercise 9-3.

除了神奇的技巧部分，这个也属于荒岛练习。如果你只有一张纸，上面包含这两个练习，你可以教的东西有很多。它涵盖了语调、音质、连读、发音、断句和语法。唯一比较有难度的部分是让学生自己造句。为了让他们尽可能多地连读，参考练习9-3中的规则。

## Chapter 10: Reduced Sounds

This is part of intonation, but instead of focusing on the peaks, you'll be looking deep into those murky valleys. Students tend to over pronounce, so you have to be vigilant about not letting them get away with it. You may find yourself unsure about what "proper" speech is, but because this program is more descriptive than prescriptive, you'll need to focus on strong intonation, letting the schwas fall where they may.

这是语调的一部分，但你要做的并不是关注"高峰"，而是深入探究那些模糊的"低谷"。学生可能倾向于过分强调每个音，所以你要警惕，不让他们侥幸逃避。你可能会发现自己不确定什么是"恰当的"言语，但是由于这个教程更倾向于描述性而不是指示性，你将需要关注重音语调，让非中央元音在可以降调的时候降调。

## Chapter 11: Word Connections

The point of this chapter is to get students away from sounding so staccato or robotic and into using the **wa-wa**, **nya-nya**, **woo-woo**, **bada-bada** sounds of spoken American English. The most important thing to stress is that, although students have learned to pronounce word by word, and, of course, that's how things are written, they have to regroup into sound groups rather than individual word groups. They have to listen for and hear whole phrases or they will miss the meaning. It's like when they say you can't see the forest for the trees—the students can't understand the meaning of the whole sentence because they are only listening for the meaning of each word.

本章的重点是让学生摆脱不连贯、僵硬的发音，而使用美语口语中的wa-wa，nya-nya，woo-woo，bada-bada这些音。要强调的最重要的一点是，虽然学生已经学会了逐个单词的发音，而且当然这就是句子的书写方式，他们还是需要把它们重组成音群，而不是词群。他们需要听完整个词组，不然不会明白它的意思。就像人们说的不能只见树木不见森林——学生们理解不了整个句子的意思，因为他们只是在听每个单词的意思。

They also have to stop intellectualizing every sound they hear—"[mēt]! What did that mean? Was it a noun (meat)? Was it a verb (meet)? An object? A subject?" By this time, the speaker has left the student in the conversational dust. The important thing to deal with is, of course, context. The identical sounds can be either logical or nonsensical: I'm meeting Bob or I'm eating Bob?

他们必须停止这种想要弄明白所听到每个音的意思的习惯——"mēt! 它是什么意思？是名词（meat 肉）吗？是动词（meet 见面）吗？是宾语？还是主语？"这时候，学生已经远远地跟不上与说话者的对话了。当然，需要学习的很重要的一点是语境。听起来相似的音可能是符合逻辑的，也可能是荒谬的：I'm meeting Bob（我在跟鲍勃见面）还是I'm eating Bob（我在吃鲍勃）？

Have each student read the five sentences in Exercise 11-1. #4, **the D** will sound fine, but #5 will probably revert to **that I**. Bring this immediately to the students' attention and have each one concentrate on making #5 sound exactly like #4. Then, explain that certain sounds are just attracted to each other, like a magnet. There are four situations for connecting words listed just below Exercise 11-1. The first one is when a word ends in a consonant and the next one starts with a vowel—they automatically link up. Have the student read the three examples, preferably from the right-hand side.

让每个学生读练习11-1中的五个句子。在读第四个句子时，the D听起来是对的，但是在读第五个句子时可能又会读成that I。立刻让学生注意这里，让每个学生第五个句子的发音和第四个一样。接着，跟他们解释有些音会互相吸引，就像磁铁一样。从练习11-1后可以看到有四种单词连读的情况。第一种是当一个单词以辅音结尾，其后的单词以元音开头时——他们会自然地连起来。让学生们读这三个例子，建议从右边开始读。

## Chapter 12: Cat? Caught? Cut?

Exercise 12-2 takes a long time, but it lets students finally break through the spelling barrier of A's, O's and U's. There are 5 **æ**, 10 **ä**, more than 50 **ə**.

练习12-2花的时间比较长，但是它会让学生最终打破A，O和U的拼写障碍。一共有5个æ，10个ä，超过50个ə。

First, have students go through and ferret out the 5 **æ** sounds, writing the symbol over the words. It is better to do it first in pencil and then use a highlighter afterwards because any mistakes result in pink on top of blue on top of green. A student reading after each color facilitates correction because that way they are not targeting too many sounds at once. Then, look for the 10 **ä** words, first in pencil, then in color. Finally, **ə**. This takes quite a bit of time, and it's better to review them line by line, rather than trying to say all of them out.

首先，让学生浏览并搜寻出5个æ音，在单词上面标注音标符号。最好能先用铅笔标注，然后再用彩色笔标，把任何出错的地方先标成绿色，然后是蓝色，最后是粉色。根据每种颜色去读单词有助于纠正学生的发音，因为他们不会一次设定太多的目标。接着，寻找10个含有ä音的单词，先用铅笔标出，再用彩色笔标出。最后是ə音。这可能要花点时间，最好能逐行复习，而不是一下子把它们都说出来。

### Cat? (5)

The **æ** sound is relatively scarce, but is highly noticeable, and has such a distinctive sound that it is not difficult to train. It's just a combination of **ä** and **ɛh**. It sometimes helps to temporarily put in a small **(y)** before **æ**, such as **kee⁽ʸ⁾æt** to make a huge exaggeration, which they can later relax into a regular **æ**. You should have them drop the jaw down (like **ä**) and then back (like **ɛh**) while pushing up the back of the tongue. Or have them say **ɛh** and leave the tongue in the same position while dropping the jaw.

æ音相对来说比较少，但却非常明显，而且它的音很特别，不难训练。它就是ä和ɛh的结合。有时候，在æ前面暂时地放一个小⁽ʸ⁾会有所帮助，例如听起来比较夸张的kee⁽ʸ⁾æt，之后他们放松地讲话时会变成正常的æ。你应该让他们把下颚向下（像ä音）且向后（像ɛh音）拉，同时将舌的后部向上推。或者让他们发ɛh音，然后让舌头停留在原位，下颚向下拉。

### Caught? (10)

The **ä** sound is easily cued to either *what you say to the doctor when he uses the tongue depressor* or the musical **lä-lä-lä**, so whenever they come to a word like **caught**, **thought**, **bought**, they can be cued with **kä-kä-kä**, **thä-thä-thä**, or **bä-bä-bä**, respectively. If a student is reluctant to fully pronounce this sound, have him put his hand under his chin to feel the jaw as it drops. The strong tendency will be to round the lips, because, after all, this is usually spelled with an **O**. Keep going back to the phonetics to break this habit.

ä音很容易给提示，它可以和"医生用压舌器让你发出的音"一样，或者跟音乐中的lä-lä-lä一样。所以，一旦有类似caught，thought，bought这样的单词，他们可以分别读作kä-kä-kä，thä-thä-thä或bä-bä-bä。如果学生不愿意完全发出这个音，那就让他把手放在下巴上感受下颚的下拉。学生很有可能会收圆嘴唇，因为毕竟拼写中通常会出现字母O。不断地回到语音的练习来打破这个习惯。

## Cut? (50+)

The schwa (a neutral vowel sound) is best done last since it is the most subtle and elusive of the three sounds, as well as the most common vowel sound in English. Because you eliminated the other two most likely candidates for confusion beforehand (æ and ä), the smoke screen is a little more readily penetrable. It is, in large part, due to the schwa that spelling is so difficult—the neutral vowel in **poss<u>i</u>ble** and **pass<u>a</u>ble** sounds identical, but needs to be spelled with appropriately different letters.

非中央元音（中性元音）最好是最后再学习，因为它是这三个音里最微妙和难以捉摸的，也是英语里最常见的元音发音。因为这样你就已经提前消除了其他两个音（æ和ä）的发音障碍，这个屏障就更容易打破了。很大程度上是因为非中央元音的拼写太难了——possible和passable里的中性元音听起来是一样的，但是需要用不同的字母进行正确的拼写。

It is pronounced "uh," which is the sound that is produced when you press on your diaphragm and don't change your mouth position at all. If it's a group that has meshed well, I have them press on each other's diaphragm, so they can hear what a neutral, unforced sound it is. The point usually comes up of the difference between ə and ʌ (as in **<u>a</u>bout** and **b<u>u</u>t**) and ä and ɔ (as in **cot** and **caught**). For practical purposes, however, we will only use the first of each pair (ə and ä), the intent of the program being to get students to sound American, rather than phonetically "perfect," which, of course, Americans are not.

它发音是"uh"，是通过按住膈肌、不改变口腔位置发出的。如果是非常默契的一组学生，我会让他们互相按住对方的膈肌，这样他们就能听到什么是中性的、自然的音。通常关键之处在于ə和ʌ的区别（正如在about和but中），以及ä和ɔ的区别（正如在cot和caught中）。然而，出于实用的目的，我们将仅仅学习使用每组的前一个音（ə和ä），因为课程的目的是让学生听起来像美国人，而不是拥有"完美的"语音，当然，美国人的语音并不是完美的。

The schwa is the noise we make when we are thinking—**uh**, **um**—for Americans, it is an unconscious, but ever-present sound.

非中央元音就是我们在思考的时候发出的杂音——uh，um——对于美国人来说，这是一种不自觉的却时刻存在的声音。

## Read Down
## 从上往下读

After the paragraph has been completely worked for all three sounds, in order to get a flow going of a single sound, I have the students read each sound group, from 1–24 without stopping. Unless, of course, they fall back into the spelling trap and mispronounce, at which point we go back to basics with the original vowel sound, and then add on the new consonants around it. For example, **ä, kä, caught** or **uh, k', cut**.

在读完练习这三个音的段落后，为了流畅地发出每个音，我让学生读每组音，从1到24不间断地读。当然，如果他们又落入了拼写的陷阱，发错了音，我们就返回练习基本的原始元音，接着加入新的辅音。例如：ä，kä，caught或uh，k'，cut。

### Read Across
从左往右读

Once they can go through the entire list smoothly, basing pronunciation on the sound they know it to be from the category, rather than from what spelling would indicate, we read across the rows, incorporating all five sounds.

当他们可以流利地读完整个列表，并把发音基于他们从每列分类中所学到的音，而不是基于拼写时，我们可以从左往右读，把五个音连起来。

### Random Reading
随意地读

As a review, we come back to this exercise and they pick words out at random which I try to guess with no clues other than their pronunciation.

作为复习，我们回到这个练习。他们随意挑选一些单词来读，我试着仅凭他们的发音来猜是哪个单词。

### The æ, ä, ə Reading
æ, ä, ə音的段落练习

There are three paragraphs in Exercises 12-4, 12-5, 12-6 for **æ**, **ä**, and **ə**, respectively. The targeted sounds are highlightened to help students realize three things:

练习12-4，12-5，12-6中共有三段话，分别练习æ，ä和ə音。需要练习的音突出标示，以帮助学生意识到以下三点：

1. How many of that particular sound there are

   这个特定的音一共有多少个

2. Where they are

   它们出现在哪些地方

3. How the sound relates to spelling

   这些发音如何与拼写联系起来

## Chapter 13: Tee Aitch

If the tongue is too relaxed and protruding, not only does it not look good, it doesn't feel good or sound right. The tip of the tongue is tense and hardly protrudes as it darts quickly out and back. Contrast **th** with **s**, **z**, and **d**, using a mirror. For the voiced **th**, have a student practice on a word like **then**. Have him say **den** and then with the exact same feeling, say the **D** sound with his tongue slightly between his teeth. This should come out a good-voiced **then**.

如果舌头太放松，伸了出来，那样不仅不好看，而且感觉不对，发音也不正确。保持舌尖的紧张度。舌尖迅速伸出和缩回，几乎不从口中伸出。将th音和s，z，d音对比，使用一面镜子来观察。对于浊音th，让学生练习读类似then这样的单词。让他读den，接着让他用相同的感觉，在发D音时，把舌头轻轻放在齿间。这样会发出一个非常标准的then音。

For an unvoiced **TH**, do the same thing with **S**. Start with **sing**, move the tongue tip forward and say **thing**. They almost can't do it wrong. A good thing about highlighting all of the **th**'s is that a student can see how frequently used the sound is, thereby allowing him to realize that even that one small sound will leave him sounding accented if he neglects it. Bear in mind that, in every word count study, **the** is the most commonly used word in the English language, comprising 6% of all utterances. Hence, with this single word pronounced wrong, 6% of a student's speech is flawed.

对于清音TH，用同样的方法使用S音帮助练习。先读sing，接着把舌尖向前伸，读thing。他们几乎都不会读错。突出显示所有th的好处是，学生可以看到这个音出现的频率有多高，这样会让他了解到，即便是这样一个小小的发音，如果他忽略了，听起来也是会有口音的。要记住，在每项对单词出现次数的统计研究中，the都是英语语言中最常使用的单词，占所有话语的6%。因此，如果这一个单词发音错误，那一个学生的话语中有6%都是有瑕疵的。

If students have trouble with the **TH** paragraph, go to Exercise 17-2. Have them read A Surly Sergeant, replacing all of the **s**'s with **th**'s. They should sound like Daffy Duck on a good day.

如果学生在练习TH的段落中有困难，那就先做练习17-2。让他们读"A Surly Sergeant"一文，把所有的s替换为th。他们听起来应该就像心情不错的达菲鸭。

When they go back to the regular **TH** paragraph, it's a lot easier. Another strange technique that works is to have students read the paragraph completely silently, but mouthing the words—and focusing on every **TH**. A mirror or a partner helps, too. Also, in Exercise 13-1, mark the 10 voiced and 2 unvoiced **th**'s. Voiced sounds are easier than unvoiced sounds for English speakers to make, so the more common sounds tend to be voiced: *the*, *then*, *this*, etc.

当他们回到正常的TH段落时，会变得简单得多。另外一个有用的奇怪技巧就是让学生默读这段话，张嘴读这些单词，但不发声——注意每个TH的发音。如果有面镜子或者有个搭档的话，也会有用。在练习13-1中，标出10个浊音和2个清音th。对于说英语的人来说，浊辅音比清辅音容易发音，所以更常见的音往往是浊音：the, then, this等。

## Chapter 14: The American T

Beddy Ba Da Bida Bedder Budder This exercise leads students through the mysteries of what looks like a [t] but sounds like a [d], or worse yet, like nothing at all. The sound of each **T** is determined by its position on the staircase (you knew it would be—you can't escape intonation). Here are six rules of thumb.

Beddy Ba Da Bida Bedder Budder这个练习会带领学生理解令人困惑的"看起来像是读t，实际上读的是d，或更糟糕的是，根本不发音"的情况。每个T的发音取决于它在音阶阶梯上的位置（你知道一定是这样的——你无法摆脱语调）。下面有六个重要的规则。

## Top of the Staircase
音阶阶梯顶部

First, they go through and notice all of the **T**'s that are just **T**'s, which are explained in Exercise 14-3 on page 128 of the student text.

首先，他们仔细查看，并发现所有的T发音就是T，这点在学生课本第128页的练习14-3中有解释。

## Middle of the Staircase
音阶阶梯中部

Then they pick out the nine **T**'s that are pronounced **D**; this is easily explained using any language that uses an apical flap (trill) for an **R** (Spanish, Italian, Russian, Indian, Korean, Japanese, etc.) as what they use as the **R** sound in the various dialects.

接着，他们会挑出9个发音是D的T。这很好解释，可以用任何在发R音时有舌尖卷舌音（颤音）的语言解释（西班牙语、意大利语、俄语、印度语、韩语、日语等），正如他们在各种方言中都使用的R音。

## Bottom of the Staircase
音阶阶梯底部

Last, they find the 7 **T**'s that aren't really pronounced at all. One of the most difficult things for students to do is get used to not letting final **T**'s and **D**'s be plosive. Tell them not to pop their final consonants, just hold the tongue in position and don't let the air out. They are used to expelling the air after **T**'s, **D**'s, **P**'s, **B**'s, etc. Use matches in class and if the flame even wavers, they can see if they have gone too far. A less flammable way to test the **T** is for each student to hold his hand in front of his face to see if he can feel his breath.

最后，他们发现有7个T是完全不发音的。对于学生来说，最困难的事情就是要习惯最后的T和D不爆破。告诉他们不要把单词末尾的辅音爆破，保持舌头的位置，不要让气流流出。他们习惯于释放以T，D，P，B等音结尾的气流。在课堂上点燃火柴，如果火焰晃动，学生就知道释放的气流过多了。另外一个不易引起燃烧的检测T音的方式，就是让每个学生把手放在脸前，看他是否能感受到自己呼出的气。

## The Held T before N
N音前面被抑制的T音

A difficult sound to produce is the **held T before an N**. The tongue goes to the **T** position, but the air is not released. Then, from the **T** position, an **N** sound is made. Not -en, just **nnn**. The sound rises quickly in pitch to the held **T** and then drops back down with the **N**. **Bitten** is pronounced **bi(t)n**. It is not pronounced **biTn** or **bi(t)ən**. On the other hand, the **D** sound before an **N** doesn't have the sharp pitch rise, contrasted in **written** and **ridden**. Commonly-used held-T words are *certain, gotten, forgotten, sentence, important*.

很难发的一个音是 "N音前面被抑制的T音"。舌头滑向T音的位置，但是不释放气流。然后，在T音的位置发出N音。不是-en，只是nnn。发音时，音高很快升到被抑制的T音，接着落回到N音。bitten发成bi(t)n，而不是biTn或bi(t)ən。另外，N音前面的D音没有音高的急剧上升，可对比written和ridden。常用的含有 "被抑制的T音" 的单词有certain，gotten，forgotten，sentence和important。

**Silent T with N**
N音附近不发音的T

In some commonly used words, the **T** just drops out completely since the **T** and the **N** are created so close together in the mouth (just behind the teeth). You'll hear this in *interview*, *advantage*, *percentage*, etc.

　　在一些常用的单词里，由于T和N在口腔中的发音位置太接近了（就在齿背），以至于T音完全不发声。你将在interview，advantage，percentage等单词中听到。

**Held T with Glottal Consonants**
声门音前面被抑制的T音

Before a throat consonant or semi-vowels, **T** is held by the back of the tongue before W, R, K, G, Y.

　　在喉辅音或半元音前，位于W，R，K，G，Y之前的T音被舌头后部所抑制而不发音。

## Chapter 15: The American R

This is one of those high-value sounds and you are going to have to get your students to use the growly throat sound of the rhotic **R**, and not let the tongue touch any other part of the mouth, particularly the alveolar ridge. The hand trick on page 138 works really well. You can also have them put a spoon on their tongue while saying *race*, *berry*, and *car*. The spoon will impede the tongue tip from reaching up and forming a consonant, instead of the more liquid vowel-type sound that is the American **R**.

　　这是核心发音之一，你需要让学生使用咆哮的喉音，也就是儿化音R。不要让舌头接触口腔的任何其他部位，尤其是牙槽嵴。第138页中介绍的利用手的技巧很有用。你也可以让他们在说race，berry和car时，把一个勺子放在自己的舌头上。勺子可以防止舌尖向上顶起形成辅音，而形成这种更加流畅的元音型的音，美音R。

## Chapter 16: The El

**The El: A Diphthong Consonant**
El：双元音辅音

The **L** presents all kinds of interesting problems. It's hard to get students to appreciate what a big, round sound it is, with the back of the tongue dropped way down while the tip is firm and anchored to the top of the mouth behind the teeth. The American **L** is ə + **L**. Indians and Russians tend to make the **L** far too quick, but too heavy. Spanish speakers make it too quick and short. Chinese speakers just leave it off the end of words. Students need to put the **el** on the two-tone double stairstep, with the second half being əl.

　　L音展示出了各种有趣的问题。让学生理解什么是响亮、圆润的音，也就是舌后部下压、舌尖紧绷并顶在牙齿后面的上颚所发出的音很难。美音L是ə音+L音。印度人和俄罗斯人倾向于把L音发得过于急促而沉重。说西班牙语的人发L音时太快、太短。说汉语的人干脆把词尾的L略去。学生需要把el音放在两个音调的两个台阶上，后半部分是əl音。

Even when the **L** is silent, because it's a voiced consonant, it has the effect of lengthening the previous vowel. Here is a five-step technique that works well.

即使L不发音，由于它是浊辅音，它也有拉长前面元音的效果。下面是一个很有用的五步技巧。

## Final El
尾音El

1. Have them talk without removing the tip of their tongue from the alveolar ridge.

   让学生说话时舌尖不要离开牙槽嵴。

2. Use a mirror to make sure that the bottom of the tongue is visible.

   对着镜子说话，确保可以看到舌头的底部。

3. Hold the nose shut to make sure that the air doesn't escape through the nose, which results in an n-like sound.

   捏住鼻子，确保气流不从鼻腔流出，那样就会有类似鼻音n的音。

4. Have them add a final, tiny schwa to finish off the **L** sound.

   让学生在L音后面加上一个微弱的非中央元音。

5. Connect the final **L** to a following vowel whenever possible (tell a story > te lə story).

   尽可能地把词尾的L跟后面的元音连读（tell a story读成te lə story）

## Chapter 17: S or Z?

This is just getting used to **z**'s in **S**'s clothing. For a general rule, students can be told that the final consonant, voiced or unvoiced, of a word determines whether the plural **S** or third person singular **S** is voiced or unvoiced.

这部分是让大家习惯于外表是S时发z音的情况。可以告诉学生，一般情况下，复数的S或第三人称单数的S是浊音还是清音取决于单词结尾的辅音是浊音还是清音。

## Chapter 18: More Reduced Sounds

Most students will pronounce *good*, **güd**, as **gūd** as in *smooth* (as well as *could*, *should*, *stood*, *look*, *took*, *book*, *cook*, *put*, *push*, *pull*, *wool*, etc.). In order to get rid of the pronounced lip movement in **ū**, work with **bic / bək / book** and **lick / lək / look** groups, which makes the throat work more than the lips. Read across **u / i / ü / ə / r**, feeling the difference between the first column words with strong, visible lip movement and the second and third column words with rear tongue and throat movement and almost no lip change whatsoever. **Ih** and **eeh** are usually paired as tense and lax vowels, but **ih**, **ü**, and **ə** are much closer, with just the tongue shifting back.

大部分学生会把good（güd）发成gūd，就像smooth中的ū音一样（会出现同样情况的单词有could，should，stood，look，took，book，cook，put，push，pull，wool等）。为了避免在发ū音时移动双唇，练习bic/bək/book和lick/lək/look两组音，让喉咙比双唇更用力。横着读u/i/ü/ə/r，感受第一栏和第二、三栏单词的区别，第一栏的单词有强烈而明显的双唇运动，第二、三栏的单词有舌后部和喉部的运动，而几乎没有任何唇部的变化。ih和eeh通常被作为成对的紧元音和松元音，但是ih，ü和ə更接近，只是舌头向后移动。

You'll have to explain to your students that it starts getting subjective here. Because **ü** is a soft, lax, or reduced vowel, it can very easily slip over into being a schwa. Therefore, some people may say either:

你要跟学生说明学到这里发音变得比较主观。因为ü是个轻柔、放松或弱读的音，它很容易就会变成非中央元音。因此，有的人会说成下面两种中的其中一种：

There's a lot tü learn,
There's a lot təlearn,

They're both correct, but a full **tū** sounds over-pronounced. It's a similar case before a vowel. To start out, it's probably better to have students make a **ü** and a glide before a vowel for clarity.

两种发音都正确，但是完整的tū听起来被过于强调了。在元音之前也一样。为了开始学习，可能最好让学生在元音之前加一个ü音和一个滑音。

...that I'm easier tü(w)understand

When they are comfortable with the sound, the concept and their own intonation, they can later reduce it further.

当他们习惯了这个音、这个概念和自己的语调，之后可以进一步减弱发音。

...that I'm easier dənderstand

If you put *used to* in the middle of the sentence, it quickly reduces to *usta*. Not at the end of the sentence, however. It sounds abruptly Southern.

如果你把used to放在句子的中间，它很快就弱读成了usta。但在句尾却不一样。它听起来立刻变得像南部人。

I ustə live in LA.
more than I used tū.

## Chapter 19: "V" as in Victory

### V Is just a Voiced F
V只是浊音的F

Just as you repaired for the American **R**, it's a good idea to relieve students of a common misconception that **B** and **V** are related. At this point, review the pairs **f/v** and **p/b** and **w**.

正如你纠正学生的美音R一样，让学生消除B音和V音有关联的误解是个好主意。这时候，复习一下f/v，p/b和w。

For some reason, though, when pressed, students come up with an over-exaggerated **V** sound that involves biting their lips too far. I explain that native Americans don't put their teeth outside of the bottom lip, but rather draw the lip up and press the front teeth against the inside of the lip. Since most people have little difficulty with **f**, again we work from unvoiced to voiced, physically holding the lip in place against the teeth, if need be. The final surprise for them is the **v** of **of**.

然而，出于某种原因，如果太用力，学生会因为咬唇咬得太厉害而形成一个过于夸张的V音。我解释一下，美国本地人不把牙齿伸到下唇的外面，而是把下唇上移，用门牙顶住下唇内侧。由于大部分人发f音有点困难，我们再次从清辅音到浊辅音来学习，如果需要的话，用手把嘴唇顶住牙齿。对他们来说最终的惊喜就是会说of里的v了。

## Chapter 20: Tense and Lax Vowels

So far, you've been through most of the vowels with **Cæt? Cät? Cɑt?** & **How Much Wüd?**, including the tense/lax vowels **ū/ü; o/a/e & i** presented in Chapters 12 & 18.

到目前为止，你已经通过Cæt? Cät? Cɑt?和How Much Wüd?部分学习了大部分的元音，其中包括紧/松元音 ū /ü，以及第12和18章介绍的o/a/e和i。

Remember, tense vowels cause facial movement; lax vowels play up and down the throat and do not cause facial movement.

要记住，紧元音会引起面部运动；松元音会引起喉部的上下运动，不会引起面部运动。

Part of the problem is that students don't double up on the sound, so when you come to any of these sounds, have the students put them on the little two-step staircase.

一部分问题是学生们不会双倍延长发音，因此当学到这些音时，让学生把它们放在两个小音阶阶梯上。

## Chapter 21: The Ridge

This section groups all of the sounds that take place at the alveolar ridge, and it's a surprisingly large number. As you have the students contrast the sounds, they should notice that the main difference is how the air comes out: popped (ch, j, t, d); hissed or buzzed (s, z, sh, zh); or glided (n, l).

这部分集合了所有位于牙槽嵴的发音，而且它们的数量大得惊人。当你让学生对比这些音时，他们应该注意到主要的区别在于气流如何流出：爆破音（ch，j，t，d）；清辅音或浊辅音（s，z，sh，zh）；或是滑音（n，l）。

## Chapter 22: Grammar in a Bigger Nutshell

This is an expansion of Chapter 9 and it's a good review for students, so they can realize how much progress they've made. They typically struggle with Chapter 9, but after going through this, when you take them back for a review, they see how easy it's become.

本章是对第9章的扩展，对于学生来讲是很好的复习，这样他们就能知道自己取得了多大的进步。他们通常在学习第9章时很艰难，但是学完之后，当你带着他们复习时，他们会发现那些内容已经变得很简单。

## Chapter 23: Practical Application

This is to transition students to the real world. For some reason, they think they should stay with a textbook much longer than they really need. Explain that once they have the tools, they should start actively applying the techniques to materials that interest them, be it podcasts, audiobooks, or talk radio. They will want to use printed material, but orient them more toward audio.

这部分是让学生向现实生活过渡。由于某种原因，他们认为需要花更长的时间来学习课本，但其实没有必要。跟他们解释，一旦他们有了工具，就应该积极地把技巧运用到那些让他们感兴趣的资料中，不论是播客、有声读物还是"脱口秀"电台节目。他们会想使用印制品，但是引导他们更多地使用音频材料。

## Chapter 24: Nasal Consonants

Fortunately, this is an easy, self-explanatory chapter. There are three nasals—lips (m), tongue tip (n), and glottal (ng).

幸运的是，这章内容简单，不需要加以说明。一共有三个鼻音——双唇音（m），舌尖音（n）和声门音（ng）。

## Chapter 25: Throaty Consonants

By the time you get here, you are reviewing sounds that have already been introduced, so like with **The Ridge**, you are getting them to focus on a particular area, while noticing vocality and air flow.

学到这部分时，你将复习已经介绍过的音，所以就像"牙槽骨"这章一样，你需要让学生关注某个特定的区域，同时注意发声和气流。

001 Read This First
002 A Few Words on Pronunciation
003 Preliminary Diagnostic Analysis
004 **Chapter 1—The American Sound**
005 Music
006 Pitch / Sound
007 The Daddy Voice
008 Sound / Pronunciation
009 Ex. 1-1: Shifting Your Voice Position
010 The Underlying Hum
011 I Closed My Eyes and Listened Carefully
012 Listening Comprehension
013 Ex. 1-2: The American Sound
014 Go-To Phrase
015 Variety Is the Spice of Life
016 Intonation and Attitude
017 Ex. 1-3: Nonverbal Intonation
018 Ex. 1-4: Sounds of Empathy
019 Warm Up with Run-Up Phrases
020 **Chapter 2—Psycholinguistics**
021 Before / After audio
022 Two Ways to Pick Up the Accent
023 Ex. 2-1: Pure Mimicry
024 Please call Stella
025 Comparing audio
026 Ex. 2-2: Are you Steadfast or Freewheeling?
027 Ex. 2-3: Mimicry
028 There was a time
029 Self Check
030 Think, Then Act
031 Ex. 2-4: Correlating Sounds
032 Gäddit
033 Ex. 2-5: Gäddit / Got it!
034 Skidiz
035 Ex. 2-6: Gathering That Empirical Evidence
036 Mathematical Notation
037 Over-Confidence
038 The "What" Factor
039 Go On, Change Your Name
040 Motivation
041 Go to Extremes
042 Your Own True Voice
043 7 Steps to a Perfect Accent
044 **Chapter 3—General Pronunciation**
045 Ex. 3-2: Combining Sounds
046 Ex. 3-3: Pronunciation & Cadence
047 Ex. 3-4: Pure Sound
048 Ex. 3-5: Regular English
049 Ex. 3-6: Pure Sound
050 Ex. 3-7: Rhyme Time
051 Mouth Positions
052 Ex. 3-8: The Pure Sound Jump Start
053 We don't have those sounds
054 Ex. 3-9: Other Characters
055 Ex. 3-10: Changing to Regular Spelling
056 The Most Common Sound in English: Uh
057 Ex. 3-11: Theodore Thurston's Theory
058 Four More Important Sounds
059 Anticipating the Next Word

060 **Chapter 4—American Intonation**
061 Ex. 4-1: Rubber Band Practice
062 The American Speech Music
063 Staircase Intonation
064 Ex. 4-2: Noun Intonation
065 Statement Intonation with Pronouns
066 Ex. 4-3: Noun and Pronoun Intonation
067 Statement vs. Question Intonation
068 Ex. 4-4: Sentence Intonation Test
069 Ex. 4-5: Four Main Reasons for Intonation
070 Ex. 4-6: Pitch and Meaning Change
071 Ex. 4-7: Individual Practice
072 Ex. 4-8: Meaning of "Pretty"
073 Ex. 4-9: Inflection
074 Ex. 4-10: Individual Practice
075 Ex. 4-11: Sticky Note Exercise
076 Overdo It
077 Ex. 4-12: Translation
078 Translation Practice
079 Intonation Contrast
080 Ex. 4-13: Create Your Own Contrast
081 Question Types
082 Ex. 4-14: Variable Stress
083 Ex. 4-15: Make a Variable Stress Sentence
084 Ex. 4-16: Yes, You *Can* or No, You *Can't*?
085 Ex. 4-17: Can or Can't Quiz
086 Application of Intonation
087 Ex. 4-18: Application of Stress
088 How You Talk
099 Ex. 4-19: Paragraph Intonation Practice
090 Ex. 4-20: Reading with Staircase Intonation
091 Ex. 4-21: Spelling and Numbers
092 Ex. 4-22: Sound/Meaning Shifts
093 Ex. 4-23: Squeezed-Out Syllables
094 Ex. 4-24: Transitions of Nouns and Verbs
095 Ex. 4-25: Transitions of Adjectives and Verbs
096 Ex. 4-26: Transitions of Adjectives and Verbs
097 **Chapter 5—Syllable Stress**
098 Ex. 5-1: Syllable Patterns
099 Syllable Rules
100 Ex. 5-2: Intonation Shifts
101 **Chapter 6—Complex Intonation**
102 Ex. 6-1: Single-Word Phrases
103 Descriptive Phrases
104 Ex. 6-2: Sentence Stress with Descriptions
105 Ex. 6-3: Two Types of Descriptive Phrases
106 Ex. 6-4: The Ugly Duckling (Descriptions)
107 Set Phrases (Compound Nouns)
108 Ex. 6-5: Sentence Stress with Set Phrases
109 Ex. 6-6: Making Set Phrases
110 Ex. 6-7: The Little Match Girl (Set Phrases)
111 Ex. 6-8: Contrasting Phrase Types
112 Ex. 6-9: Two-Word Phrases
113 Summary of Stress in Two-Word Phrases
114 Nationalities
115 Ex. 6-10: Nationality Intonation Quiz
116 Ex. 6-11: Contrasting Phrase Types
117 Ex. 6-12: Contrast of Compound Nouns

## 终极英语单词系列：

《终极英语单词12000—变身口语达人3000词》
《终极英语单词12000—成为英语学霸3000词》
《终极英语单词12000—畅读英文报刊3000词》
《终极英语单词12000—英语母语水平3000词》

（日）ALC Press Inc. 著
（免费下载图书相关音频文件）

　　"终极英语单词12000系列"由新东方从日本ALC集团独家引进，从40年累积的各类英文语料中精选而出，并根据英美人的使用频率，由浅入深分为四册。该系列已经在日本和中国台湾地区持续畅销10年，深受好评。

## 《英语词组全书》（全两册）

（韩）金正基 编著

英语词组量轻松过万，突破词汇学习难关！

◎ 英语词组大容量
◎ 词义溯源易熟记
◎ 丰富实例好素材
◎ 练习、测试重实用
◎ 词汇书、词典集一身

定价：49.8元 开本：32开 页码：832页

## 读美国中小学课本学各科词汇系列：（1–6册、全6册套装）
（免费下载图书相关音频文件）

M. A. Putlack/e-Creative Contents 编著

◎ 掌握美国中小学生必备学科词汇，读懂英文课本很轻松
◎ 读过本套书，用英文学习数学、物理、化学、历史、地理，一点都不难
◎ 读美国课本，和美国学生同步学习，像学母语一样学英文
◎ 体验美国课堂，不必远赴重洋

## 《200个一定要学的英文词根词缀》

新东方词汇研究中心 编著
（免费下载图书相关音频文件）

◎ 共收录100个常用词根、50个常用前缀和50个常用后缀
◎ 深度剖析词根、词缀的起源及含义，拆解例词，给出精到例句
◎ 所选词汇均为四六级难度，刚需实用
◎ 配有拓展词汇和阶段检测题

定价：28元 开本：32开 页码：352页

## 《英语易混词辨析——用不对词，写作怎么拿高分？》高凌 主编

◎ 共收录443组易混词，包含单词近1000个
◎ 深度剖析每组易混词在意义和用法上的异与同
◎ 搭配简明、实用的例句，并根据单词的典型应用语境精心设计小测验
◎ 适用于有一定英语基础的英语爱好者、高中生，同时为英语四六级考生提供帮助

定价：35元 开本：32开 页码：464页

## 《英语词缀词典》《英语词根词典》

（韩）金正基 编著

◎ 适合中国学生使用的词汇学习书！
◎ TOEFL、GRE、SAT、IELTS词汇，一本搞定！
◎ 两本书为相辅相成的姊妹篇，共收录了33,000多个单词和习语，词汇量之大在同类书中名列前茅，收词全面，科学，实用。

## 英语词汇速记大全系列：

《英语词汇速记大全1——词根+词缀记忆法》
《英语词汇速记大全2——词形记忆法》
《英语词汇速记大全3——同类记忆法》
《英语词汇速记大全4——词境记忆法》
（免费下载图书相关音频文件）

俞敏洪 编著

　　新东方创始人俞敏洪多年词汇研究之精华，自1999年问世以来，持续畅销，长盛不衰。囊括绝大部分常考单词，适用于各类英语考试，所选词汇具有较强的实用性和发散性，对词汇的研究独到而深刻。

## 新东方词汇进阶系列：

《Vocabulary Basic》/《Vocabulary 6000》
《Vocabulary 12000》/《Vocabulary 23000》
（免费下载图书相关音频文件）

包凡一 王玉梅 编著

◎ 明确针对性！涵盖四六级、考研、TOEFL等考试应掌握的全部核心词汇
◎ 记忆全方位！释义从多个角度详细讲解，提供多种记忆方法，帮助读者理解掌握
◎ 练习高密度！每课设置多样习题，并附有参考答案，便于随时检测学习效果
◎ 改版多亮点！例句增加准确翻译，更加贴合读者需求，进一步提升学习体验

## BEC词汇精选系列：

《剑桥商务英语(BEC)初级词汇精选》
《剑桥商务英语(BEC)中级词汇精选》
《剑桥商务英语(BEC)高级词汇精选》
新东方考试研究中心　编著

（免费下载图书相关音频文件）

◎ 精选BEC考试高频核心商务词汇，制订30天学习计划
◎ 参考历年真题，释义详尽准确
◎ 采用"词根+联想记忆法"，方法科学
◎ 给出词汇的商务例句、搭配、派生词等丰富实例，加深理解
◎ 设置听说小站、写作小站，将词汇应用于商务场景，学以致用
◎ 免费赠送英音录音，同步学习

## 《BEC 词汇词根 + 联想记忆法》
## 《BEC 词汇词根 + 联想记忆法：乱序版》
## 《BEC 词汇词根 + 联想记忆法：便携版》

（免费下载图书相关音频文件）俞敏洪　编著

◎ 参考BEC考试真题，精选商务英语常用词汇
◎ 标注词汇商务释义，总结常用商务短语和缩略语，扫清专业术语障碍
◎ 分别按正序、乱序排列单词，并推出精简便携版，方便不同读者选用

## 《21世纪办公室书信大全》

（美）Francis J. Kurdyla　著

本书精选278封商务书信，包括致谢、推销、订货、投诉、邀请、祝贺等20余种常用商务书信类型，涵盖建筑、贸易、教育、出版、金融、服务等行业，涉及经管、研发、销售、宣传等业务种类，另特别增加3封传真和13份常用商务文书，可供繁忙的商务人士随时查阅，直接套用。

定价：58元　开本：32开　页码：808页

## 商务英语跟我学系列：

《商务英语应急600词》金利　主编
《商务英语应急900句》金利　主编
《情境商务口语应急一本通》
（韩）Myungsoo Park, Jinkyu Lee 编著

三个分册系统讲解600个商务英语核心必备词汇、900个难度递增的经典商务语句和商务情境口语，可免费下载MP3录音文件，助你迅速提升商务英语水平，补充重点商务知识。

## 新概念英语之全新全绎系列：

（1–4册）（各含光盘1张）
周成刚　翁云凯　主编

◎ 按图索骥，追溯字根词源
◎ 说文解字，洞悉语句内涵
◎ 语法简述，化解疑难考点
◎ 文化拓展，补充同类知识

《新概念英语（2）精讲笔记》
《新概念英语（3）精讲笔记》
张少云　编著

◎ 遵照语言学习的普遍规律，单词入手，语法铺陈，实例巩固，步步为营
◎ 根据知识点的重要性及考查频率来安排编写体例，大而全面，精到明晰

## 英语语法新思维系列：

《英语语法新思维初级教程——走近语法》
《英语语法新思维中级教程——通悟语法》
《英语语法新思维高级教程——驾驭语法》
《英语语法新思维——名词从句超精解》
《英语语法新思维——定语从句超精解》
《英语语法新思维——句子成分超精解》
《英语语法新思维——语法难点妙解》
张满胜　著

◎ 张满胜老师多年教学实践经验和深入研究的成果
◎ 从全新的思维角度讲解和剖析各类语法知识点，帮你轻松攻克语法学习难关
◎ 探求语法规则背后深层本质，助你把语法规则内化成英语思维

《英文语法有规则：151 个一学就会的语法规则》
《英文语法有规则：151 个一学就会的语法规则（练习册）》
（日）石黑昭博　著

◎ 品牌保障：引进自培生教育出版集团，特别为亚洲英语学习者编排，在日本畅销多年
◎ 定位明确：适合初中生、高中生和一般基础语法学习者
◎ 版式编排：简明图片阐释语法内容，直观而易于理解
◎ 有学有练：配套练习册，先简述每一章的语法要点，再设置练习，方便巩固和检测

### 爱上英文系列：

《点亮心灵的句子》 俞敏洪 编著
《我的感性名言书》（韩）李秀姬 编著
《我的英语日记》（韩）南银英 编著

◎ 激励人心的名言短句，字字珠玑，
  句句经典
◎ 励志与悦读并举，为读者提供美的
  阅读体验
◎ 四色/双色创意插图，帮助读者体会
  文字意境
◎ 激发英文写作兴趣，指导日记创作

### 新东方双语书话译丛系列：

《书林辟径：邂逅生命中挚爱的书》
《书海逸趣：有书陪伴的人生不寂寞》
《护书之苦：书若安好，便是晴天》
《藏书之乐：书架上的珍宝》
《一派书心：缘何此生只爱书》
唐静 编译

　　收录古今名家关于读书、藏书、爱
书的经典美文，文章中英双语逐段对
照，译文经过精心审校；全书彩色印
刷，图片精美。

### 漫话美国系列：

（韩）李元馥 著

　　本系列包含《美国人》《美国历
史》和《美国总统》三册，作者用幽默
的漫画和地道的英语，带领读者穿越美
国200余年的历史，深入美国社会的各
个层面，全面而系统地认识这个超级大
国。想要足不出户通过阅读便通晓美
国？就来看这套书吧！

### 《狂恋美剧学口语》 邱政政 编著

（免费下载图书相关音频文件）

　　以经典美剧为素材讲解英语口语，
精选时下常见、流行的俚语、习语、句
型，将邱政政老师独创的"M7英语听说
教学法"融入其中，带领你从语音、选
词、思维和文化等多个维度学习语言精
华，纠正口语表达错误。

定价：32元　开本：16开　页码：240页

### 《美音纠音、透析与突破》

邱政政 编著

（免费下载图书相关音频文件）

　　针对中国人在美式发音上的难点和
误区，本着"语音"和"语调、节奏"
双过关的宗旨，兼顾特色音变现象，简
洁有效地列举出适合学习的美音规律和
技巧。同时运用"模仿—自觉—自然"
的学习规律，着重培养英语学习者的语
感和听觉形象。

定价：28元　开本：16开　页码：192页

### "剑桥标准英语教程系列"：

1-6级共18册，各级别包含学生用书（分为A、
B两册）和教师用书，均配有光盘并提供网站
支持。

Michael McCarthy等 编著

　　"剑桥标准英语教程"是一套针对
青少年和成人英语学习者编写的、具有
革新意义的综合英语教程。新版扩展为6
个级别，最新引入符合中高级语言学习
者需求的第5级和第6级（Viewpoint），
并对第1-4级（Touchstone）进行升级
改进，涵盖了英语初级到高级难度的内
容。课程设置前后呼应，教学方式简单
明晰，帮助英语学习者提高语言交流能
力和英语综合技能。

### 剑桥实境英语系列：

（1-4级，每级含听说、阅读、写作分册）
（听说、写作各配光盘1张）

Miles Craven等 编著

　　本丛书实用性强、覆盖面广、题材
丰富、图文并茂，可帮助英语学习者丰
富英语知识，积累语言素材，培养良好
的语言感觉，训练正确的思维方式，适
合学生自学或课堂教学。

### 《英语会话全书》（含光盘1张）

（上下全两册）（韩）李宝宁 编著

◎ 全！18大主题，182个细分话题，涵
  盖日常生活的各个方面
◎ 酷！课堂上学不到的美式英语，一种
  意思多种表达，你总比别人多会几句
◎ 值！赠送450分钟美音MP3光盘、5
  小时语音速成体验课，给你超值学习
  体验

定价：59.8元　开本：32开　页码：984页

## 《美语发音秘诀》

（含光盘1张）Ann Cook 著

◎ 用直观的图片助你理解语言现象的指导书
◎ 与现实中的语言行为一致的方法指南
◎ 蕴含绘声绘色的录音内容的发音书
◎ 讲练结合适合自学的辅导书
◎ 包含详细指导教学方法，可作为教材使用

定价：42元 开本：16开 页码：276页

## 《说出正确的口语——美音达人的语法书》

（含光盘1张）Ann Cook 著

◎ 如果你语音语调正确，一张口却都是语法错误
◎ 如果你熟知语法规则，却无法将其应用到日常交流中
◎ 如果你想要一本既讲语法规则，又教授发音技巧的书
 那么，这本书是你的理想选择！

定价：49元 开本：16开 页码：356页

## 《从零快乐学英语》

（免费下载图书相关音频文件）

李露 琚晋蓉 杨爽 编著

从成人学英语实际出发，语言浅显，内容简单实用。内容有"字母启蒙"、"点滴积累"、"认识音标"、"发音规则"、"情景对话"、"语法"等。

定价：29元 开本：32开 页码：292页

## 老外每天在用的英文系列：

《老外每天在用的生活词汇》
《老外每天在用的生活口语》
《老外每天在用的商务口语》

（免费下载图书相关音频文件）

（日）吉田研作 荒井贵和 武藤克彦 著

◎ 配有大量漫画插图，生动再现场景，身临其境轻松记单词
◎ 精选常用单词和短语，英文例句地道，讲解深入浅出
◎ 附赠可模仿练习的MP3录音，风趣生动，方便反复跟读对比
◎ 看漫画、读文字、听录音、开口说、动笔写——多种感官记忆，全方位轻松掌握

## 《生活口语表现词典》（韩）李宝宁著
## 《商务口语表现词典》（韩）李昌秀著

（各含光盘1张，附赠句型便携手册）

◎ 分别精选304组生活口语重点句型和280组商务口语重点句型，为各类常见情景提供可直接套用的"句型公式"
◎ 精心编写多个情景例句，设置大量中译英练习，辐射多种场景，活学活用，举一反三
◎ 透析中国人常犯的英语表达错误，对比正误，及时纠错。讲解商务常识，实现准确沟通

## 英语随身袋系列：

《看漫画学日常英语》
《旅游英语现学现用》
《轻松打开英语话匣子》
《英语常用句型就这58句》
《英语语法6天入门》

Bernard White，朱秀琴等 著

（免费下载图书相关音频文件）

◎ 涵盖旅游英语、漫画英语、日常会话、语法方面内容
◎ 方便携带，随时随地学习、记忆、查阅
◎ 风格轻松，零负担提升英语能力
◎ 内容基础，快速入门、易于掌握

## KET、PET、FCE官方模考题精讲精练系列：

《剑桥 KET 官方模考题精讲精练》（附 MP3）
《剑桥 PET 官方模考题精讲精练》（附 MP3）
《剑桥 FCE 官方模考题精讲精练》（附 MP3）

（英）Karen Saxby 等 著

◎ 剑桥通用英语考试官方备考资料，专业题源与讲解
◎ 科学仿真的6套官方模拟试题与透彻详尽的考试相关信息
◎ 补充技能训练与答题指导和建议
◎ 清晰、细致的答案解析和高分写作范文
◎ 时长190分钟的MP3听力练习音频光盘

# 读者反馈表

尊敬的读者：

您好！非常感谢您对**新东方大愚图书**的信赖与支持，希望您抽出宝贵的时间填写这份反馈表，以便帮助我们改进工作，今后能为您提供更优秀的图书。谢谢！

为了答谢您对我们的支持，我们将对反馈的信息进行随机抽奖活动，当月将有 20 位幸运读者可获赠**《新东方英语》**期刊一份。我们将定期在新东方大愚图书网站 www.dogwood.com.cn 公布获奖者名单并及时寄出奖品，敬请关注。

**来信请寄：** 北京市海淀区海淀东三街 2 号新东方南楼 19 层　北京新东方大愚文化传播有限公司
图书部收

邮编：100080　　　　　　　　　　　　　　　　E-mail：bj62605588@163.com

姓名：_____　　年龄：_____　　职业：_____　　教育背景：_____　　邮编：_____

通讯地址：_____　　联系电话：_____

E-mail：_____　　您所购买的书籍的名称是：_____

1. 您是通过何种渠道得知本书的（可多选）：
   □书店　□新东方网站　□大愚网站　□朋友推荐　□老师推荐　□@新东方大愚图书（http://weibo.com/dogwood）
   □其他_____

2. 您是从何处购买到此书的？　□书店　□新东方大愚淘宝网　□其他网上书店　□其他_____

3. 您购买此书的原因（可多选）：
   □封面设计　□书评广告　□正文内容　□图书价格　□新东方品牌　□新东方名师　□其他_____

4. 您对本书的封面设计满意程度：　□很满意　□比较满意　□一般　□不满意　□改进建议_____

5. 您认为本书的内文在哪些方面还需改进？　□结构编排　□难易程度　□内容丰富性　□内文版式　□其他_____

6. 本书最令您满意的地方：□内文　□封面　□价格　□纸张

7. 您对本书的推荐率：□没有　□1 人　□1—3 人　□3—5 人　□5 人以上

8. 您更希望我们为您提供哪些方面的英语类图书？
   □少儿英语类　□初高中英语类　□四六级类　□考研类　□IELTS 类　□TOEFL 类　□GRE、GMAT 类　□SAT、SSAT 类
   □留学申请类　□BEC、TOEIC 类　□实用英语类　□商务英语类　□休闲欣赏类　□英语读物类　□其他_____
   您目前最希望我们为您出版的图书是：_____

9. 您在学习英语过程中最需要哪些方面的帮助？（可多选）
   □词汇　□听力　□口语　□阅读　□写作　□翻译　□语法　□其他_____

10. 您最喜欢的英语图书品牌：_____
    理由是（可多选）：□版式漂亮　□内容实用　□难度适宜　□价格适中　□对考试有帮助　□其他_____

11. 您对新东方图书品牌的评价：_____

12. 您对本书（或其他新东方图书）的意见和建议：_____
    _____
    _____

13. 填表时间：_____ 年 _____ 月 ___ 日